Foundations for Algebra: Year 2

Managing Editors:

Elizabeth Coyner
    Bear River School
Beverly Brockhoff
    Glen Edwards Middle School

Illustrator:

Jonathan Weast
    Weast & Weast Illustration Studio
    Sacramento, California

Technical Assistance:

Bethany Sorbello
    CPM Educational Program
Thu Pham
    The CRESS Center
    University of California, Davis

Developed by CPM Educational Program

Program Directors:

Judith Kysh
    Departments of Mathematics and Education
    San Francisco State University
Tom Sallee
    Department of Mathematics
    University of California, Davis
Brian Hoey
    CPM Educational Program

v 3.0

Credits for the First Edition

Substantially Revised (2000, 2001)
by

Heidi Ackley
Steve Ackley
Elizabeth Baker
Bev Brockhoff
Ellen Cafferata
Elizabeth Coyner
Sara Effenbeck
William Funkhouser
Brian Hoey
Carol Jancsi

Judy Kysh
Kris Petersen
Robert Petersen
Edwin Reed
Stacy Rocklein
Kristie Sallee
Tom Sallee
Howard Webb
Kaye Whitney
Jon Wickham

Pilot Edition Contributing Editors (1999)

Heidi Ackley
Steve Ackley
Bev Brockhoff
Ellen Cafferata
Elizabeth Coyner
Scott Coyner
Kathleen Davies
Merci Del Rosario
Virginia Downing
Sara Effenbeck
Alice Elstien
William Ford

William Funkhouser
Bruce Grip
Stephen Inouye
Carol Jancsi
Alvin Mendle, Jr.
Pattie Montgomery
Edwin Reed
Gail Standiford
Gale Sunderland
Howard Webb
Kaye Whitney
Jon Wickham

Technical Assistance

Jennifer Buddenhagen
Grace Chen
Ankit Jain
Janelle Petersen

Jeremy Tauzer
David Trombly
Erika Wallender
Emily Wheelis

4 5 6 7 8 9 10 11 12   10 09 08 07   ISBN-10   1-931287-09-0

Printed in the United States of America   Version 3.0   ISBN-13: 978-1-931287-09-8

Foundations for Algebra: Year 2
First Edition

Table of Contents

A Note to Parents, Students, and Teachers

Welcome to *Foundations for Algebra: Year 2.*

This textbook will prepare students for future Algebra courses. It was also written to consolidate the core ideas of previous mathematics courses, so that it will serve students of varied mathematics backgrounds. The contents of this course are many of the fundamental ideas and procedures necessary to be successful in subsequent mathematics courses and many careers. Classroom teachers wrote the lessons to present these ideas in ways that have proven successful with their students. The course also meets local, state, and national curriculum standards.

The investigations, problems, and practice exercises are designed to develop the students' logical and mathematical reasoning skills. The sequence of problems leads to understanding the reasoning behind the mathematical concepts. Students complete guided investigations that explore and develop ideas, then practice them along with procedural skills in subsequent chapters. Many problems use the mathematics in situations like those encountered by students and adults in their daily activities and business settings.

In order to be successful in mathematics it is critical that students actively participate in their learning. This means that each student must read and work all of the problems. Students need to discuss mathematical concepts and the reasoning involved in the steps of their solutions. In order to provide these discussion opportunities, students are encouraged to work with a study partner and in study teams both inside and outside the classroom. It is critical that students complete ALL of the assignments, including homework, to develop their individual skills. **Homework help is available on-line at www.hotmath.com.** Equally important is that students take accurate, complete notes and ask questions about any problem, question, or concept that they find confusing or difficult to understand.

There are two additional resources that the authors designed to help students be successful in this course. The first is the mathematics Tool Kit that contains most of the ideas a student needs to know in the course. Tool Kit entries appear in the student text and in a Tool Kit booklet. The other is the *Foundations for Algebra Parent Guide*. The guide is sometimes available from the classroom teacher or the school library. It is available free through the Internet at www.cpm.org. It may also be purchased directly from CPM Educational Program for $20 plus $3 shipping (California residents please add local sales tax to the $20) by sending a check to CPM, 1233 Noonan Drive, Sacramento, CA 95822.

Getting Organized

Chapter 1

Chapter 1
Getting Organized: **DATA INTERPRETATION**

In this course you will build a foundation that will prepare you for algebra and more advanced mathematics. In this chapter you will begin to develop good work habits by becoming better organized and working with a partner or a study team. You will look at ways to <u>organize</u> <u>and analyze</u> <u>data</u> in a variety of graphs. You will begin to develop the problem solving strategy of Guess and Check.

In this chapter you will have the opportunity to:

- develop good work habits with homework.

- become accustomed to working with a partner or in a team.

- prepare your notebook for the course.

- collect, organize, display, and interpret data.

- solve word problems using Guess and Check tables to organize your solutions as preparation for writing and solving equations.

Read the problem below, but **do not try to solve it now**. What you learn over the next few days will enable you to solve it.

GO-0.   Dezzirae's oldest brother Kalani has saved enough money to buy a car. Kalani told Dezzirae, "Buying a car will actually be a good investment. I can buy it now and sell it when I need the money back. Except for buying gas, it will be almost free because I can get all my money back when I sell it."

Dezzirae looked concerned. "Kalani, I think you should collect some information before you make that kind of statement. Investing your money in a car is not a good idea!"

"I don't agree with you, Dezzirae!" Kalani replied.

Collect, organize, and analyze some data to help Dezzirae and Kalani settle their disagreement.

Number Sense	▓▓▓░░░░░░░░░░░░░░
Algebra and Functions	▓▓░░░░░░░░░░░░░░░
Mathematical Reasoning	▓▓▓░░░░░░░░░░░░░░
Measurement and Geometry	▓░░░░░░░░░░░░░░░░
Statistics, Data Analysis, & Probability	▓▓▓▓▓▓▓░░░░░░░░░

Chapter 1

Getting Organized: DATA INTERPRETATION

GO-1. You will be working in pairs or teams of four during this year. You will need to be able to work cooperatively with many different people. Working as a team is a valuable skill. Follow your teacher's instructions to interview your partner. Then you will introduce your partner to another pair. This is the first step for creating a good study team.

GO-2. On the sticky note provided by your teacher, write your name and the month and day of the month you were born (not the year). An example is pictured below. This problem and the next one will investigate the question, "What are the most common birth month and least common birth month in the class?"

Answer the following questions with your partner before taking your sticky note to the line plot your teacher has prepared. Make sure you write your answers in complete sentences.

> Marion
> April
> 21

a) Predict which month of the year will have the most birth dates in it.

b) Predict which month of the year will have the fewest birth dates in it.

c) Do you think any two people in your class will share the same birth date?

GO-3. Follow your teacher's directions about how to place your sticky note on the line plot provided for you. After everyone in class has placed their data on the line plot, answer the following questions using complete sentences.

a) Which month(s) have the most birth dates? How does the class data compare with your prediction?

b) Which month(s) have the fewest birth dates? How does the class data compare with your prediction?

c) Are there any pairs of students in your class who share the same birth date? Are you surprised?

d) Do you think students in other classes like this one will have shared birth dates? Estimate the number of pairs of students with shared birth dates.

e) Write down a career or job that might require the employee to arrange data in a line plot such as the one you just completed.

GO-4. **Mathography** A mathography is a lot like your life history, except that it is focused on mathematics in your life.

    a) On a separate piece of paper, write a letter about yourself to your teacher. The letter will help your teacher get to know you as an individual. The letter should address these three general topics: you, you as a student, and you as a math student. Remember to use complete sentences and make sure it is neat enough to be read easily. Start the letter with "Dear ...". Make sure you sign your letter. This should take between fifteen and twenty minutes to complete. Parts (b), (c), and (d) have suggestions for each of the three topics.

    b) **You**: Introduce yourself, using the name you like to be called. Describe your hobbies, talents, and interests. State your goals or dreams. What are you proud of? What else would you like to share?

    c) **You as a Student**: State the importance of school in your life. Describe yourself as a student. In what kinds of classroom activities do you excel? What kinds of activities do you find frustrating? Explain which subject(s) is/are your favorites. Tell why you like it (them). How regularly do you finish in-class assignments? How faithfully do you do your homework?

    d) **You as a Math Student**: Describe your most memorable moment in math and explain why you remember it. State your favorite math topic. Name your least favorite. Explain how you feel about math this year. What grade do you expect to earn?

GO-5. Describe each situation below with a fraction.

    a) 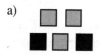   b)    c)

GO-6. Compute without using a calculator. The icon you see at left under the problem number means to compute without using a calculator.

    a) $7.5 + 3.6$ b) $9.5 - 3.8$ c) $15.4 + 14.6$

    d) $85.3 - 55.4$ e) $4(2.5)$ f) $3.5(10)$

GO-7.   The purpose of this exercise is to develop the skill of working with others when you may not always agree with their ideas.

   a)   Working alone, list two or three of your favorite items in each category.

Soft Drinks	Movies	Sports
Books	Food	Board Games
Ice Cream	School Subjects	

   b)   When you and your partner have completed your own lists, show them to each other. Your task now is to try to reach agreement on one item for each category as a team "favorite." Your team favorite may not necessarily be your own first choice. Write your agreed upon choice for as many categories as you can and list the one you could not agree on. Be prepared to describe your negotiations to the class.

GO-8.   Many students have difficulty taking notes for a math class, so we will make some suggestions to assist you with this study skill. You will keep all of your math notes together in a special place called a Tool Kit.

   When it is time to make notes, a Tool Kit icon like the one at left will be printed in the textbook under the problem number. The mathematics information will appear inside a double-lined box. The double-lined box will be printed in two places: in the textbook and in your Tool Kit. Some schools use the bound Tool Kit booklet from CPM; others photocopy the pages and have you put them in a three-ring binder. Next to the double-lined box in your Tool Kit is a place for you to make notes. Sometimes you will write or highlight key words, a phrase, or a list. Other times you will need to write one or more complete sentences. Follow the directions below each Tool Kit problem in the textbook and write neatly so your notes will be useful.

   This is your first Tool Kit entry. This information is the first of four study team guidelines.

   ### STUDY TEAM GUIDELINES

   1. **Each member of the team is responsible for his or her own behavior.**

   Make these notes in your Tool Kit to the right of the double-lined box.

   a)   Highlight the words "responsible," "own," and "behavior."

   b)   List some behaviors of a student who is following this guideline.

   c)   List some behaviors of a student who is not following this guideline.

GO-9.   Organization is a key component of success in
          almost everything you do. You will need to keep
          an organized binder for this course. Follow the
          guidelines set by your teacher.

          a)   You will need a sturdy 3-ring binder with a
                hard cover.

          b)   Put your name on the inside front cover of
                this binder. Divide your binder into
                labeled sections as directed by your
                teacher.

          c)   After you have completed this task, write "I have finished organizing my binder"
                next to this problem number on your paper for this assignment.

GO-10.

┌───┐
│   **A COMPLETE GRAPH**   │
│   │
│   Graphs are ways of displaying and comparing information. A complete graph │
│   has the following characteristics: │
│   │
│   • All graphs are **neat** and easy to read and, when appropriate, constructed with a │
│   **straightedge**.   │
│   │
│   • The units (or numbers) along the axes are clearly **labeled**.   │
│   │
│   • The axes (the vertical and horizontal number lines) are labeled with **words** that │
│   explain the numbers on the axes.   │
│   │
│   • The units (numbers marked on the axes) follow **equal intervals** on each axis.   │
│   │
│   • All graphs have a **title**.   │
│   │
│   • A key or **legend** is included when it is necessary to explain any symbols that are │
│   used in the graph.   │
│   │
│   Graphs should be drawn on graph paper or resource pages.   │
└───┘

Make these notes in your Tool Kit to the right of the double-lined box.

          a)   Highlight any characteristics of a complete graph that you have not studied before.

          b)   Write a question about any characteristics of graphs that you do not understand. Be
                sure to ask your partner or a teammate for help. If they are unable to help you, ask
                your teacher.

GO-11. Use your Tool Kit as a check-off list to help you find what is missing on each graph below. When you see the icon at left under the problem number, you will identify and correct the error that is in the problem.

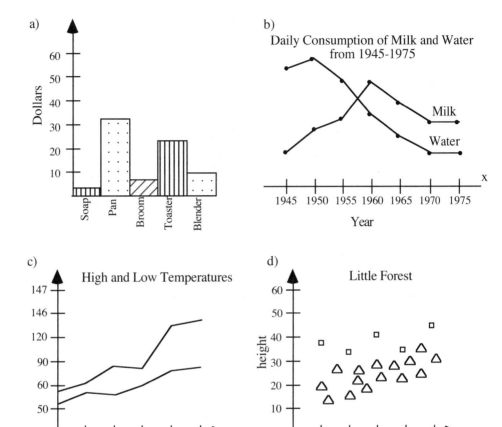

a)

b) Daily Consumption of Milk and Water from 1945-1975

c) High and Low Temperatures

d) Little Forest

GO-12. Robert and Diondra were working with fraction circles and were asked to represent thirds in two different ways. Their drawings are below. Tanisha said, "One of the pictures is incorrect." Which picture is incorrect, and why?

Note: The icon below the problem number at left indicates that the authors have included one or more errors in the problem for you to identify and correct.

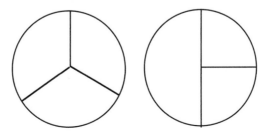

GO-13.

COMMON MEASUREMENTS

Length
12 inches = 1 foot
36 inches = 1 yard
3 feet = 1 yard
5, 280 feet = 1 mile

Volume (fluid)
8 ounces = 1 cup
16 ounces = 1 pint
2 pints = 1 quart
4 quarts = 1 gallon

Weight
16 ounces = 1 pound
2,000 pounds = 1 ton

Temperature
Fahrenheit   Celsius

212°   Water Boils   100°
98.6°   Body Temperature   37°
72°   Room Temperature   22°
32°   Water Freezes   0°

Time
60 seconds = 1 minute
60 minutes = 1 hour
24 hours = 1 day
7 days = 1 week
365 days = 1 year
52 weeks = 1 year

Centuries
1800's = 19th century
1900's = 20th century
2000's = 21st century

In your Tool Kit, highlight the measurement facts that you do not know from memory.

GO-14.   The Niesenbahn railway in Switzerland has many stair steps. It has 42 more steps than four Empire State Buildings!

a)   If the Empire State Building has 2908 steps, how many steps are in the Niesenbahn Railway?

b)   Each step in both buildings rises six inches. How many feet of climbing occurs in each building?

GO-15.   The **range** of a set of data is the difference between the largest value and the smallest value.

a)   The following scores represent the first fourteen tests that Mrs. Poppington has corrected: 62, 65, 93, 51, 55, 76, 79, 85, 55, 72, 78, 83, 91, and 82. Find the highest test score. Find the lowest test score.

b)   Find the range of the data.

c)   Explain how you determined the range. Use a complete sentence.

GO-16.   Copy each problem, then compute the sum or difference.

a)   4.3 + 2.6   b)   9.7 + 6.5   c)   1.8 + 0.3

d)   7.6 – 5.8   e)   4.3 – 2.7   f)   9.2 – 8.8

GO-17.   **Solving a Problem Using Guess and Check**

Dr. Tasha McNeil, the local orthodontist, saw eight more patients on Tuesday than on Monday. Dr. McNeil knew that the total number of patients for the two days was 44 because she had a stack of 44 folders. Each patient has exactly one folder. How many folders should be stacked in the Monday pile?

Sometimes the easiest way to get started is to guess what the answer might be and then to check to see if you are right. Guessing is a good strategy for learning more about the problem, and it will lead to algebraic solutions later in the course. The example below leads you through the four steps of a Guess and Check table. Follow along with your teacher and help Dr. McNeil find out how many folders are in the Monday pile.

Step 1:   Set up a table. The first column will contain your guess. In this case, you will be guessing the number of folders for Monday. Copy the table as shown below on your paper.

Guess Number of Folders for Monday	

Step 2:   Make a guess about the number of folders for Monday. Your first guess should be something reasonable and easy. Since you know the total number of folders is 44, it would be silly to guess anything bigger. Try guessing 10. Place your guess of 10 in the box under the heading "Guess Number of Folders for Monday."

Guess Number of Folders for Monday	
10	

Step 3:   If there were ten folders on Monday, how many folders will be in the Tuesday stack? Label the top row as shown, then write that number in the space below.

Guess Number of Folders for Monday	**Number of Folders for Tuesday**	
10		

Step 4:   Your first guess of 10 folders for Monday means there must be 18 folders for Tuesday. You can use this information to determine your next column. Label the column "Total Number of Folders" and write the total in the space below.

Guess Number of Folders for Monday	Number of Folders for Tuesday	**Total Number of Folders**	
10	18	28	

>>Problem continues on the next page.>>

Step 5: Next you check to see whether your guess gives you the correct result. The last column should be checking if the total number of folders is equal to 44. If it is not, write in "too high" or "too low." Add this information to your paper.

Guess Number of Folders for Monday	Number of Folders for Tuesday	Total Number of Folders	Check 44
10	18	28	**too low**

Step 6: Start over with a new guess. Since the last guess was too low, we need to guess something higher. Try guessing 20, then repeat steps three through five.

Guess Number of Folders for Monday	Number of Folders for Tuesday	Total Number of Folders	Check 44
10	18	28	too low
20	**28**	**48**	**too high**

Step 7: Twenty folders for Monday turned out to be too high. Now you know the solution is something less than 20 but greater than 10. Try guessing 15 and repeat the process.

Guess Number of Folders for Monday	Number of Folders for Tuesday	Total Number of Folders	Check 44
10	18	28	too low
20	28	48	too high
15	**23**	**38**	**too low**

Step 8: Fifteen is too low. Try guessing 18 folders.

Guess Number of Folders for Monday	Number of Folders for Tuesday	Total Number of Folders	Check 44
10	18	28	too low
20	28	48	too high
15	23	38	too low
18	**26**	**44**	**correct**

Step 9: You have now solved the problem. There is only one thing left to do: write the answer in a complete sentence that restates the question.

Eighteen folders should be stacked in the Monday pile.

GO-18. Using the Guess and Check table below, find two consecutive numbers that have a sum of 37. (**Consecutive** means "one after another in order," like 3 and 4.) Answer in a complete sentence.

Guess First Number	Second Number	Total of Both Numbers (Sum)	Check 37
10	(10) + 1 = 11	(10) + (11) = 21	too low

GO-19.   Parts (a) and (b) below help you solve the following problem using a Guess and Check table.

The length of a rectangle is three centimeters greater than the width. If the perimeter (distance around) equals 54 centimeters, find the dimensions (length and width) of the rectangle.

a)   In this case, a diagram would be useful. Copy the diagram at right on your paper.

b)   Copy and complete the table below. Remember to show all of your calculations and to answer using a complete sentence.

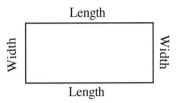

Guess Width	Length of Rectangle	Perimeter of Rectangle	Check 54
10	(10) + 3 = 13	(10) + (13) + (10) + (13) = 46	too low

GO-20.

STUDY TEAM GUIDELINES

1. Each member of the team is responsible for his or her own behavior.

2. **Each member of the team must be willing to help any other team member who asks for help.**

Highlight the words "each member" and "willing to help" in your Tool Kit.

GO-21.   Saul and Paul had to draw a line graph to show the temperature at different times of the day. Their data are in the table below right. When they compared their graphs, they were surprised to see that they were different.

a)   Whose graph is correct?

b)   Explain what is wrong with the other graph.

Note: The symbol on the base of the axis for temperature is an acceptable way to show that the graph does not begin at 0.

Time	Temperature
8:00 a.m.	68°
10:00 a.m.	76°
11:00 a.m.	78°
1:00 p.m.	85°
2:00 p.m.	87°

>>Problem continues on the next page.>>

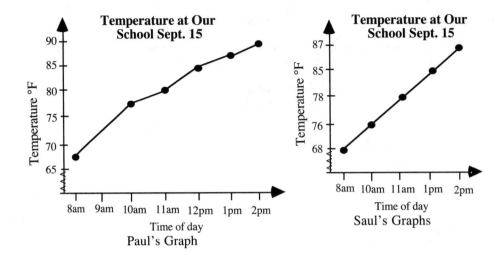

**Temperature at Our
School Sept. 15**

Temperature °F

90
85
80
75
70
65

8am 9am 10am 11am 12pm 1pm 2pm

Time of day

Paul's Graph

**Temperature at Our
School Sept. 15**

Temperature °F

87
85
78
76
68

8am 10am 11am 1pm 2pm

Time of day

Saul's Graphs

GO-22.

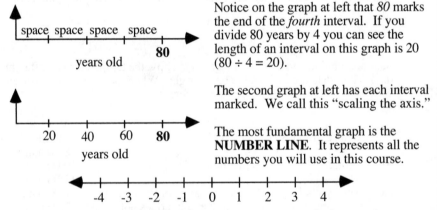

INTERVALS, SCALING AND THE NUMBER LINE

The numbers on the axes of a graph show the **SCALING** of the axes. The difference between consecutive markings tells the size of the **INTERVAL**. When you scale each axis you must use <u>equal</u> intervals to represent the data accurately. For example, an interval of 5 creates a scale numbered 0, 5, 10, 15, etc. Unequal intervals distort the relationship in the data.

space space space space

80

years old

Notice on the graph at left that *80* marks the end of the *fourth* interval. If you divide 80 years by 4 you can see the length of an interval on this graph is 20 ($80 \div 4 = 20$).

20   40   60   **80**

years old

The second graph at left has each interval marked. We call this "scaling the axis."

The most fundamental graph is the **NUMBER LINE**. It represents all the numbers you will use in this course.

-4 -3 -2 -1 0 1 2 3 4

While integer intervals are shown, fractions, π, square roots, and other numbers can be placed in the corresponding intervals.

Write the following information to the right of the double-lined box in your Tool Kit.

a)   Intervals (spacing) on an axis must be the same size.

b)   For scaling, the difference between consecutive numbers must be the same.

GO-23.   Copy the incomplete axes and fill in the missing numbers on the graphs.

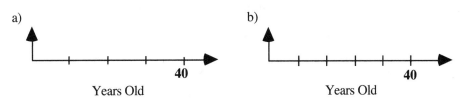

a)

Years Old

b)

Years Old

GO-24.   Mrs. Poppington is correcting math tests. Here are the scores for the first fourteen tests she has corrected: 62, 65, 93, 51, 55, 12, 79, 85, 55, 72, 78, 83, 91 and 76. Which score does not seem to fit in this set of data? Explain.

GO-25.   Kris said, "The Rawlings Rockets basketball team does not have any really tall players. These are their heights in inches: 70, 77, 75, 68, 88, 70, and 72."

a)   Which number does not seem to fit this set of data?

b)   Do you agree or disagree with Kris? Explain.

GO-26.   Sometimes a few pieces of a data set are significantly outside the range of most of the data. These data are called **outliers**. Identify the outlier(s) in the following two data sets.

a)   5, 9, 4, 6, 9, 35, 4, 7, 10   b)   84, 79, 72, 9, 80, 84, 70

c)   Explain why you chose these numbers.

GO-27.   Follow your teacher's directions for practicing mental math. There are several ways to do the problem. Which method do you think was best?

GO-28.   Follow your teacher's directions and play Logic Games with your team.

GO-29.

STUDY TEAM GUIDELINES

1. Each member of the team is responsible for his or her own behavior.

2. Each member of the team must be willing to help any other team member who asks for help.

3. **When you have a question, ask your partner or team first.**
   If no one can answer the question, then ask the teacher for help.

Make these notes in your Tool Kit to the right of the double-lined box for study team guidelines.

a) Why do you think this is a study team guideline?

b) Write an example of a question a member of the team would be able to answer.

c) Write an example of a question that your teacher would need to answer.

GO-30.

MEAN, OUTLIERS, and RANGE

The **MEAN** is the arithmetic average of a data set. One way to determine the mean is to add all values in a set of data and divide the sum by the number of values.

Example: Find the mean of this set of data: 38, 42, 50, 40, and 35.
- $38 + 42 + 50 + 40 + 35 = 205$
- $205 \div 5$ (the number of values) $= 41$, so the mean is 41.

OUTLIERS are numbers in a data set that are either much higher or much lower than the other numbers in the set.

Example: Find the outlier of this set of data: 88, 90, 96, 93, 87, 12, 85, and 94.
The outlier is 12.

The **RANGE** of a set of data is the difference between the maximum (highest value) and minimum (lowest value).

Example: Find the range of this set of data: 114, 109, 131, 96, 140, and 128.
- The highest value is 140.
- The lowest value is 96.
- $140 - 96 = 44$, so the range is 44.

The mean is generally the best measure of central tendency to use when the set of data does not contain outliers.

Make these notes in your Tool Kit to the right of the double-lined box.

a) List three kinds of data for which you might need to find the mean.

b) Create an example of a set of data that contains an outlier.

c) State the range of the data set you created in part (b).

GO-31.   Use the following data set to answer the questions below.

$$62, 65, 93, 51, 55, 12, 79, 85, 55, 72, 78, 83, 91, 76$$

a)   Find the mean of all the scores.

b)   Now find the mean without the outlier.

c)   What did including the outlier do to the mean?

d)   Find the range of the data and explain how you found it.

GO-32.   Use the following data set to answer the questions below.

$$70, 77, 75, 68, 88, 70, 72$$

a)   Find the mean of all the heights.

b)   Now find the mean without the outlier.

c)   What did including the outlier do to the mean?

GO-33.

> ### SOLVING PROBLEMS WITH GUESS AND CHECK TABLES
>
> • Read the problem carefully. Make notes or sketch a picture to organize the information in the problem.
> • Look at the question being asked. Decide what you are going to guess. Set up a table. Leave extra space for more columns in case you need them.
> • Calculate the entry for a column and label the column.
> • Continue the table until the check is correct.
> • Write the answer in a complete sentence.
>
> Example: The sum of two consecutive numbers is 29. What are the numbers?
>
> | Guess
First Number | Second Number | Total of Numbers
(Sum) | Check
29 |
> |---|---|---|---|
> | 10 | $(10) + 1 = 11$ | $(10) + (11) = 21$ | too low |
> | 20 | $(20) + 1 = 21$ | $(20) + (21) = 41$ | too high |
> | 15 | $(15) + 1 = 16$ | $(15) + (16) = 31$ | too high |
> | 14 | $(14) + 1 = 15$ | $(14) + (15) = 29$ | correct |
>
> The sum of the two consecutive numbers 14 and 15 is 29.

Answer the questions below in your Tool Kit to the right of the double-lined box.

a)   What is the easiest part of using Guess and Check tables?

b)   What is the hardest part of using Guess and Check tables?

Getting Organized: Data Interpretation   15

GO-34. Erin and Jacob decided to play a game in which Erin thinks of a number and Jacob tries to guess it. Erin says, "My number is the first of three consecutive numbers whose sum is 132." Use the following Guess and Check table and help Jacob figure out the number. Remember to answer using a complete sentence. Reminder: consecutive numbers are integers that follow one another in order, like 6, 7, and 8.

Guess First Number	Second Number	Third Number	Total of Numbers (Sum)	Check 132
10	(10) + 1 = 11	(10) + 2 = 12	(10) + (11) + (12) = 33	too low

GO-35. Casey and Karissa's father has asked them to construct a rectangular pen for their very athletic pig. They have 74 feet of fencing. Because the pig likes to run, they want the length to be one foot more than double the width. Use a Guess and Check table to help Karissa and Casey find the dimensions (both length and width) of the pen.

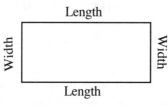

Copy and complete the table below.

Guess Width of Pen	Double the Width	Length of Pen	Perimeter	Check 74
10	2 · (10) = 20	(20) + 1 = 21	(10) + (21) + (10) + (21) = 62	too low

GO-36. Zamala made the graph shown below right and thought it looked a little unusual.

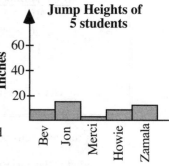

Person	Jump Height
Bev	11 inches
Jon	19 inches
Merci	6 inches
Howie	10 inches
Zamala	18 inches

a) Write a note to Zamala and tell him what he could do to improve his graph.

b) Redraw his graph using your suggested changes.

GO-37.   Copy these incomplete axes. Use your Tool Kit entry from problem GO-22 to find the missing numbers on each graph.

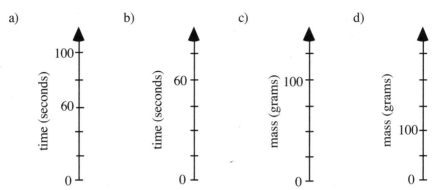

GO-38.   The longest movie ever made was called *The Longest and Most Meaningless Movie in the World*. If you sat through the entire movie, you would sit for exactly 2880 minutes.

a)   How many hours is 2880 minutes?

b)   How many days is 2880 minutes?

GO-39.   Draw a picture to represent each percent.

a)   25%   b)   75%   c) $33\frac{1}{3}\%$

GO-40.   Follow your teacher's directions for practicing mental math. Explain which solution method you liked best.

GO-41.   The **median** of a set of data is the value that is in the middle of the data set. Mrs. Poppington has just recorded these test scores in her grade book: 62, 65, 93, 51, 55, 76, 79, 85, 55, 72, 78, 83, 91, and 82.

a)   Put the test scores in order from smallest to largest.

b)   Find the median of the test scores.

c)   Explain how you determined the median. Use a complete sentence.

d)   What is the **mode** (the value that occurs most often) of the test scores?

GO-42. Edwin and Saul collected some data about test scores from a recent spelling test. They decided that a **stem-and-leaf plot** would be the best way to display their data.

The stem-and-leaf plot at right shows the test score data. With your partner, examine this stem-and-leaf plot and record your answers to the following questions.

Test Score Data

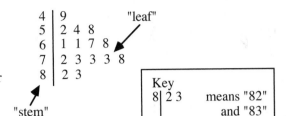

```
4 | 9              "leaf"
5 | 2 4 8
6 | 1 1 7 8
7 | 2 3 3 3 8
8 | 2 3
```

"stem"

Key
8 | 2 3   means "82"
            and "83"

a)   What is the highest score? What is the lowest score?

b)   What is the mode?

c)   How many scores are there? Write each score.

d)   What is the mean of the scores?

e)   What is the median score?

f)   What part of the score becomes the "stem"?

g)   How are the "stem" parts organized?

h)   How are the "leaf" parts organized?

i)   Why do you think this graph is called a "stem-and-leaf plot"? Be sure to answer in a complete sentence.

j)   Rotate the stem-and-leaf plot 90° counter-clockwise (that is, to the left). What kind of graph does the stem-and-leaf plot look like now?

GO-43. Follow your teacher's directions for Pencils in the Middle before starting this problem.

Edwin and Saul asked some of their classmates in third-period math class to write down the number of minutes they spend on the phone each day. Here is the data set they collected: 25, 30, 88, 12, 15, 35, 20, 5, 17, 65, 16, 12, 20, 60, 75, 93, 75, 55, 50, 45, 40, 80.

a)   Display Edwin and Saul's data on a stem-and-leaf plot.

b)   What is the greatest number of minutes spent on the phone? What is the least?

c)   Is there an even or odd number of entries? Explain how you will compute the median. What is the median?

>>Problem continues on the next page.>>

d) Find the mode (that is, find the number that occurs most often). Is there more than one number that occurs most often? If there are two modes, the data is **bimodal**. If there are three modes, the data is **trimodal**. How would you describe the mode of Edwin and Saul's data?

e) Edwin and Saul are having a disagreement about the mean. Edwin says that he added up all the minutes and the mean is 933 minutes. Saul thinks the mean is approximately 42 minutes. Who is correct? Explain why.

f) Find the mean. (The minutes really do add to 933.)

g) What are you able to see on a stem-and-leaf plot that you cannot see on a bar graph?

GO-44.

STUDY TEAM GUIDELINES

1. Each member of the team is responsible for his or her own behavior.

2. Each member of the team must be willing to help any other team member who asks for help.

3. When you have a question, ask your partner or team first. If no one can answer the question, then ask the teacher for help.

4. **Use your team voice.**

Make these notes in your Tool Kit to the right of the double-lined box.

Rewrite the fourth guideline in your own words.

GO-45.

STEM-AND-LEAF PLOT

A **STEM-AND-LEAF PLOT** is a way to display data that shows the individual values from a set of data and how the values are distributed. The "stem" part of the graph represents the leading digit of the number. The "leaf" part of the graph represents the other digit(s) of the number.

Example: Students in a math class received the following scores on their test: 49, 52, 54, 58, 61, 61, 67, 68, 72, 73, 73, 73, 78, 82, and 83. Display the test score data on a stem-and-leaf plot.

```
4 | 9        "leaf"
5 | 2 4 8
6 | 1 1 7 8
7 | 2 3 3 3 8
8 | 2 3
```
"stem"

Key
8 | 2 3   means "82"
          and "83"

Highlight the words "stem," "represents the leading digit," "leaf," and "represents the other digit(s)" in your Tool Kit.

GO-46. Display this set of data on a stem-and-leaf plot: 4.7, 3.2, 5.3, 7.2, 5.1, 7, 4.1, 3.7, 2.8, 4.3, 5.8, 6.2, 7.7, 1.5. Read all three parts below before you start your stem-and-leaf plot.

    a)   What is different about this set of data?

    b)   What digits will form the "stem"?

    c)   What digits make the "leaf"?

GO-47. One number is 17 less than another and the sum of the two numbers is 65. What are the numbers? Make a Guess and Check table and continue guessing until you find the correct answer. Remember that you must make at least four meaningful guesses. Write your answer in a complete sentence.

Guess First Number	Second Number	Sum of Two Numbers	Check 65
20	20 − 17 = 3	20 + 3 = 23	too low

GO-48. Copy each problem, then compute the sum or difference. Remember to show all your steps.

    a)   23.6 + 12   b)   16.5 + 52.43   c)   46.21 − 31.2

    d)   27.5 − 13.11   e)   94.3 − 22.6   f)   109.08 − 73.8

GO-49. Copy these incomplete axes and add their scales. You may use your Tool Kit to help find the missing numbers.

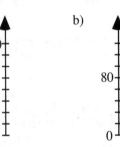
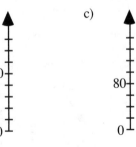

GO-50. Tanisha drew a picture to represent one-half. Natasha drew a picture to represent one-fourth. Wyman looked at the drawings and said, "Your pictures are wrong. One-half is supposed to be bigger than one-fourth." Do you agree with Wyman? Explain why or why not.

GO-51. Margaret had almost finished her homework and was finding the median of a set of numbers. She knew that there were five numbers and that the median was 21.

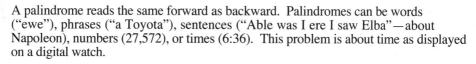

a) Four of the numbers were 1, 23, 16, and 100. What could the other number have been?

b) Suppose four of the numbers were 1, 21, 16, and 100. What could the other number have been?

GO-52. When you see the icon at left under a problem number, expect the problem to be challenging.

A palindrome reads the same forward as backward. Palindromes can be words ("ewe"), phrases ("a Toyota"), sentences ("Able was I ere I saw Elba"—about Napoleon), numbers (27,572), or times (6:36). This problem is about time as displayed on a digital watch.

a) Write down three digital watch times that are palindromes.

b) What are the least and greatest amounts of time between two times that are palindromes?

c) How many times during a 24-hour day is the time on a digital watch a palindrome?

GO-53. Follow your teacher's directions to list characteristics you and your partner or team have in common and characteristics that are unique to each of you.

GO-54.   Here are Mrs. Poppington's class test scores arranged in order from smallest to largest:
51, 55, 55, 62, 65, 72, 76, 78, 79, 82, 83, 85, 91, and 93.

   a)   Copy the list of scores on your paper.

   b)   Circle the median number.

   c)   Find the median of the <u>lower half</u> of your data, that is, the numbers to the left of the
         median. Draw a box around it. This number marks the **lower quartile** of the data
         set.

   d)   Find the median of the <u>upper half</u> of your data, that is, the numbers to the right of the
         median. Draw a box around it. This number marks the **upper quartile** of the data
         set.

GO-55.   Find the numbers that define the median and quartiles for the following sets of numbers.

   a)   10, 11, 12, 12, 12, 15, 17, 20, 21, 22, 30, 35, 35

   b)   10, 11, 12, 12, 12, 15, 17, 20, 21, 22, 30, 40, 50, 66

   c)   17, 11, 100, 35, 46

GO-56.   Another way of displaying data is called a **box-and-whisker plot**. Start with a number
line. The box-and-whisker plot is drawn above it. A box-and-whisker plot requires data
to be ordered from smallest to largest.
You also need to know the range. We will use
the data from problem GO-54 to draw a box-
and-whisker plot. An outline of a box-and-
whisker plot is shown at right to help you draw
the one for this data.

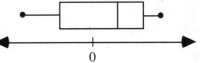

   a)   Since the range of the numbers is 42 (93 to 51), draw a number line with equal
         intervals, each interval representing five units, from 50 to 95.

   b)   Draw a vertical line segment (about two centimeters long) above the median. Write
         the number it represents below it.

   c)   Place a vertical line segment above the median of the lower half of the data. Write
         the number it represents below it.

   d)   Place a vertical line segment above the median of the upper half of the data. Write
         the number it represents below it.

   e)   Draw a box between the upper quartile and the lower quartile, using the line
         segments you drew above each quartile as the vertical sides.

   f)   Place two dots above the number line, one that labels the minimum (the smallest
         number) and another that labels the maximum (the largest number) values of the data
         set.

   g)   Draw a line segment from the lower quartile to the minimum value's dot and a line
         segment from the upper quartile to the maximum value's dot. The line segments
         extending to the far right and left of the data display are called the **whiskers**.

GO-57.   Edwin and Saul decided to collect more data from the second-period math class. They got permission from the second-period math teacher and asked 22 other students to write down the number of minutes they spent on the phone. Here are their results: 45, 37, 25, 20, 15, 13, 60, 65, 12, 8, 8, 75, 90, 100, 120, 15, 10, 20, 35, 42, 50, 35.

a)   Display Edwin and Saul's new data on a new stem-and-leaf plot.

b)   Now display the same data on a box-and-whisker plot.

GO-58.   Gracie loves to talk on the phone, but her parents try to restrict her calls. They kept records of the time she spent on the phone each day. For the past nine days the data was: 120, 60, 0, 30, 15, 0, 0, 10, and 20.

a)   Find the mean, median, and mode for the information.

b)   Which of the three measures in part (a) might give Gracie's parents the most accurate information about her phone use?

GO-59.   Marvin and Troy were talking about circles. Marvin said that the line that goes from one side of the circle to the other and passes through the center is the radius. Troy disagreed and said that line is the circumference. Help Marvin and Troy by drawing the circle and labeling the circumference, diameter, and radius.

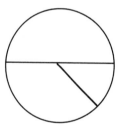

GO-60. Casey and Karissa decided to play a joke on their father and rearranged the pig pen in the shape of a triangle. They used all 74 feet of fencing to make the triangular pen. The second side of the triangle was twice the length of the first, and the third side was ten feet longer than the first. Use a Guess and Check table to find the dimensions (all three sides) of the pen.

a) Sketch a picture on your paper as shown below right.

b) Copy and complete the table. Remember to show all of your calculations and answer using a complete sentence.

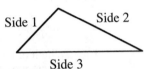

Side 1   Side 2

Side 3

Guess First Side	Second Side	Third Side	Perimeter	Check 74
10	$2 \cdot (10) = 20$	$(10) + 10 = 20$	$(10) + (20) + (20) = 50$	too low

GO-61. The length of a rectangle is five more than double the width, and the perimeter is 46 yards.

a) Sketch a picture of this situation.

b) Copy and complete the Guess and Check table, making at least four guesses to find the dimensions of the rectangle.

Guess Width	Length	Perimeter	Check 46
10	$2(10) + 5 = 25$	$(10) + (25) + (10) + (25) = 70$	too high

GO-62. Copy each problem, then compute the answer. Be sure to show all your steps.

a) $7.1 \cdot 2.5$ b) $31.2 \cdot 6$ c) $12.5 \cdot 0.02$

d) Write your answer for part (c) as a percent.

GO-63.   **Diamond Problems** With your study team, see if you can discover a pattern for the numbers in each of the three diamonds below.

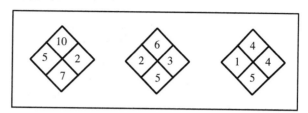

Finding patterns is an important problem solving skill used in mathematics. You will use the patterns in Diamond Problems to solve other problems later in the course.

Copy the Diamond Problems below and use the pattern you discovered to complete each of them.

a)   b)   c)   d)   e)

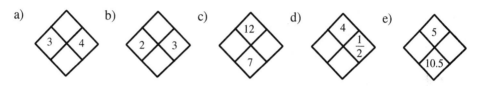

GO-64.

MEASURES OF CENTRAL TENDENCY

Numbers that locate or approximate the "center" of a set of data are called **MEASURES OF CENTRAL TENDENCY.** The mean, median, and mode are three measures of central tendency.

The **MEAN** is the arithmetic average of the data set. (See problem GO-30.) The mean is generally the best measure of central tendency to use when the set of data does not contain outliers.

The **MEDIAN** is the middle number in a set of data <u>arranged</u> <u>numerically</u>. If there is an even number of values, the median is the mean of the two middle numbers. The median is more accurate than the mean as a measure of central tendency when there are outliers in the data set.

The **MODE** is the value in a data set that occurs more often than any other value. Data sets may have more than one mode, and some do not have any mode. (See problem GO-43(d).) The mode is useful when the data are not numeric, such as showing a "most popular" choice.

Suppose the following data set represents the number of home runs hit by the best seven players on a major league baseball team: 16, 46, 21, 9, 13, 15, and 9.

The mean is $\frac{16 + 46 + 21 + 9 + 13 + 15 + 9}{7} = \frac{129}{7} \approx 18.43$.

The median is 15, since, when arranged in order—9, 9, 13, 15, 16, 21, 46—the middle number is 15.

The mode is 9, since it occurs twice and no other number appears more than once.

Highlight the words "average" (see mean), "middle number" (see median), and "occurs most often" (see mode) in your Tool Kit.

QUARTILES AND BOX-AND-WHISKER PLOTS

To find **QUARTILES**, the data set must be in order from smallest to largest. First find the median of the entire data set. Next find the median of the lower half of the data set. Finally, find the median of the upper half of the data set. The quartiles are the medians of the upper and lower halves of the data set.

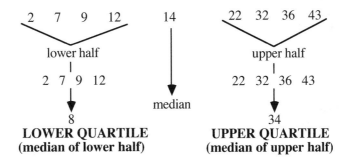

LOWER QUARTILE
(median of lower half)

UPPER QUARTILE
(median of upper half)

A **BOX-AND-WHISKER PLOT** displays data using quartiles. The plot and its parts appear below using the data above as a model. Problem GO-56 has the step-by-step directions for how to create a box and whisker plot.

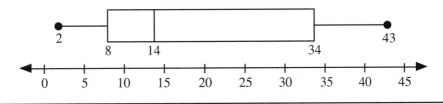

Make these notes in your Tool Kit to the right of the double-lined box.

a)   List a similarity between box-and-whisker plots and stem-and-leaf plots.

b)   List a difference between box-and-whisker plots and stem-and-leaf plots.

GO-66.

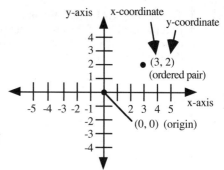

GRAPHING POINTS ON AN XY-COORDINATE GRID

Numerical data that you want to put on a two dimensional graph is entered on the graph as **POINTS**.

The points on the graph are identified by two numbers, which together make an **ORDERED PAIR** written generally as (x, y). For example, (3, 2). These two numbers are called **COORDINATES** because together they name the location of the point on the graph.

The first number of the ordered pair is the **X-COORDINATE** because it represents the horizontal distance from (0, 0).

The second number of the ordered pair is the **Y-COORDINATE** because it represents the vertical distance from (0, 0).

The ordered pair (3, 2) is located at a point that is right 3 units and up 2 units from the **ORIGIN**, (0, 0). The scaled lines are called the **X-AXIS** (horizontal) and **Y-AXIS** (vertical).

Make these notes in your Tool Kit to the right of the double-lined box.

a)   In your own words, explain what an ordered pair means.

b)   Explain how you would place the ordered pair (-4, 3) on a graph. Mark it on the graph in your Tool Kit and check with your partner or team when you return to class to be sure you did so correctly.

c)   Review the earlier Tool Kit entry that describes a complete graph.

GO-67.   Copy each problem, then compute the answer. Show all your steps.

a) $62.9 \cdot 0.7$ b) $53.2 \cdot 0.34$ c) $68.24 \cdot 7.32$

GO-68.   Erin and Jacob decided to play one more round of the "guess the number" game. Erin thought the last number she gave Jacob was too easy, so this time she said, "I'm thinking of two consecutive even numbers whose product is 528." Jacob said, "I see how you're trying to trick me, but it won't work." Use a Guess and Check table to help Jacob find the numbers. Copy and complete the table. Remember to answer using a complete sentence.

Guess First Number	Second Number	Product	Check 528
10	$(10) + 2 = 12$	$(10) \cdot (12) = 120$	too low

GO-69. Mrs. Poppington has finally finished grading her tests. The first set of scores was: 62, 65, 93, 51, 55, 76, 79, 85, 55, 72, 78, 83, 91, and 82. The last scores are: 88, 74, 97, 32, 82, 76, 59, 63, 89, and 77. Complete parts (a) through (e) for all the scores.

a) Find the median.

b) Find the range.

c) Find the mode.

d) Find the quartiles.

e) Find the mean.

f) Draw a box-and-whisker plot for the data.

GO-70. Follow your teacher's directions for practicing mental math. What new solution method did you learn today?

GO-71. Dezzirae's oldest brother Kalani has saved enough money to buy a car. Kalani told Dezzirae, "Buying a car will actually be a good investment. I can buy it now and sell it when I need the money back. Except for buying gas, it will be almost free because I can get all my money back when I sell it."

Dezzirae exclaimed, "Kalani, I think you should collect some information before you make that kind of statement. Investing your money in a car is not a good idea!"

"I don't agree with you, Dezzirae!" Kalani replied. Collect, organize, and analyze some data to help Dezzirae and Kalani settle their disagreement.

a) Your team needs to collect data on the prices of used cars. You can find this information in the want ads of the newspaper. Your teacher may have some other ideas about where you can find this information. Select one manufacturer of cars and one model. Try to pick a model of car that has been produced for a few years. Split the work among your team so that you can collect the data as quickly as possible. One member of the team should use a table like the one below to record the data for the team. You will want to have at least 15 entries in your table. Once you have collected the data, each team member needs to copy the data table.

Manufacturer of Car _____ Model of Car _____

Price of Car	Year of Car	Age of Car

b) What is the range in the prices of your data? What is the range in the ages of the cars? Use this information to scale the axes on the graph you will create in part (c).

>>Problem continues on the next page.>>

c) Enter the data on the graph. Do not connect the points. This is called a **scatter plot.** Use the example at right to help you set up your graph. Using graph paper may make it easier for you to plot the data.

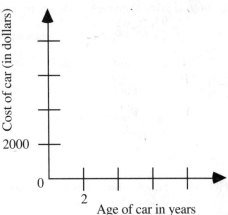

d) Examine the points on your scatter plot. Does there appear to be a relationship between the age of the car and the cost of the car? Using complete sentences, describe what you see.

e) Based on your scatter plot, what information would you give Dezzirae and Kalani to help them settle their argument? Can Kalani get all his money back if he sells his car in a couple of years? Explain why it would have been beneficial for Dezzirae and Kalani to collect and graph some data before getting into an argument.

GO-72. Your teacher will give you a resource page for this problem.

a) On the resource page, plot the following points in a bright color and draw a line through them: $(2, 40), (3, 40), (4, 40), (5, 40), (6, 40)$, and $(3\frac{1}{2}, 40)$.

b) What do you notice? Write your answer in a complete sentence.

c) Write the ordered pairs for two other points that would be on the same line as the points in part (a).

GO-73. Use the resource page provided by your teacher.

a) On the resource page, plot the following points in a bright color and draw a line through them: $(550, 72), (550, 66), (550, 69)$, and $(550, 79)$.

b) What do you notice? Write your answer in a complete sentence.

c) Write the ordered pairs for two other points which would be on the same line.

GO-74. Use the resource page provided by your teacher.

a) Label each axis.

b) Plot the following ordered pairs (points) and draw a line through them: $(-4, -4), (-2, -3), (0, -2), (2, -1), (4, 0), (6, 1)$.

c) What do you notice? Write the ordered pairs for two other points that would be on the same line.

GO-75.   Use the resource page provided by your teacher.

   a)   Label each axis. Plot the following ordered pairs: (2, 3), (-2, 3), (-2, -3), (2, -3).
        Connect the points as you plot them.

   b)   Describe the shape on your graph.

   c)   Plot a triangle on the same set of axes. List the ordered pairs needed for your
        triangle.

GO-76.   Karissa and Casey need to construct another pig pen
         for their grand champion pig named Beauty. Large
         pigs like Beauty need at least 108 square feet of living
         space. Karissa and Casey made the length 3 feet
         longer than the width and created exactly 108 square
         feet of area for Beauty. Use a Guess and Check table
         to find the dimensions (length and width) of the pen.

   a)   Sketch a picture on your paper like the one
        shown at right.

   b)   Copy and complete the table below. Remember
        to answer using a complete sentence.

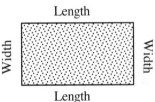

Guess Width	Length	
10	(10) + 3 = 13	

GO-77.   Copy and complete the Diamond Problems below. Notice the icon under the problem
         number at left. Use the diamond problem pattern to solve these problems.

Product

Sum

a)
    5   1.5

b)
    3.2   1.2

c)
    60
    19

d)
    13
    31

e)
    11
    25

GO-78. Organized binders do not have loose papers in them. The "Shake Test" is a technique you can use to see if your papers are locked into your binder. Hold your binder along the spine and <u>gently</u> shake it. If any papers fall out, they will need to be placed back in the binder in the correct location. You may need to purchase hole reinforcement stickers, hole-punch some papers, or simply place papers in their correct place. Work on your binder until it passes the "Shake Test." When this is completed, write "My binder has passed the shake test" next to this problem number on your paper. Your teacher may actually try the "Shake Test" on your binder tomorrow.

GO-79.

Chapter Summary As you finish a chapter, you need to reflect on the material. Your teacher is going to model one way to do that. You and your partner or team will then need to do a chapter summary of your own.

a) You will construct a concept map today for each chapter objective. Your teacher will model a topic for you.

b) Look back through your work and select two problems that illustrate what you have learned about organizing, displaying, and interpreting data. Restate the problem and show its complete solution.

c) Select a problem that you solved using a Guess and Check table. Write the problem and show the complete solution.

GO-80. Shelly and Melissa spent Saturday morning making chocolate chip cookies. They counted the cookies and discovered they had made 53 of them. Then Shelly decided to divide the cookies. Since Shelly was five years older than Melissa, it seemed natural for her to get five more cookies. Draw and label a Guess and Check table and use it to find out how many cookies were in each sister's pile. Be sure to show all four steps clearly.

GO-81. Scaling the axes to plot this set of points requires some planning: (600, 5), (750, 10), (400, 3), and (300, 0).

a) Decide the maximum and minimum values for both the x-axis and the y-axis on your graph.

b) Decide what intervals to use on each axis.

c) Draw and scale the axes so you can graph all the points.

d) Plot the points on your graph.

GO-82. You have a set of six numbers and know that five of them are 2, 24, 16, 17, and 12.

a) If you know that the median is 14, what could the missing number be?

b) If you know that the quartiles are defined by the numbers 8, 14, and 17, what could the missing number be?

GO-83. The Road Safety Committee is concerned about the number of car accidents that occur near people's homes. They want to know if it is safer to drive a long distance or a short distance. Copy the axes below, choose and label a scale with appropriate intervals, and create a scatter plot to see if there is a relationship between distance from home and the number of accidents last year.

Distance from Home	# of Accidents Last Year
2 miles	759
5 miles	680
7 miles	700
9 miles	558
12 miles	384
15 miles	135
20 miles	82

GO-84. The Road Safety Committee is impressed with your graph and now has some questions for you.

a) Since there were more accidents near homes, can we conclude that being near home causes more accidents than being farther from home?

b) Is this a **positive correlation** (as distance increases, the number of accidents also increases) or a **negative correlation** (as distance increases, the number of accidents decreases)?

c) If we see a connection between two things (like distance and accidents), does that mean one causes the other?

GO-85.   Understanding the difference between one thing being <u>correlated</u> to another and <u>causing</u> the other is important. Write TRUE if you think the item listed causes the other; write FALSE if there is a correlation but not a cause.

    a)   Being in my home causes me to fall down, because I fall down about 20 times a year at home and almost never at other people's homes.

    b)   Practicing basketball causes me to shoot free throws well, because I shoot better when I practice.

    c)   Turning on the "Seat Belt" light on the airplane causes turbulence, because whenever the light is turned on, the flight gets bumpy.

    d)   Smoking causes lung cancer, because a lot of people who smoke get lung cancer.

    e)   Being tall makes you a better speller, because a lot of people under 3 feet tall cannot spell well.

GO-86.   These questions relate to dividing by 2. Some of them may not be possible. If they are not, explain in a sentence or two why not.

    a)   Find all of the digits that could be used to make the three-digit number 5__1 divisible by 2.

    b)   Find all of the digits that could be used to make the three-digit number 3__6 divisible by 4.

    c)   If you have an even number N (divisible by 2), can the number N + 200 also be divisible by 2? Explain in a sentence or two.

    d)   If you have an odd number N (<u>not</u> divisible by 2), can the number N + 200 ever be an even number? Explain in a sentence or two.

GO-87.   Follow your teacher's directions for practicing mental math. Are you beginning to find it easier to do these type of problems? Explain.

GO-88.   Since 1904 the times for men and women in the Olympic 100-meter free-style swimming race have been decreasing. Bethany wondered if the times for the two groups would ever be the same. She needs a way to display the data to help her compare the times for men and women. The tables below show the times for the Olympic 100-meter free-style swimming races from 1904 to 2000.

>>Problem continues on the next page.>>

Men's 100-meter Free-style

Year	Athletes	Country	Time
1904	Z. De Halmay	Hungary	62.8
1908	C. Daniels	USA	65.6
1912	D. Kahanamoku	USA	63.4
1920	D. Kahanamoku	USA	61.4
1924	J. Weissmuller	USA	59.0
1928	J. Weissmuller	USA	58.6
1932	Y. Miyazaki	Japan	58.2
1936	F. Csik	Hungary	57.6
1948	W. Ris	USA	57.3
1952	C. Scholes	USA	57.4
1956	J. Hendricks	Australia	55.4
1960	J. Devitt	Australia	55.2
1964	D. Schollander	USA	53.4
1968	M. Wenden	Australia	52.22
1972	M. Spitz	USA	51.22
1976	J. Montgomery	USA	49.99
1980	J. Woithe	E. Germany	50.40
1984	R. Gaines	USA	49.80
1988	M. Biondi	USA	48.63
1992	A. Popov	Unified Team	49.02
1996	A. Popov	Russia	48.74
2000	P. Vanden Hoogenband	Netherlands	48.30

Women's 100-meter Free-style

Year	Athlete	Country	Time
1920	E. Bleibtrey	USA	73.6
1924	E. Lackie	USA	72.4
1928	A. Osipowich	USA	71.0
1932	H. Madison	USA	66.8
1936	H. Mastenbroek	Holland	65.9
1948	G. Andersen	Denmark	66.3
1952	K. Szoke	Hungary	66.8
1956	D. Fraser	Australia	62.0
1960	D. Fraser	Australia	61.2
1964	D. Fraser	Australia	59.5
1968	J. Henne	USA	60.0
1972	S. Neilson	USA	58.59
1976	K. Ender	E. Germany	55.65
1980	B. Krause	E. Germany	54.79
1984	Hogshead	USA	55.92
1988	K. Otto	E. Germany	54.93
1992	Z. Yong	China	54.64
1996	L. Jingyi	China	54.50
2000	I. deBruijn	Netherlands	53.83

>>Problem continues on the next page.>>

a) Use the resource page to draw a double-line graph for the men's and women's Olympic data. Make sure your legend clearly identifies each line.

b) What trends do you notice? (A trend is the general direction the line is headed.)

c) Do you think the women's times will eventually equal the men's times?

d) Why do you think there were no Olympic games in 1916, 1940, and 1944?

e) Why do you think the times were recorded in hundredths of a second beginning in 1968?

f) Which changed more, the men's or women's times? Why do you think that happened?

g) Write a response that Bethany might use after your analysis of the data.

h) What do you predict will be the men's and women's times in the next Olympics (2004)? Explain your prediction.

GO-89. Draw a set of axes like the one at right. Notice that there are 8 spaces on the y-axis. Put the years on the x-axis. Be careful about the interval on the x-axis. Read the "Intervals and Scaling" entry in your Tool Kit before numbering the x-axis. Make sure your graph is complete.

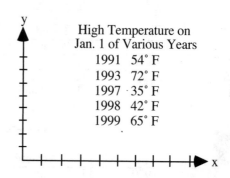

High Temperature on
Jan. 1 of Various Years
1991   54° F
1993   72° F
1997   35° F
1998   42° F
1999   65° F

GO-90. Tomatoes are sold 3 for $1.20 at Bull's Eye Market.

a) How much does one tomato cost?

b) How much would 18 tomatoes cost?

GO-91. Find the mean, median, and mode of this set of data: 7.2, 3.8, 9.4, 4.7, 1.6, 11.8, 3.8, 7.2, and 6.5.

GO-92. Look in the bottom of your backpack for any loose papers. If there are any, they should be taken out and put back in your binder. Caution: There may be papers from other classes. Put those away in their proper places as well. Try the "Shake Test" to see that everything is locked in your binder. On your paper, write, "My binder has passed the shake test."

GO-93.   Copy and complete the Diamond Problems below.

Product

Sum

a)   b)   c)   d)   e)

GO-94.   A triangle has three sides. The second side is one centimeter longer than twice the length of the first side, and the third side is two centimeters shorter than the second side. The perimeter of the triangle is 125 centimeters.

a)   Sketch a picture of this situation.

b)   Solve the problem using a complete Guess and Check process.

Guess First Side	Second Side			
10	$2(10) + 1 = 21$			

GO-95.   The product of two consecutive odd numbers is 12,099. Complete a Guess and Check table to find the numbers.

GO-96.   **What We Have Done in This Chapter**

Below is a list of the Tool Kit entries from this chapter.

- GO-8   Study Team Guidelines (also GO-20, 29, and 44)
- GO-10   A Complete Graph
- GO-13   Common Measurements
- GO-22   Intervals, Scaling, and the Number Line
- GO-30   Mean, Outliers, and Range
- GO-33   Solving Problems with Guess and Check Tables
- GO-45   Stem-and-Leaf Plot
- GO-64   Measures of Central Tendency
- GO-65   Quartiles and Box-and-Whisker Plots
- GO-66   Graphing Points on an xy-Coordinate Grid

Review all the entries and read the notes you made in your Tool Kit. Make a list of any questions, terms, or notes you do not understand. Ask your partner or study team members for help. If anything is still unclear, ask your teacher.

THE FIELD TRIP

Chapter 2

Chapter 2
The Field Trip: **INTEGER OPERATIONS AND GRAPHING EQUATIONS**

In this chapter you will begin working with integer operations. You will also discover patterns in relation to data tables, rules or equations, and graphs. In addition, you will learn about the shapes of different graphs. You will continue to record data and graph real-life situations, as well as practice the problem solving strategy of Guess and Check.

In this chapter you will have the opportunity to:

- discover and describe patterns in data tables.

- graph points in all four quadrants.

- develop integer operations for addition, subtraction, multiplication, and division.

- identify and graph linear and non-linear equations.

- continue to solve word problems using the Guess and Check problem solving strategy.

Read the problem below, but **do not try to solve it now**. What you learn over the next few days will enable you to solve it.

FT-0. **The Big Hike** At Big Tree Park, Raul, the park ranger, and Mia, the chief naturalist, each led a group hike. Raul's group hiked to Grizzly Peak, which has an elevation of 182 feet. Mia's group hiked to Mt. Sawtooth, which has an elevation of 324 feet. The elevation of their campsite is 120 feet below sea level. If Mia's group hikes downhill at a rate of 3 feet per minute and Raul's group hikes downhill at a rate of 2 feet per minute, which group will arrive at the campsite first?

Number Sense	
Algebra and Functions	
Mathematical Reasoning	
Measurement and Geometry	
Statistics, Data Analysis, & Probability	

Chapter 2
The Field Trip: INTEGER OPERATIONS AND GRAPHING EQUATIONS

FT-1.   Today you will play silent board games. The directions are below. As each silent board game is played, copy the table and the rule on your paper.

Silent Board Games
A game for the whole class.

Mathematical Purpose: To find and describe mathematical relationships.

Object: To complete the table and find the rule.

Materials: None.

How to Play the Game:
- Your teacher will start an xy relationship table on the board by filling in some of the x-values and a few of the y-values.
- The class will remain silent as you try to figure out the pattern that links each x-value to each y-value.
- Raise your hand when you think you can fill in one of the blanks. Your teacher will call on students to fill in an answer silently. Then return to your seat.
- Your teacher will erase an incorrect answer.

Ending the Game: The game ends when the table is complete and someone writes the rule.

FT-2.   Your teacher will give you instructions for the Whole-Class Graphing Activity. On the resource page provided by your teacher, make a sketch of each graph based on the large class graphs and describe what each one looks like. Add any notes to these sketches that will help you draw graphs correctly.

FT-3.   Use a Guess and Check table to solve the following problem.

Raul wanted to see if the deer population had been affected by an increase in the number of visitors to the park. He decided to count the number of visitors entering the park through each of the three gates. On Saturday, 50 more people came through the South Gate than the North Gate. There were two times as many people entering through the West Gate as the North Gate. If 3202 people visited the park that day, how many entered through each of the gates?

Copy and complete the Guess and Check table below to help you answer this question. Be sure to make at least 4 guesses. Write your answer to the question using a complete sentence.

Guess Number of Visitors Entering North Gate	Number of Visitors Entering South Gate			Check 3202
10	(10) + 50 = 60			

FT-4. Use the resource page provided by your teacher that shows a map of Big Tree Park. Match each location with a point on the diagram. Keep this map in your binder for future use.

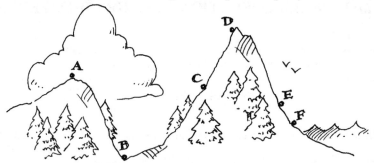

Lookout Point:	150'	Grizzly Peak:	182'
Redwood Grove:	49'	Mt. Sawtooth:	324'
Campsite:	-120'	Sea Level:	0'

FT-5. Copy each problem, then compute the answer. Show all your steps.

a) $1.234 + 0.58 + 5.316$ b) $6.1 - 1.536$ c) $4.83 \cdot 0.68$

d) $18.273 - 6.039$ e) $4.8 + 6.237 + 0.1$ f) $6.23 \cdot 0.812$

FT-6. David and his parents went on vacation. One day they drove 200 miles, traveling at the same speed the entire way. If the trip took them a total of four hours, how many miles did they drive in one hour? Show your work and write an equation.

FT-7. Here are the heights in inches of hollyhocks (tall, slender flowering plants) that are growing in the park: 10, 39, 43, 45, 46, 47, 48, 48, 49, 50, and 52.

a) Find the mean.   b) Find the mode.

c) Find the range.   d) Find the median.

e) Which measure of central tendency best represents this set of data?

f) Find the quartiles.   g) Make a box-and-whisker plot.

FT-8.   Use the resource page provided by your teacher to make your set of integer tiles. Cut out the set of squares with plus signs and the set of squares with minus signs. Store them in the envelope provided for use throughout this chapter.

FT-9.   Now that we have started a new chapter, it is time for you to organize your binder.

a)   Put the work from the last chapter in order, take it out of your binder, and store it in a separate folder.

b)   When this is completed, write, "I have organized my binder."

FT-10.   Follow your teacher's directions for practicing mental math. What new strategy did you learn today?

FT-11.   Your teacher will give several students bundles of envelopes containing unknown amounts of money. Do not open or look inside any of the envelopes until your teacher tells you to do so.

Make a table like the one below and follow the instructions from your teacher to complete it.

Envelope Label	Amount in Each Envelope	Total Amount of Money
↓	↓	

FT-12. The first stop on your field trip to Big Tree Park is a grove of redwood trees that are all different heights. Raul, the park ranger, explained that the height difference occurred because after the first tree was planted, additional trees were planted in 5-year intervals (That is, every five years). The tree nearest you is 85 feet tall, and the next one, which is five years older, is 90 feet tall. You are curious about their age, so you decide to graph the situation and use your graph to learn more about the age of the tree.

a) Use the data table like the one below on your resource page for the 85-foot tree.

					Last Year	Now	Next Year						
years (x)	-5	-4	-3	-2	-1	0	1	2	3	5	10	15	20
height (y)		81	82			85	86						

b) Fill in the height of the tree for each year, assuming the tree continues to grow at the same rate.

c) How does the height of the tree change as the years go by? Study your table and describe in words the pattern you see.

d) Write a word equation that relates the height of the tree to the number of years.

FT-13. How tall will the tree be:

a) in 30 years?   b) in 50 years?   c) in any future year?

FT-14. How tall was the tree:

a) 10 years ago?   b) 20 years ago?

c) How many years ago was the tree planted?

FT-15. Follow the steps below to graph the data from the redwood tree in problem FT-12. Start by copying the graph at right and extend the axes to represent the past and future, or use the graph on your resource page.

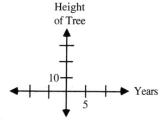

a) Scale the horizontal (x) axis by fives. Each tick mark represents five years. As you number to the right of zero, you are looking at the future. As you number to the left of zero, you are looking at the past, so -5 means "five years ago." Scale the vertical (y) axis by tens. Each tick mark will represent ten feet of height.

b) Plot the points from your table. Remember to go across to the year (x) and then move up to the height (y).

c) Connect the points to show the tree's continuous growth.

d) Does it make sense for this line to continue forever in both directions? Explain.

FT-16. Use your graph from the previous problem to answer the following questions.

a) Find the point on your graph where your line crosses the horizontal (x) axis. What is the height of the tree at this point? Record this in your table.

b) What does this point represent?

FT-17. Below is the word equation from problem FT-12.

Height = 85 + (number of years)

a) Complete a table like the one below. Show your work as modeled in the table.

Number of Years	85 + (number of years)	Height of Tree
8	85 + 8	
5	85 + 5	90
-1	85 + (-1)	
-2	85 + ( )	
-6	85 +	
-10		

b) What happens to the height of the tree as we move into the past? Why do you think this is so?

FT-18. Write a numerical expression that represents each statement. Part (a) is done for you.

a) Fourteen is added to a number x.

b) Forty-three is subtracted from a number y.

c) A number a is multiplied by five.

d) A number x is tripled, then seven is added.

FT-19.

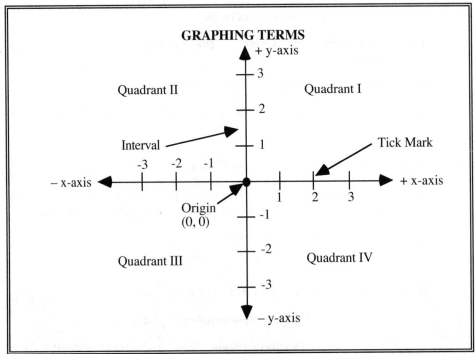

GRAPHING TERMS

Complete parts (a) through (c) below in your Tool Kit to the right of the double-lined box.

a) In your own words, describe what an interval is.

b) Tell why tick marks and a scale are needed on graphs.

c) Where on the graph is the origin?

FT-20. Copy the graphs below. In parts (a) and (b) determine the interval used between tick marks. Complete the scale by labeling the remaining tick marks.

a)

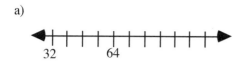

32   64

b)

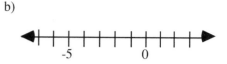

-5   0

c)

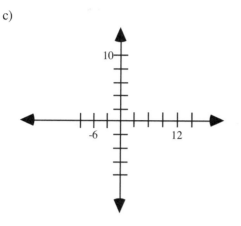

-6   12

For part (c):

i)   Label the y-axis.

ii)   Label the origin.

iii) Label Quadrant III.

iv)   Complete the scaling of both axes.

FT-21. Mia was studying some of the pond life in the park. In two hours she counted 4 more frogs than the number of turtles she saw. The number of crayfish she counted was 3 more than twice the number of turtles. She counted 75 pond animals in all. Use a Guess and Check table to find the number of turtles, crayfish, and frogs Mia counted.

a)   Copy and complete the table. Keep guessing and checking until you get the correct answer. Remember to make at least four guesses.

Guess the Number of Turtles	Number of Frogs	Number of Crayfish	Total Number of Pond Animals	Check 75
10				

b)   Write your answer in a complete sentence.

FT-22. Complete these Diamond Problems.

Product

Sum

a)

5.3   8.2

b)

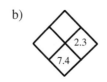

2.3

7.4

c)

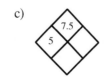

7.5

5

d)

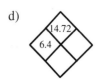

14.72

6.4

FT-23. A number n is greater than four. Which of the following graphs best represents the location of $\frac{4}{n}$ on the number line?

Note: The icon at left indicates that the problem will be in the multiple choice format.

(A)

(B)

(C)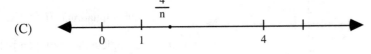

(D)

(E)   none of the these

FT-24. What is the product of seventy-two and zero?

(A) 0   (B) 1   (C) 72   (D) -72   (E) none of these

FT-25. We changed the water in our fish tank and needed to add some acid to bring the water to the right pH. We did not have any tool to measure pH, but our neighbor had a kit for his swimming pool and told us that if our aquarium held 10,000 gallons, we would need to add 6 gallons of acid. However, our aquarium holds only six gallons of water. How many <u>teaspoons</u> of acid do we need? Note: 3 teaspoons = 1 tablespoon, 16 tablespoons = 1 cup = 8 ounces.

FT-26. As each silent board game is played, copy and complete the table, then write the equation on your paper below the table. You may want to review the rules for the game in problem FT-1.

FT-27.   Represent each integer using integer tiles two different ways. Make a sketch for each model.

a)   6   b)   -2   c)   -5   d)   0

FT-28.   Use at least 12 tiles to represent each integer. Remember that you can add zero pairs to the model without changing the value of each number. Sketch a drawing for each model.

a)   5   b)   -4   c)   -7   d)   0

FT-29.   Here is another example with a diagram: 5 + (-3). Use this example as your model for solving the following problems. Draw a diagram and write an equation for each problem below the example.

+ + + + +   5

+ + + + +   5 + (-3)
_ _ _

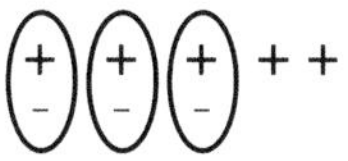

+ +   5 + (-3) = 2

ADDING INTEGERS

1.   Build your first integer.
2.   Add tiles that represent the second integer.
3.   Circle all the zero pairs.
4.   Count the uncircled tiles.
5.   Record the equation showing the sum.

---

a)   4 + (-7)   b)   -1 + (-5)   c)   -3 + 6

FT-30.   Use integer tiles to help you add the integers in each problem below. Sketch a tile drawing and write the equation for each of the following problems.

a)   -6 + (-8)   b)   2 + (-5)   c)   -3 + (-3)   d)   -2 + 3 + 5

e)   Describe the steps you used to solve part (d).

FT-31. Copy the number line below. Remember to create a reasonable scale. Draw a tick mark and label it to show when you:

Now

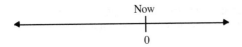

0

a) lost your first tooth.

b) started to read.

c) started elementary school.

d) started middle school.

e) started high school.

FT-32. Use the number line from the previous problem to show the following events in your life. Did the ages from the previous problem go before "Now" or after "Now" on the number line?

a) How many years ago were you born?

b) If "Now" is 0 and you were born sometime before now, what kind of integer should you use to represent when you were born? Be sure this is on your number line. It is important!

c) If "Now" is 0, in about how many years will you get your driver's license? Graduate from high school? Vote in your first election? Mark these ages on your number line and label them with the event name.

d) What kind of integers did you use to represent events in the future?

FT-33. Use the table below to complete parts (a) through (c).

in (x)	0	1	2	3	4	5	6	10	100	x
out (y)	1	3				11				

a) Fill in the missing numbers in the table.

b) Use complete sentences to describe the pattern that relates input values to output values.

c) Write the equation that represents the pattern in y-form. Be sure to include the rule in your table.

FT-34.   Use tiles to help you solve these problems. Sketch a tile drawing and write the equation
          below it.

          a)   -2 + (-3)   b)   4 + (-8)

          c)   -1 + (-5)   d)   -7 + 4 + 2

          e)   Describe the steps you used to solve part (d).

FT-35.      Candied apples are sold five for $2.00. Sandi
                                   wants three candied apples. How much will she
                                   have to pay for them? Show the steps you use to
                                   solve this problem.

FT-36.   Irving's print shop was supposed to print the number line below. Copy the number line
          and write the missing numbers below each tick mark.

          a)   Tell Irving which is larger, 5 or 8.

          b)   Tell Irving which is smaller, -7 or -3.

          c)   Tell Irving which is smaller, -10 or 2.

          d)   Finally, tell Irving how he can always determine which number is larger.

FT-37.   As each silent board game is played, copy and complete the table and then write the
          equation below the table.

FT-38. Mia explained to her study team that there are 108 wolves in the park and their number is **decreasing at a rate of three wolves per year**. She is concerned about the decline of the wolf population, so she wants your team to join her in studying the problem.

a) Copy and complete the data table or use the resource page for the wolf population from 20 years ago to help study it in the future. "Now" is represented by 0 years.

years (x)	Past Years				Now	Future Years				
	-20	-15	-10	-5	0	5	10	15	20	x
wolves (y)				123	108	93				

b) Describe the pattern in the table using complete sentences.

c) Write an equation to represent the pattern.

d) Create a graph in which "Time in Years" is on the horizontal (x) axis. It should be scaled so that one tick mark on the graph represents five years.

e) The vertical (y) axis will represent "Number of Wolves" and should be scaled so one tick mark represents ten wolves.

f) Plot the points from the data table.

g) Using a straightedge, draw a line to connect the points. Extend your line as far as possible on your graph.

h) The point where the line crosses the y-axis is called the **y-intercept**. What are the coordinates of this point?

i) The point where the line crosses the x-axis is called the **x-intercept**. What are the coordinates of this point?

FT-39. Use your pattern, the graph, and your table from the previous problem to answer the following questions.

a) When will the population be fewer than 50 wolves?

b) When would there have been 200 wolves?

c) In how many years will the wolves be gone from this park?

FT-40.   Here is another graph for you to do more independently.

input	-3	-2	-1	0	1	2	3	x
output	-6			-3		-1		

a)   Copy and complete the table above or use your resource page.

b)   Make a graph of the points.

c)   Draw a line to connect the points. Be sure to extend your line as far as possible on your graph.

d)   Name the coordinates of the x-intercept.

e)   Name the coordinates of the y-intercept.

FT-41.   Copy the diagram at right into your notebook and answer the questions that follow.

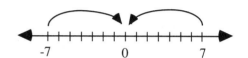

a)   What is the distance from -7 to 0?

b)   What is the distance from 7 to 0?

c)   We show that the distance from -5 to 0 is 5 using absolute value notation: |-5| = 5. Write the absolute value notation for -7 and 7.

FT-42.   Draw a number line diagram to represent the two absolute value equations below.

a) |-4| = 4   b) |8| = 8

FT-43.   Copy and complete the following equations.

a) |-17| = _____   b) |42| = _____   c) |3| = _____   d) |-10| = _____

FT-44.

ABSOLUTE VALUE

ABSOLUTE VALUE is the distance a number is from zero on the number line in either direction. We use the symbol |x| to indicate the absolute value of any number x. For example,

|-3| = 3 and |3| = 3.

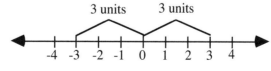

Solve for x in each part below and put your work in your Tool Kit to the right of the double-lined box.

a) |-12| = x   b) |x| = 12   c) |x| = 8   d) |x| = -4

FT-45.

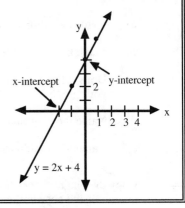

COMPONENTS OF A LINEAR GRAPH

- x- and y-axes labeled and scaled
- equation (rule) written near the line
- line extended as far as possible

x	-1	0	1	2	3	x
y	2	4	6	8	10	y = 2x + 4

x-intercept   y-intercept

y = 2x + 4

Make these notes in your Tool Kit to the right of the double-lined box.

a) Highlight the three bulleted items on the graph in your Tool Kit.

b) Write the coordinates of the points that represent the x- and y-intercepts.

FT 46. Examine the following table.

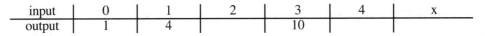

input	0	1	2	3	4	x
output	1	4		10		

a) Copy the table.

b) Look for a pattern between the input and output values. Complete the table.

c) Write the equation that represents the pattern.

d) Graph the equation.

e) Identify the coordinates for the x-intercept and the y-intercept.

f) Use your Tool Kit for "Components of a Linear Graph" to make sure your graph in this problem is complete.

FT-47. Copy and complete the table. Be sure to include the rule.

input	4	2	0	1		3	x
output		9		7	15		

FT-48. Write a numerical expression that represents each statement.

a) A negative four is added to a number.

b) A number y is multiplied by six.

c) A number c is multiplied by seven then negative five is added.

d) A number x is divided by eight.

FT-49. Use tiles to do the following computations. Sketch a tile drawing and write an equation for each one.

a) 6 + (-3)

b) 5 + (-2)

c) 7 + (-5)

d) 6 + (-8)

e) 5 + (-9)

f) 7 + (-10)

g) What pattern do you see when adding integers with opposite signs?

h) Explain how you would add 12 + (-20) without using integer tiles.

FT-50.

ADDITION OF INTEGERS

If the signs are the same, combine by adding the absolute value of each number and keep the same sign.

If the signs are different, ignore them. Then subtract the smaller number from the larger number and keep the sign of the original number that has the larger absolute value.

Example 1:
add -5 + (-3)
|-5| = 5 and |-3| = 3
5 + 3 = 8
Both signs are −, so -5 + (-3) = -8

Example 2:
add -4 + 2
|-4| = 4 and |2| = 2
4 − 2 = 2
4 is greater than 2, so -4 + 2 = -2

Put two examples of adding integers to the right of the double-lined box in your Tool Kit. One example must have at least one negative integer. When you return to class, have your partner or a teammate check that your examples are correct.

FT-51. Compute.

a) -16 + 3

b) 10 + (-91)

c) -14 + (-4)

FT-52. As each silent board game is played, copy and complete the table, then write the equation below the table.

FT-53.   Refer to the graph and table from problem FT-38.

a)   On your graph, the present year or "Now"
is represented by 0. Five years from now is
represented by 5. How was five years **ago**
represented?

b)   How many wolves were there five years ago?
Ten years ago?

FT-54.   Below is the equation for the number of wolves from problem FT-38.

Number of wolves = 108 – (3 times the number of years from now)

$$y = 108 – 3x$$

a)   Use the equation and your graph to complete the table below. A few entries are
done for you.

Number of Years (x)	108 – 3(Number of Years)	Number of Wolves (y)
-200	108 – (-600)	708
-7	108 – (-21)	129
-5		
3	108 – (9)	99
7		
10		

b)   How did you find the number of wolves 200 years ago?

c)   What happens to the number of wolves as we move into the past?

d)   Describe what happens when you subtract a negative integer from 108.

FT-55. To compute -9 – 4 using tiles, start with nine negative tiles.

The problem, -9 – 4, requires that we remove four positive tiles.

However, there are no positive tiles in the box.

a) Pairs of **+** and **–** tiles have been added to each of the following boxes. Evaluate the number that each box of tiles represent.

i) 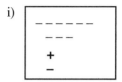   ii)    iii)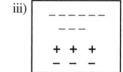

b) From which box in part (a) can four positive tiles be removed? Copy this box and remove the four positive tiles.

c) After removing the four positive tiles, evaluate the number of tiles left in the box. This is the answer to the problem -9 – (+4).

d) Compute 7 – (-2) using integers tiles. Show your drawing and write an equation.

FT-56. Use integer tiles to do the following subtraction problems. Sketch a tile drawing and write an equation for each one.

a)   -7 – (-3)   b)   -12 – 8

c)   6 – 4   d)   5 – 8

FT-57. An example of how to use a tile diagram to subtract integers is shown below. Use the diagram as a model to help solve the problems that follow.

-7 – 4

  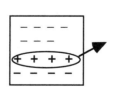

-7 – 4 = -11

a)   -6 – 5   b)   -10 – 3   c)   10 – (-5)   d)   -3 – (-7)

>>Problem continues on the next page.>>

SUBTRACTION OF INTEGERS

1. Build your first number.
2. Remove the number of tiles that represents the second number. If you cannot remove the second number, add zero pairs and try again.
3. Count the remaining tiles.
4. Record the equation showing the difference.

FT-58.   Use integer tiles to solve these problems. Sketch a tile drawing and write the equation below it.

a)   -9 – 2   b)   7 – (-4)   c)   -6 – (-8)

FT-59.   Use a Guess and Check table to solve the following problem.

On a day when they were studying the deer population, Raul and Mia decided to try to figure out the number of deer in the park. Raul counted twice as many as Mia. If together they counted 405 deer, how many deer did Mia count? How many did Raul count?

FT-60.   Complete the table for the equation y = 4x – 5, then graph the equation.

input (x)	2	3	0	1	4	x
output (y)						4x – 5

FT-61.   Complete the table for the equation y = x – 5, then graph the equation on the same axes you used in the previous problem.

input	-2	-1	0	1	3	6	x
output							x – 5

FT-62. Complete the scale for each part below.

a)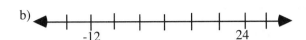

3.2   4.2

c)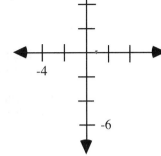

-4

-6

b)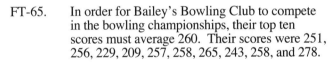

-12   24

FT-63. After looking at his partner's graph, shown at right, Jung suggested that his partner check his work. Why did Jung think that a mistake had been made?

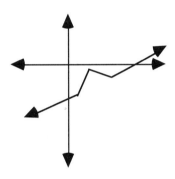

FT-64. Jon's test score was 84 correct out of 100 possible. Write his score as a percent.

FT-65. In order for Bailey's Bowling Club to compete in the bowling championships, their top ten scores must average 260. Their scores were 251, 256, 229, 209, 257, 258, 265, 243, 258, and 278.

a) What is the mean (average)?

b) Will the bowling club go to the championships? Explain how you know.

FT-66. Follow your teacher's directions for practicing mental math. What strategy did you use today?

FT-67. Today your team decided to hike to the top of Lookout Point. Take out your "Big Tree Park" resource page to help you answer the following questions.

a) What is the elevation at the campsite? At Lookout Point? At sea level?

b) If you started the hike from the campsite and you are now at sea level, how far have you hiked?

c) If it has taken one hour to hike this far, how much elevation gain have you made per minute?

d) Since you are at sea level (elevation = 0 feet), how much elevation would you have gained after one minute of hiking? After two minutes?

e) Two minutes from now is represented by positive two. How is one minute ago represented?

f) What was the elevation one minute ago? Two minutes ago?

g) Copy the following table and find the y-values for each elevation.

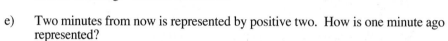

Time in Minutes (x)	Minutes Ago						Now	Minutes from Now					
	-10	-5	-4	-3	-2	-1	0	1	2	3	4	5	10
Elevation in Feet (y)							0						

h) Graph the information from the table. Put "time in minutes" on the horizontal (x) axis and "elevation in feet" on the vertical (y) axis. Scale both axes so one tick mark represents one unit (go up by ones). Then complete parts (i) through (m).

i) Use complete sentences to describe the pattern you see in the gain in elevation. Use this pattern to find the gain in elevation after 10 minutes of hiking.

j) Write the equation that describes the pattern.

k) What is the range in elevation from the campsite to Lookout Point?

l) How long will it take to reach Lookout Point?

m) Use your Tool Kit and check to see that your graph is complete. Write "My graph is complete" on your paper.

FT-68. The equation $y = 2x$ describes how y is related to x in the hiking problem.

a) Use the resource page to complete the table below exactly as shown. Use the table from the previous problem and your graph to help you.

x (time in minutes)	2(x)	y (elevation in feet)
25	2(25)	50
10	2(10)	
5		
3		
0		
-3		
-5		
-10		
-25		

b) What is true about the integers you multiplied to get a positive product?

c) What is true about the integers you multiplied to get a negative product?

FT-69. Copy and complete each table. Then explain the pattern between the input and output values using complete sentences. Finally, write the equation (rule) that describes the pattern.

a)
in (x)	28		6	0	15			360
out (y)	14	12	3		7.5	9	410	

b)
x	4	2	0			14	102
y	11	5	-1	8	20		

FT-70. Copy and complete the table below using values from -4 to 4 for the rule $y = 2x + 4$.

x (in)	-4	-3	-2	-1	0	1	2	3	4
y (out)									

a) Graph the information from the table.

b) Find the x- and y-intercepts.

c) Use your Tool Kit to make sure your graph is complete. When it is complete, write "My graph is complete" on your paper.

FT-71. Sketch a tile drawing and write an equation. Some problems will require you to add zero pairs.

a) $7 - 3$

b) $-6 - (-9)$

c) $5 + (-8)$

d) $-9 + 16$

e) $6 - 9$

f) $12 - (-5)$

FT-72.   Find the missing number that will make each equation true. Model your solution after the
          example in part (a).

          a) $x + 8 = 24$ b) $12 + z = 7$
                $16 + 8 = 24$
                $x = 16$

          c) $17 - w = 8$ d) $25 = g + (-5)$

FT-73.   Answer the questions below.

          a)   What is the length of the horizontal side
                of the rectangle? How long is the
                height?

          b)   Calculate the area.

          c)   Calculate the perimeter.

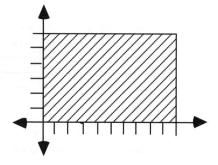

FT-74.   A full-grown ostrich weighs 345 pounds and stands 108 inches tall. Irving weighs 112
          pounds and is 5 feet tall. About how many times heavier than Irving is the ostrich? About
          how many feet taller than Irving is it?

FT-75.   Simplify and select the correct answer to $3 - 7 + 4 - 2$.

          (A)   -3   (B)   -2   (C)   1   (D)   5   (E)   none of these

FT-76.   At the end of a 147-mile trip, Pat's car had been driven a total of 3,835 miles. How
          many miles had the car already been driven at the beginning of her trip?

          (A)   2,688   (B)   3,588   (C)   3,688   (D)   3,982   (E)   none of these

FT-77.   The hikers are on their way back to camp from Lookout
Point. Their elevation is dropping at the rate of about
three feet per minute. The equation $y = -3x$ represents
the speed at which they are losing elevation.

a)   If the hikers had started at sea level (elevation = 0
feet), what would be their elevation after one
minute of hiking downhill? After two minutes?

b)   Copy and complete the section of the table below
for "Minutes in the Future".

		Minutes Ago					Now		Minutes in the Future				
x (minutes)	-10	-5	-4	-3	-2	-1	0	1	2	3	4	5	x
y (feet)							0	-3					

c)   What kind of integers did you use to represent the elevation for "minutes in the future"?

d)   What do you notice about the change in elevation?

e)   If the hikers start at an elevation of 0 and continue to hike at the same rate, how long
will it take them to reach the camp site?

f)   If "now" is represented by 0, how is 1 minute ago represented? 2 minutes ago?

g)   Go back and complete your table for "minutes ago". What was the elevation 1
minute ago? 2 minutes ago?

h)   What kind of integers did you use to represent the elevation for minutes ago?

i)   Graph the times and elevations from the table. Be sure to label your axes and show
your scaling. Put "time" in minutes on the horizontal (x) axis and "elevation" in
feet on the vertical (y) axis. Scale the x-axis by ones. Scale the y-axis by threes.

j)   Extend the line as far as you can on your graph.

k)   Use your table or the equation $y = -3x$ to find the elevation after 10 minutes of
hiking; after 30 minutes of hiking.

FT-78.   Refer to your table in the previous problem and your map of Big Tree Park.

a)   Describe how the pattern in the table is related to the equation $y = -3x$.

b)   What is the range in elevation from Lookout Point to camp?

c)   Use either the pattern from your table or the equation to find out how long it will
take the hikers to get from Lookout Point back to camp.

FT-79.   The equation $y = -3x$ describes how y is related to x.

a)   Copy and complete the table below. Complete the table exactly as shown. Use the patterns from the previous problems or your graph to help you.

x (minutes)	-3(x)	y (elevation in feet)
25	-3(25)	
10	-3(10)	
5		
3		-9
0		
-3		9
-5		
-10		
-25		

b)   What is true about the integers you multiplied to get a positive product?

c)   What is true about the integers you multiplied to get a negative product?

FT-80.   While on their hikes, students collected some tadpole specimens from the pond. The tadpoles were just beginning to develop legs. The lengths of the legs they measured were 0.45 cm, 1.3 cm, 3.1 cm, 0.78 cm, and 2.3 cm.

a)   Find the range.   b)   Find the mean.

FT-81.   Students collected one specimen of tadpoles on Monday, Tuesday, and Wednesday. Tuesday's specimen included 13 tadpoles more than the specimen from Monday. Wednesday's specimen included 27 fewer than Monday's. The total number of tadpoles collected was 1273.

a)   Set up a Guess and Check table to find out how many tadpoles students collected on Monday.

b)   Solve the problem using Guess and Check. Write your answer in a complete sentence.

FT-82.   Here is a different section of the number line. Once again, Irving needs help. Show him what numbers are needed to correctly label each tick mark on the number line.

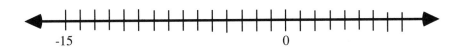

-15   0

a)   What is the largest number on this part of the number line?

b)   What is the smallest number on this part of the number line?

c)   Tell Irving how he can use the number line to determine which of the two numbers is larger than the other.

FT-83.   Solve for x.

a) $|-15| = x$ b) $|x| = 5$

c) $|x| = -7$ d) $|x| = 28$

FT-84.   Mrs. Poppington corrected more tests. Here are the scores:
51, 54, 55, 55, 62, 63, 65, 72, 76, 78, 79, 81, 82, 83, 85, 86, 91, 93, and 95. Find:

a)   the median.   b)   the upper quartile.

c)   the lower quartile.   d)   Put the data in a box-and-whisker plot.

FT-85.   Complete the following Diamond Problems.

Product

Sum

a)   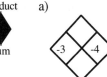   b)   c)   d)   e)

FT-86.   Use integer tiles to help you solve the following problems. Sketch the tile drawing and write the equation for each problem.

a)   -6 – 9

b)   -6 + (-9)

c)   5 – 7

d)   5 + (-7)

e)   7 – (-3)

f)   7 + 3

g)   Compare your equation in part (a) to your equation in part (b).
i)   How are they similar?
ii)   How are they different?

h)   Compare your equation in part (c) to your equation in part (d).
i)   How are they similar?
ii)   How are they different?

i)   Compare your equation in part (e) to your equation in part (f).
i)   How are they similar?
ii)   How are they different?

j)   Follow the examples in parts (a) through (f) above and rewrite the subtraction problem 12 – (-7) as an addition problem.

Narrator:	*After doing several subtraction problems with integers, Lacy exclaimed:*
Lacy:	"I've found a shortcut! I don't need to subtract. I can just add!"
Narrator:	*Her friend, Ida, who did not really like subtraction, shouted:*
Ida:	"What do you mean? Can you teach it to me?"
Narrator:	*Lacy replied:*
Lacy:	"Sure Ida, I'd be happy to. How about 3 – 5? If you were using tiles, how many zero pairs would you add?"
Ida:	"I would add two zero pairs, then take away the five positives, and combine, just like the problem says, 3 – 5. My answer is negative two."
Lacy:	"Me too, Ida. That's how I would do it if I didn't use the addition shortcut. Let's try it my way.
	"Start with three positive tiles. Then add in five negative tiles. Now circle the zero pairs and count up the tiles left over.
	"See, there are two negative tiles left over. I got the same answer as you did, negative two.
	I noticed that 3 – (5) has the same answer as 3 + (-5) so that's what I do. I just **add the opposite of the second number**, circle the zeros, and get the same answer as you."
Narrator:	*With that, Ida exclaimed:*
Ida:	"When subtracting integers, all I have to do is **add the opposite**!"
	"If the problem says 1 – 6, I can rewrite it as 1 + (-6) and I get the same answer both times. 1 – 6 = (-5) and 1+ (-6) = (-5)."

FT-87.   Rewrite each of the following subtraction problems as addition of the opposite. Then compute the answer.

a)   4 – 9   b)   5 – 7   c)   -12 – 2

FT-88.

```
┌─────────────────────────────────────────────────────────────────┐
│                RULE FOR SUBTRACTING INTEGERS                      │
│                                                                   │
│  Adding the opposite of the second number gives the same         │
│  answer as subtracting it.                                        │
│                                                                   │
│  Step One:    Change the subtraction sign to an addition sign.    │
│                                                                   │
│  Step Two:    Change the sign of the integer you are subtracting. │
│                                                                   │
│  Step Three: Use the integer rules for addition.                  │
│                                                                   │
│  Here is an example: 4 – (-5) = 4 + (+5) = 9.                      │
└─────────────────────────────────────────────────────────────────┘
```

Put two examples of subtracting integers to the right of the double-lined box in your Tool Kit. One example must have at least one negative integer. When you return to class, have your partner or a teammate check that your examples are correct.

FT-89.   Complete each subtraction problem.

a)   2 – 4   b)   6 – (-2)   c)   -7 – (-20)

FT-90.   Complete the tables for each equation. Then graph the equations on the <u>same set of axes</u>.

a) $y = x - 4$

in (x)	-3	-2	-1	0	1	2	3	x
out (y)								

b) $y = x^2$ Hint: x^2 means "x times x."

in (x)	-3	-2	-1	0	1	2	3	x
out (y)								

c)   Describe any difference(s) you see in the two graphs in relation to their equations.

FT-91.   Copy and complete the tables below using each value of x given.

a)   y = 4x

x	y
3	4(3) = 12
2	
1	
0	
-1	
-2	4(-2) = -8
-3	

b)   y = -4x

x	y
3	-4(3) = -12
2	
1	
0	
-1	
-2	(-4)(-2) = 8
-3	

c)   Use a different color for each equation and graph both of them on the <u>same</u> <u>set</u> <u>of</u> <u>axes</u>. Scale the x-axis from -3 to 3 and the y-axis from -12 to 12.

d)   What is the same about these two graphs? What is different?

e)   Look carefully at the two equations in parts (a) and (b). What do you think determines which way the line slants?

FT-92.   Exchange binders with your partner. (If you do not have time in class for this binder check, have someone at home do this check with you.)

a)   Are there labeled sections?

b)   Without actually performing the "shake test," do you think your partner's binder would survive the test? Estimate how many papers or objects might fall out.

c)   Write down one suggestion for how your partner might better organize his/her binder.

FT-93.   Refer to the table in problem FT-79. Use it to copy and complete the following statements.

a)   When you multiply two positive numbers, the product will be _____.

b)   When you multiply two negative numbers, the product will be _____.

c)   When you multiply one positive and one negative number, the product will be _____ .

FT-94.   Mrs. Poppington is trying to decide whether to require everyone to retake the Chapter 1 test. The class scores on the first test were 0, 14, 42, 63, 75, 88, 90, and 90.

a)   Calculate the mean, median, and mode.

b)   Using one of the above measures of central tendency, argue the following case: You scored 90 on the first test and want to keep your score, so you argue against a retest.

c)   Using one of the above measures of central tendency, argue the following case: You scored 14 on the test and know you can improve your score if you take the test again, so you argue for the retest.

FT-95.   At right is another section of a number line, and Irving is still confused. He does not see which number is larger. Finish scaling this section and try another approach to help him.

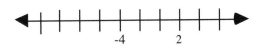

Irving can use the < (less than) or the > (greater than) symbols to order the numbers you wrote. Remember that the pointed part of the symbol points to the smaller number, and the open part opens toward the larger number.

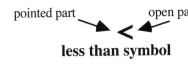

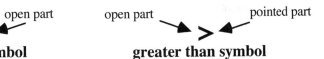

Use the < and > symbols to complete the following inequalities.

a)   2 ___ 3   b)   -2 ___ 3   c)   -3 ___ -17   d)   -17 ___ 3

FT-96.   Set up tables using values from -3 to 3 for x and graph the following two equations.

a) $y = 2x - 4$ b) $y = x^2 + 1$

FT-97.   Write a numerical equation that represent each statement.

a)   A number x multiplied by three equals negative forty-eight.

b)   Negative seven added to a number y equals negative twenty-four.

c)   Negative six subtracted from a number r is equal to seventeen.

d)   When negative twelve is subtracted from a number x the result is four.

FT-98.   Logan, who is in third grade, asked his older sister, Adrianne, what "3 · 4" means.

a)   Using complete sentences, explain how Adrianne could help Logan understand what "3 · 4" means.

b)   Draw a picture that Adrianne could use to show Logan what "3 · 4" means.

c)   Give a real-life example of when you might use "3 · 4."

FT-99.   Compute.

a)   (-2) · (-6)   b)   (-10) · (-5)   c)   (-4) · (-7)   d)   8 · 5

e)   4 · (-4)   f)   (-3) · 6   g)   3 · (-8)   h)   2 · (-11)

FT-100.   Check your solutions to the previous problem with your partner. If you have different answers, check with another pair of students. If you still disagree, get a calculator and check again. Correct any errors you may have made. If you made no errors, write "No Errors for Problem FT-99" on your paper for this problem.

FT-101.   Use your answers from problem FT-99 to answer the following questions.

a)   Look at the sign of the answers for parts (a) through (d). They should all be the same. What do all of the problems have in common?

b)   Look at the sign of the answers for parts (e) through (h). They should all be the same. What do all of the problems have in common?

FT-102.   Write the multiplication sentence and the product that go with each drawing below.

a)      b)      c)

FT-103. In the previous problems, you used the integer tiles and drawings to calculate products of integers. When you multiplied, you were adding groups of negative tiles. For example, if the problem was 3(-2), you added three groups of negative two.

a) Copy and complete the table below.

Problem	Sentence	Answer
4(-5)	Add 4 groups of -5	-20
5(-4)	Add ____ groups of ____	
6(-7)	Add ____ groups of ____	

b) Complete the sentence: Multiplication is repeated _____ .

c) What does (-3)(6) represent?

FT-104. Use tiles to find each product. Make a drawing of your work. Write the solution as an equation. Remember that the first number tells you how many groups there are and the second number tells you how many are in each group.

a) 3(-4)　　　b) 5(-2)　　　c) 4(-1)　　　d) 6(2)

FT-105. At right is a way to multiply using integer tiles in a situation in which the first integer is negative. Consider the problem (-4)(3).

a) Draw a large **neutral field**; that is, draw several pairs of positive and negative tiles. Circle and remove one group of +3. Do it again. Do it again. Do it one more time. How many times did you remove groups of +3?

b) Since multiplication shows a repeated process, the steps done in part (a) showed the problem (-4)(+3). The sentence describing the multiplication problem would be "Remove four groups of positive three." What result did you get?

FT-106. Using integer tiles, draw a large neutral field and use the same process as you did in the preceding problem.

a) Show (-5)(3). Complete the sentence: "Remove ____ groups of ____ ."

b) Show (-7)(2). Complete the sentence: "Remove ____ groups of _____ ."

c) When both integers are negative, you perform the same steps, but you remove the negative tiles. Copy this example: (-4)(-2) means "Remove four groups of -2 tiles." Copy the drawing at right, and indicate that the result is 8.

FT-107.   Copy and complete the following multiplication table.

Drawing	Product	What is left
+ + + + + + + + + ⊖ ⊖ ⊖	(-3)(-3)	
+ + + + + + + + + ⊖ ⊖ − − −		
+ + + + + + + + + ⊖ ⊖ ⊖ ⊖ −		

FT-108.

RULES FOR MULTIPLYING INTEGERS

If you multiply two integers with the **same sign**, the answer is **positive**.

If you multiply two integers with **different signs**, the answer is **negative**.

Examples: $(3)(5) = 15$; $(-3)(5) = -15$; $(-3)(-5) = 15$

Put two examples of multiplying integers to the right of the double-lined box in your Tool Kit. One example must have at least one negative integer. When you return to class, have your partner or a teammate check that your examples are correct.

FT-109.   Copy each problem and compute the product.

a) $(-3)(6)$ b) $(-7)(-3)$ c) $(-7)(-7)$

d) $(5)(-6)$ e) $(9)(-2)$ f) $(-12)(-1)$

FT-110.   Copy each problem and compute the sum.

a) $-3 + 12$ b) $10 + (-7)$ c) $12 + (-4)$

FT-111.   Rewrite each subtraction problem as an addition problem and compute the sum.

a) $-6 - (-12)$ b) $7 - (-10)$ c) $4 - 10$

FT-112. As your class was hiking, you noticed small herds of deer. The list below shows how many deer you have seen each day.

Monday 12
Tuesday 7
Wednesday 8
Thursday.........................9
Friday 15
Saturday 8

a) Determine the mean.

b) Determine the median.

c) Determine the mode.   d) Find the range for the sightings of the deer.

FT-113. Compute. Be sure to show all your work.

a) $5.62 \cdot 0.23$ b) $71.234 + 2.36 + 0.425$ c) $6.254 - 4.91$

FT-114. Complete the Diamond Problems below.

Product

Sum

a)   b)   c)   d)   e)

FT-115. Use the $<$ and $>$ symbols to complete the inequalities below.

a) $0.33 \_\_ 50\%$ b) $\frac{1}{4} \_\_ 0.20$ c) $67\% \_\_ 0.65$ d) $\frac{3}{4} \_\_ 72\%$

FT-116.   The prices for a Zippy convertible are listed in the
           newspaper as shown below to the right.

           a)   Write the data as six ordered pairs. Be careful.

           b)   What information will you plot on the x-axis?

           c)   What information will you plot on the y-axis?

           d)   Scale your axes.

           e)   Create a graph and plot the data.

Year	Price
2000	$38,500
1999	$31,000
1998	$26,000
1997	$22,000
1996	$18,500
1995	$15,900

FT-117.   Follow your teacher's instructions for practicing mental math. What new strategy did you
           use today?

FT-118.   At right is an example of a number family. Notice that each equation
           contains the same three numbers.

           $3 \cdot 4 = 12$
           $4 \cdot 3 = 12$
           $12 \div 3 = 4$
           $12 \div 4 = 3$

           Follow the same format and write number families for the equations
           below.

           a) $6 \cdot 3 = 18$ b) $2 \cdot 5 = 10$

FT-119.   Complete each of the following number families.

           a) $-7 \cdot 2 = -14$ b) $-6 \cdot (-4) = 24$

           c) $8 \cdot (-1) = -8$ d) $9 \cdot 5 = 45$

           e)   What is true about the signs of the integers you divided to get a positive quotient
                 above?

           f)   What is true about the signs of the integers you divided to get a negative quotient
                 above?

FT-120.

RULES FOR DIVIDING INTEGERS

The rules for determining the sign of the answer for division of integers are the **same as multiplication.**

If you divide two integers with the **same sign**, the answer is **positive**.

If you divide two integers with **different signs**, the answer is **negative.**

Examples: $6 \div 2 = 3$; $\frac{-8}{4} = -2$

Make these notes in your Tool Kit to the right of the double-lined box.

List two examples of dividing integers. One example must have at least one negative integer. Have your partner or a teammate check that your examples are correct.

FT-121.   Find the value of each expression.

a) $(-21) \div 7$ b) $(-42) \div (-6)$ c) $28 \div (-4)$ d) $(-63) \div (-7)$

FT-122.   Copy and complete the table using each value of x given or use the resource page. Be sure to follow the example problem and show all your steps. The answers are in the table so you can check your work. Correct any entries that you get wrong.

a)   Graph the points from the table. Make sure you have followed all the steps for making a complete graph.

b)   Describe the graph you made.

x	$y = x^2 + 1$
3	$3^2 + 1$ $(3)(3) + 1$ $9 + 1$ 10
2	
0	
-2	

FT-123.   Use what you have learned about integer addition and subtraction to rewrite the following subtraction problems as addition problems and compute the sums.

a) $-15 - (-8)$ b) $18 - (-10)$

c) $-6 - 10$ d) $12 - (14)$

FT-124.   Copy each problem and compute the answer for the indicated operation.

a) $-27 \div 9$ b) $-10 + (-5)$ c) $3 - 9$ d) $-20 + 8$

e) $(-4)(7)$ f) $(-6)(-5)$ g) $12 \div (-3)$ h) $-6 + 5 - (-6)$

FT-125. Copy and complete the table using the equation $y = 3x - 2$.

x (in)	-2	-1	0	1	2	x
y (out)						

a) If you were to graph the points from the table, what would you expect the graph to look like?

b) Graph the points. Make sure your graph is complete.

c) What does your graph look like? Does this agree with your prediction in part (a)?

FT-126. Use the graph at right to:

a) Copy the ordered pairs for each point into an xy-table.

b) Write the rule using a complete sentence.

c) Name the x- and y-intercepts.

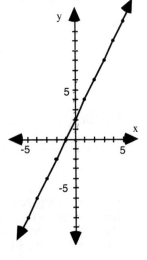

FT-127. Find the number that will make each number sentence true.

a) $x + 8 = 6$ b) $x + (-4) = 7$ c) $4a = 36$ d) $x - (-7) = 5$

FT-128. Study the following tables to determine the pattern used. Write the equation in y-form for each table. Explain how you determined the rule.

a)
x	1	2	3	4	5	6	x
y	-1	-4	-7	-10	-13	-16	

b)
x	-5	-4	-3	-2	-1	0	1	2	3	x
y	-8	-6	-4	-2	0	2	4	6	8	

c)
x	-4	-3	-2	-1	0	1	2	3	4	x
y	16	9	4	1	0	1	4	9	16	

FT-129. In the following problem two groups will be hiking. Be prepared to make a prediction about both groups. This problem will take some time. Once you have followed all of the directions for one group you will repeat the process for the second group.

The Big Hike At Big Tree Park, Raul, the park ranger, and Mia, the chief naturalist, each led a group hike. Raul's group hiked to Grizzly Peak, which has an elevation of 182 feet. Mia's group hiked to Mt. Sawtooth, which has an elevation of 324 feet. The elevation of their campsite is 120 feet below sea level. If Mia's group hikes downhill at a rate of 3 feet per minute and Raul's group hikes downhill at a rate of 2 feet per minute, predict which group will arrive at the campsite first.

FT-130. Answer the following subproblems for Raul's hiking group.

a) If they have not yet started hiking back down, what is the elevation of Raul's group now?

b) If "x" represents minutes spent hiking and "y" represents elevation in feet, write an ordered pair to represent Raul's group now. (Remember they have not started hiking yet.)

c) What is the elevation of Raul's group after one minute of hiking? two minutes? three minutes? Write an ordered pair to represent each situation.

d) Write a variable expression to represent the rate of descent as feet per minute for Raul's group. (How fast are they hiking downhill?)

e) Obtain the resource page from your teacher and complete the table for Raul's group for the first five minutes of hiking. Leave the rest of the table blank for now.

f) Use your table and what you have learned from playing silent board games to find the rule for Raul's group.

g) Follow the example on the resource page and use the rule for Raul's group to calculate the remaining values in the table. Use these values to complete your table.

h) Graph the information from the table starting with their elevation now and using all the remaining values you calculated. (Multiples of five minutes.)

i) Draw a continuous line through the points you graphed.

j) Find the range in elevation from Grizzly Peak to the campsite.

k) At a rate of descent of two feet per minute, how long will it take Raul's hiking group to reach camp?

l) According to your graph, how many minutes did it take Raul's group to reach their campsite? Does this agree with your answer in part (k)? Explain.

FT-131. Repeat all of the above subproblems for Mia's hiking group.

FT-132. Which group reached camp first? Does this agree with your prediction?

FT-133. **Chapter Summary** As you finish a chapter, you
need to reflect on how well you know the material.
Here is another way to check your understanding at the
end of a chapter.

a) Find a problem in the chapter that represents what
you have learned about each of the following
topics. Copy the problem and show the correct
solution for the problem.

- Solve a word problem using a Guess and
Check table.

- Write an equation based on a table.

- Graph a linear equation.

b) Make up two problems for each operation (+, −, · , ÷) with integers and show how to
solve your problems. Be sure to use some negative numbers.

FT-134. Match each equation to the graph it best fits. Explain how you made your decisions.

a) $y = 2x + 2$ b) $y = x^2$ c) $y = -2x$

i)   ii)   iii)

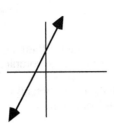   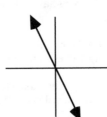   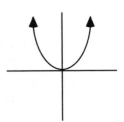

FT-135. A graph is represented by the equation $y = x^2 - 1$.

a) Complete the following data table using the equation.

in (x)	-3	-2	-1	0	1	2	3	x
out (y)								

b) On a graph, plot the values from the data table above.

CHAPTER 2

FT-136. Copy and complete the table using each value of x given. Be sure to follow the example problem and **show all your steps**. The answers are in the table so you can check your solutions. Correct any that you get wrong.

x	$y = x^2 - 2$
3	$3^2 - 2$ $(3)(3) - 2$ $9 - 2$ 7
2	2
1	-1
0	-2
-1	-1
-2	2
-3	7

FT-137. Do the following computations.

a)   -15 + 9

b)   2 + (-5) – 7

c)   -10 · (-2)

d)   9 – (-22)

e)   7 · (-4)

f)   -4 + 9 – (-31)

g)   -24 ÷ 3

h)   230 ÷ 10

i)   -52 ÷ (-13)

FT-138. Write a numerical equation that represents each statement.

a)   When seven is added to a number x, the result is three.

b)   When a number a is doubled, the result is twelve.

c)   When negative six is subtracted from a number y, the result is eighteen.

d)   When a number n is divided by seven, the result is negative two.

FT-139. Look back at your work from this chapter.

a)   Write the equations from three graphs that made straight lines.

b)   Write the equations from three graphs that made curves.

c)   How can you tell what kind of equation will give which kind of graph?

FT-140. **What We Have Done in This Chapter**

Below is a list of the Tool Kit entries from this chapter.

- FT-19   Graphing Terms
- FT-44   Absolute Value
- FT-45   Components of a Linear Graph
- FT-50   Addition of Integers
- FT-88   Rule for Subtracting Integers
- FT-108   Rules for Multiplying Integers
- FT-120   Rules for Dividing Integers

Review all the entries and read the notes you made in your Tool Kit. Make a list of any questions, terms, or notes you do not understand. Ask your partner or study team members for help. If anything is still unclear, ask your teacher.

THE MYSTERY OF THE Dual Spinners

Chapter 3

Chapter 3
Mystery of the Dual Spinners: **PROBABILITY AND FRACTIONS**

Every day you use **probability** to make decisions. Any question that starts with "What is the chance of ..." or "Should I do ..." is a question that involves probability, whether you consciously use probability or not. As you make your decisions, you are probably also using fractions or percents. As you continue to use numbers, you soon find that there are many situations that cannot be completely described only with whole numbers. Fractions, decimals, and percents are ways to describe parts of things; they are the "numbers between the integers." As you work with these kinds of numbers, you will learn how to add, subtract, and multiply them.

In this chapter you will have the opportunity to:

- use ideas from probability to gain a new perspective on addition and multiplication of fractions.

- build your understanding of addition and multiplication of fractions through the use of rectangular area models.

- review equivalent fractions and simplification of fractions.

- review the relationships among fractions, decimals, and percents.

Read the problem below, but **do not try to solve it now**. What you learn over the next few days will enable you to solve it.

MD-0. Mario and Marisa Powers are twins. For as long as they can remember, they have wanted to be federal investigators when they grow up. To their surprise, they were picked to be junior interns at the National Investigative Agency (N.I.A.) headed by Delano Franklin.

"For the final exam I will assess your skills through a color combo bingo game," said Director Franklin. "You will use a game card while I use two dice. You will need to make a prediction based on which color combinations you think will occur most often."

How should the twins label their card?

Number Sense	
Algebra and Functions	
Mathematical Reasoning	
Measurement and Geometry	
Statistics, Data Analysis, & Probability	

Chapter 3
Mystery of the Dual Spinners: **PROBABILITY AND FRACTIONS**

MD-1.   Make a number line on your paper and place the problem letter (a, b, c...) in a position that corresponds to the probability of the event happening. Part (a) is done as an example.

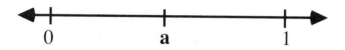

$$0 \qquad \mathbf{a} \qquad 1$$

a) It will rain today. (The reporter states there is a 50% chance of rain).

b) A Martian will walk into class now.

c) You will eat some vegetables for dinner today.

d) You will pass your math class this year.

e) You will breathe in the next 30 seconds.

f) You will be elected president.

MD-2.   Because of their great problem solving skills and inquisitive minds, Mario and Marisa Powers were picked to be junior interns at the National Investigative Agency (N.I.A.) headed by Delano Franklin.

"The first thing we want to do is assess your intuition through a color combo bingo game," said Director Franklin. "Here's how to play.

"Use a game card while I use two spinners like the ones below. After you read the game directions and study the spinners, you will need to make a predictionas to which color combination you think will occur most often. Then you will label both sides of the 16 squares according to your predictions."

Your teacher will give you a resource page so that you can play Director Franklin's color combination game.

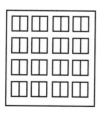

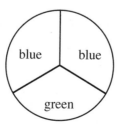

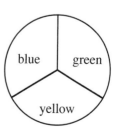

>>Problem continues on the next page.>>

a) List the combinations that are possible.

b) Predict the color combination(s) you think will occur most often. Record these predictions.

c) On the game card your teacher has given you label both parts of the 16 squares according to your predictions. You will need to repeat some of the combinations in order to fill all 16 squares.

Color-Combo-Grido I
A game for many people.

Mathematical Purpose: To study mathematical probability.

Object: To cover four squares in a row or to cover the entire game board.

Materials:
- 4 x 4 grid with squares divided in two parts.
- two spinners divided into three equal parts: Spinner 1 parts labeled blue, blue, and green; Spinner 2 parts labeled blue, green, and yellow.
- two paper clips to use as spinners, if needed

Scoring: One point for the four-in-a-row game; five points for a cover game.

How to Play the Game:
- Label all 16 squares with color combinations
- Caller spins both spinners and calls out colors.
- Circle one square matching the combination called (blue/yellow and yellow/blue are considered the same).
- Circle only color combinations that match the call.
- Keep track of each play by tallying each color combination called.

Ending the Game: The first person with four squares in a row (horizontal, vertical, or diagonal) wins; or, the first person with his/her entire card marked out wins.

MD-3. After collecting class information, answer these questions:

a) Which color combination occurred most often in your team?

b) Which color combination occurred most often in your class?

c) If you played the game 1000 times, Blue-Green will probably occur the most often. Why do you think this is true?

MD-4.   Director Franklin then explained to the twins that they would be using disguises of sunglasses and hats when on assignment. "Cool!" exclaimed Mario, "We're not allowed to wear either one at school."

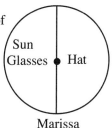

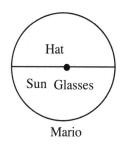

"We'll use a pair of spinners to decide who wears which disguise. Use your resource page, a paper clip, and a pencil to begin collecting data."

Marissa   Mario

First spin Marisa's spinner and then spin Mario's. Four possible combinations will occur. On your resource page, use tally marks to keep a record of how often each combination comes up. Do this 25 times. (You will have 25 tally marks recorded in your table.) In <u>this</u> experiment, <u>order</u> <u>is</u> <u>important</u>.

How many times did the spinners give you each of the disguise combinations, that is, "Glasses-Glasses," "Glasses-Hat," "Hat-Glasses," or "Hat-Hat"?

MD-5.

PROBABILITY

When you know all possible outcomes of an event, and all have the same chance of occurring, the **PROBABILITY** of an event is:

$$P(event) = \frac{\text{number of outcomes in the event}}{\text{number of possible outcomes}}$$

P(event) is the way we write that we want the probability "P" of a certain event. For example, there are 6 faces on a die. Suppose the desired event is to roll a 4. Since the number 4 appears once, we write the probability of getting a 4 as $P(4) = \frac{1}{6}$.

THEORETICAL PROBABILITY is calculated probability. If every outcome is equally likely, it is the ratio of outcomes in an event to all possible outcomes. For example, the probability of flipping a coin and getting "heads" is $\frac{1}{2}$ for each flip.

EXPERIMENTAL PROBABILITY is the probability based on data collected in experiments. For example, if you flip a coin 100 times, you will not always get 50 "heads" and 50 "tails" (the theoretical probability for 100 flips). If "heads" comes up 47 times, then the experimental probability of getting "heads" for the 100 flips would be $\frac{47}{100}$, which is close to the theoretical probability but not equal to it.

COMPOUND PROBABILITY deals with a combination of simple events.

• When <u>either</u> of two outcomes are specified (look for the word "or"), that is, <u>either</u> may happen but not both, find the probability of <u>each</u> specified outcome and <u>add</u> their probabilities.

• When <u>both</u> of two outcomes are specified (look for the word "and"), that is, the result must have <u>both</u> outcomes, find the probability of <u>each</u> outcome and <u>multiply</u> the probabilities.

Complete part (a), then do parts (b) and (c) below the double-lined box in your Tool Kit.

a) Highlight the "P(event) = " statement.

b) Write the probability of getting an odd number if you roll a die.

c) Create examples for both types of compound probability.

MD-6.   Use the information from the Tool Kit box on probability
and the results from your "Disguises" spinning
experiment to answer the following questions.

a)   About how many "Glasses-Glasses" results would
you expect after 50 spins?

b)   Write the probability of getting the "Glasses-
Glasses" combination based on your prediction for
50 spins.

c)   About how many "Hat-Hat" results would you expect after 75 spins?

d)   Write the probability of getting the "Hat-Hat" combination based on your
prediction for 75 spins.

e)   Write the probability of getting either the "Glasses-Hat" or the "Hat-Glasses"
combination based on 125 spins.

f)   Use complete sentences to explain your reasoning in part (e).

MD-7.   Copy and complete the following multiplication table or use the resource page.

x	-5	-4	-3	-2	-1	0	1	2	3
-5									
-4									
-3									
-2									
-1									
0									
1									
2									
3									

MD-8.   The least common multiple of 10 and 12 is:

(A) 2   (B) 30   (C) 60   (D) 120   (E) none of these

CHAPTER 3

MD-9. The result of combining the three fractions $1\frac{1}{8} + \frac{1}{8} - \frac{5}{4}$ is:

    (A) -1   (B) 0   (C) $\frac{5}{8}$ (D) $\frac{4}{5}$ (E) none of these

MD-10. Now that we have started a new chapter, it is time for you to organize your binder.

    a)   Put the work from the last chapter in order and keep it in a separate folder.

    b)   When this is completed, write, "I have organized my binder."

MD-11. Follow your teacher's directions for practicing mental math. There are several ways to do the problem. Which method do you think was best?

MD-12. Marisa found the spinner at right in a box of discarded game pieces.

    a)   What is the probability that she would spin red?

    b)   What is the probability that she would spin blue?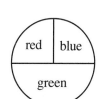

    c)   What is the probability that she would spin green?

    d)   Explain how you determined your answers.

MD-13. Your teacher will give you additional data from other classes for the Color-Combo-Grido and the Hat-Glasses spinners.

    a)   Compare the new numbers to your previous results. Write your numbers as fractions.

    b)   Do you see any differences in the data?

MD-14.   Director Delano Franklin owns four kinds of
          motor vehicles. Each type comes in two
          different colors. Marisa and Mario had to
          spin for the vehicle that they would use while
          out on investigations. Use the two spinners to
          answer the questions below.

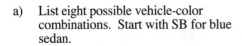
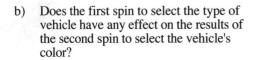

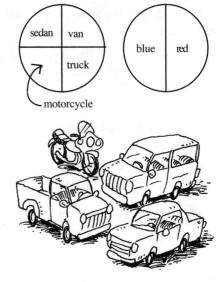

    a)   List eight possible vehicle-color
          combinations. Start with SB for blue
          sedan.

    b)   Does the first spin to select the type of
          vehicle have any effect on the results of
          the second spin to select the vehicle's
          color?

    c)   What is the probability of spinning a red
          motorcycle?

    d)   What is the probability of spinning a
          blue van?

    e)   What is the probability of spinning a blue vehicle?

MD-15.   Another way of looking at the previous problem is to use a rectangle to display the
          choices. The area of the rectangle represents the <u>sum</u> of the possibilities, that is, the sum
          of the fractional probabilities is 1. This means that the area of the rectangle equals one (1)
          square unit.

    a)   The first spinner was divided into four equal parts, so draw a rectangle and divide it
          vertically into four equal columns to represent the different vehicles. Label the top
          of each section with the name of a different vehicle.

    b)   The second spinner is divided into two equal parts, so divide your rectangle
          horizontally into two equal rows to represent the different colors. Label each row
          with a different color.

    c)   How many equal parts are there in the rectangle?

    d)   If you carefully divided the rectangle into four equal columns and two equal rows,
          what is the area of each section of the rectangle?

    e)   What is the probability of spinning each combination? Write that fraction in each
          section of the rectangle.

    f)   What is the relationship between the area of each section of the rectangle and the
          probability of getting that color combination?

MD-16. Travis prefers to drive blue vehicles. He also likes to drive vans, sedans, or trucks. Use the probability rectangle below to answer these questions.

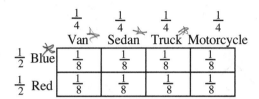

	Van	Sedan	Truck	Motorcycle
	$\frac{1}{4}$	$\frac{1}{4}$	$\frac{1}{4}$	$\frac{1}{4}$
$\frac{1}{2}$ Blue	$\frac{1}{8}$	$\frac{1}{8}$	$\frac{1}{8}$	$\frac{1}{8}$
$\frac{1}{2}$ Red	$\frac{1}{8}$	$\frac{1}{8}$	$\frac{1}{8}$	$\frac{1}{8}$

a) What is the probability that he gets a vehicle he likes?

b) What is the probability that he gets a vehicle of a color or type he does not like?

c) What is the probability that the color of the vehicle he drives is green?

MD-17. The third term in the pattern below, based on $\frac{1}{3}$, is $\frac{3}{9}$:

$$\frac{1}{3} \cdot \frac{1}{1} = \frac{1}{3}; \qquad \frac{1}{3} \cdot \frac{2}{2} = \frac{2}{6}; \qquad \frac{1}{3} \cdot \frac{3}{3} = \frac{3}{9}$$

a) What is the third term of a similar pattern based on $\frac{1}{2}$?

b) What is the fourth term of a similar pattern based on $\frac{2}{3}$? Explain how you found it.

c) What is the fifth term of a similar pattern based on $\frac{3}{4}$? Explain how you found it.

d) If a pattern is based on $\frac{4}{5}$, predict the tenth term.

MD-18. Using the idea of finding patterns in the previous problem, find the unknown number in each problem below.

a) $\frac{3}{5} = \frac{12}{x}$

b) $\frac{9}{18} = \frac{w}{6}$

MD-19.   Complete the following Diamond Problems.

 Product

Sum

a)
6   4

b)
- 6 |- 5|

c)
17
-18

d)
$\frac{1}{2}$ $\frac{1}{4}$

e)
- 30
- 2

f)
$\frac{1}{3}$ $\frac{2}{3}$

MD-20.   Draw a rectangle with a width of 5 centimeters and a length of 6 centimeters. If you draw another rectangle with a width of 6 centimeters and a length of 5 centimeters, are the two rectangles the same size and shape? Explain how you know.

MD-21.   Travis owns a blue van and a blue truck. Although he bought them both new, Travis has owned the truck for seventeen years longer than the van. If the sum of the ages of the vehicles is forty-one years, how old is the van and how old is the truck?

a)   Set up a Guess and Check table to find the answer.

b)   Show all your work and write your answer in a complete sentence.

MD-22.   What fraction of one hour (60 minutes) is represented by the following numbers of minutes? Simplify each fraction whenever possible. A sketch of a clock might help you.

a)   10 minutes   b)   15 minutes   c)   30 minutes   d)   20 minutes

MD-23.   Which of these answers is the correct simplification of $4 - (3 - 5)$?

(A) 12   (B) 6   (C) -2   (D) -4   (E) none of these

MD-24.   Mario used a pattern to write one-half many ways.

$$\text{Example: } \frac{1}{2} = \frac{2}{4} = \frac{3}{6} = \frac{4}{8} = \frac{?}{?}$$

a)   Study Mario's list. Write at least three more fractions equivalent to $\frac{1}{2}$.

b)   Marisa started a list of fractions equivalent to $\frac{1}{4}$: $\frac{1}{4} = \frac{2}{8} = ? = ? = ?$
Add five more equivalent fractions to Marisa's list.

c)   Make a list of five fractions equivalent to $\frac{1}{3}$.

d)   Make a list of five fractions equivalent to $\frac{4}{4}$.

MD-25.   List three equivalent fractions for each fraction below.

a) $\frac{24}{36}$ b) $\frac{16}{20}$

MD-26.   Read the story of the Giant **1**, then complete the assignment that follows it.

Narrator: *Marisa understood Mario's pattern
method for finding equivalent fractions
pretty well. She thought she saw an easy
way to create them.*

Marisa: Hey, Mario! Come here for a minute. I
think I see something interesting about
your pattern method.

Narrator: *Her brother, Mario, who was not thrilled
about Marisa's discovery, grudgingly
agreed to listen to her.*

Mario: Okay, okay. What do you see?

Narrator: *Marisa pointed to the example she had written on her paper.*

Marisa: Look at this! $\frac{4}{20}$ is the same as $\frac{1}{5}$, because I just multiplied the numerator of 1
by 4 to get 4.

Mario: Okay, I'm with you so far.

Marisa: Next, I multiplied the denominator of $\frac{4}{5}$ —5—by 4 and got 20. 4 over 4 is the
same as 1.

>>Problem continues on the next page.>>

Narrator: *Mario understood Marisa's method, exclaiming,*

Mario: You're right. It is one, because four divided by four is one.

Narrator: *Mario excitedly summarized Marisa's method.*

Mario: So are you saying that when you multiply the numerator and denominator by the same number, you are really multiplying the whole fraction by 1?

Marisa: You've got it, Mario. A number multiplied by 1 is always the same number, that is, an equivalent number!

Mario: You're right, Sis! What should we call this method of finding equivalent fractions?

Narrator: *Marisa pondered for a moment.*

Marisa: I know. Let's call this method "multiplying by the Giant **1**!"

Narrator: *Mario considered Marisa's idea for a moment.*

Mario: I like that, Marisa!   The Giant **1** it is! Let's try some problems.

The Giant **1** wears many disguises. What form does the Giant **1** take in each problem below?

a) $\frac{1}{3} \cdot \boxed{1} = \frac{4}{12}$

b) $\frac{3}{5} \cdot \boxed{1} = \frac{6}{10}$

c) $\frac{10}{15} = \frac{2}{3} \cdot \boxed{1}$

d) $\frac{5}{25} = \frac{1}{5} \cdot \boxed{1}$

MD-27.   When Marisa was multiplying by the Giant **1** to find equivalent fractions, she was actually using the **Identity Property of Multiplication**. The Giant **1** she used was in disguise as $\frac{4}{4}$. When she multiplied $\frac{1}{5}$ by $\frac{4}{4}$, she renamed the fraction $\frac{4}{20}$.

$$\frac{1}{5} \cdot \boxed{\frac{4}{4}} = \frac{4}{20}$$

Notice that $\frac{4}{20}$ and the original $\frac{1}{5}$ are just different names for the same number.

When multiplying by $\frac{4}{4}$, Marisa did not change the value of $\frac{1}{5}$. She just changed its name.

We can call Marisa's method the "Giant **1**" to remind us that when we multiply by the fractional forms of one (1) we are actually using the Identity Property of Multiplication.

>>Problem continues on the next page.>>

Practice using the Identity Property of Multiplication (the Giant **1**) with these problems. Write the fraction you used for the Giant **1** each time.

a) $\frac{1}{3} \cdot$ $= \frac{3}{9}$

b) $\frac{3}{5} \cdot$ ⎰⎱ $= \frac{18}{30}$

c) $\frac{5}{8} \cdot$ ⎰⎱ $= \frac{40}{64}$

d) $\frac{20}{45} = \frac{4}{9} \cdot$ ⎰⎱

e) $\frac{70}{110} = \frac{7}{11} \cdot$ ⎰⎱

f) $\frac{6}{20} = \frac{3}{10} \cdot$ ⎰⎱

MD-28.

IDENTITY PROPERTY OF MULTIPLICATION
FINDING EQUIVALENT FRACTIONS

Any number multiplied by one (1) equals itself. This is the **IDENTITY PROPERTY OF MULTIPLICATION**. That is, for any number n,

$$n \cdot 1 = n$$

This property is used to make **EQUIVALENT FRACTIONS**, that is, fractions that are equal but are written in <u>different</u> <u>forms</u>.

In general, $\frac{a}{b} \cdot \frac{c}{c} = \frac{ac}{bc}$. For example: $\frac{2}{3} \cdot \frac{4}{4} = \frac{(2)(4)}{(3)(4)} = \frac{8}{12}$.

Make these notes in your Tool Kit to the right of the double-lined box.

Write another example using the Identity Property of Multiplication to rewrite the fraction $\frac{3}{5}$.

MD-29. The electricity was out, and Mario was called to go out on an undercover mission. He had to grab some pants and a shirt from his closet in the dark. At that time there were five pairs of pants (2 jeans, 1 khaki, 2 black) and four shirts (2 gray, 1 white, 1 black) in his closet.

Draw a rectangle to organize the combinations in Mario's closet and to help you determine the following probabilities.

a) What is the probability that Mario chooses a pair of jeans and a black shirt?

>>Problem continues on the next page.>>

b) What is the probability that Mario chooses khaki pants and a white shirt?

c) Mario was hoping to get the black shirt and black pants for his midnight mission. What is the probability of that?

d) What is the probability Mario chooses black pants and a black shirt <u>or</u> jeans and a white shirt?

e) What is the most likely combination?

f) Rewrite the answers in parts (a), (b), and (c) as percents.

MD-30. What is the probability of Mario choosing a black shirt two days in a row?

MD-31. Write the first eight terms of a pattern based on $\frac{2}{3}$. Predict the 25th term of this pattern.

MD-32. Copy the problems below and use the Identity Property of Multiplication to complete the Giant **1** and replace the variable with the correct number.

a)
$$\frac{11}{22} = \boxed{\frac{11}{11}} \cdot \frac{y}{2}$$

b)
$$\frac{x}{4} \cdot \boxed{\frac{6}{6}} = \frac{6}{24}$$

c)
$$\frac{2}{3} \cdot \boxed{\frac{9}{9}} = \frac{18}{t}$$

d)
$$\frac{64}{96} = \boxed{1} \cdot \frac{8}{n}$$

e)
$$\frac{3}{6} \cdot \boxed{1} = \frac{21}{w}$$

f)
$$\frac{2}{8} \cdot \boxed{1} = \frac{12}{z}$$

MD-33. Marisa wondered if she could draw a model to understand equivalent fractions, such as $\frac{2}{3} = \frac{4}{6}$.

First, she drew a rectangle.

Then she divided the rectangle into thirds and shaded two of the thirds.

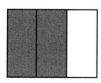

Next she divided the same rectangle into sixths and noticed that four-sixths were shaded. She could see that $\frac{2}{3} = \frac{4}{6}$ because the shaded areas were equal.

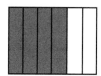

Draw models for parts (a) through (d) to represent each equivalent pair of fractions and, in part (d), replace the variable with the correct number.

a) $\frac{1}{4}$ and $\frac{2}{8}$ b) $\frac{6}{10}$ and $\frac{3}{5}$

c) $\frac{3}{4}$ and $\frac{9}{12}$ d) $\frac{4}{5}$ and $\frac{x}{10}$

MD-34. The girls' basketball team weighed the players. Their weights were 120, 122, 126, 130, 133, 147, 115, 106, 120, 112, and 142.

a)   Make a stem-and-leaf plot of their weights.

b)   What was the median weight?

c)   What was the range?

d)   What were the mean and mode?

MD-35. Marisa wanted to investigate some patterns. She wrote out some of them for you to complete.

a) $16, 8, 4, 2, 1, \frac{1}{2}$, ____ , ____ , ____

b) $27, 9, 3, 1$, ____ , ____ , ____

c) $16, 4, 1$, ____ , ____ , ____

d)   Explain the pattern for part (b) in everyday words using complete sentences.

MD-36.   The dotted line through the triangle at
          right is a **line of symmetry**. A line of
          symmetry means that the line divides the
          object into two halves which are mirror
          images of each other. How many lines
          of symmetry are on the rectangle?
          Sketch the rectangle and draw all the
          lines of symmetry you identified.

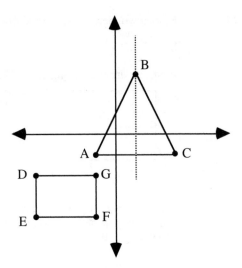

MD-37.   Starting with $\frac{24}{60}$, work backward until the fraction is in its simplest form.

MD-38.   If a pattern is based on $\frac{4}{9}$, what is the fifth term? What is the tenth term?

MD-39.   What number divided by -3 gives 12 as the result?

          (A) -36   (B) -4   (C) 4   (D) 36   (E) none of these

MD-40.   Rectangles can be used to show multiplication of fractions. Draw a rectangle. Use one
          side of the rectangle to shade one of the fractions. Use the top or bottom to shade the
          other fraction. The overlapping shading is the product.

          Example: $\frac{2}{3} \cdot \frac{1}{4}$  $= \frac{2}{12}$ or $\frac{1}{6}$

          Draw a rectangle showing $\frac{1}{5} \cdot \frac{3}{4}$.

MD-41.   Match the multiplication problem with its correct generic model. Notice that the
overlapping area represents the answer.

1.   2.   3.    4.

a) $\frac{1}{4} \cdot \frac{3}{4}$ b) $\frac{1}{2} \cdot \frac{1}{2}$ c) $\frac{1}{2} \cdot \frac{1}{3}$ d) $\frac{3}{5} \cdot \frac{2}{3}$

MD-42.   Draw a model for each of the following multiplication problems and write the answer.

a) $\frac{1}{4} \cdot \frac{1}{3}$ b) $\frac{3}{4} \cdot \frac{1}{2}$

c) $\frac{1}{4} \cdot \frac{1}{5}$ d) $\frac{3}{3} \cdot \frac{1}{2}$

MD-43. You will be playing the "Four-in-a-Row, There You Go" (Fraction Product) game, which is described below.

Four-in-a-Row, There You Go
A game for 2 to 4 people.

Mathematical Purpose: To practice fraction concepts.

Object: To cover four squares in a row, in a column, or diagonally; or, to cover the entire game board.

Materials: Game board, 2 paper clips

Scoring: One point for each "four in a row."

How to Play the Game:
- Use a fair method to decide who goes first.
- Player 1 (or Team 1) puts a paper clip on the long, narrow rectangular strip on the bottom of the game board so that it covers the fraction in the first small rectangle (usually $\frac{1}{2}$). The same player then places a second paper clip on another fraction along the bottom rectangle. Player 1 multiplies the two fractions and marks that product on the game board with an X.
- Player 2 may now move one (and only one) of the paper clips to another fraction along the bottom rectangle strip, then multiply and mark an O on the product of the two fractions on the game board.
- Players 1 and 2 take turns, each moving only one paper clip each turn and marking the product of the two fractions on the game board, until one side wins.
- Note: Not all possible answers are listed. If you choose $\frac{2}{3} \cdot \frac{1}{3} = \frac{2}{9}$ you lose a turn.

Ending the Game: The first person to get four squares in a row wins an individual game.

GAME BOARD

$\frac{1}{3}$	$\frac{8}{15}$	$\frac{1}{4}$	$\frac{3}{8}$
$\frac{2}{5}$	$\frac{3}{5}$	$\frac{3}{10}$	$\frac{1}{5}$
$\frac{1}{12}$	$\frac{1}{6}$	$\frac{2}{5}$	$\frac{1}{8}$
$\frac{4}{15}$	$\frac{12}{25}$	$\frac{1}{2}$	$\frac{3}{16}$

$\frac{1}{2}$	$\frac{2}{3}$	$\frac{3}{5}$	$\frac{1}{4}$	$\frac{3}{4}$	$\frac{1}{3}$	$\frac{4}{5}$

Your teacher will instruct you to play the game with your partner or as a class activity. When this has been completed, write "Game played" on your paper to let your teacher know you have done this activity. Include how many times you played and who won.

MD-44.   These questions relate to the "Four-in-a-Row, There You Go" (Fraction Product) game.

a)   Did you multiply the fractions by drawing out the diagram or did you use another strategy? If you used another strategy, describe it briefly

b)   Explain why you chose your strategy.

MD-45.   Look at the pair of spinners shown at right.

Spinner 1   Spinner 2

When Marisa and Mario went into Director Franklin's office, they were told that the choices for vehicles were two sedans and one truck. The colors were purple or green.

a)   Sketch a probability table for this situation.

S-sedan   P-purple
T-truck   G-green

b)   What is the probability of spinning a purple sedan (PS)?

c)   Since $\frac{2}{3}$ of Spinner 1 is sedans and $\frac{1}{2}$ of Spinner 2 is purple, write a multiplication problem to describe the probability of spinning a purple sedan.

d)   Write a problem to describe the probability of spinning a purple vehicle.

e)   What is the probability of <u>not</u> spinning a green truck?

MD-46.

MULTIPLICATION OF FRACTIONS

To multiply fractions, multiply the numerators to make the new numerator and multiply the denominators to make the new denominator. Use the Identity Property (find any Giant **1**s in the product) to simplify the resulting fraction.

In general, $\frac{a}{b} \cdot \frac{c}{d} = \frac{ac}{bd}$.   Examples: $\frac{2}{3} \cdot \frac{1}{5} = \frac{2}{15}$

$$\frac{3}{4} \cdot \frac{2}{3} = \frac{6}{12} = \left[\frac{6}{6}\right] \cdot \frac{1}{2} = \frac{1}{2}$$

Write these notes in your Tool Kit next to the double-lined box.

a)   In your own words, explain how to multiply fractions.

b)   Explain how to simplify (reduce) a fraction.

MD-47.   Copy and complete the following multiplication table or use the resource page.

	8	4	2	$\frac{1}{2}$	$\frac{1}{3}$	0
3						
6						
9						
$\frac{1}{2}$						
$\frac{1}{3}$						
$\frac{1}{4}$						

MD-48.   Use any of the strategies you have learned to find the unknown number in each problem below. Show all work.

a) $\dfrac{5}{9} = \dfrac{r}{27}$ b) $\dfrac{21}{28} = \dfrac{3}{k}$ c) $\dfrac{2}{3} \cdot \dfrac{6}{7} = x$ d) $\dfrac{3}{8} \cdot \dfrac{4}{5} = y$

e) $\dfrac{m}{12} = \dfrac{1}{4}$ f) $\dfrac{?}{?} \cdot \dfrac{3}{8} = \dfrac{12}{32}$ g) $\dfrac{c}{12} = \dfrac{3}{4}$ h) $\dfrac{3}{5} \cdot \dfrac{5}{3} = z$

MD-49   Judy likes to have a pen and a pencil when she takes notes or does classwork. Her special box contains 1 red, 1 blue, and 2 green pens. Judy also has 1 pink and 2 yellow pencils in the box. She likes to select her pen and pencil randomly. She is especially pleased when she pulls out a green pen and a pink pencil on testing days. Judy thinks this combination brings her good luck. Use the rectangle below to help you answer the questions.

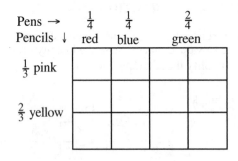

a)   What is the probability that Judy pulls out a red pen and a yellow pencil?

b)   What is the probability that Judy pulls out a blue pen and a pink pencil?

c)   What is the probability that Judy pulls out a green pen and a yellow pencil?

d)   What is the probability that Judy pulls out a blue pen and a blue pencil?

e)   Today is a test day in Judy's class. What is the probability that she pulls out her "lucky" combination?

MD-50. In her pencil box at home, Judy has four times as many pencils as pens. If she has seventy-five pens and pencils in her pencil box, how many does she have of each? Solve using a Guess and Check table.

MD-51. Which choice(s) below can you quickly identify as incorrect answers for the product of 376 and 48?

(A) 4,243   (B) 18,048   (C) 18,480   (D) 18,038   (E) none of these

MD-52. Follow your teacher's directions for practicing mental math. There are several ways to do the problem. Which method do you think is best?

MD-53. Assuming each rectangle represents one whole unit, determine the total area of the shaded regions in parts (a) and (b) below.

a)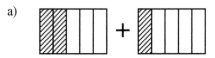

b)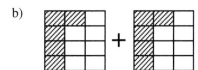

MD-54. In another pencil box, Judy has six pencils, eight markers, and three highlighters. As a shortcut we will use variables to write this as 6p + 8m + 3h. Her mom takes her to the store for more school supplies, and she comes home with a box of twelve pencils, a package of four highlighters, and one marker. If she adds the new supplies to her pencil box, how many of each type of writing utensil does she have now? Use variables to represent each type of item. Show your answer as an equation.

MD-55.   Today we will look at just one spinner. What is the probability of spinning and getting a sedan or a motorcycle?

Since sedans are represented by $\frac{1}{3}$ of the area of the spinner and motorcycles are represented by $\frac{1}{4}$ of the area of the spinner, the probability of selecting either the sedan or the motorcycle is the sum of the two areas: $\frac{1}{3} + \frac{1}{4}$.

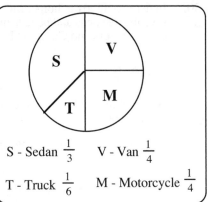

S - Sedan $\frac{1}{3}$ V - Van $\frac{1}{4}$

T - Truck $\frac{1}{6}$ M - Motorcycle $\frac{1}{4}$

This problem can be modeled using rectangles. Since the rectangles have fraction pieces of different sizes, both rectangles need to be divided into pieces that are the same size. If you visualize placing one rectangle on top of the other (while ignoring the shading for the moment), you can see the size of the pieces you need. In the example below, if you place the rectangle at right on top of the one at left, the horizontal and vertical lines create the rectangles below them. To find the sum of the fractions, write the total number of shaded pieces in relation to one rectangle.

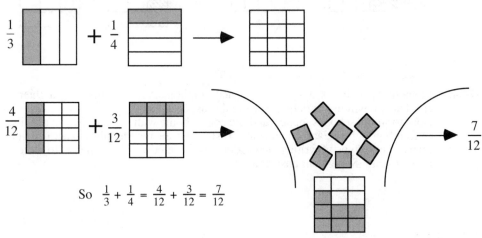

So $\frac{1}{3} + \frac{1}{4} = \frac{4}{12} + \frac{3}{12} = \frac{7}{12}$

Show how to add the following fractions using a three-step area model like the one above.

a) $\frac{2}{3} + \frac{1}{4}$

b) $\frac{1}{3} + \frac{1}{5}$

MD-56. Marisa had to miss math class to go to the dentist, so she asked Mario to explain how to add fractions. He showed her this model.

$\frac{1}{3} + \frac{1}{2}$

"First you copy the problem.

"Next draw and divide equal-sized rectangles for each fraction. Remember that one is cut horizontally and the other is cut vertically.

$\frac{2}{6} + \frac{3}{6}$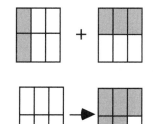

"Now redraw the rectangles with more lines, as if one rectangle is placed on top of the other one. Then shade the same areas from each of the two original rectangles.

$\frac{5}{6}$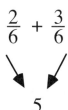

"Now you can rename the fractions as sixths, because the new rectangles are divided into six equal parts. I drew an empty rectangle with sixths.

"Finally, combine all the sixths and shade the total number of sixths in the new rectangle. Then write one fraction."

Use the fraction model Mario explained to add the following fractions.

a) $\frac{1}{4} + \frac{2}{5}$

b) $\frac{2}{3} + \frac{3}{5}$

MD-57. Now we can find the probability of selecting a truck or van (parts (a) through (c)) and a sedan or van (parts (d) through (f)) using the spinner in problem MD-55.

a) Write a fraction addition problem to show the probability of spinning a truck or van.

b) Draw a rectangle model of your addition problem.

c) Find the sum using your model.

d) Write a fraction addition problem to show the probability of spinning a sedan or van.

e) Draw a rectangle model for your addition problem.

f) Find the sum using your model.

MD-58.   Skye's Ice Cream Shoppe is Mario's favorite place
for an outing. Unfortunately, because he was late
arriving there, his friends had already ordered. He
did not know what they ordered for him. They told
him that it was either a waffle cone or a sundae and
that it was either apricot, chocolate, or blackberry.

Draw, divide, and label a rectangle to answer the
following questions.

a)   What is the probability that Mario will get something with apricot ice cream?

b)   What is the probability that he will get a sundae?

c)   What is the probability that he will get either something with chocolate or a waffle
cone with blackberry?

d)   What is the probability that he will get orange sherbet?

MD-59.   Marisa and Mario were visiting the animals at the fair when they noticed a few number
relationships. They made them into brain teasers for you.

a)   If one-half of the pigs had spots and there
were 14 pigs, how many had spots?

b)   If three-fourths of the cows had nose rings
and there were 24 cows, how many cows
had nose rings?

c)   If three-tenths of the visitors were adults
and there were 100 visitors, what number
were adults?

d)   Five-eighths of the birds were chickens. If there were 64 birds, how many were <u>not</u>
chickens?

MD-60.   Calculate the sum or difference. Simplify when possible.

a) $\frac{1}{7} + \frac{3}{7}$ b) $\frac{3}{8} + \frac{5}{8}$ c) $\frac{2}{6} + \frac{2}{6}$ d) $\frac{5}{6} + \frac{4}{6}$

e) $\frac{3}{4} + \frac{3}{4}$ f) $\frac{5}{8} - \frac{3}{8}$ g) $\frac{5}{10} - \frac{2}{10}$ h) $\frac{1}{4} - \frac{3}{4}$

MD-61.   Crystal and Cristina counted the number of letters in the last names of the students in their 7th period math class. Here is a list of their results: 9, 8, 4, 8, 7, 6, 5, 9, 7, 5, 6, 9, 8, 6, 6, 7, 7, 4, 6, and 6.

a)   What is the mean number of letters?

b)   What is the mode?

c)   What is the range?

d)   What numbers are in the upper quartile?

e)   If Crystal's last name has 7 letters, in which quartile did her name fall?

f)   What is the median number?

MD-62.   Use the < and > symbols to complete the following inequalities.

a)   -5 __ -2   b)   8 __ -1   c)   -5 __ 0   d)   -15 __ -14

MD-63.   Which number represents the product of 731 and 640?

(A) 468,840   (B) 1,371   (C) 46,784   (D) 467,840   (E) none of these

MD-64.   Complete the following Diamond Problems.

Product

Sum

a)

b)

c)

d) Bonus

MD-65. Judy has a pencil box on her desk with four blue, three red, and five yellow pencils. Her box also contains two red, one black, and three green pens. Whenever she reaches her hand in to get ready to do her homework, she randomly takes out one pencil and one pen.

a) Make a probability rectangle.

b) How many pencils does Judy have in her box?

c) How many pens does Judy have in her box?

d) What is the probability that Judy gets a blue pencil?

e) What is the probability that Judy gets a yellow pencil?

f) What is the probability that Judy gets a green pen?

g) What is the probability that Judy gets a black pen?

h) What is the probability that Judy gets a blue pencil and a green pen?

i) What is the probability that Judy gets a blue pencil and a red pen?

j) What is the probability that Judy gets a blue pencil or a red pen?

MD-66. Show how to add the following fractions using an area model.

a) $\frac{2}{3} + \frac{1}{5}$

b) $\frac{1}{4} + \frac{1}{6}$

c) $\frac{1}{3} + \frac{3}{8}$

MD-67.   You will be playing the "Four-in-a-Row, There You Go" (Fraction Addition) game. Make sure you use the new game board. You may want to review the rules in problem MD-43. In this game, however, instead of multiplying the two numbers, you add them. Also remember that some answers formed are not on the game board. When this game is completed, write "game played" on your paper to let your teacher know you have done this activity. Include how many times you played and who won.

GAME BOARD

$\frac{5}{6}$	$\frac{9}{10}$	$\frac{31}{40}$	$\frac{3}{4}$
$\frac{5}{8}$	$\frac{7}{8}$	$\frac{5}{12}$	$\frac{13}{24}$
$\frac{2}{3}$	$\frac{17}{30}$	$\frac{3}{8}$	$\frac{13}{20}$
$\frac{1}{2}$	$\frac{17}{24}$	$\frac{7}{24}$	$\frac{7}{12}$

$\frac{1}{2}$	$\frac{3}{8}$	$\frac{1}{6}$	$\frac{1}{4}$	$\frac{1}{8}$	$\frac{1}{3}$	$\frac{2}{5}$

ADDING AND SUBTRACTING FRACTIONS

To add or subtract two fractions, the fractions must have the same denominator. One way to convert two fractions with different denominators into fractions with the same denominator is to use a Giant **1**. Below are examples of adding and subtracting two fractions with unlike denominators. In general,

$$\frac{a}{b} + \frac{c}{d} = \frac{a}{b} \cdot \boxed{\frac{d}{d}} + \frac{c}{d} \cdot \boxed{\frac{b}{b}} = \frac{ad}{bd} + \frac{bc}{bd} = \frac{ad + bc}{bd}$$

ADDITION

$$\frac{1}{5} + \frac{1}{3} = \frac{1}{5} \cdot \boxed{\frac{3}{3}} + \frac{1}{3} \cdot \boxed{\frac{5}{5}} = \frac{3}{15} + \frac{5}{15} = \frac{8}{15}$$

SUBTRACTION

$$\frac{3}{4} - \frac{1}{5} = \frac{3}{4} \cdot \boxed{\frac{5}{5}} - \frac{1}{5} \cdot \boxed{\frac{4}{4}} = \frac{15}{20} - \frac{4}{20} = \frac{11}{20}$$

Answer the questions below in your Tool Kit to the right of the double-lined box.

a) What common denominator is needed to compute $\frac{1}{8} + \frac{2}{3}$?

b) Compute $\frac{1}{8} + \frac{2}{3}$ using the Giant **1**. Highlight the Giant **1**s you use.

MD-69. Using the spinner in problem MD-55, answer the following questions.

a) What is the probability of spinning either a truck or a sedan?

b) What is the probability of spinning either a truck or a van?

c) What is the probability of spinning either a motorcycle or a sedan?

MD-70. Vehicle prizes were dwindling at the prize commission car lot. There were only two sedans, three vans, and one motorcycle left. When a new shipment arrived, it contained twelve new vans, four new motorcycles, and twenty new sedans. How many vehicle prizes are now on the lot? Use variables to represent each type of item and show your answer as an equation.

MD-71. Vicki used $\frac{2}{3}$ of a cup of milk and $\frac{1}{4}$ of a cup of orange juice in her new recipe for Orange Cappuccinos. What is the total amount of milk and orange juice combined in the drink?

MD-72. Betsy had one-quarter of a dozen eggs. Her chicken laid another one-sixth of a dozen eggs. What fraction of a dozen eggs does Betsy have now if she has neither eaten nor broken any eggs?

MD-73. Ruthie did a survey among her classmates comparing the time spent playing video games to the time spent studying. The scatter plot of her data is shown at right.

a) What correlation can you make from her data?

b) Use an ordered pair to identify the outlier.

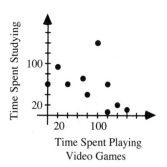

MD-74. Answer the following questions about common denominators.

a) If you were adding thirds and fourths, what denominator would you use?

b) If you were adding fifths and twelfths, what denominator would you use?

c) If you were adding eighths and sixths, what denominator would you use?

d) How do you decide which new denominator to use? Explain in a few sentences.

MD-75.   In 1991, Doug Danger jumped 251 feet on his motorcycle. Based on a classroom 30 feet long, estimate how many classroom lengths he could jump.

MD-76.   Draw a model to represent multiplying the following fractions and give the answer.

a) $\frac{1}{2} \cdot \frac{4}{5}$

b) $\frac{3}{4} \cdot \frac{2}{3}$

MD-77.   Mario found a bag of marbles. It contained five blue marbles, seven green marbles, one agate, and two steelies. What is the probability of reaching into the bag and pulling out a blue marble or a steelie? Write an equation.

MD-78.   If a certain number is to be represented by x, and x is given a value of 7, what would be the value of $\frac{x + 2}{3}$?

(A) 4   (B) 7x + 2   (C) 3   (D) x + 7   (E) none of these

MD-79.   How many hours will it take a person to travel 200 miles at the rate of 40 miles an hour?

(A) 25 hours   (B) $\frac{1}{4}$ hour   (C) 5 hours   (D) 2 hours   (E) none of these

MD-80.   Your teacher will give you a card or two to place on a number line. When all the cards are in place, draw an identical number line on your paper. Note that the number line focuses on the values between 0 and 1. Make your line long enough—at least five inches long—to fit each of the values in the correct place.

a)   Record all the numbers as they are placed on the class number line.

b)   Explain why some of the numbers name the same point.

c)   Discuss the similarities and differences between the values in the three sets of cards.

MD-81. Mario is concerned. Agent Ajax teaches the T^2 (Technology Training) course. She requires her students to earn at least 80% on tests to pass. Unfortunately, Mario only scored 39 out of 50 on the last test. He is sure that is just a little bit too low.

a) Express Mario's score as a fraction.

b) Use the Identity Property to create a fraction with a denominator of 100 to show this test score.

c) Write this fraction as a percent. (Percent means "out of one hundred.")

MD-82. Agent Ajax is a wonderfully compassionate, yet firm, teacher. While she will not make an exception on her 80% passing rule, she will allow Mario to take another test to try to improve his score. This time Mario scores 21 out of 25. Use the Identity Property of Multiplication to find Mario's score on the second test using a denominator of 100. In other words, write his score as a percent.

MD-83. Marisa is in the Fundamentals of Fingerprinting course, and the instructor, Agent Amino, is even tougher than Agent Ajax. He requires an 85% score to pass. However, he will allow students to choose the higher of two scores on the final exam. Marisa scored 43 out of 50 on one version of the final and 84 out of 100 on the other. Which score should Marisa choose?

MD-84. Tom is buying new computers for his writing team. He can buy the first five at dealer cost. The other 15 will be purchased for an extra $50 each. The cost of the computers totals $11,750. Use a Guess and Check table to find how much each of the discounted computers cost.

MD-85.   Draw a line segment on your paper that is at least 5 inches long. Divide the number line into ten equal intervals. Label the first tick mark 0.72 and the last (eleventh) tick mark 0.73. This segment represents the portion of the number line between 0.72 and 0.73. Place each of the following decimals in the proper spot on your number line.

a)   0.729   b)   0.724   c)   0.7231   d)   0.72732

e)   Round each of the numbers to the nearest hundredth. Using complete sentences, explain your strategy for rounding each number.

MD-86.   Complete the table on the resource page your teacher gives you.

Fraction	Decimal	Percent
$\frac{3}{4}$		
	0.25	
		50%
	$.3\overline{3}$	
$\frac{6}{25}$		
		80%

Fraction	Decimal	Percent
	0.4	
$\frac{5}{4}$		
	0.05	
		47%
$\frac{3}{2}$		
	0.01	

MD-87.   Look at the graph below.

a)   Enter the ordered pairs in the table below. Three pairs are done for you.

x	0	1				5		x
y	-7	-4				8		-

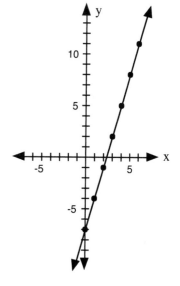

b)   Write the rule in two different ways: first using a variable and numbers, and then using words in a phrase or sentence.

c)   What are the coordinates of the y-intercept?

d)   What are the coordinates of the x-intercept? (You will have to approximate this point.)

MD-88.   Draw a square with sides of 5 units. What is the perimeter? What is the area? Be sure to label your answers.

MD-89.   Last week the low temperature in Fairbanks, Alaska was -6°. Which arrow is closest to -6° ?

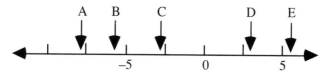

MD-90.   At one point in the last math competition, Marisa had 63 points. Then she answered a question incorrectly. The scorekeeper told her "-12 points." What was Marisa's score then?

(A) 75   (B) -12   (C) -75   (D) 12   (E) 51

MD-91.   Steve got 19 points out of 20 on his weekly quiz. Write this score as a:

a)   fraction   b)   decimal   c)   percent

MD-92. Answer the following questions about common denominators.

a)   If you were adding thirds and fifths, what denominator would you use?

b)   If you were adding halves and sevenths, what denominator would you use?

c)   If you were adding eighths and halves, what denominator would you use?

MD-93. You will be playing "Four-in-a-Row, There You Go" (Fraction Subtraction). Make sure you use the new game board shown below. The rules are similar to problem MD-43 except that you will use subtraction. Again, not all possible answers are on the game board. Make sure you always subtract the smaller fraction from the larger fraction to get a positive result. When the game is completed, write "game played" on your paper to let your teacher know that you have done this activity. Include how many times you played and who won.

GAME BOARD

$\frac{1}{8}$	$\frac{1}{6}$	$\frac{9}{40}$	$\frac{7}{20}$
$\frac{1}{3}$	$\frac{1}{10}$	$\frac{1}{12}$	$\frac{4}{15}$
$\frac{1}{4}$	$\frac{5}{24}$	$\frac{13}{30}$	$\frac{1}{8}$
$\frac{3}{8}$	$\frac{3}{24}$	$\frac{1}{24}$	$\frac{1}{12}$

$\frac{1}{2}$	$\frac{3}{8}$	$\frac{1}{6}$	$\frac{1}{4}$	$\frac{1}{8}$	$\frac{1}{3}$	$\frac{2}{5}$

MD-94. Mario decided to make some incomplete spinners to see if Marisa could figure out the missing piece.

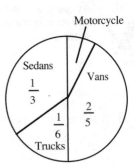

a)   Marisa said, "This is easy. All I have to do is find out what to add to $\frac{2}{5}$ to get $\frac{1}{2}$." Write a problem that shows what she needs to do.

b)   Solve the problem you wrote in part (a).

MD-95.   Mario found a partially completed spinner that Director
          Franklin was making for the next day's class. He knew that
          if he put his problem-solving skills to use, he would be able
          to figure out the missing piece. Mario decided to break the
          problem into smaller problems (subproblems).

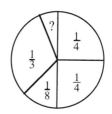

    a)   Describe the subproblems that Mario needs to solve to
          find the probability of getting the missing piece.

    b)   Solve the problem in part (a) above.

MD-96.   Marisa thought that this was such a great
          activity that she wanted to make it more
          difficult and give it to someone else. She
          decided to add "convertibles" and change the
          probabilities. There is an equal chance of
          spinning either a van or a motorcycle. What is
          the probability of spinning a van? Show all of
          your subproblems.

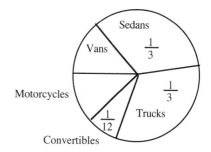

MD-97.   Jonathan was baking bread one afternoon when
          the phone rang. While he was away from the
          kitchen, his dog Flexie came through and
          knocked some of the flour out of the measuring
          cup. Jonathan had a full cup when he left and
          only $\frac{3}{8}$ of a cup when he returned. How much
          did Flexie spill?

MD-98.   Show the following values on a number line. Make the interval from 0 to 1 at least three
          inches long. Be as accurate as possible.

    a) $\frac{5}{8}$ b)   0.307   c)   42.5%

    d)   64%   e) $\frac{5}{6}$ f)   0.84

MD-99.   Marisa and Mario ordered a large pizza dinner. When it arrived, Mario quickly ate $\frac{1}{8}$ of the pizza while Marisa answered the phone. When she called Mario to the phone, their pet poodle, Precious, jumped on the table and ate two large pieces that totaled $\frac{1}{3}$ of the pizza.

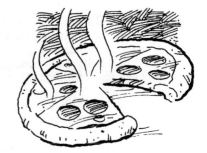

a)   Draw a model of the pizza.

b)   Write an equation to show the fraction of the pizza that was left.

c)   About what percent of the pizza was left?

MD-100.   Gale and Kaye are planning to make egg and bagel sandwiches for their group camping trip. They packed 30 eggs for breakfast. The first evening while they were out on a night hike, raccoons invaded the camp and ate some of the eggs. When the raccoons left, only $\frac{2}{5}$ of the eggs remained.

a)   What fraction of the eggs did the raccoons eat?

b)   How many eggs does this represent? Write an equation to show your work.

MD-101.   Convert the following data and write equivalent measurements.

a)   How many inches are there in 6 feet?

b)   How many inches are there in 5 feet, 2 inches?

c)   One hundred twenty-eight is how many times larger than 16?

d)   One hundred twenty-eight is how many times larger than 8?

e)   If Jon walked 16,412 feet, how many miles did he walk?

f)   Ellen walked 85,764 inches. How many miles did she walk?

MD-102. Compute.

a) -8 + (-3)   b) 4 – |-9|

c) 5 + (-7)   d) 8 + (-7)

e) -2 – |-10| f) -9 – (-5)

g) 12 – 8   h) (-3) · |-6|

i) -3 + 6   j) -20 ÷ 5

MD-103. Complete the following Diamond Problems. Hint for part (e): one factor is $\frac{1}{6}$.

Product

Sum

a)

b)

c)

d)

e)

MD-104. Use the resource page or copy and complete the tables below. Remember to show your work.

a)

A	B	A · B
3	4	3 · 4 = 12
-2	5	
-6	-3	
7	-2	
$\frac{1}{2}$	$\frac{1}{3}$	
$\frac{2}{5}$	$\frac{1}{3}$	

b)

A	B	$\frac{A}{B}$
6	3	$\frac{6}{3} = 2$
8	2	
1	2	
3	4	
2	7	
1	3	

MD-105. Look at your results from part (b) in the previous problem. Which fractions were easiest to convert to decimal form? Using complete sentences, explain why you think so.

MD-106. Marisa is back in the Fundamentals of
Fingerprinting course, and on the next exam Agent
Amino requires students to earn 83% to pass.
However, he will allow students to take two different
final exams and choose the higher of the two scores.
Marisa scored 81 out of 98 on one version of the
final and 85 out of 104 on the other.

a) Marisa is stuck. She cannot decide which
    score to take. Mario suggests, "Fractions
    mean division, right? Maybe we could just
    divide 81 by 98 on our calculator and see what
    decimal we get." Do this division, then write
    the result.

b) Marisa continues, "0.826530612... is so weird! What percent is that? I know it
    must be close to 82 or 83%, and I need to know which it is." What percent do you
    think Marisa earned? Why do you think this?

c) "Oh, I think I can answer my own question. I know that percent means 'out of a
    hundred,' so I'll round 0.826530612 to the nearest hundredth and write that as a
    fraction." To what number does Marisa round 0.826530612...? What fraction
    does she write?

d) Do parts (a), (b), and (c) for the other exam score.

e) "Oh wow!" exclaims Marisa. "Now it's obvious! I can just look at the fractions to
    see which one is better. But wait, I need to know the two percents."

    Mario counters with, "But if you know the decimals you already know the
    percents."

    Explain what Mario means.

f) Which score should Marisa choose?

MD-107. The following example shows Mario's reasoning. Mario started by noticing that
0.8173... is close to 0.82, which is just $\frac{82}{100}$. That's the secret. Remember: "Percent"
means "out of one hundred." So he knew that 0.82 meant 82%.
Convert the following decimals into percents or percents into decimals.

a) 0.48   b) 0.53   c) 0.76

d) 88%   e) 71%   f) 27.5%

MD-108. Make the conversions below. Show your work.

    a)   Change $\frac{5}{8}$ to a decimal.   b)   Change 0.307 to a percent.

    c)   Change 42.5% to a decimal.   d)   Change 64% to a fraction.

    e)   Change $\frac{5}{6}$ to a percent.   f)   Change 0.84 to a fraction.

MD-109.

FRACTIONS—DECIMALS—PERCENTS

Fractions, decimals, and percents are different ways to represent the same number.

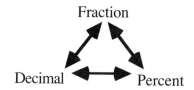

Fraction

Decimal   Percent

Examples:

Decimal to percent:

Multiply the decimal by 100.

$(0.34)(100) = 34\%$

Percent to decimal:

Divide the percent by 100.

$78.6\% \div 100 = 0.786$

Fraction to percent:

Set up an equivalent fraction using 100 as the denominator. The numerator is the percent.

$\frac{4}{5} = \frac{80}{100} = 80\%$

Percent to fraction:

Use 100 as the denominator. Use the percent as the numerator. Simplify as needed.

$22\% = 0.22 = \frac{22}{100} = \frac{11}{50}$

Decimal to fraction:

Use the decimal as the numerator. Use the decimal place value name as the denominator. Simplify as needed.

$0.2 = \frac{2}{10} = \frac{1}{5}$

Fraction to decimal:

Divide the numerator by the denominator.

$\frac{3}{8} = 3 \div 8 = 0.375$

In your Tool Kit, highlight the title (printed in italics) for each of the six ways to change the form of a number.

MD-110. Alexia's homework tonight is to design a spinner that will land on brown 35% of the time, pink 15% of the time, green 45% of the time, and purple the rest of the time.

a) What fraction of the spinner should Alexia color brown?

b) What fraction of the spinner should Alexia color pink?

c) What fraction of the spinner should Alexia color green?

d) What fraction of the spinner should Alexia color purple?

MD-111. Copy and complete the table.

$\frac{1}{6}$		
		≈ 66.7%
	0.42	
		15%
	0.357	
	0.0	
	1.0	
		200%

	1.6	
		37.5%
$\frac{1}{20}$		
		12.5%
$\frac{1}{10}$		
	0.001	
		24%
5		

MD-112. Which of the following bar graphs could represent the data from the circle graph?

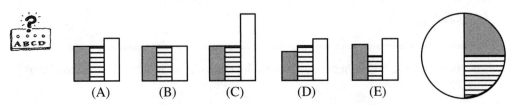

(A)   (B)   (C)   (D)   (E)

MD-113. Calculate the area and perimeter of the figure. Show all subproblems.

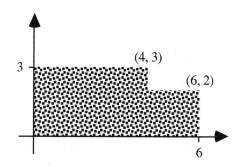

MD-114. Copy the scale at right and create a line graph for sales at the student store Monday through Friday. Notice that there are only four spaces on the vertical y-axis. You may use your Tool Kit as a model for how to set up interval(s). Put the day numbers on the horizontal x-axis. The data is shown below the graph. Remember to use your checklist to be sure your graph is complete.

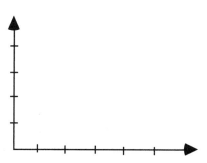

Sales at the student store:
Day 1 $41.30
Day 2 $15.90
Day 3 $92.90
Day 4 $72.00
Day 5 $85.50

MD-115. Write approximate percents for the following fractions.

a) $\frac{25}{32}$

b) $\frac{17}{40}$

c) $\frac{75}{120}$

d) $\frac{36}{140}$

MD-116. Solve the following fraction problems.

a) $\frac{1}{3} + \frac{2}{5}$

b) $\frac{3}{4} \cdot \frac{2}{3}$

c) $\frac{5}{12} + \frac{1}{6}$

d) $\frac{3}{5} - \frac{1}{10}$

e) $\frac{3}{5} \cdot \frac{3}{10}$

f) $\frac{5}{24} + \frac{3}{12}$

MD-117.

Marisa ordered pizza. There were several choices of topping: pepperoni, artichokes, olives, tomatoes, and cheese. She knew the pizza baker, so she told him to surprise her. She also told him that she only wanted two toppings. What is the probability that she will get her favorite pizza, pepperoni with artichokes?

MD-118. In the fingerprinting course, Marisa and Mario took the same test. Mario's score was 12 points less than Marisa's score. The sum of their scores was 168. Using a Guess and Check table, find out what their scores were. Write your answer in a complete sentence.

MD-119. Your teacher will give you a resource page for the game you will be playing today.

Color-Combo-Grido II
A game for many people.

Mathematical Purpose: To study mathematical probability.

Object: To cover six squares in a row or to cover the entire game board.

Materials: 6 x 6 grid with squares divided in two parts; 2 dice each with three sides colored red, two sides colored green, and one side colored yellow.

Scoring: One point for a six-in-a-row game; five points for a cover game.

How to Play the Game:
- Label all 36 squares matching individual predictions.
- Caller rolls both dice and calls out colors.
- Mark out one square matching call (red/yellow and yellow/red are considered the same).
- Mark out only color combinations that match the call.
- Keep track of each play by tallying each color combination called.

Ending the Game: The first person with six in a row (horizontal, vertical, or diagonal) wins; or, the first person with his/her entire card marked out wins.

>>Problem continues on the next page.>>

a) Discuss the game with your partner and make a prediction about what a winning card might look like.

b) Get a resource page from your teacher. Using methods learned in this chapter, analyze the color combination probabilities in the work area of your resource page. Then label your game board.

c) After the game is finished, copy the tally marks from the class game onto your resource page.

d) Compare each category that you originally put on your card to the probability found in your table.

e) Compare the class results to the probabilities you found with your probability rectangle.

f) Using complete sentences, compare the class results with the probabilities you found with your rectangle.

MD-120. The final exam in the National Investigative Agency contains a Color-Combo-Grido question. To pass the exam Mario and Marisa must analyze the situation and determine how often each combination is likely to occur.

Two dice are rolled. Each has sides colored red, red, red, green, green, and yellow.

a) When both dice are rolled, what color combinations are possible? Draw a probability rectangle, label the sides, and determine the probability of each possible combination. Give your answers as simplified fractions. Verify your answers before going on. Use these fractions to answer the following questions. Show all steps as you work.

b) Which color combination is most likely?

c) Which color combination is least likely?

d) What is the probability of getting either RR or RG?

e) What is the probability of both dice having the same color? Write an addition problem to find your answer.

MD-121. **Chapter Summary** Answer each of the following
questions to create a summary of this chapter.

a)   Show how to find five fractions equivalent to $\frac{15}{24}$.

b)   Write a clear explanation of how to add two
fractions so a student who just moved to your
school will understand. Use one of the sample
problems below or make up one of your own.
Use a rectangular area model and equations.

$$\frac{1}{4} + \frac{3}{5} \quad \text{or} \quad \frac{3}{7} + \frac{5}{9} \quad \text{or} \quad \frac{5}{8} + \frac{1}{6} \quad \text{or} \quad \frac{a}{b} + \frac{c}{d}$$

c)   The same new student does not understand multiplication of fractions. Explain what
it means to multiply two fractions, such as $\frac{2}{3} \cdot \frac{4}{5}$. Use a picture and show the steps
with numbers.

d)   Select three different percents between 1% and 100% and show how to represent
them as decimals and as fractions. Choose problems more difficult than 25%, 50%,
and 75%.

MD-122.   There are 36 green gumballs, 18 red gumballs, 22 white
gumballs, 30 purple gumballs, and 14 blue gumballs in the
gumball machine. Find the probability for each of the
following situations and write it as a percent. Show work to
support your answer.

a)   Getting a purple gumball.

b)   Getting either a purple or a green gumball.

c)   <u>Not</u> getting a green gumball.

d)   Getting either a purple or a white gumball.

MD-123.   Compute the answer to each problem.

a) $\frac{2}{7} + \frac{1}{3}$

b) $\frac{4}{5} + \frac{1}{3}$

c) $\frac{4}{9} + \frac{2}{3}$

d) $\frac{1}{4} \cdot \frac{3}{5}$

e) $\frac{4}{3} \cdot \frac{3}{4}$

f) $\frac{5}{7} - \frac{1}{3}$

MD-124. Harim has a bag with 3 blueberry and 4 raspberry gummy worms. He has another bag with 4 red licorice sticks and 2 black licorice sticks. Find the probabilities when he takes one gummy worm and one licorice stick out of each bag without looking.

a) Find the probability of Harim getting a blueberry gummy worm and a red licorice stick. Show your work. Express your answer in simplest form.

b) Find the probability of Harim getting a raspberry gummy worm and a black licorice stick. Show your work. Express your answer in simplest form.

c) Find the probability of Harim getting a blueberry gummy worm and a black licorice stick. Show your work. Express your answer in simplest form.

MD-125. Heidi has been busy with a painting project. She knows she can only spend eight hours on the project, and she estimates that she has already used two-thirds of her time. Write an equation to find how much time she has used. Make sure your answer is in hours and <u>minutes</u>.

MD-126. Calculate the following products. Write the problem, an equal sign, and the answer on your paper for each problem. (That is, write the equation with each solution.)

Note: whole numbers may be written as a fraction like this: $5 = \frac{5}{1}$.

a) $\frac{2}{3} \cdot 6$ b) $\frac{2}{5} \cdot 3$ c) $\frac{3}{4} \cdot 5$

MD-127. Barry took $\frac{1}{4}$ of $\frac{2}{3}$ of a cup of milk to make his special recipe. Write an equation to show how much he used. Show your work.

MD-128. **What We Have Done in This Chapter**

Below is a list of the Tool Kit entries from this chapter.

- MD-5   Probability
- MD-28   Finding Equivalent Fractions
- MD-46   Multiplication of Fractions
- MD-68   Adding and Subtracting Fractions
- MD-109   Fractions, Decimals, and Percents

Review all the entries and read the notes you made in your Tool Kit. Make a list of any questions, terms, or notes you do not understand. Ask your partner or study team members for help. If anything is still unclear, ask your teacher.

Going Camping

Chapter 4

Chapter 4
Going Camping: ALGEBRAIC SENTENCES

This chapter begins with a review of the order of operations. Next you will be introduced to the Distributive Property using a geometric model. Then you will use the patterns developed in Guess and Check tables to write equations with variables. Finally, algebra tiles will be used as a concrete model to help you understand simplifying algebraic expressions.

In this chapter you will have the opportunity to:

- write algebraic expressions and equations with variables.

- develop your understanding of the Distributive Property.

- evaluate algebraic expressions.

- combine like terms.

- review the order of operations by means of grouping terms.

Read the problem below, but **do not try to solve it now.** What you learn over the next few days will enable you to solve it.

GC-0.	**Hannah's Trail Mix**

Hannah, the camp cook, uses a standard recipe for trail mix that contains raisins, chocolate pieces, and peanuts. The quantity of chocolate pieces is 4 ounces more than 3 times the number of ounces of raisins. The quantity of peanuts is 5 ounces less than twice the number of ounces of raisins. What quantity of each ingredient does Hannah use in her standard recipe? Use a variable to write an equation to represent the recipe.

Number Sense		
Algebra and Functions		
Mathematical Reasoning		
Measurement and Geometry		
Statistics, Data Analysis, & Probability		

Chapter 4
Going Camping: ALGEBRAIC SENTENCES

GC-1.   Copy the Mess Hall Breakfast Menu expressions and evaluate them as your teacher gives them to you. For example, in the first entry, p + m, we let p represent the cost of pancakes and m represent the cost of milk. Likewise, the cost of each of the other items on the menu is represented by the first letter of its name. To evaluate an expression means to calculate the value.

GC-2.   Evaluate each of the following expressions:

a) $6 + 5 \cdot 8$ b) $3 \cdot 5 + 2 \cdot 10$ c) $3 + 2(4 + 7)$

GC-3.   Work with your partner to evaluate the problems below. Circle each term and show all your steps in the same way demonstrated by your teacher.

a) $17 + 3 \cdot 2$ b) $7 \cdot 2 + 4 - 2(7 + 3)$

c) $6 \cdot 2 + 3 \cdot 4 - 8$ d) $3^2 + 5(1 - 3) + 4 \cdot 5 + 1$
                                         Remember that 3^2 means $3 \cdot 3$.

e) $(8 - 12) + 10 \cdot 3$

GC-4.   You will be playing the Target Game today. You will play this game throughout the chapter, and it will help you practice using the correct order of operations. Some homework problems will refer to the game.

Target Game
A game for the whole class

Mathematical Purpose: To practice the order of operations.

Object: Use any combination of the five numbers given and any combination of arithmetic operations to reach an answer that is as close as possible to the target number.

How to Play the Game:
- Your teacher will give you five numbers and a target number.
- Arrange the five numbers in any order and use any combination of mathematical operations and grouping symbols (addition, subtraction, multiplication, division, exponents, and parentheses) to write an equation that has an answer as close as possible to the target number.
- The winner is the person who gets closest to the target number.

Ending the Game: The game ends when the teacher determines that all students have had enough time to write their best equation.

GC-5.   Simplify each expression.

a) $16 - 5(3 - 1)$ b) $3(2^2) - 8 \cdot 1$ c) $4 \cdot 5 - 2^2 + 3(5 - 4)$

GC-6.

ORDER OF OPERATIONS

An expression is organized into parts that are separated by addition (+) or subtraction (–) symbols <u>unless</u> the sum or difference is inside parentheses. Each part (a number, variable, product or quotient of numbers and variables) is called a **TERM**.

Example:

Simplify $3(6 - 3) + 4 \cdot 5^2 - 10$.

$$\boxed{3(6-3)} + \boxed{4 \cdot 5^2} - \boxed{10}$$

$$\boxed{3(3)} + \boxed{4 \cdot 5 \cdot 5} - \boxed{10}$$

1. <u>Circle</u> the terms in the expression.

$$\boxed{9} + \boxed{4 \cdot 25} - \boxed{10}$$

2. <u>Simplify</u> each term until it is one number by:

$$\boxed{9} + \boxed{100} - \boxed{10}$$

- evaluating each exponential number.

$$109 - 10 = 99$$

- performing each operation inside prentheses before doing any other operations in the term following the rule below.

- multiplying and dividing from left to right.

3. Finally, <u>combine like terms</u> by adding and subtracting left to right.

Examples of a term include 4, 3x, -2y⁴, $\frac{3x}{7}$, 4(x + 3), and 5x(x – 2)².

Make these notes in your Tool Kit to the right of the double-lined box.

a) Describe some mistakes students might make if they do not know the order of operations.

b) How will you help yourself remember the correct order of operations?

GC-7. Use the order of operations and a table like the one at right to calculate the y-values. Leave enough space on each line to show your work. Follow the example and show all your work. You do <u>not</u> need to copy the example onto your paper. Just draw two vertical and one horizontal lines to create the table workspace. Some of the answers are in your book, so you may want to use these answers to check your work and make sure you are doing the problems correctly.

x	y = 3x + 5	y
-2	y = 3(-2) + 5	
	y = $\boxed{3 \, (-2)}$ + $\boxed{5}$	
	y = $\boxed{-6}$ + $\boxed{5}$	
	y = -1	-1
0		
2		
-1		2

GC-8. You have been given the numbers 2, 3, 4, 5, and 6 in the Target Game. The target that you are trying to get is 19. Someone has already found 20 and 18.

a) Find a winning solution. b) Find another solution.

c) Are there more solutions? Check with your partner or study team members to see whether they found other solutions.

GC-9. The camp soccer teams calculate their statistics each summer. Here are the statistics for the top six teams. Round your answers to the nearest tenth.

	Games Played	Games Won	Games Lost	Goals Scored
Burn	52	42	10	162
Sizzlers	27	20	7	74
100°	28	16	12	87
Hotdoggers	30	16	14	53
Flash	33	28	5	102
Coolers	48	37	11	139

a) Find the mean number of games played by all of the teams.

b) Find the number of goals per game scored by the Coolers.

c) Find the median number of games lost for all of the teams. Which teams are closest to the median?

d) Find the median number of games won. Which teams are closest to the median?

GC-10. Lani and Will are arguing about whether $\frac{3}{6}$ and $\frac{50}{100}$ are equivalent fractions. Will says they are and Lani says they are not because you cannot use the Identity Property of Multiplication to change $\frac{3}{6}$ to $\frac{50}{100}$. Who is correct? Explain your answer.

GC-11. Use the resource page provided by your teacher to make your own set of algebra tiles. Cut out the tiles and store them in the envelope provided by your teacher.

GC-12. Now that we have started a new chapter, it is time for you to organize your binder.

a)   Put the work from the last chapter in order and keep it in a separate folder.

b)   When this is completed, write, "I have organized my binder."

GC-13. Play the Target Game and aim for a target number of 40. Use 1, 3, 4, 4, and 7. Find two solutions.

GC-14. Compute answers to the following problems in your head. Write just the answers on your paper.

a) $13 \cdot 8$ b) $10 \cdot 8 + 3 \cdot 8$

c) $7 \cdot 15$ d) $7 \cdot 10 + 7 \cdot 5$

e) $4 \cdot 198$ f) $4 \cdot 200 - 4 \cdot 2$

g)   Examine the expressions by pairs, that is, parts (a) and (b), (c) and (d), and (e) and (f).

   i)   How is each pair similar?

   ii) How is each pair different?

h)   Make up two more pairs of examples like the ones above.

GC-15. Follow the steps below to calculate the area of this rectangle.

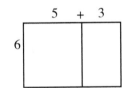

a)   Find the area (in square units) of the two smaller rectangles.

b)   Add the areas of the two sections.

c)   Find the length of the big rectangle by adding the (horizontal) lengths of the two smaller rectangles.

d)   Multiply the new length by the width.

e)   What do you notice about your answers in parts (b) and (d)?

f)   Write an equation to show that both methods give the same result.

GC-16.   Use the Distributive Property to break each problem into smaller parts, called
subproblems, then multiply and add or subtract the products.

a) $6 \cdot 31$ b) $4 \cdot 37$ c) $85 \cdot 7$ d) $50 \cdot 28$

GC-17.   Use the Distributive Property to help make working with larger numbers simpler.

a)   Explain how you could break $4 \cdot 625$ into **subproblems** to make it easier to solve.

b)   Write out your steps in the form of an equation.

c)   Compare your steps with another member of your team. Did you approach the problem in the same way or in different ways? Explain.

GC-18.

DISTRIBUTIVE PROPERTY WITH INTEGERS

- Rewrite the multiplication problem as two or more terms of products to be added or subtracted.
- Multiply the separate parts.
- Add or subtract the products.

Example 1: $6 \cdot 37 = 6(30 + 7) = 6 \cdot 30 + 6 \cdot 7 = 180 + 42 = 222$

Example 2: $3 \cdot 715$

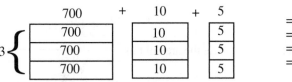

$$3 \cdot 715$$
$$= 3(700 + 10 + 5)$$
$$= 3(700) + 3(10) + 3(5)$$
$$= 2100 + 30 + 15$$
$$= 2145$$
$$3 \cdot 715 = 2145$$

Answer the question in your Tool Kit to the right of the double-lined box.

How can the Distributive Property help you with the mental math problems you do in your head? Give an example.

GC-19.   Show all your subproblems and write your answer as an equation.

a) $5 \cdot 320$ b) $4 \cdot 408$ c) $7 \cdot 906$

GC-20.   Use the picture at right to help you multiply
12 · 17. Refer to problem GC-15 if you need
help. Show all your subproblems.

	7 +	10
12	A	B

GC-21.   Travis had $\frac{3}{8}$ of a box of crackers and Shellena had $\frac{7}{8}$ of a box. They need one and a
half boxes for their party. Do they have enough? Explain your answer.

GC-22.   When Edwin's class went to the School Fair the students guessed how many jelly beans
were in a jar. Here are their guesses: 75, 80, 95, 92, 100, 72, 71, 60, 65, 88, 44, 78, 82, 83,
86, 102, 116, 101, 60.

    a)   Make a stem-and-leaf plot to display the data.

    b)   Make a box-and-whisker graph.

    c)   Which data display most clearly shows the range of the data? What is the range?

    d)   Which data display most clearly shows the mode? What is the mode?

GC-23.   Use a table like the one at right and the
order of operations to calculate the
y-values. Follow the example and show all
of your work for each y-value.

x	$y = 5 + 3(2 - x)$	y
-3	$y = 5 + 3(2 - (-3))$	
	$y = ⑤ + (3(2-(-3)))$	
	$y = ⑤ + (3(5))$	
	$y = ⑤ + ⑮$	
	$y = 20$	20
-2		17
2		
0		

Going Camping: Algebraic Sentences

GC-24. How was the Identity Property of Multiplication (the Giant **1**) used to find equivalent fractions for the problems below?

a) $\frac{2}{3} \cdot$ 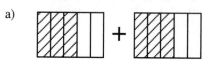 $= \frac{12}{18}$

b) $\frac{6}{7} \cdot$ **1** $= \frac{48}{56}$

c) $\frac{49}{63} = \frac{7}{9} \cdot$ **1**

d) $\frac{24}{27} = \frac{8}{9} \cdot$ **1**

GC-25. Assuming each rectangle represents one whole unit, determine the total area of the shaded parts in the problems below.

a)

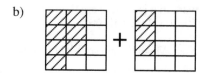

b)

GC-26. Follow your teacher's directions for practicing mental math. How are the new solution strategies helping you?

GC-27. Garret was playing the Target Game. The numbers rolled were 2, 3, 5, 6, and 7, and the target number was 31. Help Garret hit the target. Find two or three solutions and be ready to write one on the board.

GC-28. Holly Anne has a flower garden with two planting beds. She asked Chad and Scooter to help her find the total area of her garden. Here is what they did:

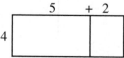

Chad's Method

$4(5 + 2)$
$= 4 \cdot 7$
$= 28$

Scooter's Method

$(4 \cdot 5) + (4 \cdot 2)$
$= 20 + 8$
$= 28$

a) Explain each step of Chad's method.

b) Explain each step of Scooter's method.

c) Which method do you prefer? Why?

GC-29. Perform the following computations.

      a) $(6 \cdot 3) + (6 \cdot 9) + (6 \cdot 1) + (6 \cdot 7) = ?$ b) $6(3 + 9 + 1 + 7) = ?$

      c)   What is the same about each problem?   d)   What is different about the problems?

GC-30. Carefully examine the rectangles at right.

      a)   What are the dimensions of Figure A?

      b)   Find the area of Figure A.

      c)   What are the dimensions of Figure B?

      d)   Find the area of Figure B.

      e)   Add the areas of Figures A and B.

      f)   What are the dimensions of Figure C?

      g)   Find the area of Figure C.

      h)   What do you notice about the combined areas of Figures A and B and the area of Figure C?

      i)   Draw a new diagram showing how Figures A and B could fit inside Figure C. Explain why this is possible.

GC-31. Use a resource page or copy the table below, then use the Distributive Property to complete it.

Factored Form	Distributed	Simplified
3(7 + 2)	3(7) + 3(2)	21 + 6 = 27
8(7 + 4)	$8 \cdot 7 + 8 \cdot 4$	
9(4 + 3 + 1)		
2(7 + 5 + 6)		
	$5 \cdot 8 + 5 \cdot 3 + 5 \cdot 9$	
6(4 + 3 + 7 + 10)		

GC-32. Try each problem using mental math and write only your answer. Then write out steps that illustrate the Distributive Property.

      a) $731 \cdot 4$ b) $3 \cdot 256$ c) $625 \cdot 5$ d) $7 \cdot 514$

GC-33. One number is five more than a second number. The product of the numbers is 2,444, and both numbers are positive. Use a Guess and Check table to find the numbers.

GC-34. The graph at right shows an example of a translation (slide). In the triangle, A (-6, -1) moved to A' (1, 2), etc.

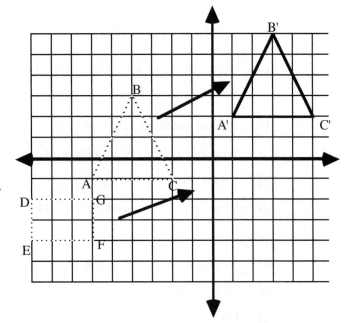

a) If B = (-4, 3) what are the coordinates of B'?

b) If rectangle DEFG slides in the same manner as the triangle, draw rectangle D'E'F'G'.

c) What are the coordinates of the vertices of the translated rectangle?

GC-35. Counselors want to paint all the cabins before the campers arrive. They are going to work different amounts of time. Chris will work five hours, Caylan will work three, Cara will work two, Rachel and Alyssa will each work four, and Levi will work six hours. If each counselor earns $6 an hour, what is the total amount the owner will have to pay to have the cabins painted? Use the Distributive Property to show how to solve this problem in two ways by completing parts (a) and (b) below.

a) Calculate how much each counselor will earn and add their earnings together. Write your answer in an equation.

b) Add all of the counselors' hours together first and then calculate the total earnings. Write your answer in an equation.

GC-36. Convert these measurements. How many:

a) inches are in 27 feet?

b) centimeters are in 14 meters?

c) weeks are in 42 days?

d) pounds are in 32 ounces?

GC-37. Draw a model for each of the following multiplication problems and give the answer.

a) $\dfrac{1}{2} \cdot \dfrac{1}{3}$ b) $\dfrac{2}{3} \cdot \dfrac{1}{4}$

c) $\dfrac{1}{5} \cdot \dfrac{2}{3}$ d) $\dfrac{4}{4} \cdot \dfrac{3}{4}$

GC-38. Below are three scatter plots. For each scatter plot, answer the following questions.

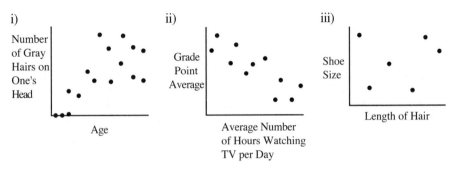

i)

Number of Gray Hairs on One's Head

Age

ii)

Grade Point Average

Average Number of Hours Watching TV per Day

iii)

Shoe Size

Length of Hair

a) What does a dot on each scatter plot represent?

b) Is there a "trend" or correlation in the group of dots? If so, describe it.

c) Write positive correlation, negative correlation, or no correlation.

GC-39. Copy the Mess Hall Lunch and Dinner Menu expressions and evaluate them as your teacher gives them to you. Each variable represents the cost of the item with the same first letter in its name.

GC-40. You have made or been provided with a set of tiles in three different sizes. These are called algebra tiles. The big square has a side length of x, the narrow rectangle has sides of length 1 (the short side) and x (the long side), and the small square has a side length of 1.

a) Trace and label the dimensions of each tile on your paper.

b) What is the area of the big square?

c) What is the area of the rectangle?

d) What is the area of the small square?

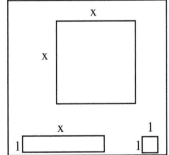

GC-41.   Remember that x can represent any number, just as the variable did in the envelope activity in Chapter 2. Remember that x has the same value <u>within</u> <u>each</u> <u>problem</u>, but its value can vary from problem to problem.

a)   Find the area of each tile in the previous problem when x = 5.

b)   Check your results with your team members. Did you agree or disagree? Explain.

c)   Why do you think x is called a **variable**?

GC-42.   Here is another example of combining like terms with a diagram. Use it as your model. Draw a diagram, then write an equation for (a) through (c) below.

$$(2x^2 + 5x + 7) + (x^2 + x + 1) = 3x^2 + 6x + 8$$

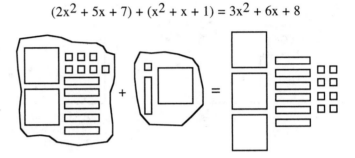

a) $(x^2 + 2x + 3) + (2x^2 + 5x + 4)$ b) $(3x^2 + 3x + 6) + (2x + 8)$

c) $(2x^2 + 10) + (6x + 2)$

HOW TO COMBINE LIKE TERMS

Group all of the tiles with the same area. Doing so models an algebraic process called **COMBINING LIKE TERMS.**

Note: The formal definition of **like terms** is two or more terms that have the same variable(s) with corresponding variable(s) raised to the same power.

Examples: 6 and 13, $2x^2$ and $-7x^2$, 4ab and 3ab.

Not like terms: 5 and 3x, 5x and $3x^2$, ab and ab^2.

List terms in order of decreasing powers.

Tile model:

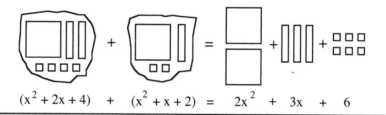

$$(x^2 + 2x + 4) \quad + \quad (x^2 + x + 2) \quad = \quad 2x^2 \quad + \quad 3x \quad + \quad 6$$

Make these notes in your Tool Kit to the right of the double-lined box.

a) Here is a real-world example of combining like terms:

If you have 8 pens and 3 pencils and your friend has 1 pen and 7 pencils, together you have 9 pens and 10 pencils.

Give two more real-world examples of combining like terms.

b) Use mathematical numbers and symbols to give three examples of like terms. Have your partner or a team member check that your examples are correct.

GC-44. Nadine and Patricia put some of their algebra tiles together in a container on the desk. Nadine put in two big squares, three rectangles, and four small squares. Patricia added two rectangles and three small squares.

a) Draw a diagram that shows the tiles each girl put in the container.

b) Write an equation to describe what is now in the container. Your equation should look like this: (   ) + (   ) = _____.

GC-45. You were busy working on a problem using four big squares, eight rectangles, and six small squares. Your partner accidentally knocked some algebra tiles off your desk. You now have one big square, three rectangles, and five small squares on your desk.

Write an algebraic equation that shows what tiles you began with, what your partner knocked off the desk, and how many tiles you have left.

GC-46. Use the Distributive Property to add parentheses and write these expressions as a product of a number and a sum. Expressions written like this are said to be in **factored form**. Here is an example to use as a model: $6 \cdot 3 + 6 \cdot 7 = 6(3 + 7) = 6(10) = 60$.

a) $8 \cdot 3 + 8 \cdot 2$

b) $31 \cdot 4 + 31 \cdot 6$

c) $25 \cdot 8 + 25 \cdot 12$

d) $7 \cdot 131 + 7 \cdot 86$

GC-47. Use the Identity Property of Multiplication (Giant **1**) to figure out the unknown number.

a) $\dfrac{3}{7} = \dfrac{r}{28}$

b) $\dfrac{24}{36} = \dfrac{4}{k}$

c) $\dfrac{2}{3} = \dfrac{x}{33}$

d) $\dfrac{n}{8} = \dfrac{42}{56}$

e) $\dfrac{m}{64} = \dfrac{1}{8}$

f) $\dfrac{4}{5} \cdot \dfrac{?}{?} = \dfrac{36}{45}$

g) $\dfrac{c}{6} = \dfrac{48}{72}$

h) $\dfrac{3}{5} \cdot \dfrac{?}{?} = \dfrac{21}{35}$

GC-48. Copy and complete the multiplication table. Put fractional answers in their simplest form.

Multiply	4	2	$\dfrac{1}{2}$	$\dfrac{1}{3}$	0
$\dfrac{1}{2}$					
$\dfrac{1}{3}$			$\dfrac{1}{6}$		
$\dfrac{1}{4}$					

CHAPTER 4

GC-49.   Ona went on a houseboat vacation. Her three-day
          rental rate was $745. She could keep the
          houseboat for any number of extra days for $150
          per day over the three-day rate. When she
          returned the houseboat, her bill was $1495. Use a
          Guess and Check table to find how many extra
          days she stayed on the river.

GC-50.   The camp cabins have two rooms. One room
          contains bunk beds and the other room is the
          bathroom.

          Draw a diagram and find the total area of the cabin
          in two ways. Assume the cabin is rectangular and
          the sleeping area measures eight feet by ten feet.
          The bathroom is eight feet by four feet. Write an
          equation to show your work both ways.

GC-51.   Complete the following fraction-decimal-percent triangles.

a)   b)   c)

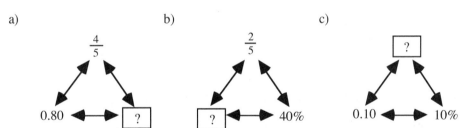

GC-52.   Use the order of operations and a table
          like the one at right to calculate the
          y-values. Follow the example given as a
          model. Show all of your work for each
          y-value.

x	y = 2x + 3(x + 1)	y
-2	y = 2(-2) + 3(-2 + 1)	
	y = (2(-2)) + (3(-2 + 1))	
	y = (-4) + (3(-1))	
	y = (-4) + (-3)	
	y = -7	-7
-1		
0		
3		

GC-53.   Claire finished her assignment early, so her teacher
    suggested that she find the last digit of the product

          $3 \cdot 3^3 \cdot 3^5 \cdots 3^{19}$. The entire product was too big
          for her calculator, but she still found the last digit.
          What is the last digit? Explain how she determined
          her answer.

GC-54.   Match each geometric figure with the algebraic expression that describes it.
          Note: "3 · x" means "3 times x" and is often written 3x. This represents 3 rows of
          length x. Sketch a quick copy of the figure and write the expression below it.

a)   b) $2(x) + 2(1)$

                        $3(x + 1)$

c)   d) $5(x + 2)$

                                            $3(x) + 3(3)$

                                                                $2(x + 4)$

                                                                $3(x) + 3(5)$

e)   f)

GC-55.   Sketch the geometric figure represented by each of the algebraic expressions.

          a) $4(x + 3)$ b) $4(x) + 4(3)$

          c)   Compare the diagrams. How do their areas compare? Write an algebraic equation
                that states this relationship. This is another example of the Distributive Property.

GC-56. Each algebraic expression below can be represented with algebra tiles in two different ways to show the Distributive Property. Use your algebra tiles to build two geometric figures for each expression. The first one has been done for you.

a) $3(x) + 3(2)$

Build $3(x) + 3(2)$.   Group them differently.

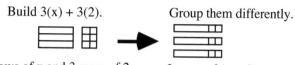

3 rows of x and 3 rows of 2   3 rows of $(x + 2)$

$3(x)$ + $3(2)$ = $3(x + 2)$

b) $2(x + 8)$ c) $4(x + 2)$

d) $5(x) + 5(4)$ e) $5(x + 6)$

f) $9(x) + 9(4)$ g) $2(4x + 7)$

h) $6(x + 3)$

GC-57.

DISTRIBUTIVE PROPERTY WITH ALGEBRA TILES

Using the Distributive Property, the area of a rectangular arrangement of algebra tiles can be represented in three different ways.

$3x + 9$ $3(x) + 3(3)$ $3(x + 3)$

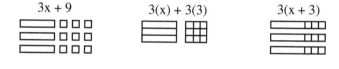

area $= 3x + 9 = 3(x) + 3(3) = 3(x + 3)$

In general, ab + ac = a(b) + a(c) = a(b + c)

Make these notes in your Tool Kit to the right of the double-lined box.

a) How is this Tool Kit entry different from the previous Tool Kit entry on the Distributive Property?

b) How is it the same?

c) How does the Distributive Property relate to area as a sum and area as a product?

GC-58. Your random numbers are 7, 2, 3, 9, and 5. Your target number is 52. Find two or three solutions that hit or come as close as possible to the target number. Show your work.

GC-59. Use the order of operations and a table like the one at right to calculate the y-values. Use the example given as a model. Show all of your work for each y-value.

x	y = 3(x + 6) – 2	y
-3	y = 3(-3 + 6) – 2	
	y = (3(-3 + 6)) – (2)	
	y = (3(3)) – (2)	
	y = (9) – (2)	
	y = 7	7
-2		
-1		
0		

GC-60. What value of x makes each equation true?

a) $x + 12 = 56$ b) $-10 + x = -32$ c) $x - 15 = 53$ d) $x + (-7) = 25$

GC-61. Several campers want to paint a mural. The wall where the mural will be painted has been divided into three sections. The height is 8 feet, and the width of each section is different. One section measures 8 feet by 6 feet. Another section measures 8 feet by 4 feet. The third section measures 8 feet by 5 feet.

a) Draw a diagram of the wall and label the dimensions of the three sections.

b) Find the area of each section.

c) Find the total area of the camp mural. Show your computation in two ways.

d) Explain how using the Distributive Property relates to finding the area of the camp mural.

GC-62. Simplify the following.

a) $\frac{1}{2} + \frac{1}{3}$ b) $1\frac{1}{2} + 1\frac{1}{3}$ c) $\frac{1}{2} + \frac{2}{3}$ d) $1\frac{1}{2} + 1\frac{2}{3}$

GC-63.   Use the Breakfast Mess Hall Menu below to help you solve these problems. Remember that we represent the cost of an item by using the first letter of its name. Copy the expressions and evaluate them.

MESS HALL MENU

BREAKFAST
Sausage $1.75
Egg $1.25
Hash Browns $1.90
Pancakes $1.75
Toast $1.35
Donut $1.50
Fruit $2.50

BEVERAGES
Juice $1.15
Milk $0.75
Cocoa $0.90

a) $3s + 2e + m$

b) $5f + j$

c) $2(h + t + p)$

d) $12d$

GC-64.   Follow your teacher's directions for practicing mental math. Write down a strategy that you like best.

GC-65.   Use the Lunch/Dinner Mess Hall Menu below to help you solve these problems. Remember that we represent the cost of an item by using the first letter of its name. Copy the expressions and evaluate.

MESS HALL MENU

LUNCH/DINNER
Hamburger $1.95
Cheese Burger $2.25
Veggie Burger $2.50
Fries $0.95
Green salad $2.05
Pasta $2.75
Taco $3.50

BEVERAGES
Small $1.05
Medium $1.65
Large $2.00
Extra Large $2.35

a)   Rasheed ordered a hamburger, fries, and a beverage, and he paid $5.25. Write an equation to represent this situation. Replace the variables for the hamburger and fries with their prices and determine the size of the beverage he ordered. Use b to represent the cost of a beverage.

>>Problem continues on the next page.>>

b) Three of his friends asked him to order each of them a cheeseburger, fries, and the largest possible beverage they could get while keeping the price under $5 apiece. Write an expression representing the new order. Use b as a variable to represent the cost of the beverage. Write this expression in two ways.

c) Find the value of b in the expression you wrote in part (b).

d) What size beverage did he order for each friend?

GC-66. Yolanda was playing a new Target Game called Integer Target Game. The integers she used were 9, -3, 8, -1, and 5. Her target was 58. How close can you come to Yolanda's target?

GC-67. Use a resource page or copy and fill in the table below using the Distributive Property.

Factored Form	Distributed	Simplified
4(x + 7)	4(x) + 4(7)	4x + 28
9(x − 1)		
2(x + 9)		
6(x + y)		6x + 6y
3(2x − 5)		
	4(y) − 4(3)	4y − 12
10(x + y)		

GC-68. The camp nurse reported 38 cases of poison oak during the first two days at camp. On the second day there were 16 more cases than the first. How many cases were there the first day? How many cases were there the second day? Use a Guess and Check table to solve this problem.

GC-69. Paul, Emilio, and Riki are three staff members at camp. Paul is three years older than Riki. Emilio is twice as old as Riki. The sum of Riki's age and Emilio's age is 81. How old is each person? Use a Guess and Check table to solve this problem. Remember to write your answer as a complete sentence.

GC-70. Today the water level in the water tank is 9 feet high. **Three weeks ago** the water level was 15 feet.

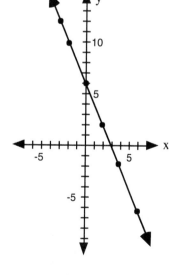

a) What is the rate the water level drops each week? Assume the rate is constant.

b) Copy the data table below and fill in the water levels for each week.

c) Graph this situation.

Time (x) (in weeks)	-3	-2	-1	0	1	2	3	4	x
Water Level (y) (in feet)	15			9					y = -2x + 9

d) Use the table or the graph to estimate during which week the water level will reach zero.

e) Use your table and graph to estimate during which week the water level was approximately 20 feet. Why is the answer negative?

GC-71. Use the graph shown below right to enter the ordered pairs in the table below.

x							x
y							

a) Write the rule in words.

b) Write the coordinates of the y-intercept. Remember that the y-intercept is where the line crosses the y-axis.

c) Write the coordinates of the x-intercept. Remember that the x-intercept is where the line crosses the x-axis.

d) Describe the direction of the line. What part of the equation tells you the direction of the line?

GC-72. Find the total area of the rectangle at right in as many different ways as you can. Explain your methods. Are there more than two ways to solve this problem?

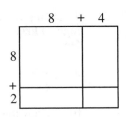

GC-73. Merci has eight money envelopes, each labeled on the outside with the letter m. All the envelopes contain the same amount of money, but Merci does not know how much. She also has six more dollars in her purse.

a) Write an expression to represent how much money Merci has.

b) When Merci opens one of the envelopes, she finds $56 inside. How much money does Merci have altogether?

c) Write an equation to represent this situation.

GC-74. Use the order of operations and a table like the one at right to calculate the y-values. Follow the example as a model. Show all of your work.

x	$y = 5 - 2x$	y
-3	$y = 5 - 2(-3)$ $y = ⑤ - ②(-3)$ $y = ⑤ - (-6)$ $y = 11$	11
2		
-1		
0		

GC-75. Complete the following Diamond Problems.

 Product

 Sum

a)

b)

c)

d)

e)

GC-76. Which choice expresses 7% as a decimal?

(A) 0.07   (B) 0.7   (C) 7.0   (D) 700   (E)   none of these

GC-77. Of the following numbers, which one best <u>approximates</u> 1084 – 108.4?

(A) 10   (B) 100   (C) 1,000   (D) 10,000   (E) none of these

GC-78.   Simplify each expression.

a) $(4x^2 + 2x + 6) + (x^2 + x + 10)$ b) $(3x + 4) + (x^2 + 6x + 2)$

c) $(6x^2 - 4x + 1) + (3x^2 + x - 7)$ d) $(2x^2 + 6) + (3x^2 - 6x)$

GC-79.   Chad has six money envelopes with an x written on the outside of each one. He knows there is the same amount of money in each envelope, but he does not know how much. He also has five more dollars in his pocket.

a)   Write an expression to represent how much money Chad has.

b)   When Chad opens one of the envelopes, he finds $16 inside. Since each envelope contains the same amount of money, how much does he have altogether?

GC-80.   The number of girls at camp was six more than twice the number of boys, and altogether there were 156 campers.

a)   Use a Guess and Check table to find the number of boys and the number of girls at camp. Write your answer in a complete sentence.

b)   Use your Guess and Check table and a variable to write an equation.

GC-81.   Johanna is planting tomatoes in the camp garden this year. At the nursery, tomato plants come in packs of six. She needs 80 plants in the garden and already has 26. How many packs of plants will she need?

   a)   Use a Guess and Check table to solve this problem. Remember to write your answer as a complete sentence.

   b)   Use your Guess and Check table to write an equation for the problem.

GC-82.   Guess Jeremiah's favorite number. He tells the campers, "If you multiply my number by 28 and then subtract 8, you end up with 160."

   a)   Use a Guess and Check table to solve for his number. Be sure to write your answer as a sentence.

   b)   Use your Guess and Check table to write an equation that represents this situation.

GC-83.

┌───┐

WRITING EQUATIONS FROM A GUESS AND CHECK TABLE

•   Make a Guess and Check table and solve the problem. Use at least four guesses, show all of your work, and write your answer in a complete sentence.

•   Put an x in your Guess column and use x to write expressions in each of the other columns.

•   Write your equation outside the Guess and Check table. You may need to use the Distributive Property and/or combine like terms.

Example: Noel and his sister, Brigitte, are both at camp. Noel is 3 years older than Brigitte, and the sum of their ages is 21. How old is Noel and how old is Brigitte? Use a Guess and Check table to solve for their ages. Write an equation.

Guess Brigitte's Age	Noel's Age	Sum of Noel and Brigitte's Ages	Check 21
10	$(10) + 3 = 13$	$(10) + (13) = 23$	too high
5	$(5) + 3 = 8$	$(5) + (8) = 13$	too low
8	$(8) + 3 = 11$	$(8) + (11) = 19$	too low
9	$(9) + 3 = 12$	$(9) + (12) = 21$	correct
x	$x + 3$	$(x) + (x + 3) = 21$	

$$(x) + (x + 3) = 2x + 3 = 21$$

Noel is 12 years old and Brigitte is nine years old.

└───┘

Make these notes in your Tool Kit to the right of the double-lined box.

List three important things for you to remember when writing equations.

GC-84. Compute.

a) -8 + 2

b) 7 - 11

c) -5 + (-8)

d) -3 - 9

e) 6 - (-5)

f) (6) · (-2)

g) -7 - 4

h) -8 + 8

i) -24 ÷ -8

j) -16 ÷ 4

GC-85. Draw a spinner that would show the results of tossing one die (singular for "dice").

a) How many sections should you have on the spinner?

b) What is the probability of landing on any one of the sections?

c) Write an equation to show that the sum of all the probabilities is equal to 1.

d) What is the probability of spinning a 4? Write your answer as a fraction and a percent.

e) What is the probability of spinning either a 2 or a 3? Write your answer as a fraction and a percent.

f) If you spin the spinner and roll a real die, what is the probability of getting a 5 and a 4? Write your answer as a fraction and a percent

GC-86. Use the order of operations and a table like the one at right to calculate the y-values. Use the example given as a model. Show all of your work.

x	$y = x^2 + 1$	y
-3		
-2	$y = (-2)^2 + 1$ $y = (-2)^2 + 1$ $y = 4 + 1$ $y = 5$	5
-1		
0		
1		

GC-87. Use a resource page or copy and complete the table using the Distributive Property. Use algebra tiles if you need them.

Factored Form	Distributed	Simplified
6(4 + x)	6(4) + 6(x)	24 + 6x
3x(x + 3)	3x(x) + 3x(3)	
6(2x + 3)		
5(2x + 4)		
	4(x) + 4(2)	
x(x + 8)		
3(2x + 2)		

GC-88. Examine the rectangle shown at right.

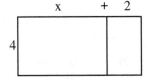

a) Express the total area of the rectangle in two different ways. Explain your methods.

b) Assume the area is 28 square units and write an equation.

c) What is the value of x?

GC-89. Margaurite wants to convince her parents to raise her monthly allowance. She decided to take a quick poll of her five best friends to see what they thought. Here are the results:

Friend	Suggested Allowance
Kari	no allowance
Wanda	$25.00
Gary	$100.00
Donna	$20.00
Jorge	$20.00

a) Calculate the mean, median, and mode for her friends' suggested allowances.

b) Calculate the range of her friends' suggested allowances.

c) Her current allowance is $30.00. Which measure of central tendency supports her argument? Why?

GC-90. Find areas A and B in the figure at right when the rectangle is cut by the lines shown. (All dimensions are in centimeters.)

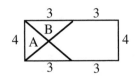

GC-91. These problems were done in class as a mental math exercise. If you were not in class, copy each problem. Close your book, and then solve.

a) $6 \cdot 55$

b) $7 \cdot 51$

c) $3 \cdot 58$

d) $31 \cdot 8$

e) $7 \cdot 39$

f) $4 \cdot 26$

GC-92.

Mr. Martin, the head groundskeeper at camp, mows the camp lawn. The lawn is rectangular, and the length is 5 feet more than twice the width. The perimeter of the lawn is 250 feet. What are the dimensions of the lawn?

a) Draw and label a diagram of the lawn.

b) Use a Guess and Check table to help you find the dimensions of the lawn.

c) Next, replace your guesses with x and write an equation to represent the problem. Show all steps as you combine like terms to simplify the equation.

d) What are the dimensions of the lawn? Write your answer in a complete sentence.

e) Use the dimensions from part (d) to find the area of the lawn. Write your answer in a complete sentence.

GC-93. Tito and Rudy were playing the "guess my number" game. Tito says, "I'm thinking of a number. If you add my number to 11 and then multiply the sum by 2, you get 47." He added, "My number is not a whole number. What is my number?"

a) Use a Guess and Check table to help Rudy find Tito's number.

b) Write an equation to represent the problem.

c) What is Tito's number? Write your answer in a complete sentence.

GC-94.   Notice that we can find the perimeter of the figure below by counting the number of
          lengths between the dots around the outside and that we can find the area by counting all
          the squares inside.

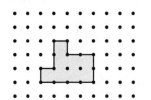

          The perimeter is 14 units.
          The area is eight square units.

          A local rancher supplies some of the food for the camp. Below are models of his land and
          the crops he grows. Find the perimeter and area for each of the figures below. Include
          "units" for perimeter and "square units" for area.

a)   Corn Field   b)   Tomato Field

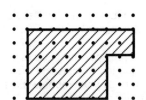   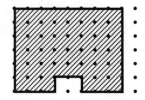

GC-95.   There are two or more ways to find the areas of the figures below. Find the area of each
          figure using at least two models. Show all subproblems.

a)   2 + 6

        4
        +
        1

b)   3 + 3 + 3

        6
        +
        3

GC-96.   Use the resource page or copy and complete the table below. Use the Distributive
          Property to complete the blank spaces. The first problem is done for you.

Factored Form	Distributed	Simplified
$7(n + 3)$	$7(n) + 7(3)$	$7n + 21$
$2(2p + 3)$	$2(2p) + 2(3)$	
$4(g - 5)$		$4g - 20$
$-2(x + 4)$		$-2x - 8$
$x(4 + 5)$		$9x$
$5x(x + 2)$		$5x^2 + 10x$

GC-97. Copy this table and use the order of operations to complete it. Use the example given as a model. Show all of your work for each y-value.

x	$y = x^2 + 2x$	y
-4		8
-3		
-2	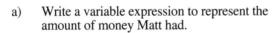 $y = (-2)^2 + 2(-2)$ $y = (-2)^2 + 2(-2)$ $y = 4 + (-4)$ $y = 0$	0
-1		-1
0		0
1		
2		8
3		

GC-98. Use your ordered pairs from the table in the previous problem to graph the equation $y = x^2 + 2x$.

a) What are the x-intercepts?   b) What is the y-intercept?

GC-99. Matt had nine money envelopes with the letter q written on the outside of each one. Each envelope contained the same amount of money. In addition to the money in the envelopes, he had 17 dollars.

a) Write a variable expression to represent the amount of money Matt had.

b) One of Matt's friends told him he knew Matt had a total of $179. Write an equation to represent the total amount of money Matt had.

c) How much money was in each of the envelopes? Write your answer in a complete sentence.

GC-100. The area of a square is 81 square inches. What is its perimeter?

(A) 36 inches   (B) 9 inches   (C) 20.5 inches   (D) 18 inches   (E) none of these

GC-101. On Monday, Jake read x pages of his book. On Tuesday, he read y pages of the book. On Wednesday, he read z pages of the book. How many pages did Jake read altogether?

(A) xyz   (B) x + y + z   (C) 3xyz   (D) 3x + y + z   (E) none of these

GC-102. Tyler was using number tiles to help him find the solution to a Target Game. The number tiles he was using were 2, 6, and 8. His target number was 7. He was so excited when he found the solution that he knocked his desk over and spilled the tiles everywhere. "I know I had the solution and I remember what it looked like, but I don't remember where each number went. I'll draw the shape of my expression to help me remember." Where had Tyler put the numbers to hit his target number of 7?

$$\frac{\square + \square}{\square} = 7$$

GC-103. The **factors** of 12 are 1, 2, 3, 4, 6, and 12. The factors of 20 are 1, 2, 4, 5, 10, and 20.

a) Write down what you think a factor is.

b) List the factors of the number 30.

GC-104. List the factors of:

a) 24   b) 15   c) 36   d) 13

GC-105. Teresa has 36 square tiles on her desk that she is arranging into rectangles. She must use all 36 tiles for each rectangle she makes.

a) Draw all the possible rectangles that Teresa could make.

b) List the dimensions (factor pairs) of each rectangle you found.

GC-106.

DISTRIBUTIVE PROPERTY

The **DISTRIBUTIVE PROPERTY** shows how to express sums and products in two ways: $a(b + c) = ab + ac$. This can also be written $(b + c)\, a = ab + ac$.

Factored form	Distributed form	Simplified form
a(b + c)	**a(b) + a(c)**	**ab + ac**

To simplify: Multiply each term on the inside of the parentheses by the term on the outside. Combine terms if possible.

To factor: Find a common factor that divides each term evenly. Then write this factor outside the parentheses and leave the remaining factors of each term written as a sum.

Note: An **integer factor** is an integer that divides another integer evenly.

Examples: Simplify: $5(x + 12)$ Factor: $4x + 6$ Factor: $6x + 3$

$$5(x + 12)$$
$$⑤(x) + ⑤(12)$$
$$5x + 60$$

$$4x + 6$$
$$2(2x) + 2(3)$$
$$②(2x) + ②(3)$$
$$2(2x + 3)$$

$$6x + 3$$
$$3(2x) + 3(1)$$
$$③(2x) + ③(1)$$
$$3(2x + 1)$$

Make these notes in your Tool Kit to the right of the double-lined box.

a)   List two examples of pairs of numbers that share a common factor.

b)   List a variable pair with a common factor. Check your examples with your partner or a teammate to verify that they are correct.

c)   Why do you think $ab + ac$ is called the "simplified form"?

GC-107.   Simplify the following problems.

a) $(2x + 4)6$ b) $7(x - 3)$

c) $-8(9x - 7)$ d) $-4(13 - x)$

GC-108.   Factor the following expressions.

a) $2x + 20$ b) $5x + 35$

c) $3x - 15$ d) $5x - 60$

GC-109.   You have been using the Distributive Property to simplify expressions throughout this chapter. Now you will reverse the order to put the expressions into **factored form**. The factors show what is being multiplied before distribution takes place. Use the Distributive Property to complete the table below. Use the resource page or your paper.

Factored Form	Distributed	Simplified
3(x + 1)	3(x) + 3(1)	3x + 3
	2(x) + 2(3)	2x + 6
		5x + 15
		6x + 12
		9c + 27
		8b + 16
		2x – 6
		-3x + 9

GC-110.   Melvin had 22 money envelopes with the letter x written on the outside of each one. Each contained the same amount of money. He also had an extra $8.00 hidden in the fold of his wallet.

   a)   Write an expression to represent the amount of money Melvin had.

   b)   When Melvin opened one of the envelopes, there was a bill for $12. Write a number that expresses the amount he owed.

   c)   Substitute the value into the expression you wrote in part (a) to determine how much money he had.

GC-111.   Katrina was using some algebra tiles. She had three large squares, five rectangles, and eight small squares on her desk. Xyrus stopped by and dropped a small bag of tiles on her desk that contained six large squares, three rectangles, and seven small squares. Write an algebraic equation to show the tiles with which Katrina started, the tiles that Xyrus gave her, and the total number of tiles she now has on her desk. To see what to write, refer to problem GC-44.

GC-112.   Copy this table and use the order of operations to complete it. Using the example given as a model, show all of your work for each y-value.

x	$y = x^2 + 2x + 1$	y
-2	$y = (-2)^2 + 2(-2) + 1$ $y = (-2)^2 + 2(-2) + 1$ $y = 4 + (-4) + 1$ $y = 1$	1
-1		
0		
1		

GC-113. Use the ordered pairs from your table in the previous problem and at least four additional pairs.

a) Graph the rule $y = x^2 + 2x + 1$. b) Describe the shape of the graph.

GC-114. The camp council is designing a patio floor for an outdoor cafeteria. They have chosen the pattern shown at right.

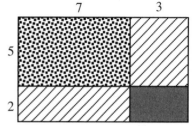

a) What is the area of the section with the 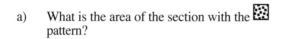 pattern?

b) What are the factors (dimensions) of the  section?

c) What is the area of the section with the ■ pattern?

d) What are the factors (dimensions) of the ■ section?

e) Notice that there are two sections of the patio in the ◩ pattern. What is the combined area of those sections?

GC-115. Write this expression as simply as you can: $\dfrac{3! + 4!}{6!}$

(5! means $1 \cdot 2 \cdot 3 \cdot 4 \cdot 5$.)

GC-116. Compute.

a) $(-1) \cdot 3$ b) $(-1) \cdot (-4)$

c) $(-1) \cdot 23$ d) $(-1) \cdot x$

e) $-1(5x + 3)$ f) $-1(x + 6)$

GC-117. Describe the effect on an integer or variable when it is multiplied by a negative one.

GC-118. Compute the product in column A and compare it with the result in column B. Follow the examples in parts (a) and (b) as you complete parts (c) through (f).

Column A (Distribute and multiply by -1.)	Column B (Take the opposite of each term inside the parentheses.)

a) $-1(x + 8) = (-1)x + (-1)(8)$
      $= -x + (-8)$
      $= -x - 8$
	$-(x + 8) = -x + (-8) = -x - 8$

b) $-1(x - 7) = (-1)(x) - (-1)(7)$
      $= -x - (-7)$
      $= -x + 7$
	$-(x - 7) = -x - (-7) = -x + 7$

c) $(-1)(2x - 11)$	$-(2x - 11) = \underline{\hspace{1.5cm}} = \underline{\hspace{1cm}}$
d) $(-1)(-3x + 10)$	$-(-3x + 10) = \underline{\hspace{1.5cm}} = \underline{\hspace{1cm}}$
e) $(-1)(2x^2 - 24x + 4)$	$-(2x^2 - 24x + 4) = \underline{\hspace{1.5cm}} = \underline{\hspace{1cm}}$
f) $(-1)(6 - 5x)$	$-(6 - 5x) = \underline{\hspace{1.5cm}} = \underline{\hspace{1cm}}$

g) Write an equation to show the relationship between $-(a + b)$ and $-a - b$.

h) Write an equation to show the relationship between $(-1)(a - b)$ and $-a + b$.

GC-119.

Chapter Summary   When you finish a chapter in a math course, you need to reflect on how well you have learned the material. It is time to think about all that you have studied and learned in this chapter.

With your partner or team, find the problem assigned by your teacher. After you have verified that you have a correct solution from your (or a teammate's) work, use the model below to create a summary poster of the mathematical idea you were assigned.

Write out the mathematical idea for your problem number and record the problem number.

Show all of the mathematical work and diagrams you used to solve the problem.

Topic: Problem #	
Solution	Explanation

Describe each step of your solution in words.

GC-120.   Joann, the camp supply manager, is ordering replacement backpacks. Based on her inventory, Joann will order twelve more green packs than blue packs, four times as many black packs as blue packs, and two times as many orange packs as black packs and blue packs together. She will order a total of 204 backpacks.

a)   Use a Guess and Check table to help you find the number of each color backpack Joann needs to order.

b)   Use your Guess and Check table to help write a variable expression to represent the number of backpacks of each color.

c)   Write an equation to represent this problem. Show all steps as you combine like terms to simplify the equation.

d)   How many backpacks of each color should Joann order? Write your answer in a complete sentence.

e)   Joann can buy the backpacks for $6.50 through a wholesale catalog company. She has a budget of $1,425. Will she be able to buy the backpacks needed? Write your answer in a complete sentence.

f)   If the backpacks are mixed together in one crate, what is the probability that Joann would unpack a black one first?

GC-121.

DISTRIBUTING A NEGATIVE ONE

When a negative one (-1) is distributed to the terms inside a pair of parentheses, the sign of <u>each</u> term is changed. For example,

$$-(3x^2 + 2x - 5) \Rightarrow (-1)(3x^2 + 2x - 5) \Rightarrow (-1)(3x^2) + (-1)(2x) - (-1)(5) \Rightarrow -3x^2 - 2x + 5$$

Answer these questions in your Tool Kit to the right of the double-lined box.

a)   How does distributing a negative one relate to subtraction?

b)   What happens to a term or number when it is multiplied by negative one?

GC-122.   Compute.

a) $-(34)$

b) $-(5x - 12)$

c) $-(2x^2 - 5x + 1)$

GC-123.   Solve the following exercises for x:

a) |-15| = x   b) |x| = 15

c) |x| = -4   d) |x| = x

e)   Use a number line to show the solutions to |x| = 7.

GC-124.   Stefano and Leo want to use different shades of blue tiles to build a rectangular mosaic
with an area of 375 square feet. Stefano suggested that the length of one side should be
10 feet longer than the length of the other side. Find the dimensions (length and width) of
their mosaic.

a)   Draw and label a diagram.

b)   Make a Guess and Check table to solve the problem.

c)   Use your Guess and Check table to write an equation.

GC-125.   Use the Distributive Property to simplify the following problems. Combine like terms
where possible.

a)   (3x + 7 + 9)2   b)   7.5(3) + 7.5(6)

c)   6(x) + 6(20)   d)   2(6) + 2(-4)

e)   4(3x – 11 + 9)   f)   1.5(3) + 1.5(6)

GC-126.   Hannah, the camp cook, uses a standard recipe for trail mix that uses raisins, chocolate
pieces, and peanuts. The quantity of chocolate pieces is 4 ounces more than 3 times the
number of ounces of raisins. The quantity of peanuts is 5 ounces less than twice the
number of ounces of raisins. Use a Guess and Check table to find the quantity of each
ingredient Hannah uses in her standard recipe.

a)   What variable would you use to represent the
quantity of raisins?

b)   Use that variable to write an algebraic
expression that represents the quantity of
chocolate pieces.

c)   Use that same variable to write an algebraic
expression that represents the quantity of
peanuts.

d)   Use the algebraic expressions you wrote in
parts (a), (b), and (c) above to write a single
expression for all the ingredients.

>>Problem continues on the next page.>>

CHAPTER 4

e)   Simplify your expression.

f)   Hannah's standard recipe makes 95 ounces of trail mix. Use your simplified expression in part (e) to write an equation that represents her recipe.

g)   Use your equation in part (f) to find the quantity (in ounces) of raisins in Hannah's recipe. Any strategy is acceptable. Show your work. h)   Now find the quantity (in ounces) of chocolate pieces and peanuts.

GC-127.   The camp director asked Hannah to put more peanuts into her trail mix.

a)   Use your variable for raisins to write a new expression for peanuts if the number of ounces of peanuts is now going to be 7 ounces more than twice the number of ounces of raisins.

b)   Find the total amount of each ingredient needed now.

GC-128.   This year 78 of the campers have decided to construct a new border around the swimming pool. Each camper will construct one block of tile pieces like the pattern shown at right. How many total tiles are needed?

This is how Chad set up the problem:

78 campers(4 waffle tiles) + 78(3 dotted tiles) + 78(2 wavy tiles) = 78(4) + 78(3) + 78(2)

This is how Scooter set up the problem:

78 campers(4 waffle tiles + 3 dotted tiles + 2 wavy tiles) = 78(4 + 3 + 2)

a)   What will Chad's answer be?

b)   What will Scooter's answer be?

c)   Who had the correct set-up? How do you know?

d)   If each tile costs $2, compute the total cost of purchasing tiles to complete the project.

GC-129.   Lauren had 12 money envelopes with the letter b written on the outside of each. Each envelope contained the same amount. She also had three dollars more in her purse. Lauren had a total of $21.

a)   Make a Guess and Check table to help you find the amount of money in each envelope.

b)   Write your answer in a complete sentence.

c)   Write an equation to represent this problem.

GC-130. Show two methods for finding the area of the rectangles below. Be sure to write and label your subproblems.

a)

5 + 7

2

b)

10 + 15

6

GC-131. Belinda has four money envelopes with the letter m written on the outside of each one. Each envelope contains the same amount of money. She also has $30 in her pocket.

a) Write an expression to represent how much money Belinda has.

b) After Belinda opens all the envelopes, she finds she has only $10 left. Assuming there was the same amount in each envelope, what amount was in each envelope?

GC-132. Allesandro and Irene were given the task of designing one of the small rectangular mosaics for the outside wall of the camp post office. They are told that the area of the planned mosaic will be 480 square inches. The short side is four inches shorter than the long side. Help Allesandro and Irene figure out the dimensions of the mosaic they will build.

a) List the pairs of integer factors of 480.

b) Use your results from part (a) and a Guess and Check table (if needed) to find the dimensions of the mosaic.

c) Use x to write an equation for this problem.

GC-133. Use the Distributive Property to simplify or factor.

a) 43(3 + 2x)

b) 8(15 – 6x)

c) 5x + 25

d) (7x – 5)4

e) 11(9 + 8x)

f) 4x – 28

GC-134. Harry wants to lead a group around the lake. He is not sure if it will be a day hike or an overnight trip. Fred tells him that if you take the distance around the lake, add 2, and multiply the answer by 15, the total number of miles will be equal to the number of campers in this session. Harry knows that there are 480 campers, so now he can figure out the distance around the lake.

a) Use a Guess and Check table to figure out the distance around the lake. Do not forget to write your answer in a sentence.

b) Use your Guess and Check table to write an equation.

c) Should the hike be a day hike or an overnight hike? Write your answer in a complete sentence.

GC-135. **What We Have Done in This Chapter**

Below is a list of the Tool Kit entries from this chapter.

- GC-6   Order of Operations
- GC-18   Distributive Property with Integers
- GC-43   How to Combine Like Terms
- GC-57   Distributive Property with Algebra Tiles
- GC-83   Writing Equations from a Guess and Check Table
- GC-106   Distributive Property
- GC-121   Distributing a Negative One

Review all the entries and read the notes you made in your Tool Kit. Make a list of any questions, terms, or notes you do not understand. Ask your partner or study team members for help. If anything is still unclear, ask your teacher.

Chapter 5

Chapter 5
The Math Club: SOLVING EQUATIONS

In this chapter you will learn how to solve equations. You will have the opportunity to see the connection between algebraic and graphic solutions. You will finish the first half of the course by reviewing the five chapters you have studied thus far.

In this chapter you will have the opportunity to:

- write and solve multiple types of equations.
- simplify expressions using the Distributive Property.
- investigate inverse operations.
- review the topics studied in the first half of the course.

Read the problem below, but **do not try to solve it now**. What you learn over the next few days will enable you to solve it.

MC-0.   The Mental Math Club is a very active club! Every year the members design a new t-shirt to wear on field trips and at math competitions. There are three companies in town that make t-shirts: *Tanks A Lot*, *Screeners*, and *Teesers*. What criteria can Diedre, the club president, use to decide from which company to order the shirts?

Number Sense		
Algebra and Functions		
Mathematical Reasoning		
Measurement and Geometry		
Statistics, Data Analysis, & Probability		

MC-1.   **Mental Math** What value of the variable makes each equation true? Solve each equation in your head.

a) $4x = 12$ b) $x + 13 = 20$

c) $5x = 35$ d) $2x = -17$

e) $3x + 7 = 15$ f) $2x + 3 = x - 8$

g)   Which equations were most difficult to solve mentally? Explain.

MC-2.   The members of the Mental Math Club want to raise money so they can take a trip. They decide to sell t-shirts with a logo. Diedre, the president of the club, calls two t-shirt vendors to find out how much it will cost to make the shirts. *Screeners* charges a setup fee of $50 to prepare the silk-screen for the logo. In addition, *Screeners* charges $7 for each shirt imprinted with the logo. The second vendor Diedre called, *Teesers*, charges $78 for the setup fee and $5 for each t-shirt.

a)   If Diedre wants to order 10 shirts to sell at school, should she buy the shirts from *Screeners* or *Teesers*? Give reasons for your answer.

b)   If Diedre wants to order 20 shirts to sell at school, should she buy the shirts from *Screeners* or *Teesers*? Give reasons for your answer.

c)   Determine the number of t-shirts that make the total cost from each vendor equal. You can use a Guess and Check table like the one below.

Number of T-Shirts	Cost at Screeners	Cost at Teesers	Same?

d)   Tell Diedre which company she should choose. Explain your reasoning so she can make the best choice.

MC-3.   Sometimes you can make a math problem easier by replacing part of it with an **equivalent** quantity. For example, you could describe the distance from San Francisco to Los Angeles as 379 miles or as 2,001,120 feet. Two expressions are equivalent if they represent the same number. Twelve inches is equivalent to 1 foot, 4 quarts is equivalent to 1 gallon, and 379 miles is equivalent to 2,001,120 feet.

a)   Thirty-two ounces is equivalent to how many pounds?

b)   One century is equivalent to how many years?

c)   Ten weeks is equivalent to how many days?

d)   Marty says her baby weighs 8 pounds. The scale shows 128 ounces. Is 8 pounds equivalent to 128 ounces? Show your work.

MC-4. For parts (a) and (b) below write an equation that shows the indicated equivalencies.

    a) How many minutes is two hours?

    b) How many seconds is two hours?

    c) Explain why 120 minutes = 7200 seconds.

MC-5. Bradley and Mindy are siblings who enjoy doing many things together. Write a numerical equation that describes each of the following situations.

    a) Bradley challenged Mindy to a basketball game. Mindy made four three-point shots. Bradley made five two-point shots and two free throws (1 point each). At that point, the score was tied. Write an equation showing that the two scores are equivalent.

    b) They continued playing for ten minutes and both scored four more two-point shots. Write an equation that shows the two new scores are equivalent. Who won?

    c) Bradley and Mindy went to the arcade. Mindy won twelve tickets on one game and eight on another. Bradley won five tickets on one game, five tickets on another game, and ten tickets on a third game. Are their totals equivalent? Write an equation to justify your answer.

    d) In the next ten minutes Bradley and Mindy each double their total tickets. Do they then have an equivalent number of tickets? Explain your answer.

    e) Bradley brought a twenty-dollar bill. Bradley spent one-fourth of his money. Mindy brought seventeen dollars but lost two dollars. Do they have equivalent amounts of money? Explain your answer.

       CHAPTER 5

MC-6. Sam plays golf at least five times a week. He records his score for each round of golf. Here are the scores for his last ten rounds:

Round	1	2	3	4	5	6	7	8	9	10
Score	73	74	67	67	74	74	72	75	66	68

a) Determine the mean, median, and mode for Sam's scores.

b) Determine the range of Sam's scores.

c) Par for the course is 72. How far from par are the mean, median, and mode?

d) Does Sam usually score above or below par? Explain.

MC-7. Bill is expecting 60 people for a barbecue. He purchased 60 burgers and 60 buns. The number of burgers is equivalent to the number of buns. Two days before the event Bill learns that 45% more people are expected to come. How many more buns and burgers does Bill need to buy?

MC-8.

EQUATIONS

A mathematical sentence with an equal sign is called an **EQUATION**. It is a relationship showing that two expressions have the same value.

Statements like 16 ounces = 1 pound, $n = 4$, $3(x - 5) = 16$, and $3(2) + 7 = 16 - 3$ are examples of equations.

Make these notes in your Tool Kit to the right of the double-lined box.

Write four equations that illustrate the equivalence of two quantities.

MC-9.   Complete the tables below and graph each of the equations. Review your Tool Kit to be
         sure you make a complete graph.

a) $y = 2x + 5$

x	0	1	2	3	-1	-2	-3
y	5	7					

b) $y = x - 2$

x	0		4	-1		2	-3	
y		-1.5			- 4			-2.5

MC-10.   Solve each equation for x. Show or explain your thinking. The ability to explain your
         methods will help you as you develop new methods for solving equations.

a) $x + 23 = 50$ b) $2x = 92$

c) $3x + 25 = 100$ d) $72 = 6x$

MC-11.   Now that we have started a new chapter, it is time for you to
         organize your binder.

a)   Put the work from the last chapter in order and keep it in a
      separate folder.

b)   When this is completed, write, "I have organized my binder."

MC-12.   Follow your teacher's directions for practicing mental math. Explain which multiplication
         strategy you like best and why you like the strategy.

MC-13.   Work backward to find the missing number.

a)   Alcania is thinking of a number. If you double it and take away four, the result
      is 28. What is Alcania's number?

b)   Omar is thinking of a number. Take half of the number, then add 12. The result is
      37. Find Omar's number.

MC-14. **Cover-Up Method** The Mental Math Club was planning a carnival to raise money. Jacob decided to run the Guess My Number booth. His good friend Carlin wanted to check out the booth before the carnival opened for business. "Try out a problem on me," said Carlin.

Jacob gave Carlin this problem: "17 more than a number is 52. Guess the number and win a prize." Carlin pictured it like this: $x + 17 = 52$

Carlin covered up the x and asked himself, "What number plus 17 equals 52? Aha," he said, "x equals 35."

$$(?) + 17 = 52$$
$$x = 35$$

He put 35 back into the equation and discovered he was right, because $35 + 17 = 52$. $(35) + 17 = 52$

"That was too easy!" exclaimed Carlin. "We won't make any money if the problems are this easy. You need to make them harder. Show me the other problems you had in mind."

Help Carlin check to see if these problems are also too easy. Use Carlin's cover-up method to solve each problem. Be sure to put your answers back into the original equations to check your work.

a) $x + 7 = 13$

b) $x - 6 = 18$

c) $y + 22 = 39$

d) $s + 25 = 155$

e) $r - 12 = 38$

f) $m - 15 = -60$

g) $x - 36 = -30$

h) $x + 40 = -10$

i) $z + \frac{5}{7} = 3$

MC-15. Jacob pulled out his second set of problems. "These are harder. Try this one."

"Four more than three times the number is 40."

Carlin pictured the problem like this: $3x + 4 = 40$

He had to break this problem down into more than one step.

First he covered up the term with the unknown. He asked $(?) + 4 = 40$
himself what number plus 4 equals 40. "Oh," he said, "That's $(36) + 4 = 40$
easy. Thirty-six plus four equals 40, so $3x$ must equal 36." $3x = 36$

However, Carlin was not finished. He still had to find out what
number the unknown x represented. So he covered up the x in $3 \cdot (?) = 36$
$3x$, asking himself, "Three multiplied by what number equals $3 \cdot (12) = 36$
36?" This was not difficult. He knew that 3 times 12 is 36, so x $x = 12$
must equal 12.

He checked his answer by substituting 12 for x. Since this was $3(12) + 4 = 40$
correct, he knew he had found the correct value for x. $36 + 4 = 40$

"These are better," claimed Carlin. "Let me see the rest of them." Use Carlin's cover-up method to check the rest of Jacob's problems. Write each step.

a) $6x - 7 = 35$ b) $3x + 8 = 23$ c) $\frac{c}{2} + 20 = 38$

d) $8x + 14 = -10$ e) $102m + 102 = 306$ f) $\frac{x}{20} + 17 = 257$

g) $3x - 2 = 13$ h) $5x + 4 = -26$ i) $2x + \frac{1}{5} = 1$

MC-16.   Ingrid bought three dozen donuts for the Mental
         Math Club meeting. Twenty-four people showed up
         for the meeting. How many donuts did each person
         get? Assume each person gets the same amount.

         a)   Which equation best represents this problem?

              (1) $x = 36 + 24$ (2) $36x = 24$ (3) $24x = 36$

         b)   Solve the equation you chose in part (a) to find
              the answer.

         c)   Is your answer for part (b) reasonable?
              Explain.

MC-17. Compute.

a) $-24 \div 6$

b) $3 + (-5)$

c) $-4 - (-6)$

d) $13 - 6$

e) $-14 \div (-7)$

f) $7 - (-8)$

g) $5 + (-2)$

h) $-8 - (-4)$

i) $(-9)(-2)$

j) $(-6)(6)$

MC-18. The number $1\frac{2}{3}$ is a mixed number that means "one whole and two-thirds of another whole." We can draw a picture to illustrate $1\frac{2}{3}$, as shown at right.

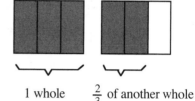

1 whole $\frac{2}{3}$ of another whole

a) How many one-thirds are in $1\frac{2}{3}$?

b) Sketch a picture to represent $1\frac{3}{4}$.

c) How many one-fourths are in $1\frac{3}{4}$?

d) Sketch a picture to illustrate $3\frac{4}{5}$.

e) How many one-fifths are in $3\frac{4}{5}$?

MC-19. Manuela is helping to prepare for the "Come as your favorite mathematician" party by filling piñatas with candy. In each piñata she includes 50 hard candies, 20 suckers, 35 jawbreakers, 60 mini candy bars, 25 sour balls, and 75 pieces of bubble gum. If Manuela is going to fill four piñatas, how many pieces of candy does she need? Write the number of candies she needs in two different ways using the Distributive Property.

MC-20. Antonio and Anna are working on a problem when they decide that they need to combine their algebra tiles in order to work it out. Antonio puts four rectangles and nine small squares on the desk. Anna puts two rectangles and three small squares on the desk. Draw a diagram and write an algebraic equation that represents what each team member put on the desk as well as the combined total.

MC-21. What is the product of $\frac{6}{7} \cdot 42$?

(A) 36   (B) 49   (C) 252   (D) 294   (E) none of these

MC-22. Which of the following integers is closest to $\frac{31}{7}$?

(A) 3   (B) 4   (C) 5   (D) 6

MC-23. These questions relate to dividing by 4. Some of them may not be possible. If they are not, explain why not in a sentence or two.

a) Find all digits that make the number 42,3__1 divisible by 4.

b) Find all digits that make the number 43,__00 divisible by 4.

c) Suppose you know that the number N is divisible by 4. (That is, there is some integer M such that $4 \cdot M = N$.) Is the number N + 400 also divisible by 4? Explain your answer using complete sentences.

d) Suppose you know that the number N is **not** divisible by 4. Can the number N + 400 be divisible by 4? Explain your answer using complete sentences.

MC-24. Follow your teacher's directions for practicing mental math. Describe the strategy you used to your partner or study team member.

MC-25. Hakim has two identical boxes of stuffed toys to use as prizes at the carnival. He has already given away 22 prizes from one box. Hakim now has 128 prizes left. How many prizes were in each box before the carnival opened? Write an equation like Carlin's from yesterday and solve it using the cover-up method.

MC-26. Carlin felt that there needed to be some problems that were even more difficult for the people who had already won at the Guess My Number booth. He wrote down the following number sentence: $3x - 15 = 30$.

He needed to change the symbols into a word clue for the booth. Carlin's translation is: "If you triple my number and subtract 15, you end up with 30. What is my number?" Change the rest of Carlin's number sentences into clues for the booth.

a) $8x + 32 = 104$ b) $\frac{x}{12} + 18 = 30$ c) $\frac{(x + 4)}{6} = 4$

d) $\frac{(x + 2)}{6} + 6 = 12$ e) $-9x - 10 = -82$

MC-27. Take Carlin's equations from the previous problem and use the cover-up method to find the missing numbers. Be sure to put the numbers back into the original equations to check that they are correct.

MC-28. Admission into the carnival is $5 for adults and $2 for children. The carnival offers a special family pack which admits 2 adults and 3 children for one price of $14.

a) If you are in a group of 12 adults and 15 children, should you buy the family pack, individual tickets, or combinations of them?

b) What should you purchase if you are in a group with 5 adults and 30 children?

MC-29. Six members of a Sumo wrestling team weighed themselves and discovered that the sum of their combined weights totaled 30 pounds less than one ton (2000 pounds). Boyd weighed 20 pounds more than twice Trede's weight. Kerber weighed 40 pounds less than Adam. Smith and Craig each weighed five pounds more than Kerber. Adam weighed 35 pounds less than twice Trede. Trede is the smallest of the six guys. Use a Guess and Check table to find out how much each player weighs.

MC-30. Janae invited five friends to her house so all six of them could make bead necklaces. She bought a bag containing 750 beads and she wants to distribute the beads evenly. How many beads does each person get? Write an equation, then solve it.

MC-31. Solve each equation for x. Check your solution.

a) $2x + 8 = 16$

b) $2 = 3x - 13$

c) $22 = 4x + 2$

d) $3x - 5 = 16$

e) $-19 = 21 + 10x$

f) $\dfrac{x - 5}{6} = 3$

MC-32.   Miranda and Tasha were responsible for ordering
         last year's Math Club t-shirts. They knew they
         had ordered 15 more red shirts than white shirts
         and twice as many blue shirts as white shirts for
         the 63 members. Unfortunately, the shirts arrived
         late and it was summer vacation. All of the shirts
         ended up in one big box because Miranda and
         Tasha were not around to sort them.

    a)   How many of each type of shirt did they
          order? (Use a Guess and Check table if
          necessary).

    b)   What percentage of the total order was red shirts?

    c)   If Miranda reaches into the box, what is the probability of pulling out a blue shirt?

    d)   If Tasha reaches into the box, what is the probability of pulling out a color other than
          white?

MC-33.   Find the missing fraction, decimal, or percent for the following problems.

    a)   b)   c)

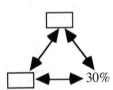 30%   0.625 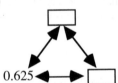 $\frac{2}{8}$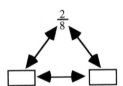

MC-34.   Add or subtract as indicated.

    a) $5\frac{3}{4} + 2\frac{3}{4}$ b) $9 - 6\frac{1}{4}$

    c) $4\frac{7}{8} + 5\frac{5}{24}$ d) $15\frac{1}{3} - 12\frac{3}{4}$

MC-35.   Simplify each of the following expressions.

    a) $(4x^2 + 2x + 1) + (x - 8)$ b) $(3x^2 - 2x + 7) - (2x^2 + 3x + 1)$

MC-36.   Use the cover-up method to solve the equations below.

    a) $2x + 5 = 25$ b) $14 = 5x - 31$ c) $4x + 22 = 6$

MC-37.   Complete these equations.

   a) $1\frac{1}{2}$ ft. = ___ inches   b) $3\frac{3}{4}$ days = ___ hours   c)   60 hours = ___ days

MC-38.   You are going to practice a system for solving equations that will be modeled by your teacher.

   a)   On the balance scale below, the circles represent cups with an unknown number of positive or negative tiles inside. The cups all have the same number of tiles in them. How many cups can we remove from both sides and still maintain balance? Use the resource page to complete the problem.

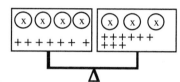

   b)   The balance scale now looks like this:

        What can we remove from (or add to) both sides to maintain the balance?

   c)   In part (b) you should have found that the scale balanced as shown at right.

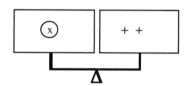

        This situation can be represented as $x = 2$. Is this the solution to the equation represented by the cups and tiles in part (a)?

   d)   Write an equation that represents the cups and tiles on the balance scale in part (a). Check to see if $x = 2$ is the solution to the equation in part (a) by replacing the x with 2 in the original equation.

MC-39.   We want to solve the following algebra problem for x: $x + 6 = 5x + 2$. Use the resource page to complete the problem.

   a)   Draw the cups and tiles on the balance scale, then write the algebraic equation on the line.

   b)   Simplify the problem on the balance scale to figure out what is in each cup. Then explain your thinking.

   c)   What is the solution to the equation?

   d)   The final step is to check your work by substituting your solution into the original equation.

MC-40.   Use the resource page to solve the equation $2x + 3 = x + 7$.

a)   Draw the picture and write the equation.

b)   Simplify the problem on the balance scale to figure out what is in each cup, then explain in words what you did.

c)   Now you have solved the equation. Check your solution by substituting the value you found into the original equation.

MC-41.   Use the resource page to solve the equation $x + 14 = 5x + 2$.

a)   Draw the picture and write the equation.

b)   Simplify the problem on the balance scale to figure out what is in each cup. Explain in words what you did.

c)   Now you have solved the equation. Check your solution by substituting the value you found into the original equation.

MC-42.   Solve the following problems. Use the resource page to show your subproblems as well as how you checked your solution.

a) $4x + 3 = 3x + 5$ b) $5x + 8 = 3x + 12$ c) $3x + 12 = 6x + 9$

MC-43.   Diedre did some trading and learned that two math club buttons plus a pencil would get her one set of markers. She also knew that one set of markers, two math club buttons, and a pencil would get her two reams of paper to make fliers announcing the t-shirt sale. She only wanted one ream of paper and had lots of markers. What did she have to trade to get one ream of paper? Use pictures or symbols to show your reasoning.

MC-44.   Solve the following equations using the cover-up method.

a) $4x + 13 = 15$ b) $5x + 8 = 40$ c) $9x - 4 = 76$

d) $3x + 11 = 13$ e) $18 + 7x = 4$ f) $20 - 6x = 2$

MC-45.   Copy each diagram and complete the scale.

a)
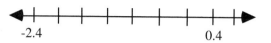
-2.4   0.4

b)
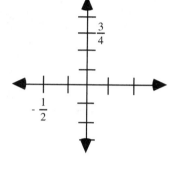

c)
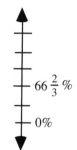

$66\frac{2}{3}$ %

0%

MC-46.   Draw and shade a picture to illustrate each number.

a) $\frac{4}{8}$ b) $\frac{3}{6}$ c) $\frac{5}{2}$

d) $1\frac{1}{5}$ e) $\frac{6}{5}$ f) $2\frac{1}{2}$

MC-47.   Set up a Guess and Check table to solve the
following problem. Write an equation. You may do
this in either order.

Matt and Paul went on a fishing trip and caught 31
fish. Matt caught one less than three times as many
fish as Paul caught. How many did each boy catch?

MC-48.   Alisa went to the store to buy ribbon and bows. There were many colors to choose from.
She decided to buy one white, three yellow, two green, and five blue bows for each box
she has to wrap. Use the Distributive Property to show two different ways to calculate the
total number of bows Alisa needs to buy if she has six boxes to wrap.

MC-49. You have eight rectangles, two large squares, and six small squares on your desk. Your partner takes away one large square, five of the rectangles, and two of the small squares. Write an equation to express what happened and how many tiles you have left.

MC-50. You are on a 650-mile trip by car. Your car used eight gallons of gas to travel the first 210 miles of the trip. If you stop at this point and fill the car's 18 gallon gas tank, will you make it the rest of the way? Show your work.

MC-51. The Poppington family is returning home after a long car trip. Chad, Emily's younger brother, is annoying the family by constantly asking, "How long 'til we get home?" Emily notices the number 135 on the mileage marker at the side of the road (mileage markers on some highways indicate distance from the beginning of a highway or from a state line). The family will be home when they reach the mileage sign with the number 375. If the car is traveling at an average rate of 60 mph, then what is the answer to Chad's question? Write an equation, solve it, and answer the question using a complete sentence. Check your solution.

MC-52. Frieda needs to earn $240 so she can go to Summer Camp. This is double the amount of money she has already saved. Write and solve an equation to find the amount of money Frieda has saved. Check your solution.

MC-53. Ginger's gas tank holds 19 gallons. She fills the tank by adding 5 gallons. Use a variable to write an equation to find the number of gallons of gas in the tank before she filled it. Check your solution.

MC-54. Solve the equation $2x + 9 = 4x + 5$ using the balance scales on your resource page.

a) Show the simplest way to keep the scales balanced.

b) Explain your reasoning in the "think clouds" and record the algebraic equations. Check your solution.

MC-55.   Solve the equation $3x + 6 - 3 = 5x + 1$ using the balance scales on your resource page.

MC-56.   As you use the resource page to do the problem, $4x + 1 = 3x - 1$, remember that adding a zero pair (+ and −) does not change the value of the equation or the balance.

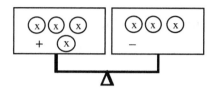

MC-57.   Solve each of the equations below, then substitute your solution for x back into the original equation to be sure that your solution is correct.

   a) $2x - 3 = 4x - 9$ b) $4x + 6 = 5x - 7$
                                                   Remember that you can add an opposite to
                                                   make zero pairs.

MC-58.   Solve each of the following problems. Be sure to show all of the steps in each solution and substitute your solution for x back into the original equation. Notice that one of the pan diagrams below has positive (+) signs, while the other has negative (−) signs.

   a)   b)

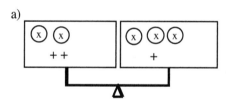   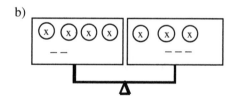

MC-59.   Carlin and Jacob just finished the last problem.

    Carlin: Hey, Jacob! I just noticed something. In that last problem you took three x's from each balance pan and got $x - 2 = -3$. Then all you have to do is use the cover-up method to finish the problem. You can just say x minus 2 is negative 3, so x has to be negative 1.

    Jacob: You're right. Let's try that system for the next problems.

Solve the following equations for x. Show all steps.

a) $2x - 2 = 4x - 8$

b) $5x + 6 = 2x + 24$

c) $4x - 5 = 2x + 27$

d) $3x - 7 = 6x - 16$

MC-60.   The perimeter of a rectangle is 48. The length is 8. Draw a diagram and solve the following equation to find the width: $48 = 2(8 + w)$.

MC-61.   Find the value of each expression. Remember the order of operations.

a) $6^2 + 4 \cdot 5 \div 2$

b) $(6^2 + 4 \cdot 5) \div 2$

c) $(6^2 + 4) \cdot (5 \div 2)$

MC-62.   Use the order of operations to complete these tables. Show all your work.

a)

x	y = 3 − 2x	y
-2	y = 3 − 2(-2)	
	y = 3 − (-4)	7
0		
2		
-1		
3		

b)

x	y = 1 − x²	y
-2	1 − (-2)²	
	1 − (4)	-3
-1		
2		
0		
1		

MC-63.   Follow the instructions below for each problem.

a)   How many one-fourths are in $4\frac{1}{4}$? Use your answer to rewrite $4\frac{1}{4}$ as a fraction with a denominator of 4.

b)   How many one-thirds are in $3\frac{2}{3}$? Use your answer to rewrite $3\frac{2}{3}$ as a fraction with a denominator of 3.

c)   How many one-eighths are in $5\frac{5}{8}$? Use your answer to rewrite $5\frac{5}{8}$ as a fraction with a denominator of 8.

d)   How many one-fifths are in $6\frac{4}{5}$? Use your answer to rewrite $6\frac{4}{5}$ as a fraction with a denominator of 5.

MC-64. Answer the following questions. Write your answer as an equation.

a) Amber has to feed her pigs 36 gallons of molasses. How many pints is this?

b) Rufina walked to the mall and back home, a total of 4 miles. How many feet is this?

MC-65. Mr. Bennett's students took a math quiz and got the following scores: 8, 7, 5, 3, 4, 7, 2, 6, and 3.

a) What is the mean score?

b) What is the median score?

c) Is there a mode? What is it?

d) What is the range of these scores?

e) If the total possible were 8 points, calculate the <u>percentage</u> grades. Round to the nearest percentage.

f) Use the percentage scores to make a stem-and-leaf plot.

g) Use the percentage scores to make a box-and-whisker plot.

h) Which data display gives Mr. Bennett information for him to decide if most students understand the material on the quiz? Explain your thinking.

MC-66. Simplify: $\frac{4}{7} \div \frac{4}{5}$

(A) $1\frac{2}{5}$ (B) $\frac{5}{7}$ (C) $\frac{16}{35}$ (D) $\frac{8}{12}$ (E) none of these

MC-67. What is 15% of 80?

(A) 8   (B) 12   (C) 15   (D) 120   (E) none of these

MC-68. Explain how you found the correct answer in each of the preceding multiple choice questions.

MC-69. Follow your teacher's directions for practicing mental math. What strategy did you practice?

MC-70. David and Rozanne have the same amount of money. David has three envelopes labeled x and an additional $15, and Rozanne has four envelopes labeled x and an additional $9. All the envelopes contain the same amount of money. How much money must be in each envelope?

a) Write an equation to show that they have the same amount of money.

b) Solve your equation to see how much money is in an envelope.

MC-71. How much is each x worth? Explain how you know.

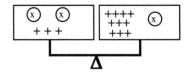

MC-72. The Mathematical Amusement Park is different from other amusement parks. Visitors encounter their first decision involving math when they pay their entrance fee. They have a choice between two plans. With Plan 1 they pay $5 to enter the park and $3 for each ride. With Plan 2 they pay $12 to enter the park and $2 for each ride.

a) Make a table like the one below to find the number of rides when the two plans cost the same.

Guess # Rides	Cost of Plan 1	Cost of Plan 2	Same (?)

b) Use x for the number of rides and write algebraic expressions for the cost of Plan 1 and for the cost of Plan 2.

c) Write an equation that shows when the plans cost the same amount.

d) Solve your equation and compare the result with the result from the table.

MC-73. Use the entries in your table from part (a) in the previous problem to set up and graph the two plans on the same set of axes.

a) Where does the line for Plan 1 cross the y-axis. Name this point with an ordered pair. Name the point where the line for Plan 2 crosses the y-axis. The point where a line crosses the y-axis is the **y-intercept**.

b) Label the coordinate of the place where the two lines intersect (cross).

c) What does the place where the lines intersect represent?

MC-74.   After your day at the park you have some film to be
          developed. Quick Photo Shop charges $2.25 plus
          $0.05 per picture for developing and printing a roll of
          film. The cost at Fast Photo Shop is $1.25 per roll
          plus $0.09 for each picture.

a)   Use the resource page to create a table like the
     one you made for the Mathematical Amusement
     Park problem. Make guesses for the number of
     pictures to see how the costs at the two photo
     shops compare.

b)   Graph the information from your table.
     What is the y-intercept for each shop?

c)   How does your graph help you decide
     when the cost is the same?

d)   Write algebraic expressions for each
     shop. Set up the equation for when the
     costs are the same. Solve the equation.

e)   Are your answers in part (c) and part (d)
     the same? Why or why not?

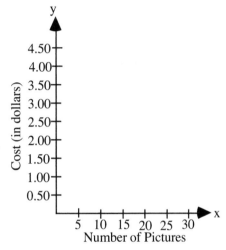

MC-75.   Solve the following equations. Be sure to show your steps and check your answers.

a) $2x + 16 = 5x + 4$ b) $6 + 3x = 2x + 13$

c) $3x - 5 = 2x + 14$ d) $5x - 5 = x + 15$

e) $2x + 18 = 3 + 5x$ f) $4x + 6 = 7x - 15$

MC-76. Mental Math Clubs (MMC) have become popular at several schools. The Einstein Foundation, a charitable organization, awarded $2,000 to the Mental Math Club at Diedre's school. The money is to be spent for a dinner honoring MMC members from several schools. Diedre calls five local hotels that have banquet facilities to ask about the prices. She reserves the Perimeter Room at the Integer Inn. The cost is $500 to rent the room. The meals cost $12 per person. How many people can Diedre invite to the dinner? Write and solve an equation and then answer the question.

MC-77. Warner won a prize of $200 to use for a membership at a local health club. The cost to become a member is $65, and the monthly membership fee is $15. How long (in months) will it be until Warner starts paying the monthly membership fee (that is, until he runs out of prize money)? Write and solve an equation.

MC-78. Addison is on page 200 in the book he is reading. Five days ago he was on page 75. Assume he reads the same number of pages each day.

a) What is his reading rate? (That is, how many pages does he read per day?)

b) Copy and complete the table below.

Time (x) in days	-5	-4	-3	-2	-1	0	1	2	3
Amount (y)	75					200			

c) Write the rule.

d) When will he finish the book, which is 417 pages long?

e) When did he start reading the book?

f) Without graphing Addison's reading rate, name the point that represents the y-intercept.

MC-79. Simplify: -5[(-2)(-3) + 9]

(A) 75   (B) 15   (C) -15   (D) -75   (E) none of these

MC-80. Which of the following is equal to $(0)(5)$?

(A) $0 - 1$ (B) $\frac{2}{0}$ (C) $0 + 3$ (D) $\frac{0}{4}$ (E) none of these

MC-81. Complete the following Diamond Problems.

Product

Sum

a) 1.3 $|-5|$

b) -4.7 -1.7

c) -0.4 -3.6

d) $|-2.3|$ -2.1

e) 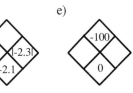 -100 0

MC-82. Write an equation to find the perimeter of this rectangle.

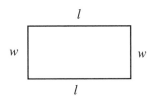

l

w w

l

MC-83. Consider the expression $3(x + 3)$.

a) What does $3(x + 3)$ mean?

b) You can represent $3(x + 3)$ with algebra tiles as shown below.

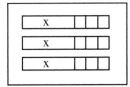

Draw three groups of $(x + 3)$.
You should see that this is $3x + 9$.

The Distributive Property allows us to rewrite a multiplication expression with parentheses as an equivalent expression without parentheses.

So $3(x + 3)$ may be rewritten as $3x + 9$.

c) With your partner, use the Distributive Property to rewrite the following expressions and model them with algebra tiles.

i) $4(x + 2)$ ii) $2(x + 5)$ iii) $3(x + 4)$

MC-84. Use the expression $3(x + 3)$ to answer the following questions.

a) Can you solve this problem to find a number value for x?

b) What happens if you make this problem $3(x + 3) = 21$? Can you solve for x?

c) Look at part (b) above. Rewrite $3(x + 3)$ as $3x + 9$ to get the new equation, $3x + 9 = 21$. Solve for x.

MC-85. Mario solved an equation and wants you to explain how he did it. Copy the solution steps he used. Next to each subproblem, give a mathematical reason that justifies how he got to the next subproblem. The first reason is given.

$4(2x + 5) = 5x + 32$	Use the Distributive Property to eliminate parentheses.
$8x + 20 = 5x + 32$	
$8x = 5x + 12$	
$3x = 12$	
$x = 4$	
$4(2 \cdot 4 + 5) = 5 \cdot 4 + 32$	
$4(13) = 52$	

MC-86. Marisa left off parts of another problem and wants you to copy and complete it by filling in either the algebraic step or writing the reason that justifies how to get to the next step in the solution.

$7x + 5 = 4(3x - 5)$ _____

_____ Add 20 to both sides of the equation.

$7x + 25 = 12x$ _____

_____ Divide both sides by 5 to have one x.

$x = 5$ _____

$7 \cdot 5 + 5 = 4(3 \cdot 5 - 5)$ Use the order of operations to simplify each side.

$40 = 4(10)$ _____

MC-87. Solve each equation. Show all subproblems.

a) $4(x + 2) = 28$ b) $2(x + 5) = 34$ c) $3(x + 4) = 30$

d) $2(x + 4) = 10$ e) $3(2x - 3) = 3$ f) $10x = 5(x + 8)$

g) $3(2x + 5) = 2x + 5$ h) $2(x - 4) = x - 7$

MC-88. Simplify the following expressions.

a) $6(x + 3)$ b) $(2x - 4)3$ c) $-2(5x - 1)$

MC-89.   Write each expression in factored form using the Distributive Property.

a)   8x + 12   b)   9x + 6   c)   -2x – 4

MC-90.   Solve each equation. Show your work.

a)   24 = 2(x + 5)   b)   90 = (2x – 8)3

c)   22 = 2(x + 4)   d)   3(2x – 1) = 9

MC-91.   Kendra notices the hard drive on her computer has
42.6 MB available for storage. She estimates she
fills up about 3 MB each month. Let x be the
number of months until the storage space on the
hard drive is filled up. Write an equation using x
and solve it.

MC-92.   Use the Distributive Property to rewrite each expression in simplified form.

a)   3(x + 6)   b)   x(x + 8)   c)   -6(7y + 4)

MC-93.   Follow the instructions for each problem.

a)   How many one-fourths are in $2\frac{1}{4}$? Use your answer to rewrite $2\frac{1}{4}$ as a fraction
with denominator of 4.

b)   How many one-thirds are in $1\frac{1}{3}$? Use your answer to rewrite $1\frac{1}{3}$ as a fraction with
a denominator of 3.

c)   How many one-eighths are in $4\frac{5}{8}$? Use your answer to rewrite $4\frac{5}{8}$ as a fraction
with a denominator of 8.

d)   How many one-fifths are in $3\frac{2}{5}$? Use your answer to rewrite $3\frac{2}{5}$ as a fraction with
a denominator of 5.

MC-94.   Tyler was working on another Target Game
problem to stump his friends at school. His
numbers were 2, 3, 4, 7, and 8. His target
number was 6. Solve Tyler's problem.

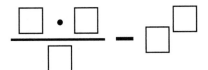

MC-95. Doreen is at camp. She wants to call home to talk to her sister about the fun she is having there, but first she needs to talk to her parents. Her phone card has $2.50 left on it. The company charges $0.20 per minute. How long can she talk to her parents and still have five minutes to talk to her sister? Let t be the amount of time she can talk to her parents. Write an equation using t as the variable to answer Doreen's question. Use a Guess and Check table if you need it. Remember to write your answer as a sentence.

MC-96. Answer the following questions and explain your answers.

a) How would you divide nine granola bars evenly among three people?

b) How would you divide seven granola bars evenly among three people?

MC-97. Solve the following equations.

a) $4x = 12$

b) $3x + 2 = 11$

c) $2(x + 4) = 8$

d) $3(2x + 8) = 40$

e) $3(2x - 3) = 6$

MC-98. The Math Club is already planning a summer field trip. They have to choose between two amusement parks. Splash City charges $5.50 for admission plus $0.75 for each ride. The cost at Wet World is $2.00 admission plus $1.25 per ride.

a) For each park, define a variable and write an equation to show the relationship between the total cost and the number of rides.

b) Create a graph for the cost at each park and locate the point where the lines intersect. What is the significance of this point? Explain.

c) Name the y-intercept for both lines. What do these points represent?

d) Use your two equations to write an equation that shows when the total cost is the same for both parks. Solve the equation. Use algebra to check your answer.

e) For what number of rides is the total cost the same at both parks? What is that cost? Be sure to put your answer in a complete sentence.

f) When the club members were asked how many rides they planned to take, the mean was 8.2 and the median was 5. Which park should they choose? Explain your reasoning.

MC-99.   Use the Distributive Property or factor to rewrite each of the following expressions.

a) $4(3x - 5)$

b) $x \cdot y + x \cdot 8$

c) $5 \cdot 2x + 5 \cdot 4 = \underline{} (\underline{} + \underline{})$

d) $-(2x + 5)$

MC-100.   Factor using the Distributive Property.

a) $8x + 12$ b) $9x + 6$ c) $-2x - 4$

MC-101.   Lynne took a taxicab from her office to the airport. She had to pay $3 per mile plus a $5 flat fee. Her total cost was $23. Write and solve an equation to find the number of miles she rode in the taxi. Write your answer in a complete sentence.

MC-102.   Use the Distributive Property or factor to rewrite the following expressions.

a) $(x + 7)5$ b) $7y - 56$ c) $-3(2x + 6)$ d) $15w - 10$

MC-103.   Complete each spinner by calculating the value of the missing fraction.

a)

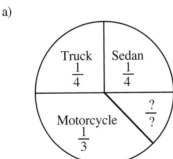

b)

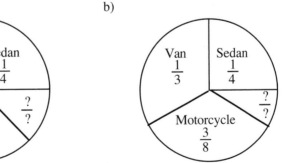

MC-104.   Carmen and Ashley wanted to make egg sandwiches for their math class. They hard-boiled 30 eggs to use. While they were out jogging, Carmen's little brother Armand ate $\frac{2}{5}$ of the eggs.

a)   How many eggs did Armand eat?   b)   What percent is this?

The Math Club: Solving Equations

MC-105. The triangles in the grid at right show an example of a reflection or flip. Point A (-5, -1) reflected to A' = (5, -1), etc.

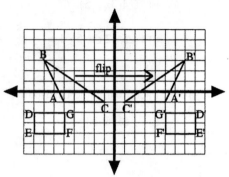

REFLECTION (FLIP)

a) If B = (-7, 3) what are the coordinates of B'?

b) What is the line of symmetry for this entire graph?

c) What are the xy-coordinates of the reflected rectangle?

d) Are the rectangles congruent? Explain.

MC-106. Solve the following equations. Be sure to show your steps and check your answers.

a) 2(x + 4) = 32

b) 3(2x − 2) = 12

c) 21 = (x + 3)2

d) 10(x − 3) = 100

MC-107. Compute.

a) -6 + (-7)

b) 2 + (-8)

c) -3 − (-12)

d) 7 · (-5)

e) -5 + 15

f) 4 − (-9)

g) 37 + (-3)

h) -11 − (-23)

i) -36 ÷ 12

j) -8 ÷ (-8)

MC-108. The Mental Math Club has not ordered the t-shirts yet. Diedre decided to call another t-shirt vendor. Her cousin told her about a place called *Tanks-A-Lot*, which charges a setup fee of $120 and an additional cost of $3 per shirt. Diedre needs to compare prices from the three different t-shirt venders: *Tanks-A-Lot, Teesers, and Screeners*.

a) Describe a way to compare the prices for the three companies.

b) Diedre has seen graphs that her mother prepared for her business presentations. She thinks a graph may be useful. Write an equation that represents the pricing for *Tanks-A-Lot*. Let x be the number of shirts and y be the total cost.

c) Complete the data table on the resource page.

Number of Shirts (x)	0	5	10	15	20	25	50
Total Cost (y)							

d) Graph the data from the table.

MC-109. Complete the table for *Teesers* and *Screeners*. Remember *Teesers* charged $78.00 for set up and $5.00 per shirt. *Screeners* charged $50.00 for set up and $7.00 per shirt.

a) Graph the *Teesers* and *Screeners* data on the same set of axes as *Tanks-A-Lot*. Use a ruler and make sure you use a different color for each line.

b) Identify the y-intercept for all 3 t-shirt vendors.

MC-110. Diedre does not know how many shirts she will need to order. Use the graphs to help Diedre decide which company she should select, depending on the size of the order.

a) Suppose Diedre wants to order 5 shirts. From what company should she order?

b) If Diedre orders 15 shirts, which company will be most economical?

c) If Diedre orders 45 shirts, which company will be most economical?

MC-111. The line representing *Teesers* crosses the line for *Tanks-A-Lot*. Write the coordinates of the point where the two lines cross. Write a few sentences explaining what this point represents.

MC-112. The cost equation for *Teesers* was $y = 78 + 5x$ and the cost equation for *Tanks-A-Lot* was $y = 3x + 120$. Write and solve one equation that will tell you the number of t-shirts when the cost for the two vendors is the same. Compare this with the result from your graph in the previous problem.

MC-113. The cost equation for *Screeners* was y = 50 + 7x. Use the same method as in the previous problem to write and solve one equation to find out when the price at *Teesers* will be the same as at *Screeners*. Compare this with the result from your equation in the previous problem.

MC-114. The line representing *Teesers* crosses the line for *Screeners*. Write the coordinates for the point where the two lines cross. Write a few sentences explaining what this point represents.

MC-115. Elle has moved to Hawksbluff for one year and wants to join a health club. She has narrowed her choices to two places: Thigh Hopes and ABSolutely fABulous. Thigh Hopes charges a fee of $95 to join and a monthly fee of $15. ABSolutely fABulous charges a fee of $125 to join and $12 per month. Which club should she join?

MC-116. Solve the following equations.

a)   12 = x – 7

b)   3x + (-4) = 2x + 9

c)   3x – 8 = 4x + (-2)

d)   2x – 6 = 1

e)   5x + 9 = 15

f)   -16 = 7 + x

MC-117. **Lida's Luscious Waffles**—Makes enough for four people.

$1\frac{3}{4}$ cups flour

$\frac{1}{2}$ cups oil

$\frac{1}{16}$ cups baking powder

$1\frac{3}{4}$ cups milk

2   eggs

Rewrite the recipe to feed families of the following sizes. Use mixed numbers when fractions are greater than one.

a)   20 people

b)   10 people

c)   2 people

d)   14 people

MC-118. Answer the questions and follow the instructions below.

a) How many one-fifths are there in $2\frac{3}{5}$? Use your answer to write $2\frac{3}{5}$ as a fraction that is greater than one.

b) Rewrite the fraction $\frac{13}{8}$ as a mixed number.

c) How many one-thirds are there in $4\frac{2}{3}$? Use your answer to write $4\frac{2}{3}$ as a fraction that is greater than one.

d) Rewrite the fraction $\frac{15}{4}$ as a mixed number.

MC-119.

MIXED NUMBERS

The number $4\frac{1}{4}$ is called a **MIXED NUMBER** because it is made from a whole number, 4, and a fraction, $\frac{1}{4}$. It is a mix of a whole number and a fraction:

$$4\frac{1}{4} = \frac{16}{4} + \frac{1}{4} = \frac{17}{4}$$

The number $\frac{17}{4}$ is a fraction that is greater than 1 because the numerator is greater than the denominator. Sometimes fractions that are greater than one are called "improper fractions." "Improper" does not mean wrong. For mathematics, keeping a fraction in its "improper form" is often more useful than changing it to a mixed number.

Make these notes in your Tool Kit to the right of the double-lined box.

a) Describe how to change a whole number into a fraction with a denominator greater than one.

b) List one example in mathematics where keeping a fraction in its improper form is more useful than changing it to a mixed number.

MC-120.

Chapter Summary It is time to summarize and review what you have learned in this chapter. Work with your partner or study team.

a) Make a list of the different ways you learned to solve equations in this chapter. Discuss the list with other team members and revise it if necessary.

b) Choose four equations from the chapter that represent the ways you learned to solve equations and progress from easier to more difficult. Copy the equations and show how to solve them.

MC-121. Use the models of balance scales below to complete parts (a) and (b).

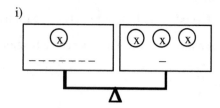

a) Write an algebraic equation for each balance scale.

b) Solve each equation.

MC-122. Solve the following equations for x. Draw the balance scale if needed.

a) $2x + 1 = 15$

b) $5x + 14 = x + (-2)$

c) $2x - 1 = 5x + 8$

d) $4x = 28 + 2x$

e) $-24 = 4x - 10$

f) $5x + 3 = 15x + (-13)$

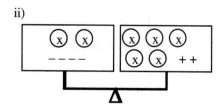

MC-123. Vicky is a high school student who repairs computers and computer networks. She charges $68 for the first hour and $28 for each additional hour of work.

a) Write an algebraic expression to represent how much Vicki charges for x hours.

b) The summer camp hired Vicky to work on computers. The camp received a bill from her that totaled $236. How many hours did Vicky work? Write an equation, solve it, and answer the question.

MC-124. Darren started folding newspapers 20 minutes before Selina arrived. By the time she arrived, he had folded 200 newspapers.

a) How many newspapers can Darren fold per minute?

b) After she arrived, Selina decided to help Darren. She can fold 15 papers per minute. How long will it be until Darren and Selina have folded the same number of newspapers?

c) If you did not use an equation in part (b), write an equation to show how many minutes it will take Selina to fold as many papers as Darren. Let m stand for the number of minutes.

MC-125. Solve the following equations. Draw a balance scale, if needed.

a) $-12 = 5x - 7$

b) $5(x + 1) = -10$

c) $15 + x = 10 + 5x$

d) $(x + 2)3 = x + (-4)$

e) $2[x + (-5)] = 12$

f) $4x + 7 = (x - 7)2$

MC-126. Use the order of operations and substitution to complete these tables. In part (b), remember to square x, then subtract.

a)

x	y = 5 − x	y
-2	y = 5 − (-2)	7
1		
0		
2		
-1		
3		
4		

b)

x	y = 5 − x²	y
-2		
3		
-1	y = 5 − (-1)² y = 5 − (1)	
2		
-3		
0		
1		

MC-127. Graph the two equations in the previous problem on the same set of axes.

a) How are the graphs and equations alike?

b) How are they different?

MC-128. Complete the following Diamond Problems.

Product

Sum

a)

b)

c)

d)

e)

MC-129. Tom is buying new computers for his writing team. He can buy the first five at a dealer discount. The other fifteen will be purchased for an extra $50 each. The cost of the computers comes to a grand total of $11,750. Find how much each of the discounted computers cost. A Guess and Check table might be useful. Write an equation.

MC-130. **What We Have Done in This Chapter**

Below is a list of the Tool Kit entries from this chapter.

- MC-8   Equations

- MC-119   Mixed Numbers

Review all the entries and read the notes you made in your Tool Kit. Make a list of any questions, terms, or notes you do not understand. Ask your partner or study team members for help. If anything is still unclear, ask your teacher.

Ray Sheo's
PRO-PORTION RANCH

Chapter 6

Chapter 6
Ray Sheo's Pro-Portion Ranch: **RATIOS AND PROPORTIONS**

In this chapter you will calculate the area and perimeter of rectangles, parallelograms, triangles, and trapezoids. You will also calculate the area and circumference of circles. You will enlarge and reduce these figures and study similarity. In your study of similarity, you will be introduced to proportions. You will learn to write proportions and solve problems using proportions. Writing and solving proportions are two very important and useful skills that will serve as a strong foundation as you continue in your study of mathematics.

In this chapter you will have the opportunity to:

- find the area of any parallelogram.
- find the area of any triangle.
- find the area of any trapezoid.
- find the area and circumference of any circle.
- reduce and enlarge figures.
- write ratios to compare items.
- write and solve proportions.
- use properties of similar figures and proportions to solve for unknown lengths, perimeters, and areas.
- use proportions to solve percentage problems.

Read the problem below, but **do not try to solve it now**. What you learn over the next few days will enable you to solve it.

RS-0.   Ray Sheo, owner of the Pro-Portion Ranch, needs to build a bridge over the Roaring River that runs through his land. He has no idea how far it is across the river, but his daughter, Maria, knows she can find out by using the properties of similar triangles. Use the drawing at right and help Maria find the distance across the river.

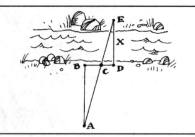

Number Sense		
Algebra and Functions		
Mathematical Reasoning		
Measurement and Geometry		
Statistics, Data Analysis, & Probability		

Chapter 6
Ray Sheo's Pro-Portion Ranch: RATIOS AND PROPORTIONS

RS-1.

CONGRUENT

Two shapes (triangles, for example) are **CONGRUENT** if they have exactly the same size and shape.

Later in the chapter we will discuss similar figures (figures that have the same shape but not necessarily the same size).

Write the following notes to the right of the double-lined box in your Tool Kit.

Name two objects in the classroom that are congruent.

RS-2.

Felipé Sheo knew that he was 60 inches tall and that his sister Maria was 5 feet tall.

Felipé said, "Hey, I'm 12 times as tall as you, since 5 times 12 equals 60." At first Maria was puzzled, but then she said, "That's not true, and I know why."

Explain in a complete sentence what Maria realized.

RS-3.

RATIO

A **RATIO** is the comparison of two quantities by division. A ratio can be written as a fraction, in words, or with colon notation. (We will use the fraction form in this class.)

$$\frac{26 \text{ miles}}{1 \text{ gallon}} \qquad\qquad 26 \text{ miles to } 1 \text{ gallon} \qquad\qquad 26 \text{ miles} : 1 \text{ gallon}$$

A ratio: • should never be written as a mixed number.

• must have units labeled when the units are different.

Highlight the fraction form in your Tool Kit to emphasize that is how we will write ratios in this class.

RS-4.   The way a ratio is stated will tell you which value is written in the numerator and which one is in the denominator. For example, if you are comparing 65 miles to 1 hour, your values will be written as $\frac{65\ miles}{1\ hour}$. The units in a ratio help you remember the order in which to write it. If you are comparing the same kinds of things, you may omit the units. For example, if you are comparing 12 feet to 8 feet, you may write the ratio as $\frac{12}{8}$. Just as fractions can sometimes be simplified, sometimes ratios can also be simplified. For example, $\frac{12}{8}$ can be simplified to $\frac{3}{2}$. Use the Identity Property of Multiplication (Giant **1**) as necessary to simplify ratios.

a)   What is the ratio of 120 miles to 3 hours?

b)   Write a ratio comparing the time it takes to drive from Atlanta to Richmond (7 hours) to the time it takes to fly (1 hour).

c)   What is the ratio of girls to boys in this classroom today?

d)   Write the ratio of 6 feet to 9 feet.

e)   Write the ratio of 90 seconds to 20 seconds.

f)   Write the ratio of 17 days to 51 days.

RS-5.   Sometimes ratios involve hours and minutes–two different units of time–or feet and inches–two different units of distance. In such cases, we need to be sure the units are the same. For example, the ratio of 8 feet to 2 yards is the same as the ratio of 8 feet to 6 feet, since 2 yards equals 6 feet or $\frac{8}{6} = \frac{4}{3}$. Write the following ratios and simplify them if possible.

a)   What is the ratio of 2 hours to 180 minutes?

b)   What is the ratio of 6 inches to 3 feet?

c)   What is the ratio of four eggs to 12 eggs?

d)   What is the ratio of eight eggs to two dozen eggs?

RS-6.

PROPORTION

An equation stating that two ratios are equal is called a **PROPORTION**.

Examples: $\frac{2}{4} = \frac{3}{6}, \frac{5}{7} = \frac{50}{70}, \frac{154}{49} = \frac{44}{14}$

Write the following notes to the right of the double-lined box in your Tool Kit.

Explain in your own words what a proportion is. Include an example of a proportion.

RS-7.   The sides of congruent figures that are arranged in
similar ways in a figure are called corresponding
sides. You may write ratios to compare the lengths
of corresponding sides of figures. For example, in
the two congruent triangles at right, side a
corresponds to side d, side b to side e, and side c
to side f. We can write the ratios $\frac{a}{d}$, $\frac{b}{e}$, and $\frac{c}{f}$.

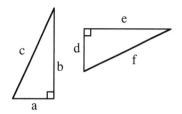

Be sure to keep the order in which you compare the corresponding sides consistent. In
the above example, sides of the triangle on the left were compared to the sides of the
triangle on the right. The short leg (left figure) matched the short leg (right figure), the
long leg (left figure) matched the long leg (right figure), and so forth.

Complete the ratios below using the corresponding sides. Assume that the pairs of
figures are congruent.

a)

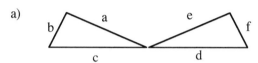

$\frac{a}{e} = \frac{?}{d}$ $\frac{c}{d} = \frac{b}{?}$

b)

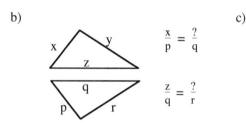

$\frac{x}{p} = \frac{?}{q}$

$\frac{z}{q} = \frac{?}{r}$

c)

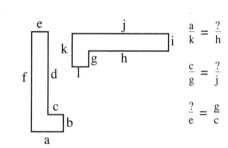

$\frac{a}{k} = \frac{?}{h}$

$\frac{c}{g} = \frac{?}{j}$

$\frac{?}{e} = \frac{g}{c}$

RS-8.   ΔABC is congruent to ΔDEF.

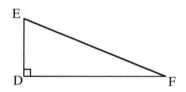

a)   If you placed ΔABC on top of ΔDEF, would all corners and edges match?

b)   Side AB and side DE are corresponding parts. These sides are in the same position
in the triangles. Which side corresponds to side AC?

c)   Which side corresponds to side BC?

d)   Angle B and angle E are corresponding angles. Which angle corresponds to angle F?

e)   Which angle corresponds to angle D?

f)   In your own words, explain what corresponding means for sides and angles of figures.

RS-9.   Jane had to find an equivalent fraction for $\frac{75}{80}$. What she wrote is shown at right. Decide with your partner whether or not Jane wrote a proportion. Explain.

$$\frac{75}{80} = \frac{15}{16}$$

RS-10.   Find an equivalent fraction to complete each proportion below.

a) $\frac{6}{15} = \underline{\quad}$ b) $\frac{13}{39} = \underline{\quad}$

RS-11.   Solve each equation.

a) $8n = 72$ b) $12e = 720$ c) $6.5y = 19.5$

d) $1.5k = 48$ e) $38t = 85.5$ f) $62w = 76.942$

RS-12.   A five-pound box of sugar costs $1.80 and contains 12 cups of sugar. Marella and Mark are making a batch of cookies. The recipe calls for 2 cups of sugar. Determine how much the sugar for the cookies costs. Use a proportion to solve the problem. Show all your work.

RS-13.   Complete the following table and graph the rule: $y = 3x - 2$.

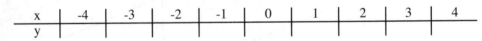

x	-4	-3	-2	-1	0	1	2	3	4
y									

a)   What is the x-intercept?   b)   What is the y-intercept?

RS-14.   Calculate.

a) $-60 \div 5$ b) $(-6) \cdot (-8)$ c) $6 - 17$

d) $-6 - 6$ e) $8 + (-13)$ f) $-14 - (-4)$

g) $-21 - 2$ h) $-12 + (-50) + 4$ i) $9 - (-17)$

RS-15. Now that we have started a new chapter, it is time for you to organize your binder.

    a)   Put the work from the last chapter in order and keep it in a separate folder.

    b)   When this is completed, write, "I have organized my binder."

RS-16. Follow your teacher's instructions for practicing mental math. What strategy did you use?

RS-17. You have used the Identity Property of Multiplication (Giant **1**) to find equivalent fractions and to solve proportions. Copy and compute the problems below. Show the values you used within the Giant **1**.

    a) $\dfrac{7}{12} = \dfrac{56}{m}$ can be solved $\dfrac{7}{12}\cdot\boxed{-} = \dfrac{56}{m}$

    b) $\dfrac{8}{3} = \dfrac{n}{48}$ can be solved $\dfrac{8}{3}\cdot\boxed{-} = \dfrac{n}{48}$

    c) $\dfrac{20}{26}\cdot\boxed{-} = \dfrac{k}{39}$

    d) $\dfrac{20}{42}\cdot\boxed{-} = \dfrac{50}{h}$

RS-18. Look at your work in the previous problem.

    a)   How were the values used within the Giant **1** in parts (c) and (d) different from the values used in parts (a) and (b)?

    b)   In part (d), how did you find the numbers in the Giant **1**? Explain.

RS-19. Solve each proportion using the Giant **1** in each problem.

    a) $\dfrac{7}{12} = \dfrac{m}{18}$ can be solved $\dfrac{7}{12}\cdot\boxed{-} = \dfrac{m}{18}$

    b) $\dfrac{5}{8}\cdot\boxed{-} = \dfrac{30}{n}$

    c) $\dfrac{2}{3}\cdot\boxed{-} = \dfrac{w}{36}$

    d) $\dfrac{4}{5}\cdot\boxed{-} = \dfrac{20}{h}$

RS-20. In the previous problem, the Giant **1** was drawn for you. As you solve the following proportions, draw your own Giant **1** if you find it helpful.

    a) $\dfrac{1}{4} = \dfrac{2.5}{n}$

    b) $\dfrac{3}{4} = \dfrac{36}{w}$

    c) $\dfrac{7}{5} = \dfrac{x}{22.5}$

    d) $\dfrac{3}{4} = \dfrac{n}{22}$

RS-21.   Copy the proportion $\frac{25}{45} = \frac{15}{27}$.

   a)   Reduce each ratio to confirm that the ratios are equal.

   b)   Multiply both sides of the original ratio by 27. You now have $27 \cdot \frac{25}{45}$ on the left side of the equation. What do you have on the right side?

   c)   Since you knew the original equation was true, how do you know the new equation is true?

   d)   Multiply both sides of the equation from part (b) by 45. On the left side of the equation you now have $27 \cdot 25$. What do you have on the right side?

   e)   Doing the two multiplications as above is known as cross multiplying. Why do you think it has this name?

   f)   How do you know that if you start with two equal ratios that you will always end up with two equal products after cross multiplying?

RS-22.   Now we want to cross multiply to confirm that some proportions are equal.

   a)   Verify that $\frac{3}{12} = \frac{5}{20}$ by cross multiplying.

   b)   Verify that $\frac{14}{49} = \frac{22}{77}$ by cross multiplying.

   c)   Suppose you know that $\frac{x}{3} = \frac{4}{6}$ is a true proportion. What true equation do you get without fractions by cross multiplying? Use this equation to find x.

RS-23. You have been using the Giant **1** to find equivalent fractions in a proportion. Some problems are easier to solve than others. For the problem $\frac{x}{30} = \frac{40}{100}$, you could not use a whole number in the Giant **1**. Instead, you can use cross multiplication to solve this proportion. The procedure is shown below for two proportions.

SOLVING PROPORTIONS WITH CROSS MULTIPLICATION

In a proportion, **CROSS MULTIPLICATION** is finding the product of the numerator (top) of one ratio and the denominator (bottom) of the other ratio, multiplying the other numerator and denominator together, and setting the products equal.

For any proportion $\frac{a}{b} = \frac{c}{d}$, after cross multiplication the result is $\mathbf{a \cdot d = b \cdot c}$.

Example: Use cross multiplication to solve for x in each proportion.

Step 1 Group any numerator and denominator elements together with parentheses if any part is a sum.

$$\frac{x}{30} = \frac{40}{100} \qquad \frac{(x+1)}{2} = \frac{3}{5}$$

Step 2 Cross multiply (multiply the numerator of each ratio by the denominator of the other ratio) to write an equation without fractions.

$$\frac{x}{30} \diagdown\!\!\!\!\diagup \frac{40}{100} \qquad \frac{(x+1)}{2} \diagdown\!\!\!\!\diagup \frac{3}{5}$$

$$x \cdot 100 = 30 \cdot 40 \qquad 5(x+1) = 2 \cdot 3$$

Step 3 Solve for x.

$$100x = 1200 \qquad\qquad 5x + 5 = 6$$

$$x = 12 \qquad\qquad\quad 5x = 1$$

$$x = \tfrac{1}{5}$$

To the right of the double-lined box in your Tool Kit, write and solve the following problems using the cross multiplication method. Be sure to show all your steps. Check your answers with your partner or team to be sure they are correct.

a) $\frac{x}{10} = \frac{42}{12}$ b) $\frac{7}{n} = \frac{4}{36}$ c) $\frac{x+2}{5} = \frac{6}{10}$

RS-24.   An airplane travels 1900 miles in four hours.

a)   Find how far the airplane travels in one hour.
       Show all of your work.

b)   Use the information from part (a) to find
       how far the airplane travels in five hours.

RS-25.   Solve for x.

a) $\frac{x + 1}{2} = \frac{21}{7}$ b) $-4x + 31 = -3(x + 6)$ c) $-64 = -4x + 2x - 6x$

RS-26.   Simplify each expression by combining like terms.

a) $2x^2 + 5 - 13x + 11x - 2x^2 + 22$ b) $-12 + x - 5x^2 + 3x^3 - 10 + 4x - 2x^3$

c) $-2x^2 + 9 - 14x - (-9x^2) + 10 + 5x^2$ d) $2x^2 + (-x) + (-2x^2)(-1) + 13x - 6x^2$

RS-27.   Repeated multiplication of the same factor can be written with exponents. Rename
           each product using exponents. Example: $5 \cdot 5 \cdot 5 = 5^3$.

a) $2 \cdot 2 \cdot 2 \cdot 2 \cdot 2 \cdot 2$ b) $3 \cdot 3 \cdot 3 \cdot 3$

c) $2 \cdot 2 \cdot 2 \cdot 2 \cdot 2 \cdot 2 \cdot 2$ d) $6 \cdot 6 \cdot 6 \cdot 6 \cdot 6$

e) $4 \cdot 4 \cdot 4$ f) $x \cdot x$

RS-28.   A week of high and low temperatures in degrees
           Fahrenheit is shown at right. Make a double line graph
           to display these data. Remember to scale and label both
           axes.

Day	Low	High
Sun	43	82
Mon	50	101
Tues	53	105
Wed	45	90
Thur	44	91
Fri	43	88
Sat	45	90

RS-29.   Rename each exponential expression as a product without exponents.

a) 4^6 b) 7^4 c) 8^7

d) 9^5 e) 2^2 f) y^3

RS-30. Hannah and Breanna were working on a problem about exponents. The problem was: "Evaluate 2^3." Hannah wrote $2^3 = 2 \cdot 3 = 6$. Breanna wrote $2^3 = 2 \cdot 2 \cdot 2 = 8$. Who is correct? Explain why.

RS-31. Calculate the area of the rectangle at right.

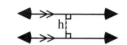

$\frac{3}{8}$ inch

$\frac{7}{8}$ inch

RS-32.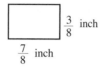

PARALLELOGRAM VOCABULARY

Two lines in a plane (flat surface) are **PARALLEL** if they never meet. The distance between the parallel lines is always the same. The marks >> indicate that the two lines are parallel.

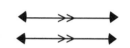

The **DISTANCE** between two parallel lines or segments is indicated by a line segment perpendicular to both parallel lines (or segments).

A **HEIGHT** (h) is the perpendicular distance:

- in triangles, from a vertex (corner) to the line containing the opposite side.

- in quadrilaterals, between two parallel sides or the lines containing those sides.

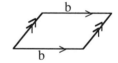

Any side of a two-dimensional figure may be used as a **BASE** (b).

A **PARALLELOGRAM** is a quadrilateral (a four-sided figure) with both pairs of opposite sides parallel.

Highlight the following key words in your Tool Kit:

a) "never meet," "distance between," and "same" (parallel);

b) "perpendicular distance" and "line containing opposite side" (height, triangle);

c) "between two parallel sides" (height, quadrilateral); and,

d) "four-sided" and "opposite sides parallel" (parallelogram).

RS-33.   Obtain the resource page from your teacher. Then
          carefully cut out the parallelogram.

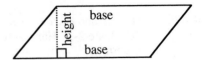

a)   Label the bases and the height as shown.

b)   Use a ruler to measure the base and height in centimeters. Label their lengths.

c)   Cut along the height to separate the triangle from the
      rest of the figure. Then move the triangle to the other
      side of the figure, as shown at right. Paste, glue, or
      tape the pieces in your notebook.

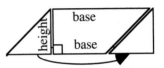

d)   What is the shape of the new figure?

e)   If you were to cut the parallelogram along
      any other placement of the height, would you
      get the same figure? Try it with the second
      parallelogram. Explain in a complete
      sentence.

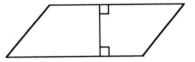

f)   Find the area of the new rectangle.

RS-34.   Discuss the difference between h and c in
          the figure at right. If A = area, use the
          variables shown to write a formula for
          calculating the area of the parallelogram.

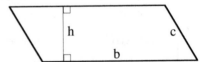

RS-35.   Tabitha's answer to the previous problem was $A = b \cdot h$. Midori's answer was
          $A = b \cdot c$. Which student was correct? Write a note to the student who had the
          incorrect answer, explaining how she can remember the correct way to calculate the
          area of a parallelogram.

RS-36.   Percent is a ratio that compares a number to 100. Follow the model shown below and express
          each of the following ratios as a percent.

          Example: $\frac{1}{5} = \underline{\quad} \%$ $\Rightarrow$ $\frac{1}{5} = \frac{x}{100}$ $\Rightarrow$ $\frac{1}{5} = \frac{20}{100}$ $\Rightarrow$ 20%.

          a) $\frac{1}{4}$ b) $\frac{3}{10}$

          c) $\frac{17}{25}$ d) $\frac{9}{5}$

RS-37.

PERCENTAGES

To solve a percentage problem you can use a proportion. There are four quantities to consider in your proportion: the percent (i.e., <u>part</u> of 100), 100, the whole, and a part of the whole. One of these quantities will be unknown.

Example: What number is 25% of 160?

$$\frac{\%}{100} = \frac{part}{a\ whole}$$

• Set up your proportion with the percent numbers on one side and the quantities you wish to compare on the other side.

$$\frac{25}{100} = \frac{x}{160}$$

• Cross multiply to write an equation without fractions.

$$25 \cdot 160 = 100x$$

• Solve for the unknown.

$$x = 40$$

a) The cost for a hotel room for three nights was $188, including $14 tax. What percent of the bill was the tax? Complete parts (i) - (iv) to the right of the double-lined box in your Tool Kit.

    i) In this case, the whole is ...   ii) The part is ...

    iii) The proportion we need to solve is ...

    iv) What percent of the bill was the tax?

b) Ian got an 80% on his math test. If he answered 24 questions correctly, how many questions were on the test?

c) Ellen bought soccer shorts on sale for $6 off the original price of $40. What percent did she save?

RS-38. Find the area of the following figures.

a)

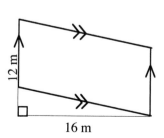

8 m

12 m

b)

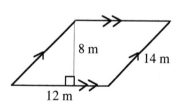

8 m

14 m

12 m

c)

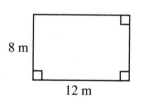

12 m

16 m

d)

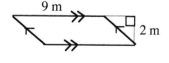

9 m

2 m

RS-39.   Make a correlation statement for each scatter plot below.

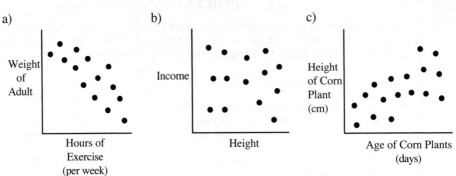

a)

Weight of Adult

Hours of Exercise (per week)

b)

Income

Height

c)

Height of Corn Plant (cm)

Age of Corn Plants (days)

RS-40.   The simplified form of $\frac{8-6}{4} \cdot 2$ is:

(A) 2.5   (B) 1   (C) -2.5   (D) 2

RS-41.   Solve the following problems.

a) $3\frac{1}{2} + 2\frac{5}{8}$ b) $\frac{26}{11} + 7$ c) $5 - 1\frac{10}{13}$

RS-42.   Here is a set of data: 17, 24, 12, 4, 7, 22, 63, 14, 7. What is the outlier?

(A) 4   (B) 63   (C) 12   (D) 14

RS-43.   Express each of the following ratios as a percent. Refer to problem RS-36 if you need help.

a) $\frac{1}{5}$ b) $\frac{19}{25}$ c) $\frac{19}{10}$ d) $\frac{3}{12}$

RS-44.   Solve each equation.

a) $\frac{2}{3} = \frac{6}{x+1}$ b) $13x - 5 = -x - 19$ c) $14x - 62 = -(-12x)$

RS-45.   Use $<, >$, or $=$ to compare the number pairs below.

a)   0.183 ____ 0.18

b)   -13 ____ -17

c)   0.125 ____ $\frac{1}{8}$

d)   -6 ____ -4

e)   72% ____ $\frac{35}{50}$

f) |-9| ____ 9

g)   -0.25 ____ -0.05

h)   -2.07 ____ -2.007

RS-46.   On your resource page find the
parallelogram that looks like the one
at right. Carefully cut it out.

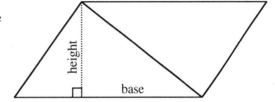

a)   Label the base and height.

b)   Use a ruler and measure the
base and height in centimeters.
Label them.

c)   Find the area of the parallelogram.

d)   Cut the parallelogram along the diagonal. What shapes did you make?

e)   Label the base and height on both triangles and glue, paste, or tape the triangles in
your notebook. What is the area of each triangle?

f)   How does the area of each of the triangles compare to the area of the parallelogram?

RS-47.   A quadrilateral with one pair of parallel sides is called a trapezoid
(see the picture at right for an example). Follow the steps below
to develop a formula for finding the area of a trapezoid.

a)   The resource page given to you by your teacher has a pair of congruent trapezoids.
Carefully cut them out.

b)   Measure the **bases** (the parallel sides) and the height of the trapezoid you cut out
and record these measurements on your cut-out piece. Use centimeters.

c)   Rotate the second copy of the trapezoid and place it "end-to-end" with the first. If
you have done this correctly, the figure should form a parallelogram.

d)   What are the base and height of this parallelogram?

e)   Find the area of the parallelogram.

f)   Using the area of the parallelogram you found in part (e), find the area of the
trapezoid. What was your last step?

RS-48.   Christa saw that she could find the area of a trapezoid without cutting. She said that the base of the big parallelogram would be the sum of the two bases of the trapezoid.

a)   Was she correct? Explain to your partner.

b)   Then Christa said that she could write the area as a formula. If t is the length of the top base and b is the length of the bottom base, then the base of the big parallelogram is b + t and the area of the big parallelogram is (b + t) · h. Using the figure from the last problem, explain to the other members of your team why Christa's method to find the area of the parallelogram is correct.

c)   Now that you know the area of the big parallelogram, what do you need to do to find the area of the original trapezoid?

RS-49.   Show how to use Christa's method to find the area of each of these trapezoids.

a)

b)

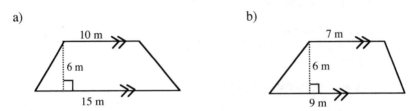

RS-50.   Ray decided to make some triangular corrals for Muggs the grumpy steer to improve his disposition. Ray will always start with a rectangle or parallelogram and fence off part of it to make the corrals. Find the area of each shaded, triangular corral.

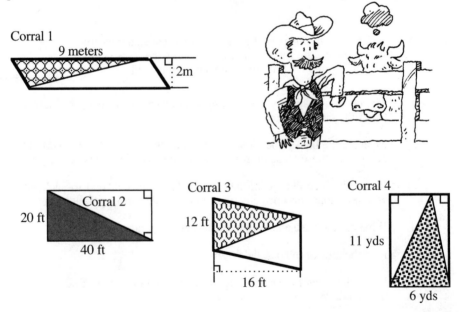

RS-51. Look at the areas you calculated in the previous problem.

    a)   In each of the corrals, what fraction of the rectangle or parallelogram is the shaded triangle? (Calculate the areas of the rectangles or parallelograms, if you need to.)

    b)   Earlier we concluded the area of a parallelogram is base · height. What can you conclude about calculating the area of a triangle?

RS-52.

AREA OF PARALLELOGRAMS, TRIANGLES, AND TRAPEZOIDS

Parallelogram	Triangle	Trapezoid
$A = b \cdot h$	$A = \frac{1}{2} b \cdot h$	$A = \frac{1}{2}(b + t) \cdot h$

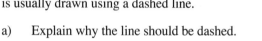

Write the following notes to the right of the double-lined box in your Tool Kit.

Calculate the area of each shape in the Tool Kit using the area formulas.

RS-53. The height of a triangle is drawn from a vertex perpendicular to the line containing the opposite side. It is usually drawn using a dashed line.

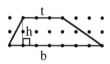

    a)   Explain why the line should be dashed.

    b)   Why is the small square drawn where the height meets the base?

    c)   Explain why the height in the second triangle does not intersect the base.

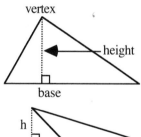

RS-54. The graph of the absolute value may surprise you. Complete the table below for the equation $y = |x| + 1$. Since $|-2| + 1 = 2 + 1 = 3$, one of the points will be (-2, 3).

x	-4	-3	-2	-1	0	1	2	3	4
y			3						

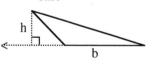

    a)   Plot the points you calculated above to get the graph of $y = |x| + 1$.

    b)   Describe the shape of the graph.

    c)   Write the ordered pair for the point where the graph changes direction.

RS-55.   For each circular object described, write the ratio $\frac{circumference}{diameter}$. Simplify each ratio.

   a)   A circle with a diameter of 49 inches has a circumference of 154 inches.

   b)   An embroidery hoop with a 14-inch diameter has a 44-inch circumference.

   c)   A plate with a 22-inch circumference has a 7-inch diameter.

   d)   Ray's watch face has a <u>radius</u> of 0.35 centimeters and a circumference of 2.2 centimeters.

   e)   Compare the simplified ratios of $\frac{circumference}{diameter}$ from parts (a) through (d). What do you notice?

RS-56.   Complete the following Diamond Problems.

Product

Sum

a)

b)

c)

d)

e)

RS-57.   **Comparing the Circumference and Diameter of a Circle** For this investigation, you will need a circular object and a flexible tape measure. Get these from your teacher.

   a)   Measure the diameter and circumference of your object to the nearest millimeter. Use the measurements your team provides to complete the first three columns of your table.

   b)   Use the data from your table to write the ratio $\frac{circumference}{diameter}$ in the fourth column.

   c)   Using a calculator, find the decimal approximations of the ratios $\frac{circumference}{diameter}$ to the nearest hundredth and enter your answers in the fifth column of the table.

   d)   Examine the last two columns. What similarity do you notice in the ratio $\frac{circumference}{diameter}$ for the different size circles?

Name of Circular Item	Circumference (millimeters)	Diameter (millimeters)	Ratio of $\frac{circumference}{diameter}$	$\frac{circumference}{diameter}$ as a decimal
any circle				

RS-58.   You know the ratio $\frac{\text{circumference}}{\text{diameter}}$ is a little more than 3. If you know the diameter of a
          circle, how could you estimate the circumference?

RS-59.   For each of the circles drawn below, estimate the circumference.

          a)   b)   c)   d)

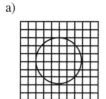   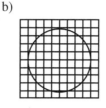   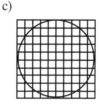   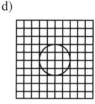

RS-60.   Pi (π) is the name of the number that is the ratio
   $\frac{\text{circumference}}{\text{diameter}}$ for any circle. Because its value is not an
          exact integer or fraction, you must use an
          approximation when you calculate with it. There are
          several different approximations you can use for π
          depending on how accurate you need to be. Below
          we examine the effects of using some of these
          different approximations.

          Suppose a circle has a diameter of 11 units.

          a)   Calculate the circumference using the π button on a calculator. Round your answer
                to the nearest hundredth.

          b)   Calculate the circumference using 3.14 for π. Round your answer to the nearest
                hundredth.

          c)   Calculate the circumference using $\frac{22}{7}$ for π. Record your answer. Then convert
                your fraction to a decimal and round your answer to the nearest hundredth.

          d)   Compare the answers to parts (a) through (c). Are the values fairly close or very
                different?

RS-61.   Raj was watching his sister Balbir do her homework. Balbir drew three circles the same size. Balbir cut the first circle in four equal pieces. She cut the second circle into eight equal pieces. Balbir cut the third circle into sixteen equal pieces. Then Balbir pasted the circle pieces on her paper as shown below.

Raj: Why are you doing that, Balbir?

Balbir: I need to find a formula for the area of a circle. Each of these 'caterpillars' is helping me do that.

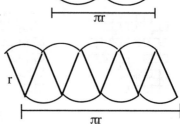

Raj: How?

Balbir: Look at the figures closely. As the number of pieces increases, you can see that they look more and more like a rectangle, right?

Raj: Yes, I see it. The area of a rectangle is base times height. What are the dimensions of these rectangles?

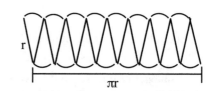

Balbir: The height of each rectangle is the radius of the circle, r. The length of the base of each rectangle is half the circumference so, it is πr.

Raj: That means that the area of the rectangle, base · height, is $\pi r \cdot r$, or πr^2.

Balbir: Since the area of the circle is exactly the same as the area of the rectangle, I'm finished!

a)   Use complete sentences to explain why the height of each rectangle is r.

b)   Use complete sentences to explain why the length of each rectangle is πr.

c)   Use complete sentences to explain why the area of the rectangle is $\pi r \cdot r$.

d)   Use complete sentences to explain why the area of the circle is πr^2.

RS-62. In a previous problem we learned that π is a number slightly larger than 3 which is not an exact integer or fraction. Since it cannot be written as the ratio of any two integers, it belongs to a special class of numbers known as **irrational** numbers. Whenever you want to be really accurate in your calculations, use the π button on your calculator which is accurate to about twelve decimal places. Modern computers have calculated π to more than four billion decimal places. Here are the first fifteen:

$$\pi \approx 3.141592653589793.$$

CIRCUMFERENCE OF CIRCLES

The **CIRCUMFERENCE** (C) of a circle is its perimeter, that is, the "distance around" the circle.

To find the circumference of a circle from its **diameter** (d), use $C = \pi \cdot d$.

To find the circumference of a circle from its **radius** (r), use $C = 2\pi \cdot r$.

Highlight "distance around the circle," "$C = \pi \cdot d$," and "$C = 2\pi \cdot r$" in your Tool Kit box.

RS-63.

AREA OF CIRCLES

To find the **AREA** (A) of a circle when given its radius (r), use the formula

$$A = \pi \cdot r \cdot r = \pi r^2$$

Write the following notes to the right of the double-lined box in your Tool Kit.

Using the area formula, calculate the area of a circle with a radius of 9.

RS-64. Calculate the circumference of the following circles, rounding each answer to the nearest tenth. All distances are in meters.

a)   diameter = 10   b)   radius = 5   c)   diameter = 15   d)   radius = 10

RS-65. Calculate the area of the following circles, rounding each answer to the nearest tenth. All distances are in meters.

a)   radius = 20   b)   diameter = 12   c)   radius = 3   d)   diameter = 15

RS-66.   Compute.

a) $\frac{2}{6} + \frac{8}{14}$ b) $\frac{3}{5} \div \frac{6}{2}$ c) $\frac{53}{60} - \frac{7}{12}$ d) $\frac{3}{5} \cdot \frac{1}{5}$

RS-67.   Susan can dig three post holes in 25 minutes. Use a proportion to determine how long it will take her to dig 14 post holes at the same rate. Round your answer to the nearest minute.

RS-68.   An unknown number is decreased by seven, and the result is multiplied by three. The final result is 27. Find the unknown number.

a)   Write an equation. A Guess and Check table might help you get started.

b)   Solve for x algebraically. Show all of your steps.

RS-69.   Jody found an $88 pair of sandals marked 20% off. What is the dollar value of the discount?

RS-70.   Simplify each fraction by eliminating Giant **1**s.

a) $\frac{3 \cdot 4}{3 \cdot 6}$ b) $\frac{7 \cdot 2}{7 \cdot 4}$ c) $\frac{8 \cdot 9}{6 \cdot 8}$ d) $\frac{16 \cdot 4}{4 \cdot 8}$

e)   Can any of your answers be simplified further by eliminating common factors? Check your answers.

RS-71.   Solve these proportions using any method you choose. (You may use a calculator, but you must show all of your steps.)

a) $\frac{10}{y} = \frac{30}{100}$ b) $\frac{18}{15} = \frac{x}{100}$ c) $\frac{4}{7} = \frac{3x - 1}{35}$

RS-72.   One method of looking at ratios is in relation to geometric shapes. Think of a copy machine and what it does to a picture when the "enlargement" button is selected. The machine makes *every length* of the picture larger by the same multiple. The angles of the enlarged figure have the same measures as the original figure. The picture below was enlarged by a factor of 3. We can also say it was enlarged by a ratio of 3 to 1. This can be written as $\frac{3}{1}$ because we are comparing the copy to the original and the sides of the copy are 3 times larger than those of the original.

> Note: For all of these problems we will keep the original size dot paper in the enlargement (or reduction) so that you may compare the sizes of the figures.

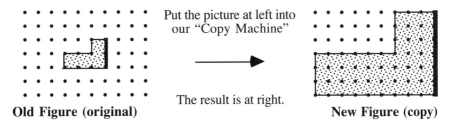

Old Figure (original)   **New Figure (copy)**

Put the picture at left into our "Copy Machine"

The result is at right.

a)   Your teacher will give you a resource page which has the original figure and the copy. These figures have six pairs of corresponding sides; one of the pairs has been darkened above.

b)   Refer to the darkened pair of corresponding sides.

   i)   What is the length of this side on the original figure?

   ii)   What is the length of this side on the copy?

c)   Write and simplify the ratio of this pair of sides in the order $\frac{\text{copy}}{\text{original}}$.

d)   Choose another pair of corresponding sides in the figure. Write and simplify the ratio of these sides in the order $\frac{\text{copy}}{\text{original}}$.

e)   Compare your simplified ratios from parts (c) and (d). What do you notice?

f)   Predict the simplified ratio you would get for another pair of corresponding sides of the two figures. Now try it. Write and simplify the ratio for the remaining pairs of corresponding sides. Was your prediction correct?

RS-73.   Geometric figures can be reduced as well as enlarged. Think of the copy machine and what it does to a picture when you select the "reduction" button. The machine keeps the angles the same size and makes *every single length* of the picture equally smaller by the same multiple. Examine the figures below and note what resulted when the copy machine reduced the original figure. The copy machine produced a copy that has sides half the size of the original side lengths. We say this picture has been reduced by a ratio of 1 to 2 or $\frac{1}{2}$. Again, we have not reduced the size of the dot grid.

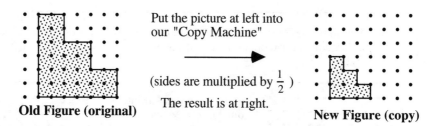

Put the picture at left into our "Copy Machine"

(sides are multiplied by $\frac{1}{2}$)

The result is at right.

Old Figure (original)   **New Figure (copy)**

a)   Locate at least three pairs of corresponding sides (there are eight in all), then write and simplify the ratio of each pair of corresponding sides in the order $\frac{copy}{original}$.

b)   Compare the ratios. What do you notice?

RS-74.   Examine the figure at right.

a)   Use dot paper to sketch the original figure. Label the dimensions.

b)   Enlarge the figure by a ratio of $\frac{4}{1}$. Label the dimensions.

c)   Write and simplify the ratio of one pair of corresponding sides in the order $\frac{copy}{original}$.

d)   Calculate the perimeter of both the copy and the original. Write and simplify the ratio of the perimeters in the order $\frac{copy}{original}$.

SIMILARITY AND SCALE FACTORS

Two figures are **SIMILAR** if they have the same shape but not necessarily the same size. In similar figures:

- the corresponding angles have the same measures *and*
- the ratios of all corresponding pairs of sides are equal.

The simplified ratio of any pair of corresponding sides in similar figures is called the **SCALE FACTOR**.

Example for two similar triangles:

$$\frac{AB}{DE} = \frac{16}{40} = \frac{2}{5}$$

$$\frac{BC}{EF} = \frac{10}{25} = \frac{2}{5}$$

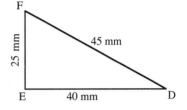

Write the following notes to the right of the double-lined box in your Tool Kit.

a) Write and simplify the ratio $\frac{AC}{DF}$.

b) What is the **scale factor** of similar figures (the ratio of their sides)?

RS-76. Patti claims she made a similar copy of each original figure shown in parts (a) and (b). For each pair of figures, write and simplify the ratios of each pair of corresponding sides in the order $\frac{copy}{original}$. Compare the ratios. Are the figures similar? (Did Patti really make a copy?) Assume that the corresponding angles are equal.

a) Original Figure   Copy

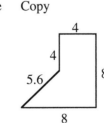

b) Original Figure   Copy

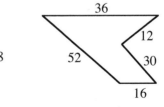

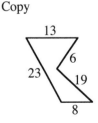

RS-77. If two figures are similar, the ratio of corresponding sides will be equal. In the two similar figures below, one side length is unknown. We write the proportion $\frac{5}{15} = \frac{x}{12}$. Solve for x.

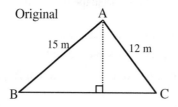
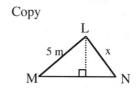

Original   Copy

RS-78. The dashed triangle ABC rotates 90° counterclockwise about vertex A. Rotate the dotted rectangle DEFG the same way about vertex D. What are the xy-coordinates of the corners of the rectangle in its rotated position?

ROTATION (TURN)

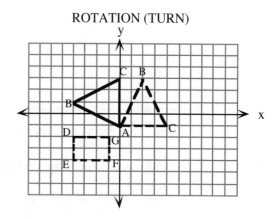

RS-79. Solve for x.

a) $100 = 2(x + 4)$ b) $-2x + 11 = 5x + 39$ c) $-66 = -4x + 2x - 6$

RS-80. Identify the base and the height of each figure, then calculate the perimeter and area.

a)

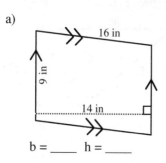

b = ____ h = ____

b)

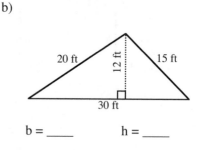

b = ____   h = ____

RS-81. Ed went to dinner with some friends and decided to leave a good tip. The bill was $51.23.

a) If he left a 15% tip, how much did he pay in all?

b) If Ed paid a total of $65, what percent tip did he leave?

CHAPTER 6

RS-82.   Complete the following fraction-decimal-percent triangles.

a)   b)   c)

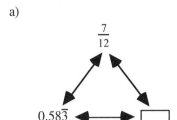

0.58$\overline{3}$

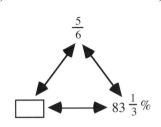

83$\frac{1}{3}$ %

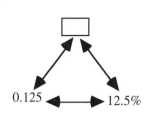

0.125   12.5%

RS-83.   Mario asked Marisa for advice on this homework problem:

Rewrite $\frac{2^3}{2^4}$ without exponents, then simplify. Marisa said, "Writing without exponents is the same as before. It's $2 \cdot 2 \cdot 2$ over $2 \cdot 2 \cdot 2 \cdot 2$." Mario said, "I see three Giant **1**s in that fraction, so it simplifies to 2. Wait! The 2 is in the denominator, so it must be $\frac{1}{2}$." "Let's check. $\frac{2^3}{2^4}$ is $\frac{8}{16}$, and that simplifies to $\frac{1}{2}$, so we're in good shape!" Rewrite the following expressions without exponents, then simplify.

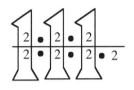

a) $\frac{10^4}{10^1}$ b) $\frac{p^5}{p^2}$ c) $\frac{3^8}{3^4}$ d) $\frac{6^3}{6^3}$

RS-84.   An example of using an exponent is $5 \cdot 5 = 5^2$. This problem is read as "five times five equals five to the second power or five **squared**." When you use the exponent 2 you can say you are "squaring" five because a square with a side of five has an area of $5 \cdot 5$, which can be written as 5^2.

a)   Write "two squared" with and without exponents. Find its value.

b)   Write "three squared" with and without exponents. Find its value.

c)   Write "four squared" with and without exponents. Find its value.

d)   Write "ten squared" with and without exponents. Find its value.

RS-85.   Ray Sheo bought the plot of land shown at right from his neighbor. Ray was not sure of all of its dimensions, but he knew the two plots were similar. Help Ray by completing parts (a) and (b) below. Remember to write your ratios in the order $\frac{new}{original}$.

Ray's New Plot   Ray's Old Plot

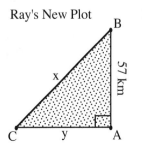

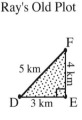

a)   The proportion $\frac{57}{4} = \frac{x}{5}$ is used to calculate the length of x. Solve for x.

b)   Write and solve a proportion to calculate the length of y.

RS-86.   We have studied the ratio of corresponding sides of similar figures. Now we will look at the ratios of perimeters of similar figures. Use the template or block provided by your teacher. There should be a different-shaped template for each member of your team.

a)   Trace your block. Label this as the original. Label each side as 1 or 2 units of length. What is the perimeter of your block? Write it near your figure.

b)   Trace your block as many times as necessary to make a similar figure with a scale factor of $\frac{3}{1}$. Make sure your enlargement is exactly the same shape as the original with each side three times as long. Label this figure as the $\frac{3}{1}$ copy. Label the length of each side of the enlarged figure. Calculate the new perimeter.

c)   Trace your block as many times as necessary to make a similar figure with a scale factor of $\frac{4}{1}$. Make sure your enlargement is exactly the same shape as the original with each side four times as long. Label this figure as the $\frac{4}{1}$ copy. Label the length of each side of the enlarged figure. Calculate the new perimeter.

d)   For each enlargement, write and simplify the ratio of the perimeters in the order $\frac{copy}{original}$.

e)   Compare your perimeter ratio with your team members who used a different shape.

f)   Explain why you would expect the ratio of the perimeter to be the same as the scale factor.

RS-87.   Go back to the original figure you traced in the previous problem. In that problem we looked at ratios of perimeters. Now we will look at ratios of areas.

a)   If the area of your original figure is one unit of area, how many units of area make up the figure with the scale factor of $\frac{3}{1}$? With the scale factor of $\frac{4}{1}$?

b)   For each enlargement, write and simplify a ratio comparing the area of the enlarged figure to the original figure. Compare your results with those of your team members.

c)   As a team, compare the answers from part (b) with the perimeter ratios for the figures. How are the area ratios and perimeter ratios related in terms of square numbers?

d)   Area is measured in square units. Explain why it makes sense that the area ratios are the square of the perimeter ratios.

RS-88.

RATIOS OF SIMILARITY

When figures are similar, the ratio of the perimeters is the same as the scale factor, $\frac{a}{b}$.

The ratio of the areas is the square of the scale factor, $\left(\frac{a}{b}\right)^2$.

The **PERIMETER RATIO** is $\left(\frac{copy}{original}\right)$ = scale factor = $\frac{a}{b}$.

The **AREA RATIO** is $\left(\frac{copy}{original}\right)$ = (scale factor)^2 = $\left(\frac{a}{b}\right)^2$.

For example, in the figures at right, the scale factor is $\frac{3}{1}$.

The perimeter ratio is
$\frac{30}{10} = \frac{3}{1}$ = scale factor.

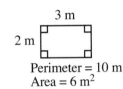

Perimeter = 10 m
Area = 6 m²

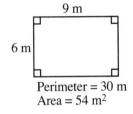

Perimeter = 30 m
Area = 54 m²

The area ratio is $\frac{54}{6} = \frac{9}{1} = \left(\frac{3}{1}\right)^2$ (the scale factor squared).

Highlight the ratios for perimeter and area in your Tool Kit.

RS-89.   Use the figures in problem RS-72.

   a)   Calculate the perimeter and area for each of the figures.

   b)   Write and simplify the ratio of the perimeters in the order $\frac{copy}{original}$.

   c)   Compare the perimeter ratio to the scale factor. What do you notice?

   d)   Write and simplify the ratio of the areas in the order $\frac{copy}{original}$.

   e)   Compare the area ratio to the scale factor. Are these ratios the same? How is the area ratio related to the scale factor?

RS-90.   Two similar triangles have a scale factor of $\frac{5}{3}$.

   a)   Find the perimeter ratio $\frac{copy}{original}$.   b)   Find the area ratio $\frac{copy}{original}$.

RS-91. One triangle at right is a $\frac{5}{1}$ enlargement of another: $\frac{copy}{original} = \frac{5}{1}$.

original

a) Find the perimeter of the original. (All measurements are in centimeters.)

b) Use a proportion to find the perimeter of the copy.

c) Use a proportion to find the area of the copy.

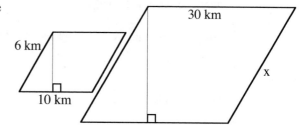

copy

RS-92. The two parallelograms at right are similar.

a) Find the missing length x.

b) Since neither height is given, you cannot calculate either area, but what is the <u>ratio</u> of the areas?

RS-93. Use dot paper to sketch a copy of the original figure shown at right. Label the dimensions.

a) Enlarge the figure by a ratio of $\frac{3}{1}$. Label the dimensions.

b) Write the ratio of one pair of corresponding sides in the order $\frac{copy}{original}$.

c) Calculate the perimeter of the copy and the original. Write and simplify the ratio of the perimeters in the order $\frac{copy}{original}$.

d) Calculate the area of the copy and the original. Write and simplify the ratio of the areas in the order $\frac{copy}{original}$.

RS-94. Solve for x.

a) $\frac{5}{8} = \frac{4x + 3}{24}$

b) $10x + 15 = 2x - 9$

c) $14x - 13 = 1 + 12x$

RS-95.   Complete the following table and graph the rule: y = -2x + 5.

x	-1	0	1	2	3	4
y						

RS-96.   The following data set contains the ages of the people living near Ray Sheo's ranch:
44, 51, 11, 21, 61, 46, 11, 55, 94, 72, 56, 15, 86, 43, 11, 33, and 23.

a)   Organize the data in order from the smallest to the largest.

b)   What is the range?

c)   Find the mean, median, and mode.

d)   Draw a box-and-whisker plot of the data.

e)   Which measure of central tendency is most useful for Ray Sheo's nephew, Rob, who is in fifth grade and hoping to have friends to play with when he visits the ranch? Explain.

RS-97.   Tofu burgers are on sale at the local Super Duper Grocery Mart at 27.5% off. The same tofu burgers are also on sale at Better Buy Supermarket at $\frac{1}{4}$ off the regular price.

a)   If a package of tofu burgers usually costs $3.59 at either store, where should Marisa shop to get the best price?

b)   What price will she pay?

RS-98.   Follow your teacher's instructions for practicing mental math. Try a new strategy today. What did you choose?

RS-99. One of the following triangles is a reduction of the other. Write and solve proportions for each of the parts below.

a) Find the length of side MN.

b) Find the length of side ML.

c) Find the ratio of the areas of the two triangles.

Original

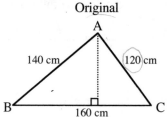

Copy

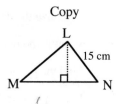

RS-100. △ABC and △DEF are similar.

a) Find x.

b) Find y.

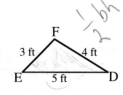

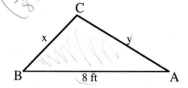

c) Find the ratio of the perimeters of the two triangles.

d) Find the ratio of the areas of the two triangles.

RS-101. Katie drew a parallelogram with a base of ten centimeters and a height of four centimeters. The other side of the parallelogram has a length of five centimeters.

a) Sketch the parallelogram that Katie drew. Label the dimensions.

b) Calculate the area and perimeter of Katie's parallelogram.

c) Katie's friend, Brooke, drew a parallelogram with every dimension three times larger. Calculate the area and perimeter of Brooke's parallelogram. Make a sketch of it if necessary.

RS-102.   The two triangles at right are similar.

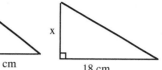

a)   Find x.

b)   Find the area of the smaller triangle.

c)   Based on ratios of similarity, use a proportion to find the area of the large triangle.

d)   Find the area of the larger triangle by using the formula for the area of a triangle.

e)   Verify that your answers to (c) and (d) are the same.

RS-103.   A triangle is enlarged by a scale factor of $\frac{10}{3}$.

a)   If the perimeter of the copy is 36 m, find the perimeter of the original triangle using the proportion $\frac{P_{copy}}{P_{original}} = \frac{10}{3}$.

b)   If the area of the copied triangle is 48 m², use a proportion to find the area of the original triangle.

RS-104.   Given two similar triangles, ΔABC and ΔDEF, use proportions to find:

a)   the perimeter of ΔDEF.

b)   the area of ΔDEF.

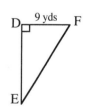

RS-105.   Use ratios of similar figures to answer the following questions.

a)   If you start with a 4-by-4 square and enlarge each side by a factor of $\frac{5}{4}$, calculate the perimeter and area.

b)   Sketch the 4-by-4 square and its $\frac{5}{4}$ enlargement. Was your answer from part (a) correct? Explain in complete sentences.

c)   Begin with a 6-by-9 rectangle and create a new smaller rectangle using a scale factor of $\frac{1}{3}$. Calculate the perimeter and area of the new rectangle.

d)   Sketch a 3-by-5 rectangle and a $\frac{3}{1}$ enlargement of the rectangle. Calculate the perimeter and area of the enlargement.

RS-106.   Identify the base and height, then find the perimeter and area of each figure below.

a)   b)

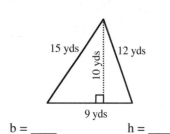

15 yds   10 yds   12 yds

9 yds

b = ____   h = ____

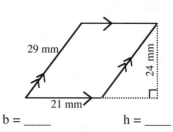

29 mm   24 mm

21 mm

b = ____   h = ____

RS-107.   Solve the following equations for x. Check your solutions.

a) $6x + 13 = 3x - 5$ b) $2 + 3x = 14 + 7x$

c) $12 + 7x = 5(x + 2)$ d) $\dfrac{3}{5} = \dfrac{x + 8}{20}$

RS-108.   Ray Sheo saw some socks on sale at the local department store. The advertised price was three pairs for $7.50.

a)   How much would he pay for one pair?

b)   How much would he pay for five pairs?

c)   How much would he pay for seven pairs?

RS-109.   Compute.

a) $\dfrac{4}{5} - \dfrac{2}{7}$ b) $\dfrac{18}{20} \cdot \dfrac{3}{2}$ c) $\dfrac{2}{3} + \dfrac{5}{8}$ d) $\dfrac{7}{9} \div \dfrac{3}{2}$

RS-110.   Complete the following Diamond Problems.

Product

Sum

a)

3.01   4.5

b)

$\frac{4}{3}$

3

c)

4

6

d)

3

4

RS-111.   In the polygons at right, all
           corresponding angles are the same and
           the side lengths are as shown.

           a) Find the ratios of the
               corresponding sides.

           b) Are the two figures similar?

           c) What is the special name for similar
               figures with a scale factor of $\frac{1}{1}$?

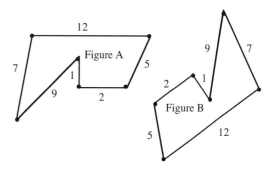

Figure A

Figure B

RS-112.   The scale factor of two similar figures is $\frac{5}{3}$. Write and solve a proportion to answer
           each of these questions.

           a)   If the perimeter of the smaller figure is 15 cm, what is the perimeter of the
                 larger figure?

           b)   If the area of the larger figure is 50 cm², what is the area of the smaller figure?

RS-113.   A pair of similar triangles is shown at right.

           a)   Write and solve a proportion to find x.

           b)   Find the area of each triangle.

           c)   Write the ratio comparing the area of the
                 small triangle to the area of the large triangle.

           d)   If you moved the smaller triangle on top of the larger
                 triangle as shown at right, would that change the
                 measurements or the ratios? Would it change the
                 solution for x? Explain.

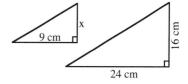

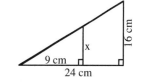

RS-114.   Examine the similar triangles at right. Decide if you want to
           compare the triangles as $\frac{\text{large}}{\text{small}}$ or as $\frac{\text{small}}{\text{large}}$.

           a)   Write and solve a proportion to find the missing leg of
                 the smaller triangle.

           b)   Find the area of each triangle.

           c)   Write the ratio comparing the area of the small triangle to the area of the large triangle.

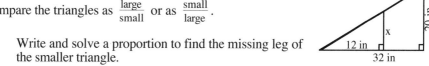

RS-115. Ray Sheo has a tall pine tree in his yard that is dying and needs to be cut down. Before he can cut it down, he needs to know how tall it is.

a) Ray decided to use what he knew about similar triangles to find the height of the tree. His first step was to stand so that the end of the shadow of the top of his head exactly matched the end of the shadow of the top of the tree. Then he measured the length of his shadow as 5 feet and the shadow of the entire tree as 65 feet. If you know that Ray is 6 feet tall, sketch and label a triangle diagram like the ones in the preceding problems. Use the information to label the parts of the diagram. Identify the two triangles.

b) Write a proportion and solve it to find the height of the tree.

RS-116. The biggest attraction at the new amusement park, World of Fun, is a huge slide that goes under the ground. To get to the top of the slide, Jon has to climb up a 56-foot ladder. Then he rides the slide to the bottom. Finally, Jon walks through a tunnel to the elevator and rides 35 feet to get back to ground level. The section of the slide that is above ground level is 77 feet long.

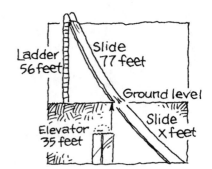

a) Use the similar triangles to find the length of the portion of the slide below ground level.

b) What is the total length of the slide?

RS-117. It is late in the day and Ray, who is 6 feet tall, casts a shadow that is 12 feet long. He is standing next to a flagpole that is 24 feet tall.

a) Sketch and label a diagram of this situation.

b) How long is the shadow of the flagpole? Explain your reasoning.

RS-118. Julia and her friend took the aluminum cans from the school recycling program and put them in five large paper bags. After school on Monday they took the cans to the recycling center and were paid a total of $12.50 for the five bags. On Tuesday they filled two more bags that were the same size as the others. How much should they expect to be paid for the two bags? Show all your work.

RS-119. Steve drives 65 miles per hour.

a) What is the ratio of miles to hours?

b) How many hours does it take for him to travel 130 miles from Portland to Tacoma?

c) How long will it take him to travel 390 miles?

d) How far can he travel in 4 hours?

e) How far can he travel in 8 hours?

RS-120. Name the four pairs of corresponding sides for these similar figures.

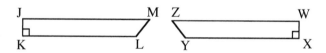

RS-121. Solve these proportions using cross multiplication. You may use a calculator, but you must show all your work.

a) $\dfrac{3 + x}{10} = \dfrac{4}{5}$

b) $\dfrac{2}{3} = \dfrac{4}{6 + x}$

c) $\dfrac{4 + x}{6} = \dfrac{3}{4}$

d) $\dfrac{8}{5} = \dfrac{2 - x}{7}$

RS-122. The problem "Simplify $\frac{2^4}{2^3}$" gave Mary and Katelyn some trouble.

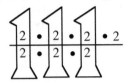

> *Mary:* The first part is easy. I'll write it without exponents. It's $\frac{2\cdot2\cdot2\cdot2}{2\cdot2\cdot2}$! But I'm stuck on the 'simplify' part.

> *Katelyn:* I see three Giant **1**s in that fraction, so it simplifies to 2.

a) Mary and Katelyn's work is shown above. Copy Mary's expanded fraction and draw Katelyn's Giant **1**s.

b) Simplify $\frac{2^4}{2^3}$ completely.

c) Use their example to simplify $\frac{3^6}{3^3}$.

RS-123. Jason was looking through his CD collection. When he sorted them by musical category, Jason found that he had 32 rock CDs, 27 classical, 18 jazz, 38 hip hop, 29 rap, 34 alternative, 78 oldies, 19 R & B, 24 gospel, and 11 country.

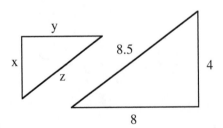

a) Make a stem-and-leaf plot of the CD data.

b) What is the mean number of CDs?

c) What is the median number of CDs?

d) What is the mode of the CDs?

RS-124. The original version of a textbook contained 1892 problems. The writers have decided to decrease the number of problems in the revised version by 23%. How many problems will they put in the revised book?

RS-125. These two similar triangles have a scale factor of $\frac{4}{3}$. Find the missing sides.

RS-126.   Use the similar figures to complete each of the parts below.

   a)   Side BC corresponds to side EF. To which
        side does side AB correspond?

   b)   To which side does side DF correspond?

   c)   Find the length of side DF.

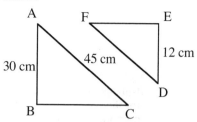

RS-127.   Ray Sheo, owner of the Pro-Portion Ranch,
          needs to build a bridge over the Roaring
          River that runs through his land. He has no
          idea how far it is across the river, but his
          daughter, Maria, knows she can find out by
          using the properties of similar triangles. Use
          the drawing at right and help Maria find the
          distance across the river.

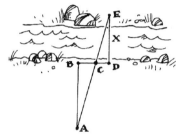

   In the diagram, the bridge is to go from D to
   E. Maria began by walking from D in a
   direction perpendicular to segment DE. After 6 feet she put a pole at point C and walked
   another 8 feet to point B. Then she turned away from the river and walked in a direction
   perpendicular to segment BD until she came to point A, which was 30 feet from point B.
   From there she could see that A, C, and E were all in a straight line. Her result was two
   similar triangles, ∆ABC and ∆EDC.

   a)   Sketch and label the figure on your paper. Be sure to include the measurements.
        Decide which parts of the two similar triangles correspond. You may want to re-
        draw the similar triangles so that they are facing the same direction.

   b)   Write a proportion and find the distance across the river.

   c)   The bridge will cost $1250 per linear foot. Calculate the complete cost of the bridge.

   d)   Ray also needs to build an approach to the bridge on each side of the river. It costs
        $17.50 per hour to operate the tractor he will need to do the work. Each approach takes
        five hours of work. How much will it cost to use the tractor to complete the work?

   e)   What is the total cost of the bridge?

RS-128.   Ray and Carmen Sheo need a new driveway 50 feet long in front of their house. The old
          driveway is 30 feet long and cost $3000. Write a proportion using $\frac{\text{cost in dollars}}{\text{feet}}$ and solve
          it to determine the cost of the new driveway. Remember to label the units.

RS-129. Ray Sheo rented the Mightee Ditch Digger so he could dig a trench for a sprinkler line. He can dig a trench 300 feet long in 2 hours. Use a proportion to find out how long it will take him to dig a trench 850 feet long.

RS-130. Isabella wants to draw a copy of a suspension bridge for the cover of her book. She wants the proportions to be correct. The real bridge has two towers which are 746 feet high (from C to D). The main span is 4200 feet long (from A to B). Isabella wants the main span of her copy to measure 21 inches long.

a) How tall will Isabella's copy be?

b) The midpoint of the roadway (point E) is 265 feet above the water. How high above the "water" will Isabella's copy be?

RS-131. Frederico wants to build a new house identical in every way except size to the house where he grew up. He wants his new house to be 1.75 times as big.

a) If his childhood home measures 50 feet long by 30 feet wide, what are the dimensions of his new house?

b) If the square footage of Frederico's childhood home is 2250 square feet (some parts of the house are two stories), what is the square footage of his new home?

RS-132. Use the circles at right to solve these problems.

a) Find the circumference of each circle.

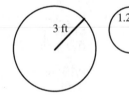

b) Find the ratio of circumferences, large to small.

c) Find the diameter of each circle.

d) Find the ratio of diameters, large to small.

e) Find the ratio of areas, large to small.

f) Are the relationships for ratios of similar polygons also true for circles? Explain.

RS-133.   Calculate the perimeter and the area of each of the figures.

a)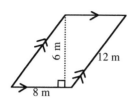

b)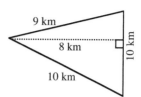

RS-134.   Combine like terms. Show all steps.

a) $3(x^2 + x) - 4x + 12x^2 - 21x + 5$ b) $-2 - 4 + 2x^2 + 60x + 5x(10 + x)$

c) $-2(10 + x) - 4 - 2x^2 + x + 5x^2$ d) $2x^2 + 60x + (-2x)(-1) + 3x - 6$

RS-135.   One day Sara, a fitness trainer, recorded the number of minutes her clients spent exercising so she could determine how long to make her classes.

42, 40, 52, 45, 55, 40, 61, 55, 50, 70, 67, 65, 37, 47, 34, 60, 59, 71, 36, 58, 33, 75, 77, 75, 35, 48

a)   Use the data above to make a stem-and-leaf plot.

b)   What is the range?

c)   What is the mode of the data?

d)   Which measure of central tendency provides the best information to help Sara plan the lengths of her classes? Explain.

RS-136.   Steve has collected 45 key rings, 25 yo-yos, and 5 CDs to be given as prizes at the school math fair. He wants to design a spinner where the chances of winning each prize are about the same as the number of prizes he has. Help him design the spinner.

a)   How many total prizes does he have?

b)   Write the number of each prize as a fraction of the total. Simplify each fraction.

c)   Use the simplified fractions from part (b) to design Steve's spinner.

RS-137.   Renata has a collection of 30 CDs, and she buys
          four new CDs each month. Her cabinet holds 150
          CDs. In how many months will Renata need a new
          cabinet for her CD collection?

          a)   Write a variable equation to represent the
               problem. A Guess and Check table might
               help you get started.

          b)   Solve the equation using algebra. Show all of
               your steps.

RS-138.   Mary was 4' 3" tall and weighed 85 pounds at the beginning of last year. Now she is 15%
          taller and 5% heavier. What are her height and weight now?

RS-139.   Follow your teacher's instructions for practicing mental math. Describe a method used
          by your partner or study team member.

RS-140.   **Chapter Summary** It is time to summarize and review
          what you have learned in this chapter. Your teacher will
          give you the format you will use.

RS-141.   Ray Sheo has two similarly shaped triangular plots of land. He needs to put some fencing
          around them. He knows the lengths of some of the sides, but he needs to know all the
          dimensions. Use the properties of similar triangles to find the unknown dimensions of
          the smaller plot of land.

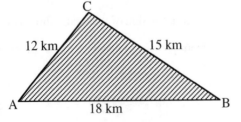

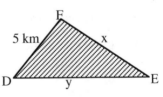

RS-142. Carmen Sheo is using a cake recipe that requires that the ratio of oil to water be $\frac{2}{3}$. If she needs $\frac{1}{2}$ a cup of oil, how much water does she need?

RS-143. Ray's son, Martin, plays for a minor league baseball team, the Cow-a-bungas. He is the star player, an outfielder with a batting average of 0.340. (Batting average is the ratio of the number of times a player gets a hit to the number of times at bat.) If Martin was at bat 570 times during the season, how many hits did he get? Remember that batting average is based on the number of hits out of 1000.

RS-144. A school cafeteria's recipe for making the day's supply of bread requires 20 cups of water for every 50 cups of flour. Write and solve a proportion to find the amount of water needed if the amount of flour is 60 cups.

RS-145. Light travels 186,000 miles per second. On average, the light from the moon takes $1\frac{1}{4}$ seconds to reach Earth. How far away is the moon?

RS-146. Each ratio below compares the circumferences of an enlarged or reduced circle to the original. Simplify each ratio by using a Giant **1** to avoid using the π key. State whether the new circle is an enlargement or a reduction.

a) $\frac{6\pi}{3\pi}$ b) $\frac{44\pi}{66\pi}$ c) $\frac{44\pi}{11\pi}$ d) $\frac{6\pi}{24\pi}$

RS-147. Zelda photocopied a rectangle that was 10 centimeters by 16 centimeters. She set the enlargement feature to 125%. Write proportions and solve them to find the new dimensions.

RS-148. Solve these proportions using cross multiplication. You may use a calculator, but you must show all of your steps.

a) $\frac{35}{70} = \frac{x}{100}$ b) $\frac{12}{33} = \frac{m}{11}$ c) $\frac{x}{15} = \frac{12}{75}$

d) $\frac{4}{32} = \frac{10.5}{x}$ e) $\frac{12}{32} = \frac{x+5}{100}$ f) $\frac{8}{3} = \frac{50}{y-7}$

RS-149. Lorca said she saved $5, which was 30% of the original price of the CD she bought.

a)   Set up a proportion that will allow you to find the original cost.

b)   Solve the proportion and find the original cost of the CD.

RS-150. The members of the Calculator Club at another school called two t-shirt vendors in their town. One store charges a fee of $55 plus $3.75 per shirt. The second store charges a $75 fee plus $2.50 per shirt. What number of t-shirts makes the total cost the same?

a)   Write an expression for the cost each company would charge for x t-shirts.

b)   Set the expressions equal to each other and solve algebraically to answer the question.

RS-151. Simplify each fraction by writing out all the factors first.

a) $\frac{42}{105}$ b) $\frac{27}{72}$ c) $\frac{35}{49}$

RS-152. Solve for x.

a) $2(x + 18) = 10$ b) $3(2x - 3) = -3$

c) $24 = 2(2x + 4)$ d) $3(2x - 1) = 9$

e) $4(2x + 1) = -28$ f) $2(x - 4) = x - 7$

g) $2(x + 8) = 3x - 3$

RS-153. **What We Have Done in This Chapter**

Below is a list of the Tool Kit entries from this chapter.

- RS-1   Congruent
- RS-3   A Ratio
- RS-6   Proportion
- RS-23   Solving Proportions with Cross Multiplication
- RS-32   Parallelogram Vocabulary
- RS-52   Area of Parallelograms, Triangles, and Trapezoids
- RS-62   Circumference of Circles
- RS-63   Area of Circles
- RS-75   Similarity and Scale Factors
- RS-88   Ratios of Similarity

Review all the entries and read the notes you made in your Tool Kit. Make a list of any questions, terms, or notes you do not understand. Ask your partner or study team members for help. If anything is still unclear, ask your teacher.

The Class Tournament

Chapter 7

Chapter 7

The Class Tournament:
DIVISION OF FRACTIONS, PERCENTS, AND FORMULAS

In this chapter you will extend your equation solving skills. You will apply these skills in several new situations and use formulas to help you solve problems.

In this chapter you will have the opportunity to:

- divide fractions.

- find percentages, both of increase and decrease.

- use formulas to solve problems.

- solve literal equations.

- solve equations that have a fraction as the coefficient of x.

Read the problem below. The class tournament will be held at the end of the chapter. Your teacher will let you know how to prepare for it.

CT-0.   It is time for the class mathematics tournament. You and your classmates will demonstrate the math proficiency you have been developing during the school year. Your assignment is to write math problems with their complete solutions and answer the math problems written by your classmates. The object of the tournament is to answer the problems correctly and earn as many points as you can for your team. Good luck!

Number Sense	
Algebra and Functions	
Mathematical Reasoning	
Measurement and Geometry	
Statistics, Data Analysis, & Probability	

Chapter 7
The Class Tournament:
DIVISION OF FRACTIONS, PERCENTS, AND FORMULAS

CT-1.   Copy the rectangles in part (a). Partition them into the given fractional parts. The first one has been done for you. You do <u>not</u> need to draw figures for parts (b) through (d).

a)

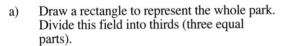

thirds   fourths   fifths

b)   If you draw a rectangle in which one-third of it is cut into 20 parts, how many parts are in the other two-thirds? How many parts is the whole rectangle cut into?

c)   If one-fourth of a rectangle is cut into 25 parts, how many parts are in three-fourths? How many parts is the whole rectangle cut into?

d)   If two-fifths of a rectangle is cut into 50 parts, how many parts are in three-fifths? How many parts is the whole rectangle cut into?

CT-2.   Solve the following equations for x.

a) $8x = 96$ b) $5x = 225$ c) $9x = 120$

d)   What operation did you use to solve each of these equations?

CT-3.   The Poppington Poppers are sponsoring a tournament. After much research, Nishi found a perfect park in which to hold the tournament. He found that it would cost $60 to rent one-third of the park.

a)   Draw a rectangle to represent the whole park. Divide this field into thirds (three equal parts).

b)   How much does it cost to rent each part?

c)   Suppose x represents the cost of renting the whole park. Write an equation that represents the situation.

d)   How much would it cost to rent the whole park? Explain how you know.

CT-4. Use the Three Way Table shown below to solve the following equations. Show three steps in your work: the fraction bar model, the equation for x from the model, and solving for x by division.

Fraction Bar	Equation for x from Model	Solving for x by Division

a) $\frac{1}{5} x = 95$ b) $\frac{1}{4} x = 56$

CT-5. Jon painted $\frac{1}{4}$ of the snack bar in 2 hours. He wanted to find how long it would take him to paint the whole snack bar.

a) Represent the situation using a Three Way Table.

b) How many hours does each part of the rectangle represent?

c) How long would it take Jon to paint the whole snack bar?

CT-6. Use a Three Way Table to solve the equation $\frac{2}{3} x = 70$. The picture at right represents this equation.

a) Copy the fraction bar on your paper. If $\frac{2}{3}$ represents 70, what does $\frac{1}{3}$ represent? Explain how you know.

b) What does x represent? Explain how you know.

CT-7. Merci has driven 100 miles, which is $\frac{1}{5}$ of the way to Salt Lake City from her house. What is the total number of miles from her house to Salt Lake City? Use a Three Way Table to solve this problem.

CT-8. Prepare your first card for the class tournament. Use the model provided by your teacher.

CT-9. Use a Three Way Table to solve the equations in parts (a) through (d). Show your work.

a) $\frac{1}{3} x = 65$ b) $\frac{1}{2} x = 43$

c) $\frac{1}{5} x = 75$ d) $\frac{1}{8} x = 25$

CT-10. What is the mean of 4, 8, 2, 6, 3, 4, 4, 5, and 9?

(A) 8   (B) 6   (C) 5   (D) 4

CT-11. The stem-and-leaf plot at right shows heights of corn plants, measured in centimeters, after a month of growth.

```
 0 | 6
 1 | 2
 2 |
 3 | 8
 4 | 5 9
 5 | 3 6 8 9 9
 6 | 0 2 5 6
 7 | 3 6 9
 8 | 0 2 9
 9 | 8 8 8 9
10 | 2 5
```

Key
1 | 2 means 12

a) Find the median.

b) Another corn plant's height is slightly greater than the median and is added to the plot. Without calculating, select the best result for each of the three problems below.

    i)   The median will: (A) Increase   (B) Decrease   (C) Stay the same

    ii)   The mode will: (A) Increase   (B) Decrease   (C) Stay the same

    iii)   The range will: (A) Increase   (B) Decrease   (C) Stay the same

CT-12. Solve for x. The variable y will be part of your answer.

    a) $10 + x = y$ b) $2x = 18 + 2y$ c) $2x - y = 8$

CT-13. Compute: $\dfrac{4^2 + 8}{3} - 3$

(A) -3   (B) 1   (C) -7   (D) 5   (E) none of these

CT-14. Complete the following Diamond Problems.

Product

Sum

    a)   b)   c)   d)   e)

CT-15. Mae and Joe baby-sit to earn spending money. Mae charges $20 for the evening and three dollars for every hour she baby-sits. Joe charges no flat rate, but his hourly fee is seven dollars an hour.

    a)   Write an expression for the cost of an evening of baby-sitting by Mae.

    b)   Write an expression for the cost of an evening of baby-sitting by Joe.

    c)   Set the expressions in part (a) equal to each other to find out after how many hours they would make the same amount of money.

    d)   If you were to choose a baby-sitter based on how much Mae and Joe charge, who would you choose and why?

CT-16. Now that we have started a new chapter, it is time for you to organize your binder.

    a)   Put the work from the last chapter in order and keep it in a separate folder.

    b)   When this is completed, write, "I have organized my binder."

CT-17. Study the following division problems and the diagrams that represent them. Answer the question below each diagram.

a) $8 \div \frac{1}{2}$ b) $8 \div \frac{1}{3}$

   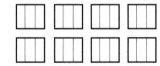

How many halves?   How many thirds?

c) $8 \div \frac{1}{4}$ d) $8 \div \frac{1}{5}$

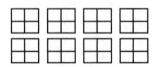   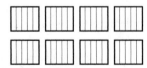

How many fourths?   How many fifths?

>>Problem continues on the next page.>>

e) $8 \div \frac{1}{6}$

f)   Use the idea from parts (a) through (e) to compute $8 \div \frac{1}{8}$ without drawing a picture. Explain how you get your answer.

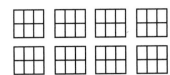

How many sixths?

CT-18.   Use your results from the preceding problem to write a multiplication problem that solves each division problem.

a) $24 \div \frac{1}{4}$

b) $8 \div \frac{1}{10}$

c) $12 \div \frac{1}{7}$

CT-19.   Set up a Three Way Table to solve the following equations. Show your work in each part. Below is an example that shows the steps involved in solving $\frac{1}{4}x = 18$.

Three Way Table

Fraction Bar Model	Equation for x from Model	Solving for x by Division
x $\frac{1}{4}$ 18 18	$x = 18 \cdot 4$ $x = 72$	$\dfrac{\frac{1}{4}x}{\frac{1}{4}} = \dfrac{18}{\frac{1}{4}}$ $x = 18 \div \frac{1}{4}$ $x = 72$

a) $\frac{1}{3}x = 24$

b) $\frac{1}{8}x = 12$

c) $\frac{1}{7}x = 10$

CT-20.   Multiply.

a) $\frac{1}{8} \cdot \frac{8}{1}$

b) $\frac{3}{4} \cdot \frac{4}{3}$

c) $\frac{2}{3} \cdot \frac{3}{2}$

d) $\frac{7}{1} \cdot \frac{1}{7}$

e)   The pairs of fractions in parts (a) through (d) are called **reciprocals**. Write three other pairs of reciprocals.

CT-21. Replace each x with the number that makes the sentence true. For part (d), rewrite the mixed number as a fraction greater than one before you find the correct value for x.

a) $\frac{1}{4} \cdot x = 1$

b) $\frac{1}{5} \cdot x = 1$

c) $x \cdot \frac{3}{8} = 1$

d) $x \cdot 2\frac{1}{4} = 1$

e) What is the result when a number is multiplied by its reciprocal?

CT-22.

| **RECIPROCAL or MULTIPLICATIVE INVERSE** |
| Two numbers with a product of 1 are called **RECIPROCALS** or **MULTIPLICATIVE INVERSES**. |
| Examples: The reciprocal of 3 is $\frac{1}{3}$; of $\frac{2}{5}$ is $\frac{5}{2}$; of $\frac{1}{7}$ is 7. |

Make these notes in your Tool Kit to the right of the double-lined box.

Why do you think the reciprocal is called the multiplicative inverse?

CT-23. Write the number shown and its reciprocal (multiplicative inverse).

a) $\frac{1}{5}$

b) $\frac{2}{3}$

c) 7

d) $\frac{4}{5}$

e) $1\frac{2}{3}$

f) $3\frac{1}{4}$

g) 1.5

h) 0.25

i) $\frac{x^2}{y}$

CT-24. Multiply each number and its reciprocal in the previous problem to verify that these numbers truly are reciprocals.

CT-25. Solve the following problems.

a) $0.93 - \frac{3}{8}$

b) $\frac{6}{10} + 3.8$

c) $6\frac{3}{5} - 3.6$

CT-26.   John has two six-sided dice. One is white; the other is green.

    a)   How many different ways are there for the two dice to land?

    b)   Make a complete outcome grid showing all the outcomes of rolling two dice. (Save this outcome grid in your notebook to use in future problems.)

Number on Green Die

		1	2	3	4	5	6
	1	1, 1	1, 2	1, 3	1, 4	1, 5	1, 6
Number	2	2, 1	2, 2	2, 3			
on	3	3, 1	3, 2				
White	4	4, 1					
Die	5						
	6						

CT-27.   Miranda called her favorite radio station to play the game "Yes or No and Why." Here is her question: "If Ray has a square plot of land that has an area of 100 square feet and all the sides are doubled, is the area also doubled? In other words, is the area now 200 square feet?"

    a)   How should Miranda answer, yes or no?

    b)   Sketch a diagram to prove your answer and explain why it supports the answer you gave in part (a).

CT-28.   Solve the following equations for x. Show your work.

    a) $2x - 3 = 5$ b) $3x + 1 = 8.5$ c) $6 = 6x - 1.2$

CT-29.   Solve the following equations. Show your work.

    a) $\dfrac{x}{4} = \dfrac{12}{16}$ b) $\dfrac{y}{12} = \dfrac{12}{144}$ c) $\dfrac{7}{n} = \dfrac{3.5}{100}$

CT-30.   Evaluate and compare. Use $>$, $<$, or $=$.

    a) $-9 + 4$ ___ $5 - 7$ b) $|-5 + 2|$ ___ $|6 - 3|$

    c) $14 - (-8)$ ___ $2 + -18$ d) $-7(-8)(-3)$ ___ $|-7(-8)(-3)|$

The Class Tournament: Division of Fractions, Percents, and Formulas

CT-31.   Prepare another card for the class tournament. Use the format given earlier.

CT-32.   Use the given diagrams to find x in parts (a) and (b).

   a) $x = \frac{1}{2} \div \frac{1}{4}$

        x indicates how many fourths there
        are in one-half.

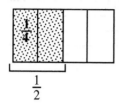

   b) $x = \frac{3}{2} \div \frac{1}{4}$

        x tells us how many fourths there are
        in three-halves.

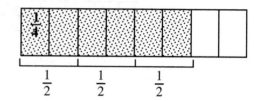

   c)   Is $\frac{1}{2} \div \frac{1}{4}$ equivalent to $\frac{1}{2} \cdot \frac{4}{1}$? Explain why your answer makes sense.

   d)   Is $\frac{\frac{1}{2}}{\frac{1}{4}}$ equivalent to $\frac{1}{2} \div \frac{1}{4}$? Why?

   e)   Is $\frac{3}{2} \div \frac{1}{4}$ equivalent to $\frac{3}{2} \cdot \frac{4}{1}$? Why?

   f)   Is $\frac{\frac{3}{2}}{\frac{1}{4}}$ equivalent to $\frac{3}{2} \div \frac{1}{4}$? Why?

CT-33.   Consider the steps shown below to solve the problem $\frac{1}{2}x = \frac{1}{3}$. Explain the mathematical
          process being done in each step.

   Step 1 $\dfrac{\frac{1}{2}x}{\frac{1}{2}} = \dfrac{\frac{1}{3}}{\frac{1}{2}}$

   Step 2 $x = \frac{1}{3} \div \frac{1}{2}$

   Step 3 $x = \frac{1}{3} \cdot \frac{2}{1}$

   Step 4 $x = \frac{2}{3}$

CT-34. Use the model in the previous problem to solve $\frac{1}{4}x = \frac{3}{4}$.

CT-35. Is there another way to solve the equation in problem CT-33? Demonstrate it.

CT-36. Riley and Tara are discussing how to simplify this expression: $\frac{1}{2} \div \frac{3}{4}$.

Riley's Solution:

$$\frac{1}{2} \div \frac{3}{4} \quad \Rightarrow \quad \frac{1}{2} \cdot \frac{4}{3} \quad \Rightarrow \quad \frac{4}{6} \quad \Rightarrow \quad \frac{2}{3}$$

Tara's Solution:

$$\frac{1}{2} \div \frac{3}{4} \quad \Rightarrow \quad \frac{\frac{1}{2}}{\frac{3}{4}} \quad \Rightarrow \quad \frac{\frac{1}{2}\cdot\frac{4}{3}}{\frac{3}{4}\cdot\frac{4}{3}} \quad \Rightarrow \quad \frac{\frac{4}{6}}{\frac{12}{12}} \quad \Rightarrow \quad \frac{\frac{4}{6}}{1} \quad \Rightarrow \quad \frac{2}{3}$$

a) Explain what Riley did to solve the equation.

b) Explain what Tara did to solve the equation.

c) Compare the two solutions above. How are they different?

CT-37. Solve the following problems using either Riley's or Tara's method. Show your work.

a) $\frac{2}{3} \div \frac{2}{5}$

b) $\frac{9}{7} \div \frac{3}{4}$

CT-38. Angela does not understand how to solve $\frac{2}{7}x = 12$. Jared claims that he found an easy way to solve this problem without even drawing pictures. He says, "All we have to do is multiply both sides of the equation by 7, because $7 \cdot \frac{2}{7}x$ is 2x, and $7 \cdot 12 = 84$, so the equation becomes $2x = 84$, which is simple to solve: $x = 42$.

a) Copy Angela's equation and discuss with your partner why Jared's method works.

b) Use Jared's method to solve $\frac{3}{4}x = 18$.

CT-39. Use Jared's method to solve the following equations. Show all steps.

a) $\frac{2}{3}x = 11$

b) $\frac{3}{4}x = 102$

c) $\frac{3}{10}x = 3.4$

d) $\frac{5}{8}x = \frac{1}{6}$

CT-40. Sarah started doing part (d) of the previous problem using Tara's method. However, she quickly got stuck. She wrote:

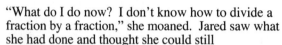

$$\frac{\frac{5}{8}x}{\frac{5}{8}} = \frac{\frac{1}{6}}{\frac{5}{8}}$$

$$x = \frac{1}{6} \div \frac{5}{8}$$

"What do I do now? I don't know how to divide a fraction by a fraction," she moaned. Jared saw what she had done and thought she could still complete the problem. He told Sarah, "Every time we could divide to solve our equations, we could also multiply to solve them. Can't we just rewrite the division as a multiplication problem using the reciprocal?"

Copy Sarah's work and complete it by rewriting the last step as multiplication using the reciprocal.

CT-41.

SOLVING EQUATIONS WITH FRACTIONAL COEFFICIENTS

Once an equation has been simplified so that the variable is isolated with a fractional coefficient, divide both sides by the fractional coefficient or multiply both sides by its reciprocal.

Example 1: $\frac{1}{4}x = 12$

Example 2: $\frac{3}{4}x = 12$

Solution A:

$$\frac{\frac{1}{4}x}{\frac{1}{4}} = \frac{12}{\frac{1}{4}}$$

$$x = 12 \div \frac{1}{4}$$

$$x = \frac{12}{1} \cdot \frac{4}{1}$$

$$x = 48$$

Solution B:

$$\frac{1}{4}x = 12$$

$$\frac{4}{1} \cdot \frac{1}{4}x = 12 \cdot \frac{4}{1}$$

$$x = \frac{48}{1}$$

$$x = 48$$

Solution A:

$$\frac{\frac{3}{4}x}{\frac{3}{4}} = \frac{12}{\frac{3}{4}}$$

$$x = 12 \div \frac{3}{4}$$

$$x = \frac{12}{1} \cdot \frac{4}{3}$$

$$x = \frac{48}{3} = \frac{16}{1}$$

$$x = 16$$

Solution B:

$$\frac{3}{4}x = 12$$

$$\frac{4}{3} \cdot \frac{3}{4}x = 12 \cdot \frac{4}{3}$$

$$x = \frac{48}{3} = \frac{16}{1}$$

$$x = 16$$

Make these notes in your Tool Kit to the right of the double-lined box.

a) Which solution method do you prefer? Why?

b) How are the methods the same?

CT-42. Solve the following equations. Put one of these examples in your Tool Kit.

a) $\frac{1}{4}x = \frac{1}{8}$

b) $\frac{1}{9}x = \frac{1}{3}$

c) $\frac{2}{3}x = \frac{5}{6}$

CT-43. Solve for x. Show your work.

a) $x = \frac{1}{2} \div \frac{1}{4}$

b) $x = 3 \div \frac{1}{3}$

c) $\frac{2}{3} \div \frac{5}{6} = x$

d) $3x - 24 = -15$

e) $6 = 6x - 18$

f) $4x - 7 = x + 5$

g) $2(x + 8) = -34$

CT-44. Travis rolls his socks together in pairs and keeps them in his drawer. He has four pairs of black socks, six pairs of white socks, one pair of blue socks, one pair of gray socks, and three pairs of brown socks. Because of a power outage, he must take a pair out of the drawer in the dark. What are his chances of getting a pair of brown socks? Express your answer as both a fraction and a percent. Show your work.

CT-45. Solve the following equations. Remember to distribute first.

a) $21 = (x + 3)2$

b) $3(2x - 2) = 2$

c) $4x - 5 = 4(2x - 3)$

d) $-2(x + 4) = 5(x - 1)$

CT-46. Complete the following Diamond Problems.

Product
◆
Sum

a)

b)

c)

d)

CT-47. Prepare another card for the class tournament.

DIVISION OF FRACTIONS

To divide fractions, multiply by the reciprocal of the divisor.

Example 1: $\dfrac{7}{6} \div \dfrac{2}{3} = \dfrac{7}{6} \cdot \dfrac{3}{2} = \dfrac{21}{12}$ or $\dfrac{7}{4}$

Example 2: $\dfrac{\frac{2}{3}}{\frac{5}{6}} = \dfrac{2}{3} \cdot \dfrac{6}{5} = \dfrac{12}{15}$ or $\dfrac{4}{5}$

Make these notes in your Tool Kit to the right of the double-lined box.

a)   Highlight the divisor in each of the examples.

b)   Rewrite example 2 as a division problem with a division sign ($\div$).

CT-49.   Write an equation or use a Guess and Check table to solve the following problem.

During one season, two apple trees and three pear trees produced a total of 126 pieces of fruit. Each apple tree produced the same number of apples, and each pear tree produced two more pieces of fruit than either apple tree. How many apples did each of Ray's apple trees produce in one season? Complete the table below and answer in a complete sentence.

CT-50.   Jon has $1500 in a special savings account that is earning interest at the **simple interest rate** of 3%. Jon will get 3% of $1500 (0.03 · $1500 = $45) in interest this year. At the end of the year, he will have $1545. Sometimes people are paid simple interest for more than one year. If Jon earned 3% simple interest for 5 years, he would have earned $45 · 5 = $225 in interest in that time.

The formula for the amount of money Jon would have after t years is $45t. In general, the formula is

$$A = P + I = P(1 + rt)$$

where:
- A stands for the amount of money at the end of t years.
- P stands for the principal, the amount of money Jon has now (P = $1500).
- I stands for the interest earned.
- r stands for the interest rate (r = 3% or 0.03).
- t stands for the time in years that the money has been in the account (t = 2 years).

a)   Use the formula to calculate how much money Jon will have after 2 years.

b)   Use the formula to calculate how much money Jon will have after 6 years.

CT-51.   Annie's goal is to have $2500 saved after two years. She has $2350 in the bank today. The bank will pay 3% simple interest on the money for two years. Will Annie reach her goal? Explain.

CT-52.   Samantha is twelve years old and has inherited $8000 from her grandfather to pay for college in six years. Her bank pays 5% **compound interest**. That is, the bank pays interest not only on the original principal, but also on the interest already earned.

a)   Complete the table to find out how much money Samantha will have at the end of each year.

Time (years)	Amount at Beginning of Year	Interest Paid	Amount at End of Year	Year-End Amount in Terms of Yearly Beginning Balance	Year-End Amount in Terms of Principal
1	$8000	$400	$8400	$8000 \cdot (1.05)$	$8000 \cdot (1.05)$
2	8400	420	8820	$8400 \cdot (1.05)$	$8000 \cdot (1.05)^2$
3				$1.05)$	$8000 \cdot (1.05)^3$
4				(1.05)	$8000 \cdot (1.05)^4$

b)   Where does the 1.05 come from?

c)   Use the pattern you see in the far right column to figure out how much money Samantha will have in 5 years. Then figure out how much money she will have in 6 years.

d)   Samantha's younger sister Tabitha got $5000 from her grandfather. She decides to put her money into a bank that pays 6% compound interest for 10 years. Write the formula to compute the total amount of money she will have after 10 years and use your calculator to find it.

CT-53.   From the previous problem, you know that the amount of money you have in a savings account that uses compound interest will be more than the amount of money you have in an account that uses simple interest. The formula for computing the amount of money in an account with compound interest is

$$A = P(1 + r)^t$$

where:
- A stands for the amount of money at the end of t years.
- P stands for the principal, the amount of money Samantha has now (P = $8000).
- r stands for the interest rate (r = 5% or 0.05).
- t stands for the time in years the money has been in the account (t = 6 years).

a)   Use the formula to calculate how much money Samantha will have after 3 years. Compare this with your answer from CT-52.

b)   Use the formula to calculate how much money Samantha will have after 5 years.

CT-54.   Mary wants to have $8500 for a car when she is 21. She has $6439 in a savings account earning 4% compound interest. Mary is 13 now.

a)   Use the formula to find out how much money Mary will have when she is 15. Use t = 2.

b)   How much money will Mary have when she is 17? Use t = 4.

c)   Will Mary have enough money for the car when she is 21? Use t = 8.

CT-55.   Randy and Rita are twins who are planning to enter college in five years. They have $2000 to put in a savings account. They can invest the money at 4.5% simple interest or at 4.3% compound interest. Which interest rate should they choose? Show your work to support your answer.

CT-56.   Randy and Rita's baby sister, Rachel, has been given $1000 to put into a savings account. Her parents have to decide whether to put the money in a bank that pays 6% simple interest or 5% interest compounded annually. Use the information on your resource page to graph the amount of money that Rachel would have in her account over the next 15 years until she leaves for college.

CT-57.

SIMPLE INTEREST

SIMPLE INTEREST is interest paid only on the original amount of the principal at each specified interval (such as annually). The formula is I = Prt, where I = Interest, P = Principal, r = rate, and t = time.

Example: Teresa invested $1425.00 (principal) in a savings account at her local bank. The bank pays a simple interest of 3.5% annually (rate). How much money will Teresa have after 4 years (time)?

$$I = Prt \quad \Rightarrow \quad I = (1425)(0.035)(4) = \$199.50$$

$$\Rightarrow \quad P + I = \$1425 + \$199.50 = \$1624.50$$

Teresa will have $1624.50 after 4 years.

Make these notes in your Tool Kit to the right of the double-lined box.

a)   How would you find how much money Teresa would have after 10 years?

b)   In the Tool Kit box containing the formula I = Prt, highlight the line that includes what each variable represents.

CT-58.

COMPOUND INTEREST

COMPOUND INTEREST is interest paid on both the original principal and the interest earned previously.

The formula for compound interest is $A = P(1 + r)^t$, where A = total amount including previous interest earned, P = principal, r = interest rate, and t = time.

Example: Teresa found another bank that paid 3.5% (rate) compounded annually. If she invests $1425.00 (principal), how much money will she have after four years (time)?

$$A = P(1 + r)^t \quad \Rightarrow \quad A = 1425(1 + 0.035)^4$$
$$\Rightarrow \quad 1425(1.035)^4 = 1425 \cdot 1.1475 = \$1635.22$$

Teresa will have $1635.22 after 4 years.

Make these notes in your Tool Kit to the right of the double-lined box.

Should Teresa have her interest compounded annually or should she receive simple interest? Why?

CT-59. Judd was curious. He asked, "How would you solve the equation: $\frac{1}{6}x = \frac{1}{2}$?" Show him how to solve for x and state its value.

CT-60. Solve the following equations for x.

a) $\frac{1}{16}x = \frac{1}{4}$

b) $\frac{1}{3}x = \frac{1}{4}$

CT-61. Consider Renzi's method for solving the following problem. Explain what he has done in each step to get his solution.

Step 1 $\quad \frac{5}{8} + 2\frac{3}{4}$

Step 2 $\quad \frac{5}{8} + \frac{11}{4}$

Step 3 $\quad \frac{11}{4} \cdot \frac{2}{2} = \frac{22}{8}$

Step 4 $\quad \frac{5}{8} + \frac{22}{8} = \frac{27}{8}$

Step 5 $\quad 3\frac{3}{8}$

CT-62. Follow the steps Renzi used to add the numbers in each problem.

a) $\quad 3\frac{3}{5} + \frac{7}{10}$

b) $\quad \frac{2}{3} + 4\frac{4}{9}$

c) $\quad \frac{2}{5} + 1\frac{3}{4}$

CT-63. Stacy and Noel are discussing whether or not Renzi's method would work with subtraction problems. Try these to find out.

a) $\quad 2\frac{1}{8} - \frac{1}{4}$

b) $\quad 4\frac{3}{10} - 1\frac{1}{5}$

CT-64.   Alisa was riding her bike home from the baseball field. She wondered how long it would take her to get to her house. She noticed she was $\frac{2}{3}$ of the way home after $\frac{1}{2}$ an hour.

a)   Write an equation to represent Alisa's problem.

b)   What is the reciprocal of $\frac{2}{3}$?

c)   Show that $\frac{2}{3}$ and $\frac{3}{2}$ are reciprocals. Use your Tool Kit entry for help.

d)   Solve Alisa's equation. How long will it take her to get home?

CT-65.   Prepare another card for the class tournament.

CT-66.   Complete the following fraction-decimal-percent triangles.

a)

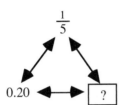

b)

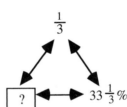

c)

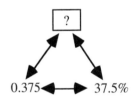

CT-67.   Solve each proportion for x. Show all your steps.

a) $\frac{3}{4} = \frac{84}{x-3}$

b) $\frac{x}{7} = \frac{3}{5}$

c) $\frac{x}{100} = \frac{5}{8}$

d) $\frac{21}{100} = \frac{x}{15}$

CT-68.   Erika, the head of the Booster Club, thinks the club can make money by selling shirts. She can buy a shirt for $6.00.

a)   Erika wants to mark up (increase) the price by 50%. How much would a shirt cost with a 50% increase?

b)   The Booster Club also sells caps. The club can buy a cap for $3.00. If the club sells a cap at a 50% increase, how much will they charge for a cap?

CT-69.   Snack bars make their profit by selling each product for more than its purchase price. The operators of a snack bar purchase products at wholesale prices. To determine the selling price of an item, they increase the wholesale price of it by a certain percentage. This amount of increase is the **markup**.

Snack	Wholesale Unit Price
Chips	$0.25
Pretzel	$0.25
Hot Dog	$1.00
Fruit Bowl	$0.70
Sunflower Seeds	$0.35
Popcorn	$0.55
Candy Bar	$0.38
Bottled Water	$0.25
Soda	$0.25
Coffee	$0.25
Sports Drink	$0.50

Steve, the Snack Bar Committee chairperson, wants to make a profit of at least 40% on each item. Some of the items and their wholesale unit prices are listed in the table at right.

Determining the **selling price** of a $0.25 bag of chips is a two-step process.

a)   Determine the amount of money represented by the 40% markup by finding 40% of $0.25.

$$\frac{\%}{100} = \frac{part}{a\ whole} \qquad \frac{40}{100} = \frac{m}{\$0.25}$$

b)   Add the markup to the wholesale price to determine the selling price.

CT-70.   Use the resource page or make a complete table. Use the work shown for the chips and the candy bar as a model. Show all of your work.

Item	Wholesale Unit Price	Markup at 40% Rate	Selling Price
Chips	$0.25	$\frac{40}{100} = \frac{m}{\$0.25}$ $m = \$0.10$	$0.25 + $0.10 = $0.35
Hot Dog	$1.00		
Fruit Bowl	$0.70		
Sunflower Seeds	$0.35		
Popcorn	$0.55		
Candy Bar	$0.38	$\frac{40}{100} = \frac{m}{\$0.38}$ $m = \$0.15$	$0.38 + $0.15 = $0.53

CT-71.   Listed below are four wholesale unit prices. Calculate each selling price if the wholesale unit prices will be marked up 70%. Show your work.

a) $0.85

b) $1.25

c) $2.40

d) $0.95

CT-72. Simplify the expressions. Write each whole number as a fraction greater than one, then add or subtract. Do not write your answers as mixed numbers; leave them in fraction form.

a) $2 + \frac{2}{3}$

b) $3 + \frac{2}{5}$

c) $5 - \frac{3}{4}$

d) $\frac{3}{8} - 2$

CT-73. Write an equation for each of the following fraction bar models. Then find x.

a)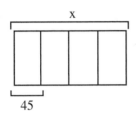

b)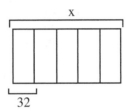

CT-74.

MARKUP and SELLING PRICES

The amount that the cost of an item will increase is called a **MARKUP**. This increase is based on a percentage of the cost.

The **SELLING PRICE** is the sum of the original cost and the markup.

Example:
The wholesale price of a pen is $0.70. To ensure a profit, Angela must mark up the wholesale price by 35%. Determine the markup and selling price.

$$\frac{\%}{100} = \frac{part}{a \ whole} \qquad \frac{35}{100} = \frac{m}{\$0.70} \qquad markup = \$0.2450 \approx \$0.25$$

$$selling \ price = wholesale + markup = \$0.70 + \$0.25 = \$0.95$$

In your Tool Kit highlight the two lines in the example that show how to find the markup and selling price.

CT-75. Solve for x. Show your work.

a) $\frac{1}{6}x = 25$

b) $\frac{2}{3}x = \frac{1}{2}$

c) $\frac{3}{4}x = 9$

d) $12x = 4$

CT-76. Look at the outcome grid you made in problem CT-26 for rolling one green and one white die. Ellen is playing a game that requires her to roll the two dice and add together the values shown.

a) What is the fractional probability that her sum would equal 2? In other words, find P(2).

b) P(3) = ?   c) P(4) = ?   d) P(5) = ?   e) P(6) = ?

f) P(7) = ?   g) P(8) = ?   h) P(9) = ?   i) P(10) = ?

j) P(11) = ?   k) P(12) = ?

l) Do the answers in parts (a) through (k) show all the possible ways for two dice to land? If you were to add the fractional probabilities, what should the sum be? Check your results above by adding the answers from parts (a) through (k). If the sum does not equal the number that you think it should, check your outcome grid for errors and add again.

CT-77. Solve for x.

a) $2x - 9 = 3$

b) $0.25x = 12$

c) $2x - 6 = 10$

d) $\dfrac{5}{7} = \dfrac{x + 2}{20}$

CT-78. Daniel has a scale drawing of his patio that he needs to paint. He knows the width of the patio is 10 feet, but the scale drawing is in inches.

a) Find the length of the patio. Show your steps.

b) Find the area of the patio so Daniel knows how much paint to buy.

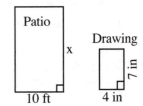

c) One can of patio paint covers 125 square feet. How many cans of paint will Daniel need?

CT-79. Joshua is saving $2 each week. If he starts with $5, how many weeks will it take for him to reach $34? Write an equation and solve it. A table or a graph may be helpful.

CT-80. Prepare another card for the class tournament.

CT-81. Follow your teacher's directions for practicing mental math.

CT-82. Consider which discount is better for each item.

a) Would you rather buy a $12 t-shirt that is advertised as 30% off or $\frac{1}{3}$ off? Why?

b) Would you rather buy a $50 glove that is advertised as 40% off or $\frac{1}{4}$ off? Why?

CT-83. Cheryl is the manager of a furniture store which is having a 25% off sale. Joyce is an employee and Rhonda is a customer. Cheryl and Joyce also receive employee discounts on their purchases. The **discount**, a percent or fraction of the original price, is subtracted to find the final cost of the item. Copy and complete the table showing each person's discount as a percent, a decimal, and a fraction.

	Cheryl's Discount	Joyce's Discount	Rhonda's Discount
Percent	50%		
Decimal		0.40	
Fraction			

CT-84. A rain coat costs $250. Find how much the coat will cost with the following discounts.

a) 50% b) 25% c) 10% d) 5%

CT-85.   Kathy, the snack bar manager, needs to determine the end-of-tournament sale prices. One of the items to be discounted by 25% is a $1.40 hot dog. She asked Myrna and Fern to calculate the discounted prices for her. Kathy was pleased to find that Myrna and Fern, with their math teams, had accurately calculated the discounts in two different ways.

Myrna's Team		Fern's Team	
25% of $1.40 x = discount amount		25% of $1.40 d = sale price	
$\dfrac{\%}{100} = \dfrac{part}{whole}$		$100\% - discount (\%)$	
$\dfrac{25}{100} = \dfrac{x}{\$1.40}$	1)_____	$100\% - 25\% = 75\%$	1)_____
x = $0.35	2)_____	$\dfrac{75}{100} = \dfrac{d}{\$1.40}$	2)_____
$1.40 − $0.35 = $1.05	3)_____	d = $1.05	3)_____
Sale price is $1.05.		Sale price is $1.05.	

a)   Explain what Myrna's team did in each of their steps (1 through 3) to find the sale price of the hot dogs.

b)   Explain what Fern's team did in each of their steps (1 through 3) to find the sale price of the hot dogs.

c)   Compare the two methods above. How are they different?

CT-86.   Find the discount and sale price of the items below. Round up to the nearest cent. Show your work. Use both methods from problem CT-85 for part (a). Use either method for parts (b) and (c).

a)   Price: $25.75   b)   Price: $5.99   c)   Price: $0.95
       Discount: 35%   Discount: 25%   Discount: 30%

CT-87.   Dave was a "shop-till-you-drop" kind of person and had a great time at the mall.

a)   He purchased a $45 tie at 40% off. Calculate the selling price. How much did he save?

b)   He purchased a pair of $65 pants at 30% off. Calculate the selling price. How much did he save?

c)   He also purchased an $84 dress for his wife at one-third off. Calculate the selling price. How much did he save?

d)   How much did Dave spend on all his purchases? How much did he save?

CT-88.

DISCOUNT AND SALE PRICE METHODS

Method #1

- Determine the percent of discount.
- Write a proportion.
- Calculate the discount by solving the proportion.
- Subtract the discount from the original selling price.

Your answer is the sale price.

Method #2

- Determine the percent of discount.
- Subtract the percent discount from 100%. This is the percentage to be paid.
- Write a proportion. Solve to find the sale price.

Your answer is the sale price.

Example: Find the sale price of a $55 shirt sold at a 25% discount.

Method #1:

$$\frac{25}{100} = \frac{x}{55}$$

$$(100)(x) = (55)(25)$$

$$100x = 1375$$

$$x = \$13.75 \text{ (discount)}$$

$$\$55 - \$13.75 = \$41.25 = \text{sale price}$$

Method #2:

$$100\% - 25\% = 75\%$$

$$\frac{75}{100} = \frac{x}{55}$$

$$(100)(x) = (55)(75)$$

$$x = \$41.25$$

In your Tool Kit highlight the steps in the method you will use.

CT-89.   Find the sale price of a $ 0.65 bag of peanuts sold at a 30% discount. Do the problem twice, using each method once.

The Class Tournament: Division of Fractions, Percents, and Formulas   273

CT-90.   Find the new sale prices for the following snack bar items. For the final few hours of the tournament, the discount will be 45%. Round your answer to the nearest cent.

a)   Chips: $0.35   b)   Hot Dog: $1.40

c)   Popcorn: $0.77   d)   Candy Bar: $0.53

e)   Do these seem like prices a snack bar would charge? Why or why not? What do you think the snack bar manager would do about the awkward prices?

CT-91.   Kaitlin's family spent $60.25 at the fair. If it cost $10 for all of them to get in, and the tickets for the rides were $0.75 each, how many rides did the family go on? Write and solve an equation to represent this problem. Be sure to answer in a complete sentence.

CT-92.   Find the perimeter and area of the two triangles below.

a)   b)

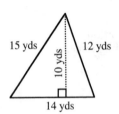

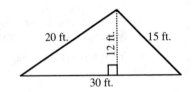

CT-93.   Write the reciprocal of each of the following numbers.

a)   5   b) $\frac{4}{5}$ c) $\frac{6}{7}$

d) $\frac{2}{3}$ e)   7   f) $1\frac{1}{3}$

CT-94. Rob lives in northern Arizona and recorded the following high and low temperatures for a two-week period last winter. (Temperatures are recorded in degrees Celsius.)

Day	1	2	3	4	5	6	7	8	9	10	11	12	13	14
Low Temperature	-8	-6	-6	-5	-2	4	12	10	8	0	-1	-3	-9	-8
High Temperature	4	6	8	8	10	10	16	16	15	9	4	6	-1	-5

a) Find the mean, median, and mode for the low temperatures.

b) Which average best represents the low temperatures? Explain.

c) Find the range for the low temperatures. What does the range indicate about the temperatures?

d) Find the range, mean, median, and mode for the high temperatures.

CT-95. Prepare another card for the class tournament.

CT-96. A regular newspaper measures 60.96 centimeters by 38.1 centimeters. The largest newspaper was the *HetVolk*, printed in Belgium in 1993. It measured 142 centimeters by 99.5 centimeters. How many times larger was the area of *HetVolk* than a regular newspaper?

CT-97. Solve the following problems.

a) Eight is what percent of 40?

b) Fifteen is 30% of what number?

c) What is 42% of 87?

d) Sixteen is what percent of 157?

CT-98. Find the <u>differences</u> between the following values.

a) 217 and -198

b) $1\frac{2}{3}$ and $\frac{3}{4}$

c) $0.59 and $1.25

CT-99.   Myrna and Fern's teams are practicing for the class tournament by giving each other problems to solve. Each team solved this problem: A shirt purchased wholesale for $15 has been marked up 80%. What is the new price?

Myrna's Team

$$\frac{80}{100} = \frac{x}{\$15.00}$$

$$100x = 1200$$

$$x = \$12.00$$

$$\$15.00 + \$12.00 = \$27.00$$

Fern's Team

$$100\% + 80\% \text{ (increase)} = 180\%$$

$$\frac{180}{100} = \frac{x}{15.00}$$

$$100x = 2700$$

$$x = \$27.00$$

a)   Compare the two solution methods. How are they different? Explain in complete sentences.

b)   How are the methods above similar to those used in problem CT-85? How are the methods different? Explain in complete sentences.

c)   Which method do you prefer? Why? Explain in complete sentences.

CT-100.    Duane is an old-timer who helps out around the baseball field. Melissa started talking to him and discovered some interesting facts. When Duane was a child, frozen juice bar were 2¢. Now they are 60¢. Matinee movies were $0.75. Now they are $4.50. Bread was 24¢ for a small loaf. Now it is $2.19. Gasoline was 19¢ per gallon. Now it is $1.58 per gallon.

Below is how to find the percent increase of a frozen juice bar.

1)   Find the amount of increase: 60¢ − 2¢ = 58¢

2)   Set up a proportion to find the percent, following the formula:

$$\frac{58 \text{ (amount of increase)}}{2 \text{ (original price)}} = \frac{x \text{ (percent)}}{100}$$

3)   Solve the proportion: $58 \cdot 100 = 2x \Rightarrow 5800 = 2x \Rightarrow 2900 = x$

The price of this frozen juice bar has increased by 2900%!

Find the percentage increase for the other items listed above.

CT-101. Sometimes prices go down. Duane remembers when he bought his first calculator for $110. If calculators are now available for $5.75, what is the percentage decrease? Remember to compare the difference to the starting amount.

CT-102. Mighty Max weighed in at 135 pounds for wrestling. By the time the season ended, he weighed 128 pounds. What was the percentage decrease of his weight?

CT-103. Find the percentage increase or decrease of each of the following items:

Item	Original Price	Current Price	Percentage Increase or Decrease
Milk	$0.25	$2.25	
Candy Bar	5¢	55¢	
Computer	$2000	$1200	
Hamburger	19¢	89¢	

CT-104. What is the meaning of a percentage increase that is greater than 100%?

CT-105.

PERCENTAGE INCREASE OR DECREASE

Determine the amount of increase or decrease, then set up a proportion and solve for the percentage.

$$\frac{\text{amount of increase or decrease}}{\text{original price}} = \frac{\text{x (percent)}}{100}$$

Example 1:

Bread increased from $0.29 to $2.89.

$2.89 - 0.29 = $2.60

$$\frac{x}{100} = \frac{\$2.60}{\$0.29}$$

$0.29x = 260$

$x \approx 897\%$

Example 2:

Phones decreased from $59 to $4.95.

$59 - \$4.95 = \$54.05

$$\frac{x}{100} = \frac{\$54.05}{\$59}$$

$59x = 5405$

$x \approx 92\%$

Highlight the proportion you use to find the amount of increase or decrease in your Tool Kit.

CT-106. A tank top decreased in price from $12.50 to $10.50. What is the percentage decrease?

CT-107. The town's population has grown from 11,567 to 28,760 over a period of fifteen years. By approximately what percent has the town grown in that time?

CT-108. One item for sale in the snack bar is a miniature glove that gets larger when soaked in water. The package says its size increases 600%. If the glove is two inches long, how long will it be once it is put in water?

CT-109. Carol is buying a hat for $9.95 with a sales tax of 5%. What will be the total cost after the tax is added?

CT-110. Complete the following table.

Problem	What is missing? (part, whole, or %)	Write a proportion.	Solve for x.
What percent of 70 is 14?			
Twelve is 3% of what number?			
25% of 48 is what number?			

CT-111. Prepare another card for the class tournament.

CT-112.

> # FORMULAS
>
> A **formula** is a shorthand way of writing a general mathematical statement or rule. When writing formulas, variables are assigned to represent the various parts of the rule or statement.

Write a formula for each of the following statements in your Tool Kit to the right of the double-lined box.

a) One-sixth of your Earth weight is your weight on the Moon. Let e represent Earth weight and m represent Moon weight.

b) Distance is equal to the rate of speed times the time it takes to travel. Use d for distance, r for rate of speed, and t for the time it takes to travel.

c) The interest (dollars you earn) for a savings account that pays simple interest is equal to the amount of money deposited (principal) times the percentage rate times the amount of time the money is invested. Use I for interest, P for principal, r for rate, and t for time.

d) The circumference of a circle is the product of the diameter and π. Use C for circumference and d for diameter.

e) A batting average is found by taking the total hits made and dividing it by all of the times at bat (excepting walks, hit batters, and sacrifices). Use H for hits and AB for times at bat.

CT-113. Sometimes an equation has two or more variables. Look at each pair of problems below. How are they alike? How are they different? In each equation the goal is to solve for x. Work with a partner and solve each equation. Assume that none of the variables equal zero.

a) $5x + 4 = 14$ and $mx + 4 = 14$

b) $2x + 5 = 6$ and $nx + 5 = 6$

c) $3x - 8 = 16$ and $cx - 8 = 16$

CT-114. Solve the equations below. For equations with more than one variable, you may want to circle the variable for which you are solving. This will help remind you that it is the variable you want left by itself.

a) Solve for x: $\$6.25x = \$50$.

b) Solve for x: $\$6.25x = y$.

c) Solve for r: $D = rt$

d) Solve for d: $C = \pi d$

e) Solve for y: $x = ay$

f) Solve for r: $d = 2r$

g) Solve for a: $F = ma$

CT-115. Look back in your Tool Kit and find the formula for the area of a trapezoid.

a) Write the formula for the area of a trapezoid.

b) Find the area of the trapezoid at right.

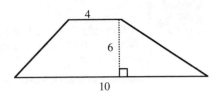

CT-116. Calculate the area of each of these trapezoids. Show all your steps.

a)

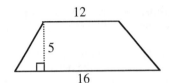

b)

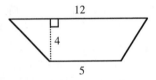

CT-117. Work with your partner. Give your partner step-by-step instructions for how to solve part (a), and he or she will record what you say. Exchange roles for part (b).

a) $6x + 36 = 150$

b) $\$3.65x + \$0.25 = \$11.20$

CT-118. Perform the following unit conversions. Remember you can use your Tool Kit.

a) Explain how to convert 72 inches into feet.

b) Explain how to convert 192 ounces into pounds.

c) Tim wrote, "To change feet into miles, multiply by 5,280." Carolan said, "Tim, you're way off! You divide by 5,280." Who is correct? How do you know?

CT-119. Use the equation $y = 2x + 3$ to find the values for y in the table below.

x	-3	-1	0	2	4
y					

a) Graph it.

b) What is the x-intercept?

c) What is the y-intercept?

CT-120. Solve for x.

a) $4x + 6 = 26$

b) $ax + 6 = 26$

c) $15x = 135$

d) $gx = 135$

e) $\$0.25x + \$4.50 = \$14.75$

f) $\frac{5}{6}x = 35$

CT-121. A box contains 15 yellow, 15 orange, and 15 green tennis balls. If Izzy draws a tennis ball at random out of the box, what is the probability that he drew either a green or an orange tennis ball? Show your work and express your answer as a percent.

CT-122. Find the designated areas of the following circle. The shaded region is one-eighth of the circle.

a) What is the area of the unshaded region of the circle?

b) What is the area of the shaded region?

c) In a few sentences explain each of the steps you followed to answer parts (a) and (b).

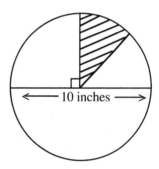

10 inches

CT-123. Solve for x.

a) $45x = 630$

b) $2(48 + x) = 160$

c) $0.32x = 175$

CT-124. Solve for the indicated variable.

a) Solve for w :

$s = w + m$.

b) Solve for t :

$d = rt$.

c) Solve for b :

$A = \frac{1}{2}bh$.

CT-125. Prepare another card for the class tournament.

CT-126. Write down the positive integers as shown below. Which column will contain the number 500 ?

$$\begin{array}{ccc} 1 & 2 & 3 \\ 6 & 5 & 4 \\ & 7 & 8 & 9 \\ 12 & 11 & 10 \end{array}$$

CT-127. Follow your teacher's directions for practicing mental math. Write the new strategy you learned.

CT-128. Howie is driving from Minneapolis to Indianapolis. He plans to drive 65 miles per hour. How far can he travel in 7 hours? Copy and complete the table below.

Time (hours)	1	2	4	7	9
Distance (miles)					

a) Do you see a pattern in the table to help you find a rule? What was your rule or formula? Write it in the form "Distance Traveled = ..."

b) If Minneapolis is 575 miles from Indianapolis, how long will it take him to drive there at 65 miles per hour?

c) If Howie drove 70 miles per hour for 7 hours, how far would he travel?

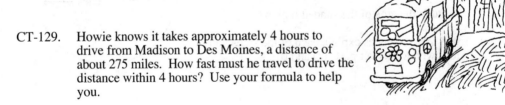

CT-129. Howie knows it takes approximately 4 hours to drive from Madison to Des Moines, a distance of about 275 miles. How fast must he travel to drive the distance within 4 hours? Use your formula to help you.

a) What is t ?

b) What is d ?

c) Fill in the numbers you know and solve your equation to let Howie know how fast he has to drive.

CT-130. Next year, teams will be invited to a math tournament from all over the state. To help them decide if they want to enter the tournament, a driving distance time chart will be included in the announcement.

Copy the driving distance time chart and use the formula you wrote in problem CT-128 to fill in the missing information.

City	Distance (miles)	Rate of Speed (mph)	Time (hours)
West Valley		70	4.5
Willow Springs	183	70	
Center City	247		3.8
Highland Park	48	60	

CT-131. Your teacher recently announced that the class mathematics tournament would take place in a few days. You and your classmates have had the opportunity to demonstrate the math proficiency you have been developing over the school year by writing math problems with their solutions. The object of the tournament is to answer the problems correctly to earn as many points as you can for your team.

Tomorrow is the tournament day! Follow the instructions below to prepare for the tournament.

a) Using the review cards you have created throughout this chapter, select the two cards you think are your best. Make sure that your solutions are correct and complete.

b) Exchange these cards with a partner. Help each other ensure that all the information and the solutions on your cards are correct.

c) Work together to select the best cards from the team to give to your teacher. Your teacher will tell you how many cards to select.

d) Give these cards to your teacher.

e) Write "Cards have been selected" on your paper.

CT-132.

DISTANCE, RATE, TIME

DISTANCE (d) equals the product of the rate of speed (r) and the time (t).

$$d = r \cdot t$$

Example: Find the rate of speed of a passenger car if the distance traveled is 572 miles and the time elapsed is 11 hours.

$$572 \text{ miles} = r \cdot 11 \text{ hours} \implies \frac{572 \text{ miles}}{11 \text{ hours}} = \text{rate} \implies 52 \text{ miles/hour} = \text{rate}$$

Make these notes in your Tool Kit to the right of the double-lined box.

Give two real-world examples when you could use this distance formula.

CT-133.　Solve the following problems.

　　　a)　Find the time if the distance is 157.5 miles and the speed is 63 mph.

　　　b)　Find the distance if the speed is 67 mph and the time is 3.5 hours.

CT-134.　Find the batting average for Dynamic David. He had 20 hits in 62 at bats.

CT-135.　Solve the problems below.

　　　a)　$\frac{3}{8} x = 12$　　　b)　$\frac{5}{6} \div \frac{2}{5}$　　　c)　How much is a markup of 25% on a price of $6.99?

CT-136.　A triangular shaped playground has a height of 23 meters and a base of 32 meters. Write the area formula for a triangle and use this to determine the area of the playground.

CT-137.　Ellen is playing a game that requires her to roll two dice and add them together. Use the outcome grid you made in problem CT-26 for rolling one green die and one white die to answer the following questions.

　　　a)　What is the probability of rolling 7 or larger? P(7 or larger) = ?

　　　b)　What is the probability of rolling 6 or less? P(6 or less) = ?

　　　c)　What is the probability of rolling an odd or an even number? P(even or odd) = ?

　　　d)　What is the probability of rolling 1? P(1) = ?

　　　e)　What is the probability of rolling 4 or 5? P(4 or 5) = ?

　　　f)　Trixie wants to play a game in which she wins with a sum of 3 or 6 and you win with a sum of 2 or 12. She says this is fair because you both have two winning numbers. Is this game fair? Explain.

CT-138. Use the resource page or copy the table below, then simplify each fraction by eliminating Giant **1**s. Rewrite your answer using exponents if necessary. The first one is done for you.

	Original Expression	Eliminate Common Factors	Simplified Expression
a)	$\dfrac{6 \cdot x \cdot x}{3 \cdot x \cdot x \cdot x \cdot x}$	$\dfrac{2 \cdot \cancel{3} \cdot \cancel{x} \cdot \cancel{x}}{\cancel{3} \cdot \cancel{x} \cdot \cancel{x} \cdot x \cdot x}$	$\dfrac{2}{x^2}$
b)	$\dfrac{x \cdot x \cdot x}{x}$		
c)	$\dfrac{21 \cdot x \cdot x \cdot x}{7 \cdot x}$		
d)	$\dfrac{a \cdot a \cdot a \cdot b}{a \cdot b}$		
e)	$\dfrac{16\pi r^2}{4r}$		

CT-139. Rewrite the following products using exponents.

a) $4y \cdot 4y \cdot 4y \cdot 4y$

b) $3x \cdot 3x \cdot 3x$

c) $4a \cdot 3a$

d) $3ab \cdot 4ab^2$

CT-140. **Rules for the Class Tournament**

Your teacher will assign you to a team and give you a color-coded card with a number. The color represents your team. The number is your player number. When the teacher calls your number, it will be your turn to work with another student on your team to answer a question correctly.

Your teacher will assign your team a space on the chalk or white board. Be sure you work in that space only. Follow all rules concerning replacing the chalk or marker, circling the answer, and erasing your work after the points have been awarded. You will lose points if you forget.

• Appoint a scorekeeper for your team.

• When you are a member of the audience, remember that yelling or blurting out an answer will cause your team to lose points.

• Your teacher will tell you how many points will be awarded for correct solutions and how many points will be deducted for not following the rules.

• Consult with your teammates and make sure you all understand the answer. Remember to ask the teacher for clarification if you all have the same question.

• If there are no further questions, you are ready to play. Good luck!

CT-141. To promote the tournament Ida made a rectangular banner with a length of 320 centimeters and a width of 450 centimeters. Then other students made more flags based on Ida's. For each of the other flags, calculate the new dimensions, then calculate the new perimeter and area.

a) Each dimension of Amy's flag is 25% larger than Ida's.

b) Each dimension of Maria's flag is 30% smaller than Ida's.

c) Each dimension of Kristyn's flag is $1\frac{1}{2}$ times larger than Ida's.

CT-142. Design a dart board for a dart tournament that meets the following conditions.

a) $\frac{1}{4}$ is red

b) 15% is green

c) 0.4 is yellow

d) the rest is blue

e) If you threw 100 darts and they all hit the board, what is the probability of hitting:

   i) red?   ii) green?   iii) yellow?   iv) blue?

f) If you threw 120 darts and they all hit the board, how many darts would hit each color?

   i) red   ii) green   iii) yellow   iv) blue

CT-143. Anita charges $12.00 to mow her neighbor's lawn. Whenever her neighbor wants additional work done on the yard, Anita charges $4.50 per hour. How many extra hours did she work if the total amount she charged the neighbor was $43.50? Write and solve an equation to answer the question.

CT-144. Anita's mother insists that she put 30% of her earnings into a college fund. Find the total amount she puts into the fund for 3 mowings and five extra hours of yard work.

CT-145. Solve for x. Show your work.

a) $x + 32 = 5x - 12$

b) $100 = 5(2x + 9)$

c) $10x = 2(x + 4)$

d) $4(3x - 8) = 2x + 21$

CT-146. You decide to visit the Mathematical Amusement Park again on a special plan. Your choices are Plan 1, in which you pay $7.50 to enter the park and $1.10 per ride, or Plan 2, in which you pay $12.50 to enter the park and $0.60 per ride. Write an equation to determine the number of rides that would make the total cost equal for the two plans. Then solve the equation.

CT-147. There are 18 chocolate chip cookies, 12 oatmeal cookies, and 10 raisin cookies in a cookie jar. If Miguel takes a cookie from the jar without looking, what is the probability that he does <u>not</u> get a chocolate chip cookie? Show work to support your answer.

CT-148. Kirby has $75 in a savings account. He had only $55 in the account 4 weeks ago. He wants to buy a guitar for $185. Assume he has been saving the same amount of money each week.

a)   At what rate is he saving money each week?

b)   Copy the data table below and fill in the account totals for each week.

Time (x) in weeks	-4	-3	-2	-1	0	1	2	3
Amount (y) in dollars	$55				$75			

c)   Graph this situation.

d)   Use the table or the graph to determine when the amount in his account will be $185.

e)   Determine when Kirby started saving money.

CT-149. Find the following distances, rates, or times.

Distance	Rate of Speed	Time
	45 mph	1.5 hours
362 miles	68 mph	
128 miles		2.5 hours
72 miles		$\frac{3}{4}$ hours

CT-150. A rectangle is graphed so that two of the sides are on the x- and y-axes and the vertex opposite the origin is at (-4, 6). Graph the rectangle.

a) In which quadrant is the rectangle?

b) What are the dimensions of the rectangle?

c) If the dimensions are increased by 40% and two sides of the rectangle stay on the x- and y-axes, what are the coordinates of the vertex opposite the origin?

d) What is the percentage increase of the perimeter and the percentage increase of the area?

CT-151. A floor plan for the snack bar is shown at right, but it is too large. Reduce the figure by reducing all the measurements by 30%. (All measurements are given in feet.) Then calculate the percentage decrease of the new area.

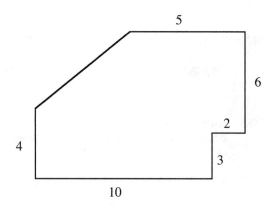

CT-152. **What We Have Done in This Chapter**

Below is a list of the Tool Kit entries from this chapter.

- CT-22   Reciprocal or Multiplicative Inverse
- CT-41   Solving Equations with Fractional Coefficients
- CT-48   Division of Fractions
- CT-57   Simple Interest
- CT-58   Compound Interest
- CT-74   Markup and Selling Prices
- CT-88   Discount and Sale Price Methods
- CT-105   Percentage Increase or Decrease
- CT-112   Formulas
- CT-132   Distance, Rate, Time

Review all the entries and read the notes you made in your Tool Kit. Make a list of any questions, terms, or notes you do not understand. Ask your partner or study team members for help. If anything is still unclear, ask your teacher.

Gold Strike!
at Dried Up Creek

Chapter 8

Chapter 8
Gold Strike At Dried-Up Creek:
THE PYTHAGOREAN THEOREM, SURFACE AREA, AND VOLUME

In this chapter you will work with right triangles and use them to solve complex problems. You will also work with cubes and nets to learn about surface area and volume.

In this chapter you will have the opportunity to:

- identify right triangles.

- develop and use the Pythagorean Theorem.

- use the technique of subproblems to solve complex problems.

- find the surface area and volume of prisms and cylinders.

Read the problem below, but **do not try to solve it now**. What you learn over the next few days will enable you to solve it.

GS-0.   **The Mine Shaft**

Sourdough Sam was given a gold mine. To get the gold, Sourdough Sam's mining company will build a sturdy entry platform for the new mine shaft. The platform will be a rectangular prism 4 feet high with a base 20 feet by 15 feet. The concrete for the platform will be poured around a cylindrical hole 6 feet in diameter. The miners will be lowered through the hole to get to the vein of gold. Sam needs to know how many cubic feet of concrete to order and how much it will weigh.

Number Sense	
Algebra and Functions	
Mathematical Reasoning	
Measurement and Geometry	
Statistics, Data Analysis, & Probability	

Chapter 8
Gold Strike At Dried-Up Creek:
THE PYTHAGOREAN THEOREM, SURFACE AREA, AND VOLUME

GS-1.   Calculate.

a) $3^2 + 4^2$ b) 5^2 c) $5^2 + 12^2$ d) 13^2

GS-2.

RIGHT TRIANGLES

A **RIGHT TRIANGLE** is a triangle in which the two shorter sides form a right angle. The shorter sides are called **LEGS**. Opposite the right angle is the third and longest side called the **HYPOTENUSE**.

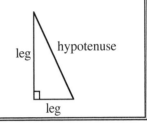

Make these notes in your Tool Kit to the right of the double-lined box.

a)   Highlight "the shorter sides are called legs" and "longest side called the hypotenuse."

b)   How many degrees are in a right angle?

GS-3.   Mr. Wrangler gave each of his sons, Luke and Duke, square-shaped property around triangular lakes. He knew Luke wanted more shoreline, so he gave Luke two smaller pieces on the shorter sides of the lakes. Duke wanted less shoreline and lots of wide open space. Therefore, his father gave him the big square of land on the long side. Luke was sure he had more land because he had two pieces of land on each lake. Duke's piece on the lake was largest, so he was sure he had more.

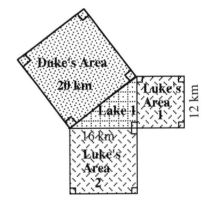

Using the diagram at right, help Luke and Duke settle their disagreement.

a)   What shape is the lake?

b)   Copy the table below. You will also need this table for the next problem. Find the area of each square around Lake 1. Record the data in the table.

c)   Compare the sum of the area of Luke's land with the area of Duke's land. Was it split fairly?

Lake	Luke's Areas			Duke's Square Area
	Square 1	Square 2	Total Area	
1				
2				
3				

GS-4.   Luke and Duke received property around two other lakes on the Wrangler property.
          Their land here is shaped like the property around Lake 1.

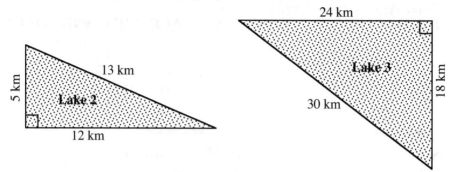

a)   Draw Lakes 2 and 3 and sketch the surrounding square plots of land. Remember
       that Luke has two pieces of land on the shorter sides of each lake. Duke has one
       piece of land on the longest side of each lake. Label each plot of land with the name
       of the owner. What is the shape of each lake?

b)   Find the area of each square around Lakes 2 and 3. Record the data in the table
       from the previous problem.

c)   Compare the sum of the areas each brother received. Was the land split fairly?

GS-5.   Mr. Wrangler used a formula to ensure the land would be split fairly. The formula
          describes the relationship between the legs and hypotenuse of any right triangle.
          Answer the following questions using the diagram and table information for Lake 1.

a)   How does the <u>sum</u> of the squares of the leg lengths compare with the square of the
       length of the hypotenuse?

b)   Write an equation describing the relationship of the two shorter legs and the
       hypotenuse. This formula is called the **Pythagorean Theorem**.

c)   If you were given the area of one of the square pieces of land, how would you find
       the length of the side?

d)   Suppose one of the squares had an area of 64 km². What is the length of its side,
       that is, the distance along that portion of the lake?

GS-6.   This activity will help confirm the relationship between the legs and the hypotenuse of a
          right triangle.

a)   Copy the table below, leaving room to fill in the blanks.

triangle	length of leg 1	length of leg 2	length of hypotenuse	$(\text{length of leg 1})^2$ $+$ $(\text{length of leg 2})^2$	$(\text{length of hypotenuse})^2$	equal?
1)	5	12				
2)	6	8				
3)	9	12				

>>Problem continues on the next page.>>

b) On graph paper, use a ruler to <u>carefully</u> draw right triangles that have the leg lengths in the table. Use the side of one square of graph paper as one unit.

c) Measure the length of each hypotenuse using a graph paper ruler. Record these lengths in your chart. Check your measurements with your study team.

d) Complete the table by squaring the leg lengths and the hypotenuse length. Then check your answers with your study team.

e) Does the relationship between the numbers in the last column in the table match the one described by the Pythagorean Theorem?

GS-7. Use the Pythagorean Theorem to determine whether the lengths listed below form a right triangle. Explain your reasoning.

a) 15 feet, 36 feet, and 39 feet

b) 20 inches, 21 inches, and 29 inches

c) 8 yards, 9 yards, and 12 yards

d) 4 meters, 7 meters, and 8 meters

GS-8.

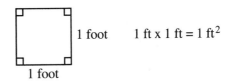

MEASUREMENT IN DIFFERENT DIMENSIONS

Measurements in one dimension are labeled as cm, ft, etc.

————————————
1 foot

Measurements in two dimensions are labeled as cm^2, ft^2, etc.

1 foot   1 ft x 1 ft = 1 ft^2
1 foot

Measurements in three dimensions are labeled as cm^3, ft^3, etc.

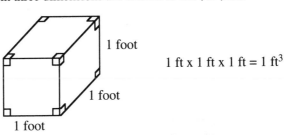

1 foot

1 ft x 1 ft x 1 ft = 1 ft^3

1 foot

1 foot

Make these notes in your Tool Kit to the right of the double-lined box.

Highlight each shape and the corresponding units.

PYTHAGOREAN THEOREM

The **PYTHAGOREAN THEOREM** states that for any right triangle, the sum of the squares of the lengths of the legs is equal to the square of the length of the hypotenuse.

(leg 1)² + (leg 2)² = (hypotenuse)²

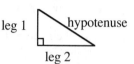

Example:

$$(3)^2 + (4)^2 = (x)^2$$
$$9 + 16 = (x)^2$$
$$25 = (x)^2$$
$$5 = x$$

Make these notes in your Tool Kit to the right of the double-lined box.

a) Highlight the formula for the Pythagorean Theorem.

b) Is it possible to find the length of one leg if you are given the lengths of the other leg and the hypotenuse? If so, how?

GS-10. Find the areas of the following shapes. If you can, also find the perimeters. If you cannot, explain why you cannot.

a)

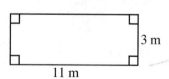

b)

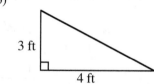

c)

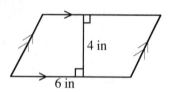

d)

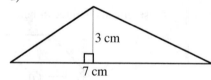

GS-11. Solve the following equations.

a) x + 3 = -5

b) x + 4 = 3x

c) 2x − 5 = -3

d) 2x − 1.5 = 7

GS-12. The Wild West Frontier Park now offers an unlimited day pass. For $29.00, visitors can go on as many rides as they want. The original plan charged visitors $8.75 to enter the park plus $2.25 for each ride. Write an equation to determine the number of rides that would make the total cost equal for the two plans. Solve the equation.

GS-13. Convert the following percents to decimals.

a) 35%

b) 17%

c) 4%

d) 2.5%

e) 65.8%

f) 0.09%

GS-14. Write out the following expressions without exponents and compute their values.

a) 2^2

b) 2^3

c) 4^2

d) 3^4

e) 7^3

f) 5^4

GS-15. Jack noticed there was a sale on Quadrunners. The salesperson said the company was cutting the price for that weekend, so Jack got an 8% discount.

a) If the usual price of the Quadrunner was $4298, what amount did Jack pay with the 8% discount?

b) If the store sold three Quadrunners that weekend, how much money was saved in all by the three customers?

GS-16. Write the inverse operation that will "undo" each of the operations below. Operations that undo another operation are called **inverse operations**.

a) addition

b) division

c) subtraction

d) distributing

e) multiplication

f) factoring

GS-17. Copy and complete the following table or use the resource page. Addition and subtraction are each used twice, once each way.

First #	What was done to the first number to get the second number?	Second #	What can be done to the second number to get the first number again?
60		2	
x		3x	
47		40	
1		97	
36		6	

What do the two columns you filled out have in common? What is different about them?

GS-18.   Use graph paper to complete the following problems.

a)   How many different rectangles with whole number dimensions can you make that have an area of 12 square units? Sketch them on graph paper and label their dimensions.

b)   Can you make a square with an area of 12 if you use whole numbers for the lengths of the sides? If so, what are its dimensions? If not, explain why not.

c)   How many different rectangles that have an area of 16 can you make using whole numbers for the length and width? Sketch them on graph paper and label their dimensions.

d)   Can you make a square with an area of 16? If so, what are its dimensions? If not, explain why not.

e)   How many different rectangles with whole number dimensions can you make that have an area of 40? Sketch them on graph paper and label their dimensions.

f)   Can you make a square with whole number dimensions that has an area of 40? If so, what are its dimensions? If not, explain why not.

g)   What is the next largest area after 40 for which you could make a square with side lengths that are whole numbers? What are its dimensions?

h)   What is the next smallest area under 40 for which you could make a square with side lengths that are whole numbers? What are its dimensions?

GS-19.   Area numbers that can make a square are called square numbers or **perfect squares**. If the following numbers are perfect squares, list the dimensions of the square they make.

a)   Is 16 a perfect square?   b)   Is 54 a perfect square?

c)   Is 1 a perfect square?   d)   Is 81 a perfect square?

GS-20.   Complete a table like the one below to record all the square numbers (perfect squares) from 1 to 100.

Side Lengths of the Square	1	2	3	4	5	6	7	8	9	10	x
Area of the Square											

GS-21.   Study the example shown at right. It contains a mathematical symbol that might be new to you.

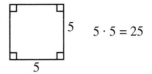

$5 \cdot 5 = 25$

a)   Copy the new mathematical symbol.

b)   What does the $\sqrt{}$ symbol indicate should be done to the square area, 25?

$\sqrt{25} = 5$

c)   What is the name of this symbol?

This is "unsquaring" or the inverse of squaring.

GS-22.   Just as $\overline{)}$ means dividing and is the inverse of multiplying, $\sqrt{}$ is a mathematical symbol that tells us to do the inverse of squaring. When the area of a square is given, we "unsquare" it to find the dimensions (that is, the lengths of the sides of the square). The inverse of squaring is called the **square root**. To show "unsquaring" or finding the square root, use a **radical sign**, $\sqrt{}$.

a)   Sketch a square. Label the area 36 square units. Do not label its dimensions.

b)   Write the area under a $\sqrt{}$. This means that we want to know the dimensions of a square with an area of 36. We are going to find the square root of 36.

c)   What are the lengths of the sides of the square you drew in part (a)?

d)   Use your expression with the $\sqrt{}$ in part (b) and your answer in part (c) to write an equation.

GS-23.   Copy each radical expression below and simplify it by finding the square root. (How long are the sides of squares with these areas?)

a) $\sqrt{49}$ b) $\sqrt{100}$ c) $\sqrt{144}$ d) $\sqrt{64}$

GS-24.

```
╔══════════════════════════════════════════════════════════╗
║                SQUARING AND SQUARE ROOT                    ║
║                                                            ║
║  When a number or variable is multiplied by itself, it is  ║
║  said to be SQUARED.                                       ║
║                                                            ║
║  For example, $6 \cdot 6 = 6^2 = 36$, $a \cdot a = a^2$.   ║
║                                                            ║
║  The SQUARE ROOT of a number or variable is the factor     ║
║  that when multiplied by itself results in the given       ║
║  number. Use a radical sign, $\sqrt{\phantom{x}}$, to show ║
║  this operation.                                           ║
║                                                            ║
║  For example, $\sqrt{49}$ is read as "the square root of   ║
║  49" and means, "Find the positive number that multiplied  ║
║  by itself equals 49." $\sqrt{49} = 7$, since $7 \cdot 7 = 49$. ║
║                                                            ║
║  When finding the area of a square you are squaring the    ║
║  number that represents the side length. When the area of  ║
║  a square is known, you determine its dimensions by        ║
║  finding the square root of a number.                      ║
╚══════════════════════════════════════════════════════════╝
```

Make these notes in your Tool Kit to the right of the double-lined box.

a)   List two other pairs of mathematical operations that are inverses (opposites) of each other.

b)   Highlight the information in the Tool Kit that tells you how to read the square root sign.

GS-25.   Find each square root. Write your answer as an equation.

a) $\sqrt{81}$ b) $\sqrt{16}$ c) $\sqrt{25}$ d) $\sqrt{121}$

GS-26.

```
╔══════════════════════════════════════════════════════════╗
║                  BASES AND EXPONENTS                       ║
║                                                            ║
║  Bases and exponents are used to write a number or         ║
║  expression in exponential form: $a^n$. The BASE, a, is a  ║
║  factor (number or variable expression) raised to a        ║
║  power. The EXPONENT, n, is sometimes called the power     ║
║  and indicates how many times the base is used as a        ║
║  factor.                                                   ║
║                                                            ║
║  In general, $a^n$ means a multiplied by itself n times.   ║
║  For example, $2^4$ means $2 \cdot 2 \cdot 2 \cdot 2$.     ║
║  The base is 2 and the exponent is 4.                      ║
╚══════════════════════════════════════════════════════════╝
```

Make these notes in your Tool Kit to the right of the double-lined box.

Write another example of a number in exponential form.

GS-27.   Simplify, then name the base and the exponent.

a) 3^7 b) 8^5 c) $5(9 - 6)^3$

GS-28.   Ann is measuring some fabric pieces for a quilt. Use th[e]
 her find each of the missing lengths below:

a)

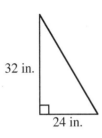

32 in.

24 in.

b)

44 ft

c)

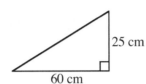

25 cm

60 cm

d)

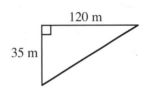

120 m

35 m

GS-29.   Determine the positive value that makes each equation true.

a)   If $x^2 = 36$,
      $x = ?$

b)   If $x^2 = 65$,
      $x = ?$

c)   If $x^2 = 84$,
      $x = ?$

d)   If $x^2 = 13$,
      $x = ?$

GS-30.   Sourdough Sam was in the hills prospecting for
 gold when he ran out of water. He walked two
miles west, where he found a stream. He followed
the stream north three miles. He looked down and
saw something glittering. Gold! He had left all of
his prospecting gear back at his campsite, so he
walked directly back to it. How far did he have to
go?

a)   Copy the diagram at right and use the
      Pythagorean Theorem to write an equation
      represented by the triangle to solve the problem.

b)   Solve your equation to find out how far away
      Sam's campsite is.

gold

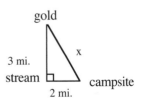

3 mi.

stream

x

campsite

2 mi.

...d to hide the gold where no one else would find it. He ...a nearby tree to use it as a reference point, then went ...paces east and fifteen paces south. How far from the tree ...m bury the gold?

Draw a diagram and label it.

b) Write and solve an equation to find how far from the tree he buried the gold.

GS-32. 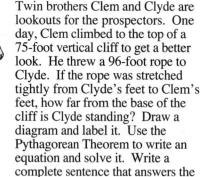 Twin brothers Clem and Clyde are lookouts for the prospectors. One day, Clem climbed to the top of a 75-foot vertical cliff to get a better look. He threw a 96-foot rope to Clyde. If the rope was stretched tightly from Clyde's feet to Clem's feet, how far from the base of the cliff is Clyde standing? Draw a diagram and label it. Use the Pythagorean Theorem to write an equation and solve it. Write a complete sentence that answers the question.

GS-33. Write an equation, then find the missing length in each diagram.

a)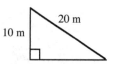

20 m

10 m

b)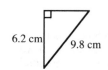

6.2 cm

9.8 cm

GS-34. Sourdough Sam's wife, Ann, thought about visiting one of her quilting friends on her way home from town. To do so, she would have to travel 24 km south to her friend's house and then 32 km west to her home. Instead, she decided to go straight home. What is the distance directly to her home? Write and solve an equation to find the distance.

GS-35. The hypotenuse and one leg of a right triangle are 65 and 60 meters.

a) What is the length of the third side?

b) Find the area and the perimeter of the triangle.

GS-36. Rosie and Josie are sisters from Ann's quilting club with a problem similar to that of Luke and Duke. They will be sharing the square plots of land around a lake (shown at right). Rosie will get the two square plots of land on the shorter sides, and Josie will get the square plot of land on the longer side.

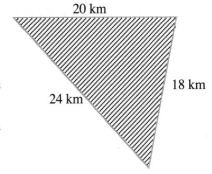
20 km
24 km
18 km

a) Find the area of Josie's piece. Find the area of Rosie's pieces combined.

b) Is this a fair share? Why or why not?

c) What is different between Luke and Duke's lakes and Rosie and Josie's?

GS-37. Compute each value.

a) 6^5

b) 4^7

c) 1.5^3

d) 0.04^2

e) $(2 + 3)^4$

f) $2(3 + 4)^3$

GS-38. Samantha, the owner of Noble Ranch, must pay taxes on her land. She calculated the acreage as 5920 acres. The tax rate is four cents per acre. The government has sent her a bill showing that she owes $281.60 in taxes. Help Sam decide if her tax bill is accurate.

a) Calculate Samantha's tax bill.

b) What conclusions can you make about Samantha's tax bill? Include the amount of tax Samantha should pay in your explanation.

GS-39. Nestor, a local farmer, also received a tax bill for his homestead. The tax rate is $25.60 per square mile or four cents per acre. His taxes amount to $15.60. Use the diagram at right and the questions below to find the area of Nestor's farm. Decide if his tax bill is accurate.

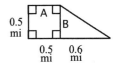
A B
0.5 mi
0.5 mi   0.6 mi

a) What is the area of Nestor's farm in square miles? Show all subproblems.

b) What is the area of Nestor's farm in acres? A square mile is equal to 640 acres.

c) Compute Nestor's tax bill. Is his tax bill accurate? Explain.

GS-40.   Follow your teacher's directions for practicing mental math.

GS-41.   Obtain a resource page from your teacher for the next two problems. Find the length of
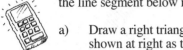
          the line segment below right by completing parts (a) through (c).

          a)   Draw a right triangle with the line segment
                shown at right as the hypotenuse.

          b)   How many units long are the legs?

          c)   Use an equation to find the length of the line
                segment (hypotenuse).

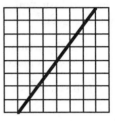

          Find the lengths of each of the following segments. Be sure to show all your work.

          d)   e)

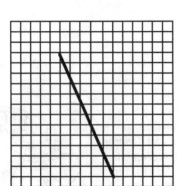   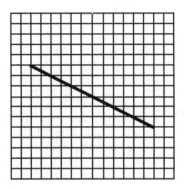

GS-42.   The Claude-Hopper family has decided to build pens for
          their animals. To keep the different animals separated
          from each other, they need to build four pens. The pigs
          are to be kept in a square pen with a side length of 15
          feet. The mule pen will also be square and will measure
          36 feet on each side. The third square pen is for the
          oxen. In the middle is a right triangular pen for the
          chickens. Find the total area of the four pens.

          a)   Copy and label the drawing of each animal pen.

          b)   The calculation of the area of each pen is a
                subproblem that helps answer the question.

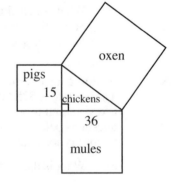

                                          >>Problem continues on the next page.>>

Solve each of the five subproblems.

i)   What is the area of pig pen?

ii)   What is the area of the mule pen?

iii)   What is the hypotenuse of the chicken pen?

iv)   What is the area of the chicken pen?

v)   What is the area of the oxen pen?

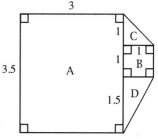

c)   Use your answers from part (b) to find the total area of the farm pens.

GS-43.   Use subproblems to solve the problem below. Copy and label the drawing. List the subproblems, then solve each one.

Regal Ranch has four agricultural sectors: Sectors A and B are rectangles; sectors C and D are right triangles. Measurements are shown in miles.

a)   What is the total area of the ranch in square miles? Show the subproblems you use.

b)   One square mile is equal to 640 acres. How many acres is Regal Ranch?

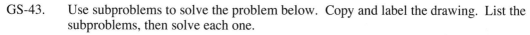

GS-44.   Clem and Clyde set up a tent at the base of Lookout Peak. They pounded a stake in the ground five feet from the center pole so they could attach a rope to it. If the rope they attached to the very top of the center pole was 13 feet long, how tall was the center pole? Draw and label a diagram. Show all your work as you solve this problem.

Breaking a large or complex problem into smaller parts is a problem solving strategy called **SUBPROBLEMS**. This strategy means to solve each part and put the smaller parts back together to answer the original question.

Example: Find the area of this figure.

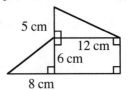

Subproblem 1:

$\frac{1}{2} \cdot 12 \cdot 5 = 30$
area of first triangle = 30 cm^2

Subproblem 2:

$6 \cdot 12 = 72$
area of rectangle = 72 cm^2

Subproblem 3:

$6 \cdot 8 = 48$
$48 \div 2 = 24$
area of second triangle = 24 cm^2

Subproblem 4:

$30 + 72 + 24 = 126$
Sum of the areas = 126 cm^2

Make these notes in your Tool Kit the to right of the double-lined box.

Draw a figure that would need to be broken into smaller parts to find its area. Write the subproblems you would have to solve.

GS-46.   Clem and Clyde staked out a claim for land just outside Bovine Gulch. The boundaries form a square, a rectangle, and a right triangle. Find the total area of their land in square miles and tell them how much fencing they need to fence the outside of their land.

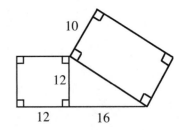

GS-47. Jo Jo plays third base and Dano plays first base on the Stickball Cactus League team. Jo Jo is standing at third base and throws the ball to Dano. How far apart are the bases? Draw a picture to help you. The distance between each base is 90 feet.

GS-48. Find the total area of the rectangle and right triangle combination shown at right. Be sure to show all your subproblems.

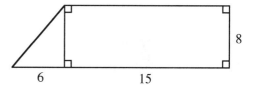

6   15   8

GS-49. Find the lengths of each of the following segments. Be sure to show all your work.

a)

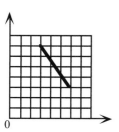

0

b)

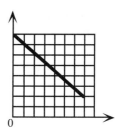

0

GS-50. A right triangle has a base of 15 cm and an area of 90 cm². Find its perimeter. Show all your subproblems.

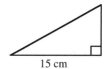

15 cm

GS-51.   The figure shown at right is made up of a right triangle and a rectangle.

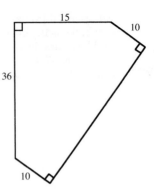

a)   Draw a line to help divide the figure into two subproblems.

b)   Use the dimensions given to find the area of the triangle, the rectangle, and the whole figure. Be sure to show all your subproblems.

GS-52.   Plot the points P(0, 0) and T(4, 4) on a square grid.

a)   Find all the squares that have P and T as two of the four vertices.

b)   Find the sum of the areas of these squares.

GS-53.   Try to make a square out of 20 tiles. Is it possible?

a)   What is the area of the largest square you can make with 20 tiles? What are the lengths of its sides?

b)   How many more tiles would you need to make the next biggest square? What is the area of this square? What would be the lengths of its sides?

c)   Why does it make sense that $\sqrt{20}$ is between 4 and 5?

d)   Do you think $\sqrt{20}$ is closer to 4 or to 5? Explain your reasoning.

GS-54.   The area of a square is 60 square units, so the length of the side is not a whole number.

a)   Between which two whole numbers is the side length?

b)   Between which two whole numbers is the side length of a square that has an area of 32?

c)   Between which two whole numbers is the side length of a square that has an area of 8?

GS-55. Between which two whole numbers is each of the following square roots? To which whole number do you think it is closer? (For example: $\sqrt{125}$ is between 11 and 12 and is closer to 11.)

a) $\sqrt{40}$　　b) $\sqrt{95}$　　c) $\sqrt{3}$　　d) $\sqrt{200}$

e) $\sqrt{59}$　　f) $\sqrt{75.5}$　　g) $\sqrt{154}$　　h) $\sqrt{320}$

GS-56. Describe your method for estimating the approximate value of a square root when the number is not a perfect square.

GS-57. Spencer and Reba were comparing their answers from an earlier problem. They agreed that $\sqrt{40}$ was between 6 and 7. Spencer said, "I think $\sqrt{40}$ is about 6.5, since 40 is about halfway between 36 and 49." Reba's estimate of $\sqrt{40}$ was $6\frac{4}{13}$. Spencer was astonished. "How on earth did you come up with *that* number?"

"Easy," replied Reba. "I just looked at the patterns in the building squares problem GS-20. I know that 40 tiles is 4 more than 36, and 36 is the perfect square of $6 \cdot 6$. I also know that I need 13 more tiles to get from 36 to 49, and 49 is the perfect square of $7 \cdot 7$. I figured that 40 tiles is enough for a square that is 6 by 6, and I have **4** out of the **13** tiles that I need for a square that is $7 \cdot 7$. It makes sense to me that a good estimate of $\sqrt{40}$ is $6\frac{4}{13}$. What do you think, Spencer?" Spencer was not so sure. He wanted to check the value on a calculator.

a) Use your calculator to make a decimal approximation of $\sqrt{40}$. Round your answer to the nearest hundredth (0.01).

b) How close to your answer from part (a) is Spencer's estimate of 6.5?

c) Convert Reba's estimate of $6\frac{4}{13}$ to a decimal. How close is Reba's estimate?

GS-58. Use Reba's method to approximate the following square roots. Copy and complete the table. Express your answer as a mixed number, then compare your mixed number with a calculator approximation.

	$\sqrt{45}$	$\sqrt{50}$	$\sqrt{91}$	$\sqrt{110}$	$\sqrt{150}$	$\sqrt{15}$
Mixed Number						
Converted to a Decimal						
Calculated to the Nearest 0.01						

GS-59.   Find the total area and perimeter of the figure at
           right. Be sure to show all of your subproblems.

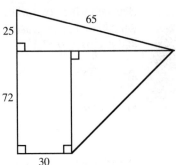

GS-60.   Jon invested $500 at 3.8% compound interest
           per year. How much money will he have at the
           end of six years?

GS-61.   Find the length of the missing side of each of these right triangles.

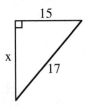

a)

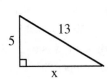

b)

c)

GS-62.   Solve these equations for x. Check your answers.

a)   (x + 4.5)2 = 32   b)   6 + 2.5x = 21   c)   3x + 8.4 = 19.2

GS-63.   Sara finds a sweater for $49.99. If she has $54 and sales tax is 8%, does she have
           enough money to buy the sweater?

GS-64.   Look at the graph at right. Copy the table
           and enter the ordered pairs for the points
           marked on the line. Then write the
           equation for the line in the last space in
           your table.

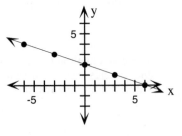

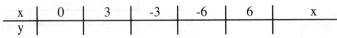

x	0	3	-3	-6	6	x
y						

GS-65.   Follow your teacher's directions for practicing mental math.

GS-66.   Your teacher will give you two resource pages per study team. Each member of your study team will cut out one figure, fold it along the bold lines and tape it together. Put all four three-dimensional objects where all members of the team can examine them.

a)   How many faces do your prisms have, excluding the top and bottom (shaded faces)?

b)   Describe the faces of your prism.

c)   What do you notice about the bases (top and bottom) of the prisms?

d)   Describe the shaded bases (top and bottom) of the prisms your team made. What are their shapes?

e)   Prisms are named by the shape of their bases. List the names of the prisms.

GS-67.

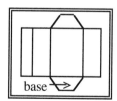

PRISMS

A **PRISM** is a three-dimensional figure composed of polygonal faces (called sides or lateral sides) and two congruent, parallel faces called bases. No holes are permitted in the solid. The remaining faces are parallelograms (or other special quadrilaterals). A prism is named for the shape of its base.

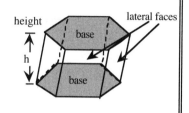

Your study team built models of four different prisms. Since you will need to refer to these prisms to help you solve future problems, you will now make your own set of the prisms to place in your Tool Kit. Rather than taping the edges together to form solid models, you should leave them untaped so they can lay flat for storage and be "popped up" when the model is needed.

Cut out each of the four prisms from the resource pages you received from your teacher. Fold and unfold along the bold-faced lines, then attach one base of each prism to your Tool Kit page with tape (or glue).

In your Tool Kit to the right of each model sketch each of its faces.

GS-68.   Sam put $1000 worth of gold in a savings account. He will earn 3.5% compound interest per year. How much money will he have in three years?

GS-69.   Carol went on another shopping spree. She bought a pair of $65 jeans at 40% off, a $24 tank top at $\frac{1}{4}$ off, and a pair of $35 shoes at 30% off. How much did she save? How much did she pay for all three items?

GS-70.   In 1997 a box of 300 glass marbles sold at Ronna's auction house for £2760. At the time, £1 (British pound) was worth $1.57. What did the box of marbles sell for in U.S. dollars?

GS-71.   Find the length of the missing side.

a)

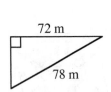

72 m

78 m

b)

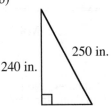

250 in.

240 in.

GS-72.   Solve for x.

a) $\frac{1}{2} = \frac{5x}{10}$

b) $\frac{3x}{9} = \frac{x + 2}{6}$

c) $\frac{x + 2}{5} = \frac{2x + 1}{3}$

GS-73.   Find each of the following.

a) $|-15| + |-26|$

b) $- |-40|$

c) $|0.5| + |-1\frac{1}{2}|$

d) $|24| + |-15|$

GS-74.   The diameter of the large circle is 18 cm.

a)   What is the area of the shaded circle?

b)   What subproblems did you do to find the answer?

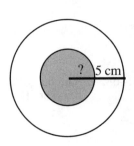

GS-75. Look at this drawing of a box, which is also called a rectangular prism. It is one inch high (thick).

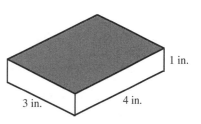

1 in.

3 in.   4 in.

a) If you had several one cubic inch blocks (1" x 1" x 1"), how many blocks would you need to completely fill the rectangular prism?

b) What is another name for the number of blocks needed to fill the prism?

c) What kinds of units are used to label volume?

GS-76. We have added layers to the prism from the previous problem.

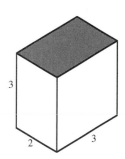

a) How many layers have been added? How many total layers are in this prism?

b) Let h stand for the height of the prism. What is the value of h?

c) What are the dimensions of the base in this figure?

d) Let A stand for the <u>area</u> of the base. What is the value of A?

e) In the previous problem you calculated that it would take 12 blocks to fill the prism when it was 1 layer high. Now that it is 5 layers high, how many blocks do you think it will take to fill it completely? Explain how you arrived at your answer.

f) Using V for volume, h for height (number of layers), and A for the area of the base, write a formula for finding the volume of a prism.

GS-77. Examine the prism at right.

a) What is the area of the base (A)?

b) What is the height (h)?

c) Calculate the volume of this prism.

GS-78.   The figure at right is a triangular prism.

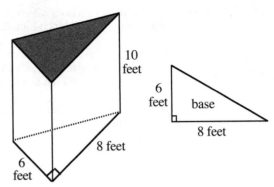

a)   Find the area of its base.

b)   Find its volume.

GS-79.

VOLUME OF A PRISM

The **VOLUME** of a prism is the area of either base (A) times the height (h) of the prism.

V = (Area of base) · (height)

V = Ah

Example:

   Area of base = (2 in.)(3 in.) = 6 in.^{2}

   (Area of base)(height) = (6 in.^{2})(4 in.) = 24 in.^{3}

   Volume = 24 in.^{3}

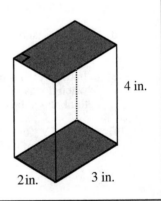

Describe how to find the area of the base for a triangular prism in your Tool Kit to the right of the double-lined box.

GS-80.   The height of a prism whose base is shown at right is 35 units.

a)   Find the area of the base of the figure.

b)   What is the volume of the prism? Show your work.

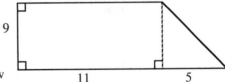

GS-81.   Find the length of each of the following segments. Be sure to show all your work.

a)

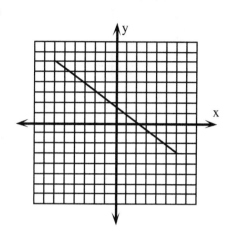

b)

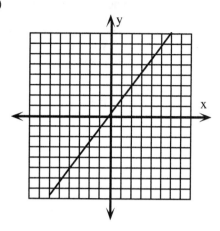

GS-82.   Delbert's parents said he watches too much television on the weekends. He wanted to show them that he watches about the same amount as his peers. Delbert collected information from ten students about how much time they spend watching television. From one weekend, the students reported viewing times of 240, 0, 60, 30, 120, 900, 65, 90, 240, and 195 minutes.

a)   Find the mean, median, and mode of these times.

b)   Suppose the student who reported 900 minutes had not come to school, so Delbert only had the other nine reported times. Compute the new mean, median, and mode.

c)   Which of the measures of central tendency is most useful for Delbert to convince his parents he is not watching too much television?

GS-83.   Listed below are sets of side lengths for triangles. Determine if each set of dimensions would result in a right triangle.

a)   42   144   150   b)   45   108   117

c)   7   19   25   d)   56   216   225

GS-84.   A bag contains 11 red, 5 yellow, and 7 purple marbles. Find the probability of drawing a purple marble followed by a red marble. The purple marble was not put back in the bag.

GS-85. Examine the figure at right.

a) Find the area of the figure. List all your subproblems and show your work.

b) If the figure represents the base of a prism of height 7 inches, what is its volume?

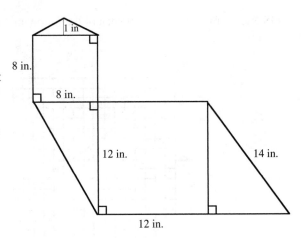

GS-86. Take out your Tool Kit and turn to your entry on prisms. Use the dimensions on your rectangular prism (4 by 6 by 20) to answer the following questions.

a) Find the area of the shaded top (base).

b) Find the area of the shaded bottom (base).

c) Find the areas of each of the lateral faces.

d) Find the sum of the areas of all of the faces and bases.

e) Why do you think this number is called the **surface area** of this rectangular prism?

GS-87. Now you will calculate the surface area of the other three pop-up prisms. Refer to problem GS-86 for the subproblems and to the pop-ups in your Tool Kit. All dimensions are in centimeters. The bases of the pop-up prisms are:

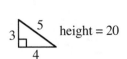
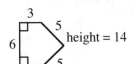
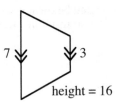

a) What is the surface area of the triangular prism?

b) What is the surface area of the pentagonal prism?

c) What is the surface area of the trapezoidal prism?

GS-88.   The base of your prism can be used to find its volume.

a)   Calculate the base area of each prism.

b)   What is the height of each prism?

c)   What is the total volume of each prism? Be sure to label the volume in cubic units.

d)   Explain how you calculated the volume of each prism.

GS-89.   Consider the drawing at right. All the angles are right angles.

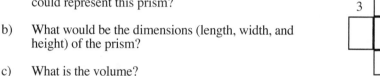

a)   Imagine folding along the bold lines. Sketch the prism it would cover. Which of your pop-up models could represent this prism?

b)   What would be the dimensions (length, width, and height) of the prism?

c)   What is the volume?

d)   Find the area of all of the faces, including the bases. List the subproblems used to find these areas.

e)   What is the total surface area (the sum of all of the faces and bases)?

GS-90.

SURFACE AREA OF A PRISM

The **SURFACE AREA** of a prism is the sum of the areas of all of the faces, including the bases. Surface area is expressed in **square units**.

Example: Find the surface area of the triangular prism at right.

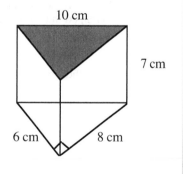

Subproblem 1: Area of the two bases

$$2\left[\tfrac{1}{2}(6 \text{ cm})(8 \text{ cm})\right] = 48 \text{ cm}^2$$

Subproblem 2: Area of the three lateral faces

Area of face 1: $(6 \text{ cm})(7 \text{ cm}) = 42 \text{ cm}^2$
Area of face 2: $(8 \text{ cm})(7 \text{ cm}) = 56 \text{ cm}^2$
Area of face 3: $(10 \text{ cm})(7 \text{ cm}) = 70 \text{ cm}^2$

Subproblem 3: Surface Area of Prism = sum of bases and lateral faces

$$48 \text{ cm}^2 + 42 \text{ cm}^2 + 56 \text{ cm}^2 + 70 \text{ cm}^2 = 216 \text{ cm}^2$$

>>Problem continues on the next page.>>

Make these notes in your Tool Kit to the right of the double-lined box.

a) Why is surface area expressed in square units?

b) In your own words describe what "surface area" means.

GS-91. Find the surface area of a rectangular prism with a base of six feet by five feet and a height of seven feet. Use your pop-up model as a guide. List the subproblems needed to solve this problem.

GS-92. Miss Lilly rode the stagecoach to Bovine Gulch. When the stage arrived, she discovered that her trunk of valuable quilt fabrics had fallen off the stage. If the trunk was a rectangular prism that measured 2 feet by 3 feet by 1.5 feet, what was its volume?

GS-93. The drawing shown at right represents the piece of brown paper Miss Lilly used to wrap Clem and Clyde's present. All angles are right angles.

a) Draw a sketch of the box that can be wrapped in this paper without any waste or overlap. Label its dimensions.

b) Find the surface area of the box.

c) Find the volume of the box.

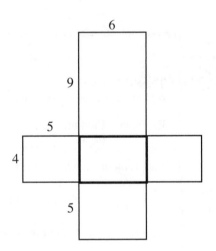

GS-94. Find the area and perimeter of the figure shown at right. List each subproblem and show your work.

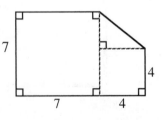

GS-95.   Describe how to find the third side of a right triangle if you know the length of:

a)   the hypotenuse and one leg.   b)   both of the legs.

GS-96.   Find the volume of the prism with the base
shown at right and a height of 8. List the
subproblems before you begin.

7.6

10   21.25

GS-97.   Solve the following equations for x. Check your solution.

a) $6x + 8 = x - 12$ b) $1000 = -20x + 400$

c) $-6x - 1 = 125$ d) $\dfrac{x - 11}{25} = \dfrac{24}{30}$

GS-98.   Solve $2r = d$ for r.

GS-99.   Find the diameter of a circle if the radius is 7.58 centimeters.

GS-100.   Solve for d: $C = \pi d$.

GS-101.   The radius of a circle is 6.5 centimeters.

a)   Find the circumference.   b)   Find the area.

GS-102.   Find the volume of a prism that has a base area of 20.3 square centimeters and a height of
17.75 centimeters.

GS-103. Make a sketch of the two paper cylinders shown at right. Label the height of each one and write, "I think this one will have more volume" under the cylinder you believe will have more volume.

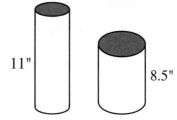

11"

8.5"

GS-104. Examine the cylinders above right. Each cylinder has been constructed from a piece of paper that measures $8\frac{1}{2}$ inches by 11 inches.

a) In your notebook, make a sketch of the <u>base</u> of the tall cylinder and label the circumference. Write under the lateral area its sketch for each.

b) Calculate the diameter and the radius of the tall cylinder. Add these measurements to your sketch. Find the area of the base. Show your work.

c) Make a sketch of the base of the short cylinder and label the circumference. Fill in the lateral area.

d) Calculate the diameter and the radius. Add these measurements to your sketch, then find the area of the base. Show your work.

GS-105. Refer to the diagram of the cylinders in problem GS-103. Imagine that you cut one inch off the bottom of the <u>tall</u> cylinder so that you now have a new cylinder with the same base that is exactly one inch tall.

a) Make a sketch of this cylinder.

b) How many one-inch squares would it take to cover the <u>base</u> of this cylinder?

c) If you had one-inch cubes, how many cubes would it take to <u>fill</u> this cylinder?

d) What do you notice about your answers to parts (b) and (c)? Explain your observation.

e) Can you use the information from parts (b) through (d) to find how many cubes it would take to fill the original <u>tall</u> cylinder? Explain your method.

GS-106. Imagine that you cut one inch off the bottom of the <u>short</u> cylinder so that you now have a new cylinder (with the same base) that is exactly one inch tall.

a) Make a sketch of this cylinder.

b) Use the process in parts (b) through (e) of the previous problem to find the volume of the original short cylinder.

GS-107. Ann and Nan were writing formulas for finding the volume of a cylinder. Ann wrote, "V = Ah." Nan wrote, "V = $\pi r^2 h$." Their math teacher examined their work and announced that they were both correct.

a) Compare the two formulas. What do variables V, A, and h represent? What does πr^2 represent?

b) Explain why Ann and Nan are both correct.

c) Express A in terms of πr^2 in the first formula.

GS-108.

VOLUME OF A CYLINDER

The **VOLUME OF A CYLINDER** is found by multiplying the base area (A) times the height (h).

Volume = (Area of base)(height)
$$V = Ah = (\pi r^2)(h)$$

Example:

Find the volume of the cylinder at right.

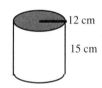

$A = \pi(12)^2 = 144\pi$
$V = 144\pi(15) = 2160\pi \approx 6785.84 \text{ cm}^3$

Look at the example in the Tool Kit. To the right of the double-lined box, explain why the answer is given as cm^3.

GS-109. Draw a diagram and find the volume of a cylinder that has a radius of 15.3 centimeters and a height of 12 centimeters.

GS-110.   Answer these questions and show your work.

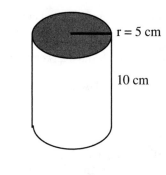

a)   What is the area of the base of the cylinder
      above right?

b)   What is the volume of that cylinder?

c)   Find the area of the base of the cylinder
      below right.

d)   Find the volume of that cylinder.

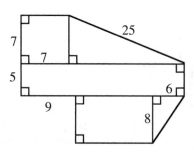

GS-111.   Use the figure at right.

a)   Find the total area. Be sure to show
      all your subproblems.

b)   If the figure is the base of a prism
      with a height of 14, find the volume.

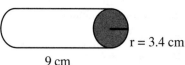

GS-112.   Find each of the following.

a) $-|-93|$ b) $|-20| + |63|$ c) $|-\frac{1}{2}| - |-\frac{1}{2}|$ d) $|102| - |97|$

GS-113.   Write and solve a proportion for the following problem.

In a recent survey for the student council, Dominique found that 150 students out of a
total of 800 students on campus did __not__ like soda. If half of the student body was going
to attend a dance, how many students could she expect would want soda?

GS-114.   Jian has two large bags of candies: the first one has 100 red jellybeans and 300 black
jellybeans; the second one has 200 red jellybeans, 100 black jellybeans, and 300 green
jellybeans. He grabs a bag at random, reaches into it and pulls out one jellybean.

a)   What is the probability that it is green?

b)   What is the probability that it is red?

GS-115. Find the area of a rectangle with the given dimensions.

a) base = $4\frac{1}{2}$ mm, height = $1\frac{1}{5}$ mm   b) base = 1.26 m, height = 5.6 m

GS-116. Find the area of a circle with the given dimension.

a) radius = 1.3 cm   b) diameter = 5.5 m

GS-117. Find the circumference of a circle with the given dimension.

a) radius = 7.3 cm   b) diameter = 8.5 m

GS-118. Below is the net of a cylinder. Find the total surface area (the area of the three separate pieces added together) of the cylinder's net. (A **net** is a two-dimensional unfolded picture of a three-dimensional object.)

a) The height of the cylinder is 7.2 cm. The longer side of the rectangle is the same measurement as what part of the circle?

b) Show the subproblems you used to find the total area of this cylinder (that is, the surface area of all three pieces).

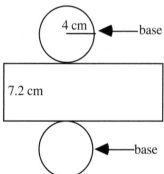

GS-119. Use the net at right to answer the questions below. It is not drawn to scale.

a) What is the circumference of the base of this cylinder?

b) Use your answer to part (a) to find the radius of the base.

c) Find the total surface area of this cylinder.

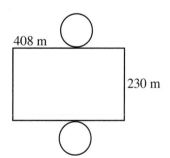

GS-120.   Which of the cylinders matches the net?

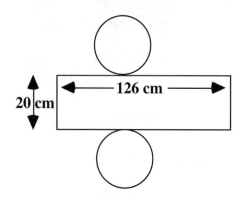 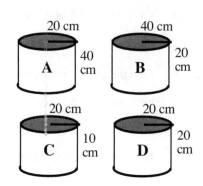

GS-121.   Find the surface area of a soda can with a radius of 5 centimeters and a height of 18 centimeters. Sketch and show your work. List the subproblems you used.

GS-122.   Explain in your own words how to find the surface area of a cylinder.

SURFACE AREA OF A CYLINDER

The **SURFACE AREA OF A CYLINDER** is the sum of the two base areas and the lateral surface area. The formula for the surface area is:

$$S.A. = 2\pi r^2 + \pi dh$$
$$= 2\pi r^2 + 2\pi rh$$

where r = radius, d = diameter, and h = height of the cylinder.

Example:

Find the surface area of the cylinder at right.

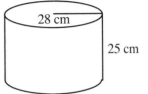

Subproblem 1:   Area of the two circular bases

$2[\pi(28 \text{ cm})^2] = 1568\pi \text{ cm}^2$

Subproblem 2:   Area of the lateral face

$\pi(56)25 = 1400\pi \text{ cm}^2$

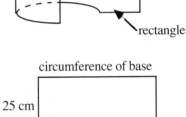

Subproblem 3:   Surface area of the cylinder

$1568\pi \text{ cm}^2 + 1400\pi \text{ cm}^2 = 2968\pi \text{ cm}^2$
$\approx 9324.25 \text{ cm}^2$

Make these notes in your Tool Kit to the right of the double-lined box.

a)   How is finding the surface area of a cylinder different than finding the surface area of a prism?

b)   How is it the same?

GS-124.   Find the diameters of the following circles. Show your work.

a)   A circle with a circumference of 31.40 cm.

b)   A circle with an area of 56.5 square inches.

c)   A circle with a radius of 8.16 meters.

GS-125. The figure at right represents the base of a prism with a height of 12.

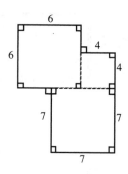

a) Find the area of the base. Show all subproblems.

b) Find the volume of the prism.

GS-126. Luke Wrangler added a rectangular gate to the fence he built around his homestead. The gate was 6 feet high and was reinforced with a 10-foot diagonal board.

a) Draw a diagram of the gate and the diagonal. Be sure to label your drawing.

b) Find the width of the gate.

GS-127. Archimedes the Arachnid was a spider who so admired his namesake, the great Greek mathematician, that he made all his webs very geometric. One day, he made a web like the one below right by going 1 centimeter from his starting point S to point A, spinning a strand, making a 90° turn, going one more centimeter (to B), and then going back to his starting point (S). Then he went along the web back to B, made a 90° turn, and spun webs one more centimeter (to C), and then back to S. He kept doing this until he had spun a 6-centimeter strand on his return to point S. How many strands did he spin? Note that a strand is the distance between two points. The problem asks how many strands, not the sum of their lengths.

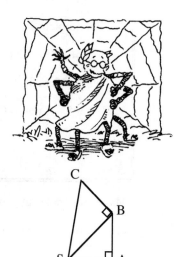

GS-128. **The Mine Shaft**

Sourdough Sam was given a gold mine. To get the gold, Sourdough Sam's mining company will build a sturdy entry platform for the new mine shaft. The platform will be a rectangular prism 4 feet high with a base 20 feet by 15 feet. The concrete for the platform will be poured around a cylindrical hole 6 feet in diameter. The miners will be lowered through the hole to get to the vein of gold. Sam needs to know how many cubic feet of concrete to order and how much it will weigh.

a) How many cubic feet of concrete will be needed to build the platform?

b) If concrete weighs 120 pounds per cubic foot, how much will the platform weigh?

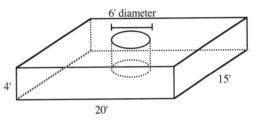

c) If each donkey cart can haul 350 pounds of concrete, how many cart loads will be needed?

d) If the entire platform including the center hole (but not the bottom) is painted, what area will the paint cover?

GS-129. **Chapter Summary**

Like many other gold miners' wives, Sourdough Sam's wife, Ann, spends many evenings quilting while Sam is at the mine. You will help her with her most recent project. Take the colored paper your teacher provides and create an individual summary quilt piece. Choose one of the main ideas of this chapter and a representative problem. As you have done in other chapters, write a clear explanation of your solution. You must include a picture or diagram.

GS-130. Find the length of the missing side in each triangle below.

a)

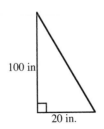

100 in
20 in.

b)

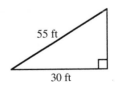

55 ft
30 ft

GS-131.   This figure represents the base of a prism with a height of 6.

   a)   Find the area of the base. Show all subproblems.

   b)   Find the volume of this prism.

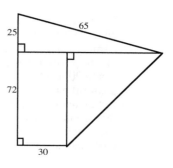

GS-132. $\sqrt{30}$ is between:

   (A) 5 and 6   (B) 4 and 5   (C) 3 and 4   (D) 6 and 7

GS-133.   Mrs. Wrangler is planning a birthday party for her grandson, Arnold, at the Bar K Ranch.
           It costs $75 for up to 12 children and $8.50 for each additional child. Arnold wants to
           invite 15 friends. How much will Mrs. Wrangler have to pay for Arnold's party?

GS-134.   The horse trough at Sam's mine looked very much like a rectangular prism with no top. It
           measured eight feet long by three feet wide by two feet deep. It had recently rained, so the
           trough was completely full. How much water was in the horse trough?

GS-135.   The figure at right is a barn at the
           Wrangler Ranch. Use the following
           information and the dimensions shown
           on the drawing to find the surface area
           of the barn so that Luke and Duke will
           know how much whitewash to buy. It
           is 28 feet from the ground to the top of
           the roof. They will not whitewash the
           door, window, floor, or roof. List the
           subproblems needed to find the total area
           to be whitewashed.

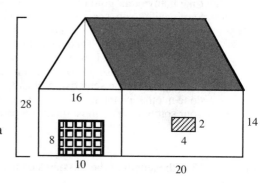

GS-136.   The Wranglers built a barn, a storage shed, and a house. The storage shed was 70 paces
           due east from the house. The barn was 240 paces due south of the storage shed. How
           many paces is it from the barn to the house? Draw and label a diagram and show all
           subproblems.

GS-137. Find the volume of the cylinder at right. Explain the steps that you followed.

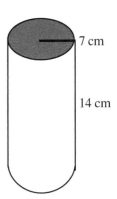

7 cm

14 cm

GS-138. Solve the following equations.

a) $x = \dfrac{4}{5} \div \dfrac{1}{2}$

b) $x = 6 \div \dfrac{7}{8}$

GS-139. **What We Have Done in This Chapter**

Below is a list of the Tool Kit entries from this chapter.

- GS-2   Right Triangles
- GS-8   Measurement in Different Dimensions
- GS-9   Pythagorean Theorem
- GS-24   Squaring and Square Root
- GS-26   Bases and Exponents
- GS-45   Subproblems
- GS-67   Prisms
- GS-79   Volume of a Prism
- GS-90   Surface Area of a Prism
- GS-108   Volume of a Cylinder
- GS-123   Surface Area of a Cylinder

Review all the entries and read the notes you made in your Tool Kit. Make a list of any questions, terms, or notes you do not understand. Ask your partner or study team members for help. If anything is still unclear, ask your teacher.

Chapter 9

Chapter 9
College Bound: **SLOPES AND RATES OF CHANGE**

In this chapter you will extend your knowledge of data tables, writing equations, and graphing. As you work on this chapter, you will see that many mathematical ideas are intertwined. You will be able to describe and identify linear graphs from their equations or data tables and write linear equations from linear graphs or data tables. You will apply these skills in problem solving contexts and real-life situations.

In this chapter you will have the opportunity to:

- find the rate of change of a set of data.

- use slope triangles to find the rate of change of a line.

- write equations from graphs and data tables.

- graph lines using the slope and the y-intercept.

- graph and solve inequalities.

Read the problem below, but **do not try to solve it now**. What you learn over the next few days will enable you to solve it.

CB-0. George and Ben are two friends who make extra money parking cars at concerts and sporting events at the big arena near their homes in Indianapolis. They both want to go to college to become architects. Ben wants to go to Indiana-Purdue University at Fort Wayne, but George wants to start at the local community college and transfer in two years. Both are worried about the expense of college since neither of their families can afford to help. Use the information provided to decide if the boys will earn enough to be able to attend college.

Number Sense

Algebra and Functions

Mathematical Reasoning

Measurement and Geometry

Statistics, Data Analysis, & Probability

Chapter 9
College Bound: SLOPES AND RATES OF CHANGE

CB-1.   Complete the table and write the rule.

x	-1	0	1	2	3	4	5	x
y	4	1	-2	-5				

a)   How can you tell from the table if the graph is a line or a curve?

b)   Graph the data.

c)   Describe the direction of the graph as it goes from left to right.

CB-2.   **Cash on Hand (Part One)**

Kristie, Samantha, Connie, and Julie are four friends who work part-time in one of the concession stands at the arena. One Saturday, each girl earned $15. Over the next week:

a)   Kristie saves an additional $2.50 per day.

b)   Samantha saves an additional $1.50 per day.

c)   Connie spends $2 per day.

d)   Julie neither spends any of her money nor saves any additional money.

Construct a table like the one below or use the resource page provided by your teacher to show the changes for each girl's cash on hand over the next seven days. Let the x-value represent the days and let the y-value represent the cash on hand. Use the table below to help get you started. Day 0 is Saturday.

Day (x)	0	1	2	3	4	5	6	7	x
Kristie	$15								
Samantha	$15								
Connie	$15								
Julie	$15								

e)   How much money will Kristie, Samantha, Connie, and Julie each have on the following Saturday (the seventh day)?

f)   Write an equation for each girl's situation that shows how much money she will have on any given day.

CB-3.   **Cash on Hand (Part Two)**

On the resource page your teacher gives you, create a graph to compare the girls' financial situations by following the directions below.

a)   On the same set of axes, graph the cash on hand for Kristie, Samantha, Connie, and Julie. Use a different color for each girl's graph. Label each graph with the name of the girl and the equation.

b)   What is similar about the four graphs?

c)   Compare the graphs of Kristie and Samantha. How are they alike? Describe the direction of the graph for both girls. How are the graphs different?

d)   Now compare Connie's graph to Kristie's and Samantha's graphs. Describe what you see.

e)   Compare Julie's graph with the others. Describe what you see.

CB-4.   **Cash on Hand (Part Three)**

The girls have another friend, Maleya. Maleya does not work with them at the concession stand and did not earn any money that day. However, she has been able to save $2.50 from baby-sitting each day since Sunday.

a)   Construct a table or use the resource page provided by your teacher for Maleya, then add her data to the graph you made for the other girls. Remember to label the line with her name and equation.

b)   Compare Maleya's graph to Kristie's graph. Will Maleya and Kristie ever have the same amount of money at the same time? Explain your answer.

c)   When will Maleya have more money than Connie? When will she have more money than Julie?

d)   Will Maleya ever have more money than Samantha? How can you tell?

CB-5.   Use the graph shown below to answer the following questions.

a)   Compare and contrast lines L, M, N, and K. Be as detailed as possible.

b)   Which line appears steepest?

c)   Which lines appear to have the same steepness?

d)   How is line K different from the other lines?

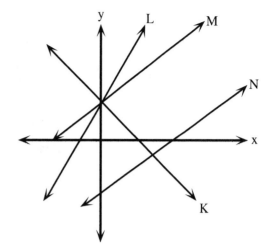

CB-6.

DESCRIBING LINES

Lines are described by their steepness and direction as they are viewed from left to right. Lines that go up show a positive rate of change. Lines that go down show a negative rate of change.

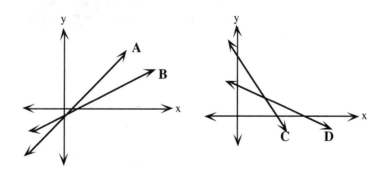

a)   Copy the graphs above.

b)   Compare the steepness of lines A and B, C and D, then A and C.

c)   Describe the direction of these lines. Which lines go up? Which go down?

CB-7. Lucy is a vendor selling boxes of popcorn at the arena. The table at right shows how many boxes of popcorn she sells throughout the day.

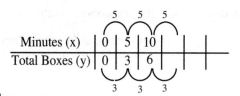

Minutes (x)	0	5	10		
Total Boxes (y)	0	3	6		

a) Assuming she continues to sell popcorn at this rate, copy and complete the table at right.

b) What pattern do you see in the table?

c) At what rate is she selling popcorn? Express your answer in boxes per minute.

d) How many boxes of popcorn will she sell in one hour?

CB-8. Find the area and perimeter of the triangle at right.

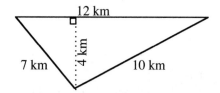

CB-9. On a radio show Polly won a $250 gift certificate to a local health club. The cost to become a member is $99, and the monthly membership fee is $16.50. How long can Polly use the health club before she runs out of money from her gift certificate? Write an equation and solve it.

CB-10. Solve for x.

a) $\frac{1}{2}x - 3 = -7$

b) $\frac{1}{2}x + \frac{1}{4} = 3$

c) $\frac{5}{8}x + \frac{2}{3} = 1\frac{11}{12}$

d) $\frac{x}{3} = \frac{21}{7}$

CB-11. Complete the following Diamond Problems.

Product

Sum

a)

b)

c)

d)

CB-12.   Now that we have started a new chapter, it is time for you to organize your binder.

a)   Put the work from the last chapter in order and keep it in a separate folder.

b)   When this is completed, write, "I have organized my binder."

CB-13.   Mr. Drawsalot is the landscape architect for the new museum near the local sports arena. He was asked to draw a picture of what the front of the building would look like five years after its completion. A row of trees will be planted along the front of the building. The trees will be three feet tall when planted, and in his drawing the trees will be 13 feet tall.

a)   Assuming the trees will grow the same amount each year, copy and complete the table below. Let $x = 0$ be the year the trees are planted.

Year (x)	0	1	2	3	4	5	x
Height (y)	3					13	

b)   Graph the information from your table and label it with its equation. Make sure you are careful and accurate. You will use your graph again later in the chapter.

c)   What is the change in time from one x-value to the next?

d)   What is the change in height from one y-value to the next?

e)   What ratio describes the growth rate of the trees? Write this **rate of change** as a ratio with units.

f)   What part of the equation shows the rate of change?

g)   Analyze your data table as shown below. Mark the rate of change across the table.

$$\text{rate of change} = \frac{\text{change in height}}{\text{change in time}}$$

Year (x)	0	1	2	3	4	5	x
Height (y)	3	5	7	9	11	13	2x + 3

+1   +1

+2   +2

CB-14.   Continue using your marked data table to answer the following questions.

a)   Add year 10 and year 20 to your data table.

b)   What is the change in time from year 5 to year 10? What is the change in height from year 5 to year 10? Write the **rate of change** (five-year growth rate) as a ratio with units.

c)   Compare the ratio you wrote in part (b) to the ratio you wrote in part (e) of the previous problem. What do you notice? What conjecture can you make?

d)   If the bottom of the sign for the museum is 35 feet above the ground, how many years will it take for the trees to reach the sign?

e)   If the sign is 12 feet tall, in how many years will the trees block it?

CB-15.   One of the overflow parking lots at the old baseball
         stadium holds 280 cars. Corey is working as a
         parking lot attendant at the overflow lot. His shift
         will end when the lot is emptied. The baseball game
         is sold out, so the overflow lot is full.

   a)   Assuming that cars leave at the same rate, copy
         and complete the table below. Write the rule
         for the relationship.

Time in Minutes (x)	0	3	6	9	12	x
Number of Cars in Lot (y)	280	247	214			

   b)   What is the change in the x-values? What is the change in the y-values?

   c)   Use your answers in part (b) to write a ratio to express the rate that the number of
         cars in the lot changes. Is this a positive or negative rate? Be sure to include units
         and simplify your ratio.

   d)   Compare your ratio and your equation. Which part of the equation shows the rate
         of change?

   e)   Graph the information from the table. Label the line with its equation. Describe the
         direction of your graph.

   f)   Make a conjecture about the rate of change between any two points on your line.

   g)   If Corey's shift ends when there are no more cars on the lot, at what time will
         Corey's shift be over if the game ends at 3:30 p.m.?

CB-16.   Antoinette had a carton with a dozen eggs in it. She weighed the carton with different
         numbers of eggs and got the weights shown in the table below.

Number of eggs	12	9	6	3
Weight (ounces)	43	34	25	16

   a)   Make a graph showing the weight of the eggs vs. the number in the carton.

   b)   Looking at your graph, find the rate at which the weight increases as the number of
         eggs increases.

   c)   Where does the line cross the y-axis?

   d)   What is the meaning of where the line crosses the y-axis?

336   CHAPTER 9

CB-17.

<table>
RATE OF CHANGE

RATE OF CHANGE is a ratio that compares the amount one quantity changes as another quantity changes.

$$\text{Rate of Change} \ = \ \frac{\text{change in one quantity}}{\text{change in the other quantity}}$$
</table>

In your Tool Kit highlight the formula for rate of change.

CB-18.   As you move from left to right along the hypotenuse of each triangle, which one is going up? Which one is going down?

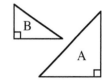

CB-19.   Sherice can fill lemonade cups at a rate of four cups per minute.

a)   How many cups can she fill in 6 minutes?

b)   How many cups can she fill in 10 minutes?

c)   If Sherice fills c cups in t minutes, write an equation which relates c and t.

d)   Sketch a graph to show the relationship between time and the number of cups filled. Which value is on the horizontal axis? Which value is on the vertical axis? Label your graph.

CB-20.   You are given two values in the following table. Assuming that the rate of change is constant, complete the table.

x	-6	-3	0	3	6	9	12	15	x
y			2	0					

a)   How can you tell from the table if the graph is a line or a curve?

b)   Graph the relationship in the table.

c)   Describe the direction of the line.

d)   Calculate the rate of change between x = 0 and x = 3. Remember the formula for rate of change: rate of change $= \dfrac{\text{change in y-values}}{\text{change in x-values}}$.

e)   Calculate the rate of change between x = -3 and x = 9.

f)   Identify the x- and y-intercepts.

CB-21. Use the symbol < or > to complete the following inequalities.

a) -16 ___ -19   b) |-18| ___ -11   c) -12 ___ 0

CB-22. Martin finds a sweater for $39.99 plus tax. The tax rate is 8.25%. If Martin has $42, does he have enough money to buy the sweater?

CB-23. Armand and Benito want to go to the camp store to buy snacks for their hike. They pull the change out of their pockets and find that they have a total of $2.50. Benito notices that they have twice as many dimes as they have nickels and two more quarters than nickels. Write an equation that represents the total amount of money they have in terms of nickels. Find out how many nickels, dimes, and quarters they have to spend on their snacks. A Guess and Check table might help you get started.

CB-24. For the following problem, you will need your graph from problem CB-13. Follow the steps below and use the graph to find the rate of change between the age of a tree and its height.

a) Plot and label points A(2, 7) and B(5, 13).

b) Draw a right triangle that has segment AB as its hypotenuse. This right triangle that helps you determine the rate of change between any two points on the line is called a **slope triangle**.

c) Find the number of feet the trees have grown between points A and B.

d) Find the number of years that have elapsed between points A and B.

e) Find the rate of change between the points A and B on the graph.

CB-25. Repeat the process in the previous problem for the points C(1, 5) and D(7, 17) to find the slope of the line through the points C and D.

CB-26. Imagine any two points on the line passing through the points A, B, C, and D in the previous problems. What would be the slope of the line (rate of change) between any two points on the line? Give a reason for your answer.

CB-27. Read the following information and use it to answer the questions that follow.

CALCULATING THE SLOPE OF A LINE

You can calculate the slope of a line using the same methods you used to find the rate of change.

1. Pick any two points on the line.

2. Draw a slope triangle.

3. Use the slope triangle to find the <u>vertical</u> change between the first and second points along the y-axis.

4. Use the slope triangle to find the <u>horizontal</u> change between the first and second points along the x-axis

5. Use the equation $\text{slope} = \dfrac{\text{change in y-values}}{\text{change in x-values}}$. Substitute the values from steps 3 and 4.

6. If the graph goes up from left to right, the slope ratio is positive. If the line goes down from left to right, the slope ratio is negative.

Use the method above to help you find the slopes of the following lines. Identify the x- and y-intercepts for each line.

a)

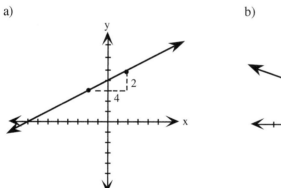

b)

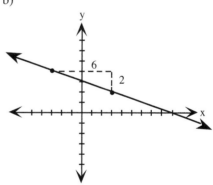

>>Problem continues on the next page.>>

c)

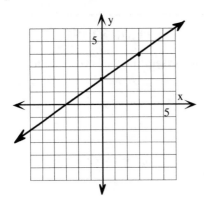

d)

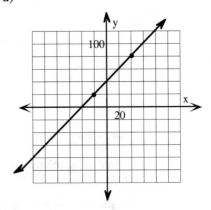

e)

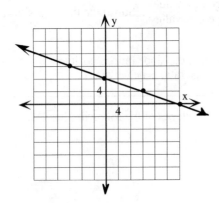

f)

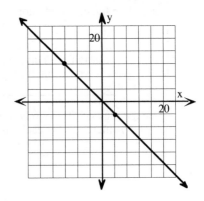

CB-28.   Several lines are graphed on the set of axes below right. For each line locate one point where the line crosses exactly through the corner of a graph paper square as it does at the origin. Use this point to find the rate of change (slope) and complete the table on the resource page provided by your teacher. Compare the results of the two columns for each equation.

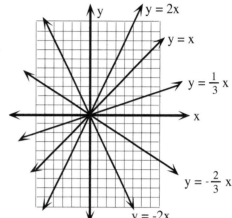

Equation	Rate of Change	Coefficient of x
$y = x$		
$y = 2x$		
$y = \frac{1}{3}x$		
$y = -2x$		
$y = -\frac{2}{3}x$		

CB-29.   Find the slope of each line segment below.

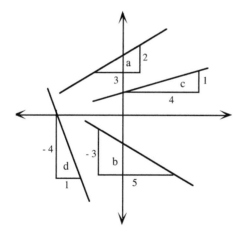

CB-30.   Evaluate.

a) $-44 - 55$ b) $100 + (-60)$ c) $83 - (-15)$

d) $34 - 42$ e) $-11(-10)$ f) $285 + (-642)$

CB-31.   Find the perimeter and area of each figure.

a)   b)   c)

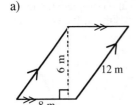   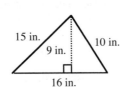   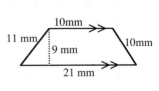

CB-32.   Solve for x.

a) $\frac{2}{3}x + \frac{2}{3} = \frac{2}{3}$ b) $x + \frac{3}{4} = 3\frac{2}{3}$

CB-33.   A toy car cost $1.89 before a television special. After the television special, the price jumped to $2.50. By what percent did the price increase?

CB-34.   Determine the compound interest earned on $220.00 invested at 3.25% compounded annually for 6 years.

CB-35.   A number pattern begins -5, -3, etc. with the numbers increasing by 2 each time. The sum of the reciprocals of the terms is $\frac{16}{63}$. How many terms are in the pattern?

CB-36.   Use what you have learned in the past few problems to figure out the slope of the line for each of the following linear equations. Also decide whether the graph of each line is increasing or decreasing.

a) $y = \frac{1}{2}x + 2$ b) $y = 2x - 4$ c) $y = -\frac{1}{3}x + 4$

d)   Which graph goes up most steeply? Which goes down most steeply?

CB-37.   Below right are the graphs of five equations. Use the graphs and the equations to complete
the table. The "constant" is the term in the equation without the variable.

Equation	Constant	Coordinate of y-intercept
y = x		
y = x + 2		
y = x + 5		
y = x – 2		
y = x – 6		

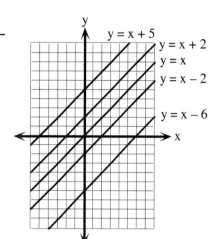

CB-38.   Use the table in the previous problem and compare the y-intercept of each line to the constant
number in each equation. What is the relationship between the y-intercept of
the line and the equation?

SLOPE OF A LINE AND LINEAR EQUATIONS

The **SLOPE** of a line is the rate of change between any two points on that line. It represents both steepness and direction. The slope ratio states the rate at which the relation between the two quantities is changing. The sign of the ratio indicates whether the rate of change is increasing (+) or decreasing (−).

$$\textbf{slope} = \frac{\text{vertical change}}{\text{horizontal change}} = \frac{\text{change in y-values}}{\text{change in x-values}}$$

Some textbooks write the ratio $\frac{\text{vertical change}}{\text{horizontal change}}$ as $\frac{\text{rise}}{\text{run}}$.

All equations of straight lines can be put in the form

$$y = (\textbf{coefficient})x + (\textbf{constant number})$$

where the **coefficient of x** is the rate of change (or **slope**), and the **constant number** is the **y-intercept**.

This form of a linear equation is called the **SLOPE-INTERCEPT FORM** and is written $y = mx + b$, where m is the slope and b is the y-coordinate of the y-intercept (0, b).

Example:

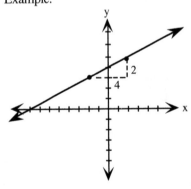

$$\text{slope} = \frac{\text{vertical change}}{\text{horizontal change}} = \frac{5 - 3}{2 - (-2)} = \frac{2}{4} = \frac{1}{2}$$

$$\text{y-intercept} = (0, 4)$$

$$y = \frac{1}{2}x + 4$$

In your Tool Kit, highlight:

a) the words in the ratio that tell you how to find slope.

b) the slope and y-intercept (found in the example).

CB-40.   Use what you have learned in the past few problems to find the y-intercept of each of the following equations.

a) $y = 2x - 4$

b) $y = \frac{1}{2}x + 2$

c) $y = -\frac{1}{3}x + 4$

d) $y = 3x + 1$

e) $y = -\frac{3}{2}x + 5$

f) $y = \frac{3}{4}x - 3$

g)   Which graph goes up most steeply? Which goes down most steeply?

CB-41.   Use the scale graph at right with the three points A(0, 250), B(150, 600), and C(150, 250) to answer the following questions.

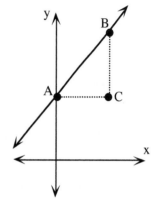

a)   What kind of triangle is $\triangle ABC$?

b)   What is the distance from A to C? C to B?

c)   What is the slope of line AB?

d)   Write the equation of the line.

e)   What is the distance from A to B?

f)   What is the area of $\triangle ABC$?

CB-42.   The groundskeeper of the arena kept track of the temperature from 6 a.m. to 6 p.m. during a day with a short heavy rain. He recorded the temperature every hour. Study his graph and use it to answer the questions below.

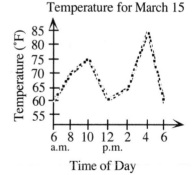

Temperature for March 15

a)   When did the temperature increase?

b)   When did the temperature increase most quickly? Explain how you know.

c)   When did the temperature decrease? Explain how you know.

d)   What was the rate of change of the temperature from 4 p.m. to 6 p.m.? Show your work.

CB-43.   The local donut shop has an automatic donut machine that makes dozens of donuts per
          hour. The table below shows the number of donuts made throughout the day up to
          different times.

Time	7:00	7:30	8:00	8:30	9:00
Number of Donuts	1280	1520	1760	2000	2240

a)   Draw a graph showing the number of donuts made in relation to the time. Scale the
      y-axis using an interval size of 200. Let 0 time on the x-axis represent 6:00 a.m.

b)   At what rate does the machine produce donuts?

c)   Where does the line cross the y-axis?

d)   What is the meaning of where the line crosses the y-axis?

CB-44.   What time does the donut shop in the previous problem start making donuts?

CB-45.   Al bought a computer for $2200 in July. Now the same model sells for $1650. By what
          percent did the price decrease?

CB-46.   Use proportions to solve the problem below. Show all steps.

          Ray bought 36 feet of wire for $24. How much will he have to pay for 90 feet of wire?
          How many feet of wire can he buy for $150?

CB-47.   Determine the simple interest earned on $118.00 invested at 5.25% for 8 years.

CB-48.   Solve the following equations.

a) $4x + (-3) = -27$ b) $3(2x - 3) = -15$

c) $21 = 2(x + 4)$ d) $2(2x - 15) = -20$

e) $4(x + 2) = 2x - 9$ f) $x + (-7) = 3(x + (-2))$

CB-49.   Use the equation $y = \frac{3}{2}x + 1$ to complete parts (a) through (d) below.

a)   Make a table and complete it. Use integer values for x from -3 to 3.

b)   Graph the equation using the values from your table.

c)   What is the rate of change as determined by the table?

d)   What is the slope of the line?

e)   What is the y-intercept of the line?

CB-50.   For each of the following equations, identify the slope and y-intercept. Then tell whether the line will have a positive or negative slope and what this says about the line.

a) $y = 3x + 6$ b) $y = -\frac{4}{5}x + 2$ c) $y = 0.75x - 4$ d) $y = -\frac{1}{3}x$

CB-51.   Ping and Xiu were graphing some lines for homework when Ping noticed that Xiu was working much more quickly than he was. Ping asked Xiu to show him her shortcut. Xiu explained, "If you want to graph $y = \frac{1}{2}x + 2$, just start by putting a point at 2 on the y-axis for the y-intercept, and then counting up one and over two to the right. The 'up one and over two' comes from the rate of change $\frac{1}{2}$ in the equation."

Use Xiu's shortcut to graph the equations below on the same set of axes.

a) $y = -\frac{1}{3}x + 4$ b) $y = \frac{5}{3}x - 2$ c) $y = \frac{3}{4}x + 1$

CB-52.   Use Xiu's shortcut to graph the equation $y = -\frac{2}{3}x + 2$. Label the line with its equation.

CB-53.   Points A, B, and C lie on the same line.

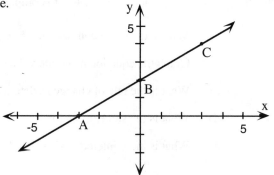

a)   Using points A and B, draw
     the slope triangle to find the
     slope of the line.

b)   Using points B and C, draw
     the slope triangle to find the
     slope of the line.

c)   Using points A and C, draw
     the slope triangle to find the
     slope of the line.

d)   Which of the points on a line should you use to find its slope? Explain your answer.

e)   Identify the x- and y-intercepts.

f)   Write an equation for this line. What part of the equation shows the slope of the
     line? How does the other part of the equation relate to the graph?

CB-54.   The last soccer game of the season has been scheduled to
          start at 1:00 p.m. at the arena. A special celebration will
          follow the game. Gary and his two friends have tickets to
          the game and have agreed to meet at the stadium. They all
          decided to leave their houses at noon and meet in the
          parking lot.

     Gary lives 20 miles from the arena. Due to traffic, he
     can only average about 40 miles per hour.

     Luis lives only 5 miles from the arena. He decides to
     ride his bicycle to avoid the traffic. He averages about
     6 miles per hour on his bike.

     Leonard lives 15 miles from the arena. He manages to avoid all traffic, averaging
     45 miles per hour for the trip.

a)   Make a table for each person above, showing the distance they have traveled at each
     time. Let x represent time (in minutes) and y represent the distance from the arena.

	Minutes	0	10	20	30	40	50
Distance	Gary	20					
from	Luis	5					
Arena	Leonard	15					

b)   Construct a single graph. Let the x-axis represent time (in minutes) and the y-axis
     distance (in miles) from the arena. Let 1 grid mark equal 2 units (either miles or
     minutes). Graph all three trips on the same graph in different colors.

c)   What is the slope of the line for each person (rate of change)?

d)   Will they all arrive in time for the 1 p.m. celebration? Explain.

CB-55.   Complete the following Diamond Problems.

 Product

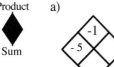 Sum

a)

b)

c)

d)

CB-56.   Identify the slope and y-intercept of these linear equations. Use them to graph lines without making a table.

a) $y = \frac{1}{2}x - 5$

b) $y = -\frac{5}{3}x + 4$

c) $y = 3x - 4$

CB-57.   Solve for x.

a) $\frac{2}{3}x = 45$

b) $\frac{3}{5}x = 60$

c) $2x + 3 = -x + 8$

d) $8 = -4 + 3(3x + 5)$

CB-58.   Ms. Beade had each team in her class measure the length of a team member's pencil. The class was divided into seven teams, so there were seven measurements (in centimeters): 7.5, 13.2, 17.0, 6.5, 9.8, 8.7, and 9.3. Use the data to:

a)   prepare a stem-and-leaf plot.

b)   prepare a box-and-whisker plot.

CB-59.   Several lines are graphed on the axes below. Using your previous observations about rates of change, match each line to an equation in the table on the resource page.

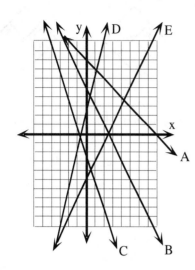

Equation	Line
$y = 2x - 5$	_____
$y = 4x + 2$	_____
$y = -2x + 5$	_____
$y = -3x - 2$	_____
$y = -x + 8$	_____

CB-60.   Hank's great-great-grandfather buried a gold piece that was worth $2 in 1890. Suppose it doubled in value every 10 years that it was buried.

a)   How much would it be worth in 2000?

Date (year)	1890	1900	1910									2000
Value ($)	2											

b)   Add another row to your table and write your answers in exponential notation.

Exponent Form	2^1			2^4								

c)   Graph the data. Put the date on the horizontal (x) axis and the value on the vertical (y) axis. Scale your axes appropriately.

d)   Does it make sense to connect the points here?

CB-61.   A survey was conducted before the last student council election, and 350 out of 900 students said they would vote for Jamie. One out of how many students said they would vote for Jamie?

CB-62.   Victor took his skateboard to the repair shop last week to get it fixed. The woman from the repair shop called at 5:00 p.m. to tell Victor that his skateboard was fixed and ready to be picked up. Victor wants to pick up his skateboard today before the repair shop closes at 5:30 p.m. It is now 5:10 p.m. and the repair shop is across town, $4\frac{1}{2}$ miles from Victor's house. Victor can ride his bicycle to the shop at an average speed of 15 miles per hour. Will Victor be able to pick up his skateboard today? Show how you get your answer.

CB-63.   George and Ben are two friends who make extra money parking cars at concerts and sporting events at the big arena near their homes in Indianapolis. They both want to go to college to become architects. Ben wants to go to Indiana-Purdue University at Fort Wayne, but George wants to start at the local community college and transfer in two years. Both are worried about the expense of college since neither of their families can afford to help.

Ben's older sister, Marie, says that in her job they use graphs to estimate. She will show George how to use these ideas to decide if he will have enough money to attend college. She uses Ben's savings book to show George how to do it. Here is how to use Marie's idea.

Month	Feb.	Mar.	April	May	June	July	Aug.	Sept.	Oct.	Nov.
Balance	$61	$179	$285	$401	$524	$627	$748	$857	$971	$1085

a)   Make a scatter plot showing the balance in Ben's savings account on the first of each month. Let February be Month 0 on your graph.

b)   Use a ruler to draw a line of best fit (a straight line that goes through the "middle" of the pattern of the points) for the months from February through November. What is the slope of the line of best fit? What does this slope represent?

c)   About how much can Ben be expected to save if he works through August 1 of next year?

CB-64.   George did not start parking cars until July 1, when he had $209 in his savings account. Here is a list of his monthly savings balances.

Month	July	Aug.	Sept.	Oct.	Nov.
Balance	$209	$334	$451	$581	$706

a)   Make a scatter plot showing the balance in George's savings account on the first of each month. Let July be Month 0 on the graph.

b)   Draw a line of best fit for the months from July through November. What is the slope of your line? What does this slope represent?

c)   George is going to keep working at the arena until college starts in August. If George saves about the same amount each month, how much will he save by August 1 of next year?

CB-65.   George's school counselor gave him a sheet with information about expenses at Indianapolis Community College. George has qualified for a Pell Grant. In the last problem, he got a reasonable estimate of how much he will save during the year parking cars. Use that information and the information at right to determine if he has enough money yet to afford to attend the community college.

Community College	
Costs	
Tuition (1 year)	$1986
Books	600
Gas for car + parking	800
Clothes, personal, etc.	900
Total Cost	$4286
Sources of Income	
Pell Grant	$2100
Savings(from arena job)	
Total Income	

CB-66.   Ben's school counselor calculated the expenses at Indiana-Purdue University at Fort Wayne (IPFW) including tuition, books, housing, and some personal spending money. You estimated how much money he will save parking cars through the year. He has received a Pell Grant and has qualified for a $3025 loan. How much more will he need to save?

IPFW	
Total Cost	$8818
Sources of Income	
Pell Grant	$2400
Loan	$3025
Savings (from arena job)	
Total Income	

CB-67.   George has been offered a second job for next summer that will not interfere with his arena job. He will net $6 per hour helping a friend sweep out stores. Calculate how many hours George will need to work at this rate to have enough money for college.

CB-68.   If Ben needs to earn about $1300, how many hours will he need to work at $6 per hour?

CB-69.   What is the slope of the equation $y = \frac{3}{5}x + 2$? Where would this graph cross the y-axis? Explain.

CB-70.   Calculate the following sums and differences.

a) $3\frac{1}{2} + 2\frac{5}{8}$

b) $\frac{26}{11} + 7$

c) $5 - 1\frac{10}{13}$

CB-71.   Use the graph at right to describe the
          savings habits of each student. For
          example, from the graph you know that
          Rhonda starts with $4 and Lauren saves
          $3 every two weeks.

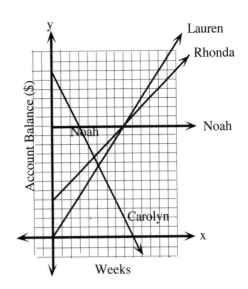

CB-72.   Ray Sheo keeps track of the height of his fast-growing corn. His records are shown in the
          table below.

Day	0	2	4	6	8	x
Height (cm)	2	7.5	13	18.5	24	

a)   What is the growth rate of Ray's corn? Is this number always the same?

b)   If you graph the points in this table, will it make a line or a curve? Explain how you
      know.

c)   In how many days will the corn be 47 centimeters tall?

d)   If Ray harvests the corn when it reaches 3 meters, when will he harvest it?

CB-73.   The simplified form of $\left(\frac{8+6}{7}\right) - 7$ is:

          (A) 5   (B) 1   (C) -5   (D) 2

CB-74.   Solve for x.

          a) $3x + 2(x - 6) = 3x + 8$ b) $3 - 4(x + 1) = 12x + 3$ c) $0.8x = 68$

CB-75. Lucian is driving to Fort Lauderdale. Assuming he averages 52 mph, determine how far he has gone after the following amounts of time.

a)   3 hours   b)   6 hours   c) $\frac{1}{2}$ hour   d) $4\frac{1}{2}$ hours

CB-76. Joshua wants to have a huge collection of baseball cards. Currently he has 175 cards. His plan is to use his allowance to buy a pack of 12 cards each week.

a)   The current week is 0 in the table below. Complete the table.

Week	0	1	2	3	4	5
Baseball Cards	175					

b)   Calculate the rate of change. Is the graph a line?

c)   From the table, can you determine the y-intercept? How do you know?

d)   Write an equation to represent the total number of cards (y) in terms of weeks (x).

CB-77. Follow your teacher's directions for practicing mental math.

CB-78. Use the inequality signs to answer the following problems.

a)   -3 ___ 2   b)   -3 ___ -6

c)   0 ___ -7   d)   -2 ___ 0 ___ 7

CB-79. You have been working with the < and > signs. We can modify the signs to include the possibility that the two values are equal: ≤ and ≥. The ≤ sign means less than or equal to. The ≥ sign means greater than or equal to.

For example, x ≥ 6 means x is greater than 6 or equal to 6. This is how it is graphed on a number line:

-6   0   6

Graph each inequality:

a)   x ≥ 5   b)   x ≤ 5

CB-80. Ben told Marie that he had an amount of money in his wallet that was less than $20. He asked her how to write this as an inequality. Marie said, "The amount of money you have is unknown to me, so let's call it x. The symbol for 'less than' looks like this: <, so write x < 20." On a number line, x < 20 looks like this:

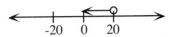

-20   0   20

a) Graph the following problems using Marie's method.

i)   x = 5   ii)   x > 5

iii) x < 5   iv)   x ≥ 5

b) How are graphs (ii) and (iv) different?

c) What does the filled-in circle mean?

d) What does the open circle mean?

CB-81. Ben asked Marie how to decide which way to draw the arrows for the inequality x ≥ 6. She told him that to decide which direction the arrow goes, first locate the point, 6, on the number line. Next check to see whether 5 or 7 makes the inequality true, since each of these numbers is located on a different side of 6.

a)   Is 5 ≥ 6?   b)   Is 7 ≥ 6?

The arrow goes toward 7, since 7 made the inequality true.

CB-82. The temperature for the day is predicted to be no higher than 75° F and no lower than 50° F. This graph represents the inequality 50° ≤ x ≤ 75°.

25 30 35 40 45 50 55 60 65 70 75 80

a) What do you think this graph means?

b) What would the graph for the inequality 45° < x ≤ 70° look like?

CB-83. Corey's car needs 12 gallons of gas to go 220 miles.

a) How much gas is needed to go 0 miles?

b) Construct a graph that shows g, the number of gallons of gas used (y-axis), compared to m, the number of miles driven (x-axis).

c) Using your graph, estimate how much gas will be needed to go 70 miles.

d) Estimate how many miles can be driven with 10 gallons of gas.

e) Use proportions to find exact answers to parts (c) and (d).

f) How many miles per gallon does Corey's car get? Show your work.

CB-84. Corey wanted to be able to figure out how much gas it would take him to go a certain number of miles. He decided he would rather write and solve the linear equation than solve a proportion.

a) Knowing that he could go 220 miles on 12 gallons of gas, use your knowledge of proportions and slope to write the equation that represents this. Use x for miles and y for gallons.

b) What is the slope of the equation? Compare the slope with the proportions in part (e) of problem CB-83. What do you notice?

CB-85. George had to buy a book for a class he needed to take to study for college entrance exams. Marie told him that the cost of the book was at least $10 but no more than $20. Write the possible cost of the book as an inequality.

CB-86. Ben's school needed vans for a field trip. Each van can hold no more than 9 students. Make a number line graph to show the number of students that can travel in a van. Remember that $x \le 9$ and that no van can have part of a student.

a) Discuss with your partner whether your graph should have a line with an arrow or something different.

b) Describe what your graph looks like.

CB-87.   Graph the following inequalities.

   a) $x \geq 6$ b) $x < -7$

   c) $0 \leq x \leq 8$ for all whole numbers   d) $-7 < x \leq 10$

CB-88.   The answers in this problem are not numerical. Use the variables a, b, c, and/or d to
          answer each question.

   a)   What are the coordinates of F?

   b)   What are the coordinates of G?

   c)   What is the area of ΔAHG?

   d)   What is the slope of segment AG?

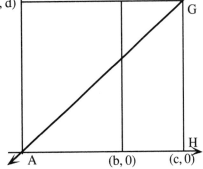

CB-89.   On a piece of graph paper, plot the following points and connect them: A(-3, -4),
          B(2, 4), and C(5, -4).

   a)   What is the area of ΔABC?

   b)   What is the perimeter of ΔABC?

   c)   Calculate the slope of each side of the triangle.

CB-90.   Evaluate.

   a) $18 \cdot 2 + 3 \cdot 2 \div 6 + |{-6}|$ b) $27 - |{-3} \cdot 7|$ c) $3 + 6 \cdot 9 - 3 \cdot 5$

   d) $-11 + 4 \cdot 7 - |11|$ e) $13 - 2 \cdot 6 + 3^2 \cdot 4$ f) $3 \cdot 7 - (4 \cdot 2)^2 + 6^2 \cdot 2$

CB-91.   Solve these problems. Show your steps.

   a) $2x - 8 = |26|$ b) $3x + 5 = |{-20}|$

   c) $4x + 12 = 32$ d) $8x - 16 = -32$

CB-92.   Ben's little sister, Clarisse, came home with a math problem she could not do. She asked Ben to help her.

The problem was $x + 4 \geq 10$. She told Ben that she could solve equations but not inequalities. Ben told her that solving inequalities is a lot like solving equations. Here is Ben's method.

- Write the inequality as an equation and solve in the usual way:
  $x + 4 = 10$, so $x = 6$.

- Put a solid dot at $x = 6$ on a number line.

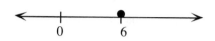

- Test (substitute) a point in the <u>original</u> inequality to see if it makes the inequality true. Zero is one of the easiest numbers to test: $0 + 4 \geq 10 \Rightarrow 4 \geq 10$, which is false.

- Since 0 made the inequality false and 0 is to the left of 6, all points to the right of 6 must be true for $x + 4 \geq 10$, so draw a line with an arrow to the right of 6.

The graph shows the solution, $x \geq 6$.

CB-93.   Solve and graph these problems.

a) $x + 5 > 7$ b) $7 > x + 5$

c) $x - 6 \geq -12$ d) $2x - 8 \leq 26$

e) $8 - 2x \leq -26$ f) $3x + 5 \leq |-20|$

g) $4x + 12 < 32$ h) $16 - 8x < -32$

CB-94.   Kindra would like to have more than $1500 in her savings account.

a)   If she starts with $61 in her savings account, write an inequality to show how much she wants to have.

b)   Solve the inequality in part (a).

c)   How much does Kindra need to save?

CB-95. The new Olympic-sized pool is closed for its annual cleaning and only about 10,000 gallons of water are left in the bottom. It is time to refill it. The pool holds 640,000 gallons and can be filled by the usual pipes at 2000 gallons per minute. A fire hose can also be used to pump up to another 1000 gallons per minute if desired.

   a) What are the minimum and maximum rates of filling the pool?

   b) Find the shortest and longest times it can take to fill the pool.

   c) On the same set of axes, draw two lines that show the possible amounts of water in the pool after x minutes. Be sure to show where the pool is full.

   d) Write the equations of the lines you drew in part (c).

CB-96. Solve and graph the following inequalities.

   a) $2x + 5 \geq 10$ b) $4 \leq x - 2$

   c) $3x - 9 < -12$ d) $-12 < x - 9$

CB-97. Graph these lines on the same set of axes.

   a) $y = \frac{3}{5}x - 4$ b) $y = -\frac{1}{2}x + 1$

CB-98. Gail bought her cap for $7.50, which was $\frac{1}{3}$ off the original price. What was the original price? (Hint: What part of the original price is $7.50?)

CB-99. Solve the following equations.

   a) $5x + 4 = 3x + 2.5$ b) $\frac{3}{4}x - 3 = -5$ c) $-\frac{2}{5}x - 1 = 9$

CB-100. A prism is 23.5 inches tall. The base of the prism is a right triangle with legs that are 5 inches and 3.75 inches long. Draw and label a diagram. What is the volume and surface area of the prism? Show your subproblems.

CB-101. Use the graph below to answer the following questions.

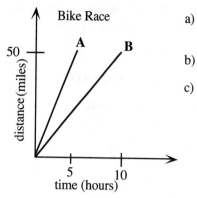

a) Which bicyclist, the one at point A or the one at point B, is traveling at the greater rate?

b) Find the coordinates of point A and point B.

c) What is the average rate in miles per hour for the bicyclist at point A? What is the average rate for the bicyclist at point B?

CB-102. In 45 minutes, Ishmael can ride his bicycle 12 miles. Assume he rides at a steady rate.

a) How long does it take him to ride 4 miles?

b) How far will he ride in 60 minutes if he continues at the same rate of speed?

c) What is Ishmael's average speed in miles per hour?

CB-103.   **Chapter Summary**

It is time to summarize and review what
you have learned in this chapter. In teams
or with a partner, you will be making a
mobile. Choose examples from the
chapter for the following topics: slope, rate
of change, y-intercept, and inequalities.

Your team should divide the work in order
to complete the mobile in one class period.
For each topic, the mobile must have a
concept label and a sample problem. See
the example at right. You may put the four
topics back to back to get all of them on
one mobile.

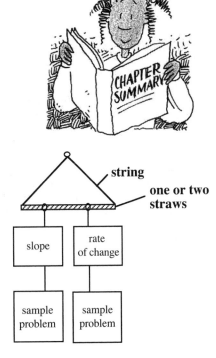

CB-104.   Mai has a small bottle with 2 cups of orange juice. While waiting for chemistry lab to
start, she pours out different amounts and then weighs the bottle and the juice left in it.
Here are the weights she recorded.

Number of Cups Left in Bottle	2	$1\frac{3}{4}$	1	$\frac{1}{2}$
Weight (in ounces)	21	$16\frac{3}{2}$	12	$7\frac{1}{2}$

a)   Draw a graph showing the weight vs. the number of cups left in the bottle.

b)   Find the slope of the line you drew in part (a). Is the slope positive or negative?

c)   What does the slope represent?

d)   Where is the y-intercept?

e)   What is the meaning of the y-intercept?

CB-105. Complete the table below for the equation $y = -|x + 4| - 3$.

x	-6	-4	-1	0	2	3	5
y							

a) Predict the shape and orientation of the graph.

b) Graph the equation.

c) Was your prediction in part (a) correct? What part of the equation determined the orientation of the graph?

CB-106. Brian's Sports Memorabilia Company puts together specialized packages with clothing and equipment from the customer's favorite sports team. The company can put together packages at a constant rate. An order has been placed for 100 packages. Each package costs $750. The company inventory for April is listed below.

Day	3	6	9		
Completed Packages	42	44	46		

a) Fill in the next two sets of data.

b) What is the rate of change (packages/day)?

c) What is the shape of the graph?

d) What is the slope of the line?

e) What is the y-intercept of the line?

f) What does the y-intercept represent in this problem?

g) What is the equation of the line?

h) How many days will it take to have 100 packages completed?

CB-107. A line is determined by the points (1, 2) and (2, -1).

a) Draw a slope triangle and determine the slope.

b) Use the slope pattern to find another point on the line with integer coordinates.

c) Find the distance between the first two points.

CB-108.   For each line find the slope, the y-intercept, and give the equation.

a)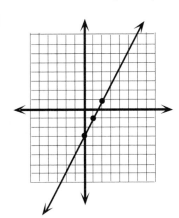

b)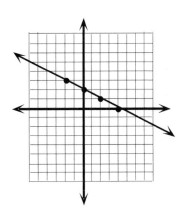

CB-109.   Use the slope and y-intercept to graph each line.

a) $y = -\frac{2}{3}x - 1$ b) $y = \frac{1}{2}x + 2$ c) $y = 3x$

CB-110.   Why can't you use slope-intercept form to graph $y = x^2 - 2$?

CB-111.   Graph each inequality.

a) $x \geq 3$ b) $x < -2$ c) $-2 \leq x < 3$

CB-112.   Solve and graph each inequality.

a) $2x + 1 \leq 5$ b) $7 > 3 - x$ c) $3x + 7 > x - 1$

CB-113.   On a set of axes scaled by tens,

a)   Plot the points (-24, 40) and (36, 60). Use a ruler to draw the line between them.

b)   Estimate the y-intercept.

c)   Draw a slope triangle to find the slope of the line.

d)   What is the equation of the line?

CB-114.   **What We Have Done in This Chapter**

Below is a list of the Tool Kit entries from this chapter.

- CB-17   Rate of Change

- CB-39   Slope of a Line and Linear Equations

Review all the entries and read the notes you made in your Tool Kit. Make a list of any questions, terms, or notes you do not understand. Ask your partner or study team members for help. If anything is still unclear, ask your teacher.

Modeling Growth

Chapter 10

Chapter 10
Modeling Growth: EXPONENTS, SCIENTIFIC NOTATION, AND VOLUME

This chapter brings the course to a close by using several ideas with three-dimensional figures. You will have the opportunity to apply scale factors to create enlargements and reductions of items you select. This project will reinforce previous work with surface area and volume. Your teacher will give you detailed directions about this project; for now, begin to look for an everyday item like a cereal box, bar of soap, canister of snack foods, or similar items that you would like to use for the enlargement and reduction project in this chapter. You will need to have your selection approved by your teacher.

You will also continue to use subproblems to practice various topics in multi-step problems. Finally, you will tie together the notion of exponents and apply them to large and small numbers.

In this chapter you will have the opportunity to:

- work with very large and very small numbers.

- simplify exponential expressions.

- investigate the change in volume of three-dimensional figures when the dimensions are enlarged or reduced.

- investigate growth patterns of surface area and volume in relation to increases and decreases in dimensions.

- study the graphs of equations containing squared and cubed numbers.

Read the problem below, but **do not try to solve it now**. What you learn over the next few days will enable you to solve it.

MG-0. **Cracker Snacks**

The Clifford Snack Company produces cracker canisters. Their snack-size canisters are similar to full-size canisters but have been reduced by a scale factor of $\frac{2}{5}$. Use the dimensions of the full-size canisters to calculate the surface area and volume of both the full-size and the snack-size canisters.

Number Sense	
Algebra and Functions	
Mathematical Reasoning	
Measurement and Geometry	
Statistics, Data Analysis, & Probability	

Chapter 10
Modeling Growth: EXPONENTS, SCIENTIFIC NOTATION, AND VOLUME

MG-1.   Use the set of cube template resource pages your teacher gives your team to make six cubes of different sizes. Do not seal the lids shut, because the cubes need to be nested for storage. When you finish, write in your notebook, "Cubes built."

MG-2.   Get the Cube Growth resource page from your teacher. Record the scale factors and edge lengths for Cubes A through F. For this problem we will agree that Cube C (the colored one) has an edge length of one unit. Thinking about how many edge lengths of Cube C fit along the side of Cube D will help you fill in the table. Then complete parts (a) and (b) below.

Name of Cube	Scale Factor	Length of One Edge	Surface Area of One Face	Volume of Cube
A				
B				
C (Unit Cube)	$\frac{1}{1}$	1 unit	1 unit ^{2}	1 unit ^{3}
D				
E				
F				
Rule				
Extensions				

a)   Complete the remaining columns for cubes A through F. You will find it easier to begin with cubes D through F and leave cubes A and B for last.

b)   Using the patterns developed in the Cube Growth resource page, write a rule for each column in terms of x. Then use those rules to complete the remaining rows in the table.

MG-3.   Use the rectangular prism shown below right to complete parts (a) through (d) below.

a)   Calculate the surface area of the prism. Show all your subproblems.

b)   Explain why the exponent for area is 2 (that is, cm^2).

c)   Calculate the volume of the prism.

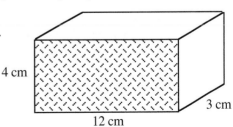

4 cm

12 cm

3 cm

d)   Explain why the exponent for volume is a 3 (that is, cm^3).

MG-4.   Copy and complete the chart of these cubed numbers.

Exponent Form	Factored Form	Standard Form
2^3	$2 \cdot 2 \cdot 2$	8
3^3		
	$4 \cdot 4 \cdot 4$	
		125
6^3		
7^3		
	$8 \cdot 8 \cdot 8$	
9^3		

MG-5.   Copy and complete the table below.

Original Form	Factored Form	Simplified Form
$5^2 \cdot 5^5$	$(5 \cdot 5)(5 \cdot 5 \cdot 5 \cdot 5 \cdot 5)$	5^7
$2^2 \cdot 2^4$		
$3^7 \cdot 3^2$		
$x^3 \cdot x^5$		
$x^3y^2 \cdot xy^2$		

a)   For each example, compare the bases of the original expression to the base(s) of the simplified expression. What do you notice?

b)   For each example, compare the exponents of the original form to the exponent(s) of the simplified form. What do you notice?

c)   Simplify $20^{12} \cdot 20^{51}$ without writing the factored form. Describe your process.

MG-6.   State the slope and y-intercept for the equation of each line below.

a) $y = -\frac{5}{3}x - 2$

b) $y = 4x - \frac{5}{12}$

MG-7.   Solve each inequality and sketch the graph of the solution on a number line.

a) $4x - 10 < 6$

b) $3x - 4 \le 5x - 8$

MG-8.   Is 3^5 the same as $3 \cdot 5$? Explain.

MG-9.   Now that we have started a new chapter, it is time for you to organize your binder.

a)   Put the work from the last chapter in order and keep it in a separate folder.

b)   When this is completed, write, "I have organized my binder."

MG-10.   Use the data in problem MG-2 to make three graphs on the large axes on the resource page your teacher gives you. For this problem we will let each x-value represent a scale factor and examine how it changes for length, area, and volume. Draw one graph comparing scale factor to edge length, $y = x$ for $0 \le x \le 11$; one comparing scale factor to area, $y = x^2$ for $0 \le x \le 11$; and one comparing scale factor to volume, $y = x^3$ for $0 \le x \le 5$. You will need to calculate additional values for $x = 10$ and $x = 11$. Write the rule by each graph, then complete parts (a) through (c) below.

a)   Which graph is the flattest when the scale factor is 5?

b)   Which graph is the steepest when the scale factor is 5?

c)   Explain why the curve for the volume data becomes so much steeper than the curve for the surface area data.

MG-11.   Graph the three equations in the previous problem on the small axes on the resource page for $0 \le x \le \frac{3}{2}$ for intervals of $\frac{1}{4}$. A data table is included for $x = \frac{3}{4}$, $x = \frac{5}{4}$, and $x = \frac{3}{2}$.

a)   What point(s) is (are) common to all three graphs?

b)   Why are the curves below the straight line ($y = x$) for the scale factors $0 < x < 1$?

MG-12. Label the dimensions of the prism at right where it appears on the resource page your teacher gives you.

Original
Prism

a) Find the surface area and volume of the original prism. Record the results on your resource page.

b) Label the dimensions of each of the enlargements. Use the scale factors $\frac{2}{1}$ and $\frac{3}{1}$.

c) Calculate the surface area and volume for <u>each</u> of the two enlargements. Record your answers on the resource page.

d) Write and simplify a ratio comparing the surface area of each enlargement to the surface area of the original.

e) Write and simplify a ratio comparing the volume of each enlargement to the volume of the original.

f) Continue sketching, labeling, and calculating the surface area and volume for prisms enlarged by the scale factors on the resource page.

MG-13. Refer to your table in problem MG-2 to help you answer the questions below.

a) How do the surface area ratios compare to the enlargement ratios?

b) How do the volume ratios compare to the enlargement ratios?

c) Compare your results in parts (a) and (b) to your graphs in problem MG-10.

RATIOS OF DIMENSIONAL CHANGE

For any pair of similar figures or solids with a scale factor $\frac{a}{b}$, the enlargement and reduction relationships are:

Length (one dimension)	Area (two dimensions)	Volume (three dimensions)
$\frac{a}{b}$	$\frac{a^2}{b^2}$	$\frac{a^3}{b^3}$

Example 1:   Example 2:

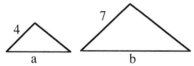

length: $\frac{a}{b} = \frac{4}{7}$ length: $\frac{a}{b} = \frac{2}{3}$

area: $\frac{a^2}{b^2} = \frac{4^2}{7^2} = \frac{16}{49}$ area: $\frac{a^2}{b^2} = \frac{2^2}{3^2} = \frac{4}{9}$

volume: $\frac{a^3}{b^3} = \frac{2^3}{3^3} = \frac{8}{27}$

Length ratios apply to sides, edges, and perimeters of figures.

Area ratios apply to surface area of solids and the area of two-dimensional regions.

Highlight the three basic ratios and their headings (length, area, and volume) in your Tool Kit.

MG-15. Copy and complete the table. Use the Giant **1** to simplify the factored form.

Original Form	Factored Form	Simplified Form
$\dfrac{5^5}{5^2}$	$\dfrac{5 \cdot 5 \cdot 5 \cdot 5 \cdot 5}{5 \cdot 5}$	5^3
$\dfrac{2^4}{2^2}$		
$\dfrac{3^7}{3^4}$		
$\dfrac{x^5}{x^3}$		
$\dfrac{x^3 y^2}{x y^2}$		
$\dfrac{x^5}{x}$		

a) For each example, compare the exponents in the original form to the exponents in the simplified form. What do you notice?

b) Simplify $\dfrac{20^{51}}{20^{12}}$ without writing the factored form. Describe what you did in detail.

MG-16. Practice estimating square roots by writing your estimate as a mixed number and as a decimal, then using your calculator to check your estimate. Be sure to write your estimate before you use your calculator. Round your answers to the nearest hundredth (0.01). You should have three answers for each problem.

a) $\sqrt{45}$

b) $\sqrt{260}$

c) $\sqrt{650}$

d) $\sqrt{57}$

MG-17. Howie and Steve are making cookies for themselves and some friends. The recipe they are using will make 48 cookies, but they only want to make 16 cookies. They have no trouble reducing the amounts of flour and sugar, but the original recipe calls for $1\frac{3}{4}$ cups of butter. Help Howie and Steve determine how much butter they will need.

MG-18. I am thinking of a number. If you multiply it by $\frac{1}{3}$ and then add 13, the result is 94. Write an equation and solve it to find my number.

MG-19. Simplify the expression $5 + 2^2 \cdot 3 - 3.75(5 - 4)$.

MG-20. Use subproblems to calculate the area of the figure at right. List each subproblem and show your work.

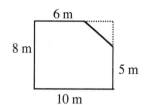

6 m

8 m

5 m

10 m

MG-21. Graph each of the following equations on the same set of axes.

a) $y = \frac{4}{3}x - 3$

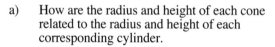

b) $y = -\frac{1}{3}x + 2$

r = 1.35

MG-22. Your teacher will lead a demonstration about the volume of cones.

a) How are the radius and height of each cone related to the radius and height of each corresponding cylinder.

h = 11

b) Sketch the two cones in your notebook. Label the radius and height of each one.

r = 1.75

c) Estimate which cone you think will have the greater volume. Write "I think this one will have more volume" below the cone you believe has more volume.

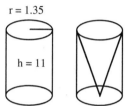

h = 8

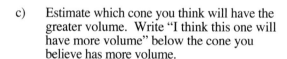

d) How many cones full of rice were needed to fill its corresponding cylinder?

e) Based on your teacher's demonstration, describe how the volume of a cone compares to the volume of a cylinder of the same base and height.

f) Find the volume of each cone.

MG-23. On a separate sheet of paper, write the instructions for how to find the volume of the cone shown at right.

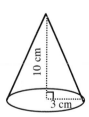

a) Trade papers with your partner. Follow the instructions your partner wrote to find the volume of the cone.

10 cm

b) Let your partner know if the instructions were clear and easy to follow. Give suggestions for how the instructions could have been better.

3 cm

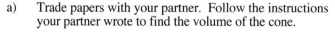

MG-24. Get a resource page from your teacher. Let each member of your study team calculate the data for one of the cones shown. If there are absent team members, divide the remaining work among those who are present. The first cone is shown below.

Cones	Scale Factor	Area of Circular Base	Ratio of Areas $\frac{New}{Original}$	Volume Cubic Units	Ratio of Volumes $\frac{New}{Original}$
6 cm 2 cm	1	12.56 cm²	$\frac{12.56}{12.56}$	25.12 cm³	$\frac{25.12}{25.12} = \frac{1}{1}$

a) Complete each row of the table. Write the ratios twice, both as a decimal and as a ratio.

b) Share your results with your team so that all team members have a complete set of data. Check to make sure the data is correct.

c) Compare your results for the ratios of the area and volume to the Tool Kit entry in problem MG-14. Be sure your results are consistent with the basic relationships there.

MG-25. Refer to the graph at right to answer the following questions.

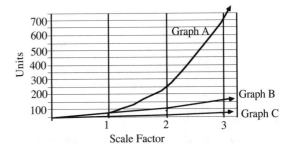

a) Which graph represents the height of the different cones?

b) Which graph represents the area of the base of the different cones?

c) Which graph represents the volume of the different cones?

d) Explain how you determined your choices for parts (a), (b), and (c).

MG-26.

VOLUME OF A CONE

Every cone has a volume that is one-third the volume of the cylinder with the same base and height. To find the volume of a cone, use the same formula as the volume of a cylinder and divide by three. The formula for the volume of a cone of base area A and height h is:

$$V = \frac{A \cdot h}{3}$$

When the base of the cone is a circle of radius r, the formula is:

$$V = \frac{\pi r^2 h}{3} \quad \text{or} \quad \frac{1}{3}\pi r^2 h$$

Highlight the equation to calculate the volume of a cone in your Tool Kit.

MG-27. Find the volume of a cone with a height of 8 feet and a radius of 5 feet. Draw a sketch and show your work.

MG-28. Copy and complete the table.

Original Form	Factored Form	Simplified Form
$(5^2)^5$	$(5 \cdot 5)(5 \cdot 5)(5 \cdot 5)(5 \cdot 5)(5 \cdot 5)$	5^{10}
$(2^2)^4$		
$(3^7)^2$		
$(x^3)^5$		
$(x^3 y^2)^2$		

a) For each example, compare the exponents in the original form to the exponent(s) in the simplified form. What do you notice?

b) Simplify $(20^2)^{51}$ without writing the factored form. Describe in detail what you did.

MG-29.   Sketch the prism at right on your paper.

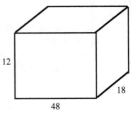

a)   Calculate the surface area and volume.

b)   Suppose you wanted to know the surface area and volume of a prism with dimensions $\frac{1}{2}$ those of the prism at right. You could find the new surface area by writing the equation $\frac{1^2}{2^2} = \frac{\text{surface area}}{3312}$. Find the surface area of the new prism, then use a similar proportion to find its volume.

c)   What would be the new surface area and volume if you reduced the original dimensions to $\frac{1}{3}$ the size of the original prism?

MG-30.   The regular size Yummy Soup can has a rectangular label like the one shown at right.

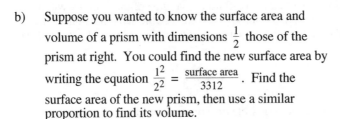

a)   Assuming that the label cannot overlap, find the diameter and radius of the can.

b)   Find the dimensions of the label on the family size can if it is $\frac{7}{5}$ of the size of the regular size can.

c)   Explain how to find the volume of any reduced figure without using volume formulas.

MG-31.   Shante is painting a building with 33 identical offices. If she uses 14 gallons of paint for the first six offices, how much paint will she need to paint all 33 offices?

MG-32.   Follow your teacher's directions for practicing mental math. Write the new strategy you learned.

MG-33.   Read the rules below for Pair Up, the game you will be playing today. As you play, you
         must record each turn you take on your paper.

Pair Up
A game for two people.

Mathematical Purpose: To simplify expressions with exponents.

Object: To make card pairs by matching each problem with the simplified
exponential expression.

Materials: Pair-Up cards: Problem Deck and Solution Deck

Scoring: One point for each correct match. Two points for each correct match if
the card contains an asterisk. Card pairs with asterisks (rule cards) are
worth two points because they use the laws of exponents.

How to Play the Game:
*   Spread the solution cards face up in the shape of a rectangle..
*   Designate Player One and Player Two.
*   Player One draws a card from the deck, copies the problem on his or her
    paper, and simplifies it. Player One then finds the simplified solution card
    to match. Player One earns one point after Player Two verifies the cards
    match. If Player One's solution is incorrect, s/he loses his/her turn.
*   Player Two may try using the same expression. If Player Two is
    successful, Player Two is awarded the point.
*   Now it is Player Two's turn. Player Two repeats the same steps.

Ending the Game: The game ends when all of the card pairs are gone.
Whoever has the most points wins.

MG-34.   After playing Pair Up, complete each question below.

   a)   Record the scores for you and your partner.

   b)   Who won?

   c)   Locate the card pairs with asterisks and lay them out so that all players can view
         them. These pairs are the laws of exponents represented with symbols. Write a
         word sentence for each of these rules.

   d)   Which exponent rules did you find most difficult?

MG-35.

LAWS OF EXPONENTS

$$x^a \cdot x^b = x^{(a+b)} \qquad (x^a)^b = x^{ab} \qquad \frac{x^a}{x^b} = x^{(a-b)}$$

$$x^0 = 1 \qquad (x^a y^b)^c = x^{ac}y^{bc}$$

These rules hold if $x \neq 0$ and $y \neq 0$.

For each rule, there are three card pair examples in the game. Choose one example for
each of the rules and copy it into your Tool Kit.

MG-36. Use the laws of exponents to simplify the following problems.

a) $(x^2)(x^5)$ b) $x^7 \cdot x^5$ c) $y^8 \cdot y^6$ d) $y^7 \div y^4$

e) $\dfrac{x^3}{x^1}$ f) $x^3 \cdot x^4$ g) $m^{13} \cdot m^{14}$ h) $x^{32} \cdot x^{59}$

MG-37. Donald has been taking care of his neighbor's cat every day for two weeks while the neighbor is on vacation. Donald is being paid $2 per day.

a) How much did Donald make for the two weeks?

b) The neighbor calls to say that the family wants to stay another two weeks and wants Donald to continue to take care of the cats. Donald agrees, but he wants to change the pay rate. He says, "Will you pay me 2¢ for the first day, 4¢ for the second day, 8¢ for the third day, and so on for the two weeks?" The neighbor agrees readily and thinks to herself, "Wow! What a great deal! I guess Donald didn't do too well in math." Is the neighbor right or does Donald know his math? Organize the information in a table to support your answer.

Day Number	Amount Earned	Total Earnings
1	$0.02	$0.02
2	$0.04	$0.06
3	$0.08	$0.14

c) Copy and continue the table above to show Donald's earnings for the next 14 days. Use the data to make a graph. Scale your axes appropriately. Label the horizontal axis "Days" and the vertical axis "Total Amount Earned."

d) Does your graph support your answer to part (b)? Explain why or why not.

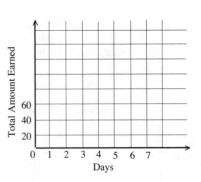

MG-38. Find the volume of the cone at right. You will need to use the Pythagorean Theorem to find the height. Show your work. (The answer is not 376.8 cubic centimeters.)

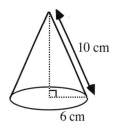

10 cm

6 cm

MG-39. The graph at right represents the number of books that are in each of several students' backpacks and how much each backpack weighs. Answer the following questions after studying the graph.

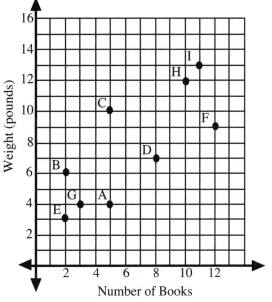

a) How many backpacks do you see represented on the graph?

b) Of all the backpacks graphed, which one weighs the median weight?

c) Of all the backpacks graphed, which one has the median number of books in it?

d) What is the mode for the weight?

e) What is the mode for the number of books?

f) Write a correlation for the scatter plot.

MG-40. Blanca is making a one-foot square ceramic tile for her art class. In the upper left corner she wants to put a design that is $\frac{1}{3}$-foot by $\frac{3}{4}$-foot. What is the area her design will cover? Draw a sketch of the entire tile and then shade the part that will contain her design.

MG-41. Complete the following Diamond Problems.

Product

Sum

a)

$\frac{1}{x}$ $\frac{2}{x}$

b)

x^0 3

c)

1   2.5

d)

0.375 $\frac{1}{5}$

e)

$-35x^2$ $5x$

MG-42. Use the laws of exponents to simplify the following problems.

a) $x^{31} \div x^{29}$

b) $(x^4)^2$

c) $(y^2)^3$

d) $(x^5)^5$

e) $\dfrac{x^3}{x^3}$

f) $(x \cdot y)^2$

g) $(x^2 \cdot y^3)^3$

h) $(2x)^4$

MG-43. Below is a cone and two cylinders. All have the same radius. Use your knowledge of cones and cylinders to calculate mentally the volume of each cylinder.

Cone volume:
25 cubic cm

a)

Cylinder A

b)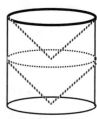

Cylinder B

MG-44. Follow your teacher's example and complete the table for powers of 10.

a) In the table you have constructed, you should see a pattern. Use the pattern to decide how many zeros 10^7 will have. How many zeros will 10^{23} have?

b) How would you write 10^{-7}?

c) How would you tell someone to write 10^{50}? 10^{-50}? Do not actually write the numbers; just write a sentence telling someone how s/he would write them.

Powers of 10	Standard Form
10^4	
10^3	
10^2	100
10^1	10
10^0	
10^{-1}	

MG-45. Multiply.

a) $9.23 \cdot 10$ b) $9.23 \cdot 10^2$ c) $9.23 \cdot 10^3$ d) $9.23 \cdot 10^4$

e) Without computing, what do you think $9.23 \cdot 10^{10}$ would be?

f) Write a sentence describing in words what happens to the decimal point when you multiply a number by 10^4.

MG-46. Predict where you think the decimal point will be after these factors are multiplied. Record your prediction. Use your calculator to check your answers. Organize your work in a table like the one below.

Factors	Prediction	Check
$78.659 \cdot 10^2$		
$346.387162 \cdot 10^5$		
$24.68931 \cdot 10^8$		

Describe where the decimal point of a number moves after multiplying the number by a power of 10 with a positive exponent.

MG-47. Predict where you think the decimal point will be after these factors are multiplied. Use your calculator to check your answers. Organize your work in a table like the one below. Notice the negative exponents.

Factors	Prediction	Check
$3471 \cdot 10^{-3}$		
$689.32 \cdot 10^{-5}$		
$72187.65 \cdot 10^{-6}$		

Describe the decimal point movement when multiplying by a power of 10 with a negative exponent.

MG-48. Predict where you think the decimal point will move after these numbers are divided. Record your prediction. Use your calculator to check your answer. Organize your work in a table like the one shown.

Numbers	Prediction	Check
$3471 \div 10^3$		
$689.32 \div 10^5$		
$72187.65 \div 10^6$		

a) Compare your answers to those in problem MG-47.

b) Write a sentence or two explaining the relationship between multiplying a number by a negative powers of 10 and dividing by positive powers.

MG-49. Make a three-dimensional sketch of the product package that you and your team members will be enlarging and shrinking.

a) Measure your product package and include its dimensions on your sketch. If your product package is a rectangular prism, you will need to label the height and the length and width of its base. If it is a cylinder, you will need to label the height and the radius of its base.

b) Calculate the surface area and volume of your product package.

MG-50. Use the resource page provided by your teacher to do the exercises below.

a) Sketch two intersecting lines and mark the intersection. Name the geometric figure that marks the intersection of two lines.

b) Darken two different intersecting edges on the cube. Name the geometric figure that marks the intersection of two edges.

c) Find and darken a pair of parallel edges on the cube and shade the face that contains them.

d) Darken two parallel edges on the cube that are not part of the same face and sketch in the plane that contains them.

e) Darken a pair of edges on the cube that are **skew lines** (lines in three-dimensional space that do not lie in the same plane, do not intersect, and are not parallel).

f) Shade a pair of intersecting faces on the cube and darken the edge that marks the intersection. Sketch the dotted lines that indicate the line is infinite.

g) Shade three intersecting faces on the cube. Name the geometric figure that marks the intersection.

MG-51.   Name the geometric figures formed by the intersection of:

  a)   two distinct lines.   b)   two distinct planes.   c)   three distinct planes.

MG-52.   Angela bought a set of cylindrical canisters for her
          kitchen. The largest one, shown at right, has a diameter
          of seven inches and a height of 15 inches.

  a)   Sketch the canister and label its dimensions.

  b)   Calculate the volume of the canister.

MG-53.   Inside the large canister from the previous problem is a
          smaller canister that is mathematically similar to the

          original. The smaller canister has $\frac{4}{5}$ the height and

          diameter of the large one.

  a)   Sketch and label the dimensions of the smaller
        canister.

  b)   Find the volume of the smaller canister.

MG-54.   The Top Grade Gasoline station buys gasoline for $1.15
          per gallon. The station used to sell 5000 gallons per day
          at $1.41 per gallon. The owner recently raised the price to
          $1.49 per gallon but now sells only 4000 gallons per day.

  a)   How has the price change affected Top Grade
        Gasoline's daily profits?

  b)   By what percentage did the total revenue from sales change?

MG-55.   Solve for x.

  a) $\frac{1}{2}(6x + 4) = 2x - 11$ b) $\frac{2}{3}x + 12 = x - 15$ c) $2\frac{1}{3}x + 1 = \frac{1}{3}x + 29$

MG-56.   Michael brought a bag of sand back from the
          seashore for Janessa's sandbox. On the way to
          the car, the bag developed a hole and he lost one-
          third of the sand. When he got home, he
          discovered he had lost an additional two-fifths of
          the sand. What was the total loss of sand?

MG-57.   Solve each inequality and sketch the graph of the solution on the number line.

          a) $46 > \frac{2}{3}x + 32$ b) $13 - 3x \geq 25$

MG-58.   Find the product: $\frac{2}{3} \cdot \frac{3}{4} \cdot \frac{4}{5} \cdot \, ... \, \cdot \frac{99}{100}$.

MG-59.   Sketch the rectangular prism shown at
          right. Label the dimensions and calculate
          the surface area and volume. Show all
          your subproblems.

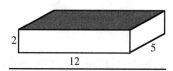

          a)   Enlarge the dimensions by a factor of 100%. Sketch and label the enlarged prism.
                Calculate the new surface area and volume. Show all your subproblems.

          b)   Explain how you could have calculated the new surface area and volume without
                using the area and volume formulas.

          c)   What is the percentage increase in surface area? What is the percentage increase in
                volume? Use a proportion to find out. Using your Tool Kit on percent increase
                might help you get started.

MG-60. With all the enlarging and reducing of things going on in class, Leigh had a dream that he shrunk his dog, Mantra, a large Malamute. In his dream, Mantra's new volume was 36,000 cubic centimeters.

a) Use a proportion to calculate the percent decrease in volume if Mantra's original volume was 182,250 cubic centimeters.

b) Calculate the volume of Leigh's backpack if its dimensions are 15 centimeters by 30 centimeters by 45 centimeters.

c) Will the shrunken dog fit in Leigh's backpack? Explain.

d) What would Mantra's volume be if her new dimensions were only $\frac{1}{9}$ of her original dimensions?

MG-61. Rink's favorite drink, Aloha Pineapple Juice, is packaged in a can like the one shown at right. Even after drinking it, he always feels thirsty. He wants the company to package the juice in a larger can.

a) If the company enlarges the dimensions of the can by a ratio of $\frac{4}{1}$, how much juice would the can hold? Show your work or explain how you got your answer.

b) Does it seem likely that the company will make a can that size? Explain.

MG-62. The label of the Aloha Pineapple Juice can is seven inches high and has an area of 140 square inches. What is the diameter of the can?

MG-63. In a sentence, precisely describe the following numbers in words so that someone reading what you describe could write them without seeing all of the digits.

a) The mass of the sun is approximately 1,990,000,000,000,000,000,000,000,000,000 kg.

b) The mass of an electron is approximately 0.00000000000000000000000000000911 kg.

MG-64. Some scientists use very large and very small numbers. They have a simplified way of writing these numbers called **scientific notation**.

a) In scientific notation, the mass of the sun is approximately $1.99 \cdot 10^{30}$ kg. Compare this number to the one in MG-63 part (a). Explain what was done to write it in scientific notation.

b) The mass of an electron is approximately $9.11 \cdot 10^{-31}$ kg in scientific notation. Compare this number to the one in the previous problem part (b). Explain what was done to write it in scientific notation. In particular, what does the negative exponent mean?

MG-65.

> ## SCIENTIFIC NOTATION
>
> **SCIENTIFIC NOTATION** is a way of writing very large and very small numbers compactly. A number is said to be in scientific notation when it is written as the product of two factors as described below.
>
> - The first factor is less than 10 and greater than or equal to 1.
> - The second factor has a base of 10 and an integer exponent (power of 10).
> - The factors are separated by a multiplication sign.
> - A positive exponent indicates a number whose absolute value is greater than one.
> - A negative exponent indicates a number whose absolute value is less than one.
>
> | Scientific Notation | Standard Form |
> |---|---|
> | $5.32 \cdot 10^{11}$ | 532,000,000,000 |
> | $2.61 \cdot 10^{-15}$ | 0.00000000000000261 |

Write the following numbers in scientific notation and record them in your Tool Kit to the right of the double-lined box.

a) 370,000,000

b) 0.0000000000076

MG-66. Lani bought ice cream to eat on her way home. She remembered that she needed to buy fish food, so she set the cone in a cup holder in her car and went back into the store. It took longer than she thought it would, and by the time she got back to her car, the ice cream had melted completely.

6cm   7cm   Ice cream

Cone
12 cm

Show your work for each problem below.

a) Calculate the volume of the ice cream "scoop" (the cylinder).

b) Calculate the volume of the cone.

c) Did the melted ice cream overflow the cone or is it all in the cone? Why?

d) What minimum cone height would hold all the ice cream? Write an equation or use a Guess and Check table.

MG-67. Copy and complete the chart of these cubed fractions.

Exponent Form	Factored Form	Standard Form
$\left(\frac{1}{2}\right)^3$	$\frac{1}{2} \cdot \frac{1}{2} \cdot \frac{1}{2}$	$\frac{1}{8}$
$\left(\frac{1}{3}\right)^3$		
$\left(\frac{1}{4}\right)^3$		
$\left(\frac{1}{5}\right)^3$		
$\left(\frac{2}{3}\right)^3$		
$\left(\frac{3}{4}\right)^3$		
$\left(\frac{2}{5}\right)^3$		
$\left(\frac{4}{5}\right)^3$		

MG-68. In Payne's class, seven students had three siblings, six students had two siblings, nine students had one sibling, and three students had no siblings. What is the mean number of siblings for students in Payne's class?

MG-69. The difference $\dfrac{3^2 + 7}{4} - \dfrac{8 - 4^2}{2}$ is:

(A) 8   (B) -4   (C) 0   (D) -5

MG-70. Simplify.

     a)   -3 + 0.05   b)   -7 + (-2.8)   c)   7 + (-10.6)   d)   -5.8 + 2

MG-71. Determine which of the quantities below is larger. Do the problem in your head, without a pencil or paper. Describe your method in detail.

     Which is larger: $\dfrac{1}{3} + \dfrac{2}{4} + \dfrac{2}{5} + \dfrac{5}{11}$ or 2?

MG-72. Margy thought that her family's cookie canister was too small, so she decided to buy a new one. She told her son Chris that the canisters were similar. Margy asked Chris to find the percent increase in volume of the new canister. Solve this problem for Chris.

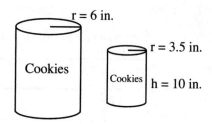

     a)   Use a proportion to find the height in inches of the larger cookie canister. Round your answer to the nearest tenth.

     b)   Calculate the volume of both canisters and the percentage the volume increased.

MG-73. **Cracker Snacks**

The Clifford Snack Company produces cracker canisters. Their snack-size canisters are similar to full-size canisters but have been reduced by a scale factor of $\frac{2}{5}$. Use the dimensions of the full-size canisters to calculate the surface area and volume of both the full-size and the snack-size canisters.

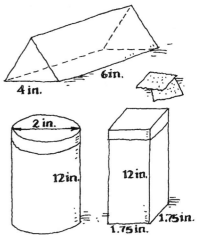

a) Full-size cracker canisters come in shapes and sizes like the equilateral triangular prism, square-based prism, and cylinder shown at right. Calculate the surface area and the volume of each full-size cracker canister.

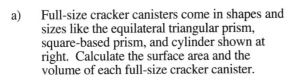

b) Sketch the snack-size canisters and record the new dimensions if they have been reduced by a factor of $\frac{2}{5}$. Calculate the surface area and volume of each of the snack-size canisters.

MG-74. Copy and complete the table below.

Standard Form	Scientific Notation
568,000,000,000,000,000,000,000,000,000	
	$1.11 \cdot 10^{-15}$
30,000,000,000,000	
99,810,000,000,000,000,000,000,000	
	$4.72 \cdot 10^{-9}$
	$1.2 \cdot 10^{2}$
0.0000000000000000034	

MG-75. Use the laws of exponents to simplify the following problems.

a) $x^4 \div x^3$ b) $(x^3)^4$ c) $(2y^2)^3$ d) $(x^2)^4$

e) $\dfrac{x^2}{x^{-3}}$ f) $(xy^2)^2$ g) $(x^2y^2)^4$ h) $(2x)^3$

MG-76. Solve the following equations.

    a) $x + \dfrac{3}{4} = 6\dfrac{5}{6}$
                      b) $\dfrac{1}{2}x + \dfrac{3}{4} = 1$

MG-77. Simplify.

    a) $\dfrac{3}{4} \cdot 5\dfrac{1}{5}$
         b) $\dfrac{11}{4} \cdot -2\dfrac{1}{3}$
         c) $-\dfrac{1}{3} \div \dfrac{2}{5}$

    d) $\dfrac{1}{8} \cdot (0.6)$
         e) $\dfrac{-112}{2} \cdot \dfrac{1}{6}$
         f) $-2\dfrac{2}{3} + \dfrac{1}{7}$

MG-78. First-place trophies cost $8.25 each. What is the total cost of a first-place trophy if there is a tax of 8%?

MG-79. What percent of 25 is 13? Show your work.

MG-80. Darrel and Rosemary built their new home in the shape of the diagram below. (All of the measurements are in feet.)

    a)   Find the total area of their home. Be sure to show all of your subproblems.

    b)   Find the area of their circular pool.

    c)   If the dimensions of their lot are 150 feet by 175 feet, what is its perimeter?

    d)   What is the area available for a driveway, walkways, and landscaping?

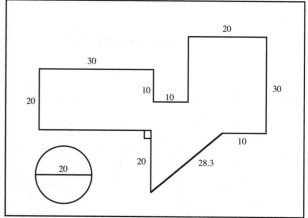

MG-81. Take out the product package that your team has selected. Use the measurements and product sketches to help you continue.

a) Discuss with your study team members the scale factor you want to use to enlarge the size of your product package and the scale factor you want to use to reduce the size of your product package. Record the scale factors you have chosen.

b) Decide with your team members who will construct the enlarged product package and who will construct the reduced product package. Record your decision.

c) For your package, make a sketch of the "new" product package. Be sure to include the new dimensions.

d) For your package, calculate the surface area of your "new" product package and write the ratio of the new surface area to the original surface area. Simplify your ratio.

e) For your package, calculate the volume of your "new" product package and write the ratio of the new volume to the original volume. Simplify your ratio.

f) Have your other team members check your calculations.

g) Obtain the materials you will need to build your "new" product package.

h) Use your measurements from MG-49 to make a template for your "new" product package. You may need to use several sheets of tag board depending on your enlargement factor.

i) Carefully cut out the template and fold or glue the pieces together.

j) Use construction paper and crayons or markers to draw the label for your "new" product package. Be sure your label is also drawn to scale.

MG-82. Match each expression below with its correct answer.

a) $2 \cdot 2 \cdot 2$ 4

b) x^4 $2^2 \cdot 3^2$

c) $5h$ $3x$

d) 36 $x \cdot x \cdot x \cdot x$

e) $\sqrt{16}$ 8

f) $x + x + x$ $5 \cdot h$

MG-83.   Simplify each of the following expressions.

a) $2^2 + 3^2$ b) $7^2 \cdot 7 \cdot 7$ c) $4^2 + 5^2$

d) $8^2 + 7^2$ e) $(2^2 + 6)^2$ f) $3^2 + 5^2$

g) $x - x$ h) $3 \cdot 3 \div 3$ i) $4x + x - 2x$

MG-84.   Simplify the following expression. Show each step and explain in words what you did.

$$\frac{3 - 2(5 - 1) + 3}{9 - 7}$$

MG-85.   Juan found that 20 new pencils weigh 12 ounces. How much will 50 new pencils weigh?
Set up a proportion and solve it.

MG-86.   The perimeter of this triangle is 47 cm. Solve for x and
compute the length of each side. Show your equation.

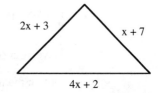

$2x + 3$ $x + 7$

$4x + 2$

MG-87.   Bethany just bought an amazing Cube-o-saurus. The
package says, "Soak in water overnight and the
cube-o-saurus will get an amazing eight times larger."
The cube-shaped dinosaur starts out about one
centimeter on a side. Bethany is looking forward to
seeing the 8-centimeter long creature. The next
morning she finds the Cube-o-saurus is the same
shape and only 2 centimeters long, 2 centimeters tall,
and 2 centimeters wide. Was the Cube-o-saurus
falsely advertised? Is the new shape eight times larger?

MG-88.   Ned and his family are at a restaurant for dinner. The bill is $87 and they want to leave a
tip of 15% of the bill. Set up a proportion and solve it to find how much of a tip Ned's
family should leave.

MG-89.   Answer the comparison questions below.

   a)   How many times larger is $3 \cdot 3 \cdot 3$ than $3 + 3 + 3$?

   b)   How many times larger is $\frac{1}{3} + \frac{1}{3} + \frac{1}{3}$ than $\frac{1}{3} \cdot \frac{1}{3} \cdot \frac{1}{3}$?

MG-90.   Which is larger: 2^5 or 5^2 ? Explain how you know.

MG-91.   Follow your teacher's instructions for practicing mental math.

MG-92.   How much larger is $\frac{1}{2} + \frac{1}{2} + \frac{1}{2}$ than $\frac{1}{2} \cdot \frac{1}{2} \cdot \frac{1}{2}$?

MG-93.   Angela needed $\frac{1}{8}$ of a piece of material that was $\frac{2}{3}$ of a yard long. What was the length of her piece?

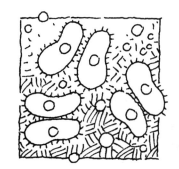

MG-94.   A bacteria cell splits in half to form two cells. Eventually those two cells will grow and then split in half to form four cells. This process is repeated over and over again every twenty minutes, three times every hour.

   a)   Draw a sketch of each generation for the first four splits. Copy the table below to help you record the number of cells at each generation.

Time	0:20	0:40	1:00	1:20	1:40	2:00
Splits	1	2	3	4	5	6
Total Cells	2	4				
Total Cells (exponential form)	2^1	2^2				

   b)   Extend your table to Time = 4:00 and complete it. You do not have to draw the generations.

Time						
Splits						
Total Cells						
Total Cells (exponential form)						

>>Problem continues on the next page.>>

c)   What exponential pattern do you notice?

d)   By the end of the eleventh hour, how many cells will there be? Write your answer in scientific notation.

e)   After 24 hours, how many cells will there be? Use your calculator to find the answer, but remember that for very large numbers your calculator will display scientific notation. Many calculators show scientific notation as 1.3^{03} meaning $1.3 \cdot 10^3 = 1300$. Rewrite the calculator display for the number of cells at 24 hours in proper scientific notation and in standard form.

MG-95.   When Jason arrives for his shift as a toll taker for the Pacific Bridge, he finds that there are 44 dollars in his cash drawer. Cars begin coming through the toll booth, and soon he is very busy. After half an hour, Jason has a spare moment and counts the money in his drawer. He finds that the drawer contains $178.

a)   Since each car pays $2 to cross the bridge, determine how many cars have come by his booth during his shift.

b)   At the same rate, how many cars will come by Jason's booth during his six-hour shift?

MG-96.   What is the range of the data set 114, 728, 364, 487, 546, 1478, 287, 98, 821 ?

(A) 1380   (B) 1478   (C) 1191   (D) 547

MG-97.   Complete the following Diamond Problems.

Product   a)   b)   c)   d)   e)

Sum

MG-98.   Caylan used a third of a tank of gas to drive to the ocean. On her way to take her cousin home, she used a fourth of a tank. If her tank holds 18 gallons and she gets 30 miles per gallon, how many more miles can she drive?

MG-99.   **Chapter Summary**   As you finish a chapter, you
need to reflect on how well you know the material.
Find a problem in the chapter that represents what
you have learned each of the following topics. Copy
the problem and show the correct solution for the
problem. Explain why you selected the problem.

- Volume and surface area of a prism

- Volume of a cone

- Laws of exponents

- Scientific notation

MG-100.   **Course Summary**   Your teacher will assign each team a chapter to summarize.

a)   For the chapter assigned to you, list the objectives from the front of the chapter.
Restate them in your own words.

b)   List the Tool Kit entries from the end of the chapter.

c)   With your team, select five problems from the chapter that you think best represent
the objectives and the Tool Kit.

d)   Write out the solutions for the problems.

e)   Prepare a poster to present to the rest of the class that shows the chapter objectives
(in your words), the Tool Kit list, and the five problems with their solutions. Be
ready to explain why you chose those particular problems and how they illustrate
important ideas from the course.

MG-101. Your job is to create some new problems for the final exam. Your teacher will assign your team another chapter. Use the five problems selected for that chapter as a basis for writing the new problems. Sometimes you can do this by just changing some numbers. Sometimes you will need to change the whole problem. Two examples are given below.

Find the area.

Old:

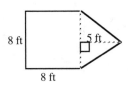

New:

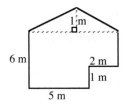

Solve the equation.

Old: $5(x - 3) = -7x + 18$ New: $-3(x - 5) = -2x + 10$

a)   With your team, write one different problem that is similar to each of the five poster problems.

b)   Solve each of the problems your team wrote.

MG-102. Find the surface area of the hexagonal prism shown at right. Dividing the hexagon into smaller parts and using subproblems will help.

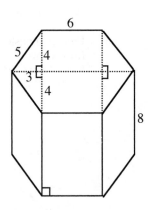

a)   Find the area of the hexagonal bases by answering parts (i) through (iii). The two obtuse triangles are congruent and the region in the middle is a rectangle.

   i)   Find the area of the four congruent triangles.

   ii)   Find the area of the two congruent rectangles.

   iii)   Find the area of the hexagonal bases.

b)   Find the area of the lateral faces by answering parts (i) and (ii).

   i)   What are the dimensions of the lateral faces?

   ii)   Write an equation to find the total area of the lateral faces.

c)   Write an equation that gives the total surface area.

d)   How could you have used other subproblems to find the area of the hexagonal bases?

MG-103. Light travels faster than sound. That is why you see lightning before you hear thunder during a thunder storm. The amount of time that passes between seeing the flash of lightning and hearing the thunder can actually tell you how far away the storm is. For example, if you see lightning and then hear thunder 10 seconds later, the lightning was about two miles away.

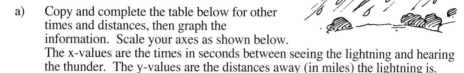

a) Copy and complete the table below for other times and distances, then graph the information. Scale your axes as shown below. The x-values are the times in seconds between seeing the lightning and hearing the thunder. The y-values are the distances away (in miles) the lightning is.

x (time in seconds)	5	15	40			5n
y (distance in miles)	1	3		4	$4\frac{1}{2}$	

b) How could you use your graph to find how far away a storm is if the time lapse is $2\frac{1}{2}$ seconds?

c) If it took 25 seconds to hear the thunder, how far away is the lightning?

d) If you were 12 miles away from the storm, about how long would it take you to hear the thunder after seeing the lightning flash?

e) Why does it make sense that the graph goes through the point (0, 0)?

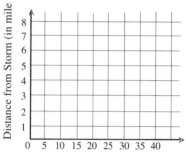

Distance from Storm (in mile)

0 5 10 15 20 25 30 35 40
Time to Hear Thunder (in seconds)

MG-104. A group of mountain climbers hears thunder 30 seconds after they see the lightning.

a) About how far are the climbers from the storm?

b) Two minutes later the mountain climbers hear thunder again, but now they hear the thunder 20 seconds after they see the lightning. Now how far are they from the storm?

c) How fast is the storm traveling?

MG-105. Cheryl and Jeremy are playing a game in which they use two dice. They must subtract the numbers on each die. The number rolled on the second die is subtracted from the number rolled on the first die. Copy and complete the chart showing all of the possible differences.

a) What is the probability that Cheryl will roll a difference of 2 or 0?

b) It is now Jeremy's turn. What is the probability that he will roll a difference of 4 or -5?

c) What is the probability that Cheryl or Jeremy will roll a difference of zero?

d) What is the probability that Cheryl or Jeremy will roll a difference that is greater than 5?

Differences of Two Dice

	First Die					
	1	2	3	4	5	6
1	0	1	2	3	4	5
2	−1					
3	−2					
4	−3					
5	−4					
6	−5					

(Subtract Second Die)

MG-106. Use the laws of exponents to simplify each expression.

a) $x^5 \cdot x^4$

b) $\dfrac{n^{12}}{n^3}$

c) $(y)(3y^2)$

d) $(x^3)^2$

e) $\dfrac{x^4}{x^1}$

f) $\dfrac{y^2 x^6}{xy}$

g) $\dfrac{n^{-2}}{n^5}$

h) $(2x^3)^3$

MG-107. There are 36 green gumballs, 18 red gumballs, 22 white gumballs, 30 purple gumballs, and 14 blue gumballs in the gumball machine. Answer the following questions using percentages. Make sure you show your work.

a) What is the probability of getting a purple gumball?

b) What is the probability of getting either a purple or a white gumball?

c) What is the probability of <u>not</u> getting a greengum ball?

MG-108. **What We Have Done in This Chapter**

Below is a list of the Tool Kit entries from this chapter.

- MG-14   Ratios of Dimensional Change
- MG-26   Volume of a Cone
- MG-35   Laws of Exponents
- MG-65   Scientific Notation

Review all the entries and read the notes you made in your Tool Kit. Make a list of any questions, terms, or notes you do not understand. Ask your partner or study team members for help. If anything is still unclear, ask your teacher.

Appendix A
Making the Order of Operations Formal: MATHEMATICAL NAMES

INTRODUCTION

So far in this book, we have tried to help you understand the ideas behind what you are doing. Now is the time to give the formal names to what you already understand, so that when someone asks you for a reason for your actions, you can give them a name for your reason—rather like being able to name a period in history (early Roman Empire) or a scientific effect (evaporation). Therefore, much of this Interlude will be telling rather than asking you to work on problems. Then, after we have told you the names that mathematicians give certain ideas, we will give you some examples and then more problems for practice.

BACKGROUND

Mathematicians did not just sit down one day many years ago and make up the properties we will be talking about. Each of these properties comes from working with the whole numbers (0, 1, 2, 3, ...) and seeing the rules which always work for them. One such rule is $A \cdot B = B \cdot A$ for any two natural numbers A and B. This is not a surprise to you. You have known for a long time that, for example, $3 \cdot 4 = 4 \cdot 3$. What is different, however, is that many years ago, people studying algebra decided it was important to give this rule a name (the Commutative Property) and—this is the important part—to say that this rule works for <u>all</u> numbers. We use this property when we work with any kind of numbers: positive, negative, fractions, and even some kinds of numbers you may not know yet, like complex numbers. But once you have learned these rules and learned how to use them, you can be sure that they will always work. So the rule we gave earlier ($A \cdot B = B \cdot A$) is true even if A and B are these other kinds of numbers.

THE PROPERTIES OF ARITHMETIC OPERATIONS AND THEIR FORMAL NAMES

Additive Identity This is just the number zero (0). The name comes from the fact that when you add zero to any number, you get the same number you started with. That is, $x + 0 = x$ for any number x. This property is actually how the additive identity is defined: z is the additive identity if, for every number x, $z + x = x + z = x$. But you know it is the number zero.

Additive Inverse An inverse operation in general is about undoing. Suppose you have the number 4 and want to add something to it to get zero (the additive identity). The number you would have to add would be -4. So we say that -4 is the additive inverse of 4. Similarly, the additive inverse of -3 is 3 since $(-3) + 3 = 0$. So, just like the previous definition, we say that for any number x, we get its additive inverse y if $x + y = y + x = 0$.

Multiplicative Identity The number one (1). Just as adding the additive identity to a number does not change it, multiplying a number by the multiplicative identity does not change that number. So w is the multiplicative identity if, for every number x, $w \cdot x = x \cdot w = x$.

Multiplicative Inverse Suppose you have the number 4 and want to multiply it by something to get 1 (the multiplicative identity). You would have to multiply by $\frac{1}{4}$. So we say $\frac{1}{4}$ is the multiplicative inverse of 4. Similarly, the multiplicative inverse of $\frac{1}{8}$ is 8 since $8 \cdot \frac{1}{8} = 1$. Formally, y is the multiplicative inverse of x if $x \cdot y = y \cdot x = 1$. An important fact to know is that zero does not have a multiplicative inverse, but it is the only number which does not.

Distributive Property You have worked with this property a lot so far, and it is enormously important in algebra where you will need it almost every day. It relates addition and multiplication and says that $x \cdot (y + z) = x \cdot y + x \cdot z$. Usually you would just write $x(y + z) = xy + xz$, but we put in the multiplication signs to emphasize the multiplicative aspects of this property.

Commutative Property We referred to the commutative property above. It simply says that the order in which you add or multiply does not matter. That is, for any two numbers x and y, it is true that $x + y = y + x$ and $x \cdot y = y \cdot x$. Technically, there are two properties here: the commutative property of addition and the commutative property of multiplication. We will refer to both of them under the single name, "Commutative Property."

Associative Property This is one property that has probably never occurred to you ever to doubt. It says that if you have three numbers to add (or to multiply), if you add the first two and then add the sum to the third, you get the same answer as if you add the second and third and then add that sum to the first. Here it is in symbolic form remembering that we do operations inside of parentheses first, $(x + y) + z = x + (y + z)$ and $(x \cdot y) \cdot z = x \cdot (y \cdot z)$ or, if we write it without the multiplication symbol, $(xy)z = x(yz)$. So, for example, $(3 + 4) + 5 = 7 + 5 = 12$, which is also the answer of $3 + (4 + 5) = 3 + 9$. Again, technically, there are two properties here: the associative property of addition and the associative property of multiplication. We will refer to both of them under the single name, "Associative Property."

EXAMPLES

Example 1. Find $20 \cdot 12$. We know that $12 = 10 + 2$, so by the Distributive Property, we know that $20 \cdot 12 = 20 \cdot (10 + 2) = 20 \cdot 10 + 20 \cdot 2 = 200 + 40 = 240$.

Example 2. Simplify $2x + 4 + 7x$. By the Commutative Property, we know that $4 + 7x = 7x + 4$. Now the problem becomes $2x + 7x + 4$. Using the usual order of operations, we solve this as $(2x + 7x) + 4$. Using the Distributive Property, $(2 + 7)x + 4 = 9x + 4$.

Example 3. Show that $\frac{3}{4}$ and $\frac{24}{32}$ represent the same number. Using the Multiplicative Identity, $\frac{3}{4} \cdot 1 = \frac{3}{4}$. But when we write 1 as the Giant **1**, $\frac{8}{8}$, we see that $\frac{3}{4} \cdot \frac{8}{8} = \frac{24}{32}$. Thus, $\frac{3}{4} = \frac{24}{32}$.

PROBLEMS

MN-1.   Name the rule that allows us to do each of the following operations.

a) $4 + (5 + (-5)) = (4 + 5) + -5$ b) $5 \cdot 3 = 3 \cdot 5$

c) $3(x + 5) = 3x + 3 \cdot 5$ d) $14 + (-3) = -3 + 14$

e) $5 \cdot \frac{1}{5} = 1$ f) $\frac{2}{3} \cdot \frac{1}{6} = \frac{1}{6} \cdot \frac{2}{3}$

g) $x + 7z = 7z + x$ h) $13 + 0 = 13 + (-10 + 10)$

i) $7(x + yz) = 7x + 7yz$ j) $(z - w) \cdot 8 = 8 \cdot (z - w)$

k) $t + 0 = t$

MN-2.   Name the operation that allows us to do $1 \cdot 7 = 7 \cdot 1$.

(A) Multiplicative Inverse   (B) Distributive Property

(C) Commutative Property   (D) Additive Identity

MN-3.   Name the operation that allows us to do $1 \cdot 7 = 7$.

(A) Multiplicative Identity   (B) Distributive Property

(C) Commutative Property   (D) Additive Identity

MN-4.   Name the operation that allows us to do $3 + (4 + 5) = 3 + (5 + 4)$.

(A) Multiplicative Identity   (B) Associative Property

(C) Distributive Property   (D) Commutative Property

MN-5.   Name the operation that allows us to do $3 + (4 + 5) = (3 + 4) + 5$.

(A) Multiplicative Identity   (B) Associative Property

(C) Distributive Property   (D) Commutative Property

MN-6.   Name the operation that allows us to do -3 + 0 = -3.

    (A) Additive Identity   (B) Additive Inverse

    (C) Distributive Property   (D) Associative Property

MN-7.   Name the operation that allows us to do -3 + 0 = -3 + (-6 + 6).

    (A) Additive Identity   (B) Additive Inverse

    (C) Distributive Property   (D) Associative Property

WHY A NEGATIVE TIMES A NEGATIVE IS A POSITIVE

Earlier in the course we gave an argument of why a negative integer times a negative integer is a positive integer which was primarily based on the idea that multiplying, say, $(-3) \cdot (-5)$ could be thought of as <u>taking</u> <u>away</u> 5 of the negative tiles and doing it 3 times. While most students come away from this demonstration knowing what the rule is and having a good idea why it works, the argument is more of a teaching device than a formal proof. Now, however, with the formal properties we introduced above, we can give a complete and formal demonstration of this fact.

The central idea in our proof uses the distributive property and the additive identity. We give two arguments which are actually exactly the same except that one is a purely formal proof which really uses algebra while the other one just uses a particular pair of numbers x and y. Reading over this proof will probably be difficult for most students, but if you think you might want to be a mathematician someday, it is never too early to get started. It will probably be easier if you start with the proof for Statement 1 that involves numbers. Then go to the more general one that uses variables.

Statement 1   If x is a positive number and y is a negative number, then xy is negative.

We assume everyone knows three facts:
*   If x and z are positive numbers, then their product is a positive number.
*   The additive inverse of a positive number is negative and the additive inverse of a negative number is positive.
*   If x is any number, then $x \cdot 0 = 0$.

Reasons that Statement 1 is true using a particular pair of numbers.

Suppose $x = 5$ and $y = -3$. Then the additive inverse of y is 3 since $(-3) + 3 = 0$. Now see what happens when we multiply $5 \cdot ((-3) + 3)$. We are going to treat $5 \cdot (-3)$ as an unknown and get information about it.

By the Distributive Property, we know that $5 \cdot ((-3) + 3) = 5 \cdot (-3) + 5 \cdot 3$. However, we also know that $5 \cdot ((-3) + 3) = 5 \cdot 0 = 0$. (Recall we assumed that $x \cdot 0 = 0$ for any number x.)
Therefore, the two products $5 \cdot (-3)$ and $5 \cdot 3$ are additive inverses since they add up to 0. But earlier we agreed that since 5 and 3 are positive, we know their product is positive. So their additive inverse—here $5 \cdot (-3)$—must be negative. So, at least for these two numbers with different signs, their product is negative.

Reasons that Statement 1 is true using algebra.

As stated, we assume that x is positive and y is negative. The additive inverse of y is (-y), which we know is positive. Now see what happens when we multiply x · (y + (-y)). We are going to treat x · y as an unknown and get information about it.

By the Distributive Property, we know that x · (y + (-y)) = x · y + x · (-y). However, we also know that x · (y + (-y)) = x · 0 = 0. Therefore, the two products x · y and x · (-y) are additive inverses since they add up to 0. But earlier we agreed that since x and (-y) are positive, we know their product is positive. So their additive inverse—here x · y—must be negative. Thus for any two numbers x and y, with x positive and y negative, their product is negative.

Now (at last) we are ready to show that a negative times a negative is a positive.

Statement 2 If x and y are negative numbers, then xy is positive.

Reasons that Statement 2 is true using a particular pair of numbers.

Suppose x = -5 and y = -4. Then the additive inverse of y is 4 since (-4) + 4 = 0. Now see what happens when we multiply (-5) · ((-4) + 4).

By the Distributive Property, we know that (-5) · ((-4) + 4) = (-5) · (-4) + (-5) · 4. However, we also know that (-5) · ((-4) + 4) = 5 · 0 = 0. Therefore, the two products (-5) · (-4) and (-5) · 4 are additive inverses since they add up to 0. But since (-5) is negative and 4 is positive, by what we learned from Statement 1, we know their product is negative. So their additive inverse—here (-5) · (-4)—must be positive. So, at least for these two numbers with negative signs, their product is positive.

Reasons that Statement 2 is true using algebra.

As stated, we assume that x and y are both negative. The additive inverse of y is (-y), which we know is positive. Now see what happens when we multiply x · (y + (-y)).

Again, by the Distributive Property, we know that x · (y + (-y)) = x · y + x · (-y). However, we also know that x · (y + (-y)) = x · 0 = 0. Therefore, the two products x · y and x · (-y) are additive inverses since they add up to 0. But since x is negative and (-y) is positive, by what we learned from Statement 1, we know their product is negative. So their additive inverse—here x · y—must be positive. Thus for any two negative numbers x and y, their product is positive.

PROBLEM

MN-8. In what we just did, we assumed that you knew that x · 0 = 0 for any x. Actually, you can prove this statement, too, using the Distributive Property and the Additive Identity. As a hint, multiply the statement 1 + 0 = 1 on both sides by x and see what happens.

Appendix B
Here are Constructions: COMPASS CONSTRUCTION

HC-1.   Today you will use a compass and straightedge to construct geometric figures. A straightedge is a line segment maker; a compass is a circle maker.

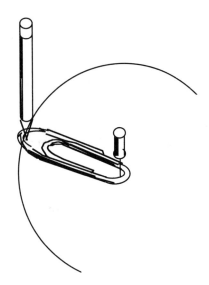

   a)   Use a paper clip as a compass to make some circles. You may choose to use two pencils, one to draw and one to anchor the center of the circle. A push pin also works well to hold the center in place.

   b)   Use one loop of the paper clip at a time to make two different circles with the same center. These are called **concentric** circles.

   c)   Now use the plastic grid compass provided by your teacher (or the kind of compass your teacher specifies) in a similar manner and make some circles.

   d)   Make four concentric circles using the plastic grid or other compass.

HC-2.   Toward the bottom edge of a new sheet of paper, make a line that is about the same length as the one below and label point A near the left part of the line.

   a)   Center your compass on point A and use it to make a "slash" across the line the same distance from A as shown above. Find the point where the slash mark intersects the line and label it point B. This slash mark is a little piece of a whole circle. It is called an **arc**.

>> **Problem continues on next page.**>>

b)   Next we will make an equilateral triangle. Start with your compass still centered at point A and mark an arc the length of line segment AB ($\overline{AB}$) above the center of the line as shown in the drawing.

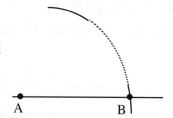

c)   Center the compass at point B. Use the same length and make another arc that intersects the one from part (b). Label the point of intersection C, as shown in the diagram.

d)   Use your straightedge to draw $\overline{AC}$ and $\overline{BC}$ to make ∆ABC. What kind of triangle is this?

HC-3.   Follow the steps below to construct ∆JKL.

a)   Start by drawing a long line. Mark and label a line $\overline{JK}$ as you did $\overline{AB}$ in the previous problem.

b)   Now center your compass at point J and choose any length that is more than half of the length of $\overline{JK}$ and not the same as $\overline{JK}$. Make two arcs above the center of the line segments from K, as you did in the previous problem.

c)   Label the point of intersection L. Use your straightedge to draw $\overline{JL}$ and $\overline{JK}$ to complete the triangle.

d)   What kind of triangle is this?

HC-4.   Next we will construct an **angle bisector**.

a)   Draw an angle and label its vertex Q.

b)   With the center of your compass at the vertex, draw an arc that intersects both sides (rays) of your angle and label the intersection points P and R respectively.

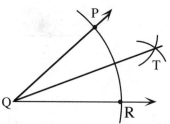

c)   Center your compass at point P and make an arc mark out beyond your arc but in the interior of the angle.

d)   Repeat part (c) from point R to intersect the first mark you made. Label this point T.

e)   Line up the intersection of the two arc marks (point T) and the vertex and draw the angle bisector from Q through T.

HC-5.   In this problem we will construct a **perpendicular bisector** of a segment. Start with a line segment and label its endpoints, S and T.

a)   A perpendicular line makes right angles with another line. What is a bisector?

b)   Center your compass at point S and then at point T and make two pairs of crossing arcs as you did in problems HC-2 and HC-3, one above and the other below the line segment.

c)   Draw a line connecting the two pairs of crossing arcs. This line is the perpendicular bisector of the line segment $\overline{ST}$.

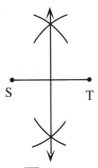

d)   Mark the point where the perpendicular bisector intersects $\overline{ST}$. Label it M and draw in the right angle box. Point M is the **midpoint** of $\overline{ST}$.

HC-6.   Use your compass to draw a circle.

a)   Mark a point A on the circle and center your compass at point A. Using a length the same as the radius, mark point B.

b)   Continue around the circle using the length of the radius and marking C, D, E, and F.

c)   Now carefully draw $\overline{AB}$, $\overline{BC}$, $\overline{CD}$, $\overline{DE}$, $\overline{EF}$, and $\overline{FA}$. Each of these is a **chord** in the circle.

d)   What geometric figure is created by the chords?

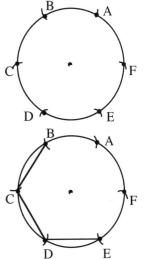

HC-7.   Construct a circle with the same six markings as in problem HC-6. Connect three of the points with chords so that an equilateral triangle is formed.

HC-8.   Construct a circle with the same six markings as in problem HC-5. We are going to make a twelve-sided figure, a **dodecagon**.

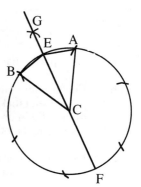

a)   Draw ∠ACB with its vertex at the center of the circle. This is called a **central angle**.

b)   Construct the angle bisector of ∠ACB. Draw the chords from points A and B to the point where the angle bisector intersects the circle (point E).

c)   You do not need to draw the whole bisector. The important points are E and F, where the bisector crosses the circle and bisects the two arcs. What is the special name for $\overline{EF}$?

d)   Use the method from part (c) to bisect the other arcs and draw a regular dodecagon.

HC-9.   Start again with a circle. This time we will construct a square.

a)   Draw a diameter $\overline{EF}$.

b)   Construct the perpendicular bisector of the diameter.

c)   Mark the points B and D where the perpendicular bisector intersects the circle.

d)   Use your straightedge to connect the four points B, D, E, and F to make a square.

HC-10.   Start with a construction like the one you did in problem HC-9. Now construct an octagon by using the same method as you used in problem HC-8, where you got twelve sides after starting with six sides.

HC-11.   How could you use what you did in problem HC-10 to construct a 16-sided figure? Make that 16-sided figure now. You may want to start with a larger circle.

HC-12.   In one circle, construct a triangle, a hexagon, and a dodecagon.

HC-13.   In one circle, construct a square, an octagon, and a dodecagon.

HC-14.   Use the construction methods you have learned so far and your straightedge to connect points to make the following figures. Use a large circle on a whole sheet of paper to start each.

a)   Construct a pattern like the one below in a larger size.

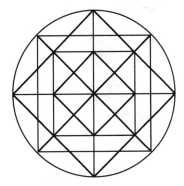

b)   Construct a pattern like the one below in a larger size.

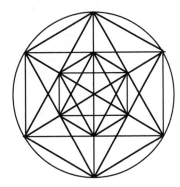

c)   Shade one or both of your constructions in parts (a) or (b) to make a symmetric design.

HC-15.   Select one (or more) of the following designs to construct in a larger size. All of the
         construction makings have been erased, so you will need to do some problem solving to
         decide how these designs were constructed using only the constructions you have learned.

Here are Constructions: Compass Construction

GLOSSARY

absolute value: (| |) The distance of a number from zero on the number line. It is always non-negative. (53)

acute angle: An angle with a measure greater than 0° and less than 90°.

acute triangle: A triangle with all three angle measures less than 90°.

addition: (+) An operation that tells how many objects there are when two sets are combined. The result is the number of objects in the two sets together, called a sum. In arithmetic, the word "object" usually means "number." (49)

adjacent angles: Angles which share a common side and vertex but no common interior points.

algebra: A branch of mathematics that uses variables to generalize the rules of numbers and numerical operations.

algebraic expression: Variables and constants, joined by addition or subtraction. Examples: 3x or 2x + 4 (129)

algorithm: A fixed rule for carrying out a mathematical procedure. Example: To find the average of a set of values, find their sum and divide by the number of values.

altitude of a triangle (height): The perpendicular distance from a vertex to the opposite side (or its extension) of a triangle.

angle: A geometric figure made up of two rays or line segments that have the same endpoint.

angle bisector: A ray that divides an angle into two congruent parts. (409)

arc: The portion of a circle between two points on a circle. (408)

area: The measure in square units of the interior region of a plane figure or the surface of a three-dimensional figure. (156)

area of a triangle: To find the area of a triangle, multiply the length of the base (b) by the height (h) and divide by two. $A = \frac{1}{2} bh$ (221)

area of a circle: $A = \pi r^2$, where r is the length of the radius of the circle. See area. (225)

associative property for addition: Changing the grouping of the numbers does not change the result in addition. Example: $(5 + 3) + 7 = 5 + (3 + 7)$ (402)

associative property for multiplication: Changing the grouping of the numbers does not change the result in multiplication. Example: $(5 \cdot 3) \cdot 2 = 5 \cdot (3 \cdot 2)$ (402)

average (mean): The sum of given numbers divided by the number of numbers used in computing the sum. Example: The average of 1, 4, and 10 is $(1 + 4 + 10) \div 3 = 5$. (14)

axis (pl. axes): A number line which can be used to indicate a position of a point, based on its coordinates. (28)

base of an exponent: The number used as the factor in an exponential expression. Example: $5^2 = 5 \cdot 5$. The number 5 is the base. (298)

base: For a triangle, the base may be any side, although usually it is the bottom one. For a trapezoid, the two parallel sides are the bases. For a cylinder or prism, either one of the two congruent parallel faces may be the base while for a pyramid or cone, the base is the (flat) face which does not contain the vertex (where all the sides come together). (215, 221, 309)

bimodal: A set of numbers that has two modes. (18)

box-and-whisker plot: A graphic way of showing a summary of data using the median, quartiles, and extremes of the data. (27)

certainty: When an event will definitely happen. The probability of a certain event is 1.

center: (or center point) The point equidistant from all points on a circle. (407)

central angle: An angle whose vertex is the center of a circle. (410)

chord: A line segment that connects two points on a circle. (410)

circle: The set of all points in two dimensions that are the same distance r from a fixed point P. The fixed point P is called the center of the circle and the distance r is called the radius. (222)

circumference: The distance around the outside of a circle. You can calculate circumference from the diameter (d) or the radius (r). $C = \pi d = 2\pi r$. (225)

coefficient (numerical): The numeral part of a term, such as 6 in 6x. (260)

combining like terms: When working with an expression, terms that are exactly the same except for their coefficients can be combined into one quantity. Terms are combined by addition and subtraction of the coefficients. Example: $3x^2 + 2y + 6 + 4y - 2x^2 = x^2 + 6y + 6$. (141)

common: Shared. (159)

common factor: A common term factor: (1) in arithmetic, the integers multiplied are called factors; (2) in algebra, a monomial or polynomial that is a factor of a polynomial. For example: $10x + 15 = 5(2x + 3)$. Five is the common factor. (159)

common multiple: A number that is a multiple of the two or more numbers. Example: 24 and 48 are common multiples of 3 and 8. (86)

commutative property: The property of an operation such that changing the order of the numbers does not change the result of the operation. Examples: $3 \cdot 4 = 4 \cdot 3$ or $7 + 8 = 8 + 7$

compass and straightedge (construction with): A geometric construction. The straightedge is only used to draw line segments. The compass is used to transfer equal distances and draw arcs and circles. (407)

complementary angles: Two angles whose sum is 90°.

complementary probabilities: Two probabilities are complementary if their sum is one.

complex fraction: A fraction with a fraction in the numerator and/or the denominator.

composite figure: A shape made of several simpler figures.

composite number: A number with more than two factors.

compound interest: Interest paid on both the principal and previous interest earned which accumulates over time. It can be calculated by using the formula $B = p(1 + r)^t$, where B is the balance, p is the principal, r is the annual rate, and t is the time in years the account earns interest. (265)

cone: A three dimensional figure with one circular base and one vertex. (375)

congruent: Figures which have the same size and shape. (207)

conjecture: An educated guess based on data, patterns, and data. Scientists use the term hypothesis.

consecutive: In order. Example: 8, 9, 10 are consecutive numbers. (10)

constant: A numerical term which does not change.

coordinate: See ordered pair.

coordinate grid (system): A two dimensional system formed by two perpendicular number lines that intersect at their zero points. The location of a point is given by first stating the horizontal location (x) and then the vertical location (y), written as an ordered pair, (x, y). (28)

correlation: A measure of interdependence of two sets of data. (33)

corresponding parts: Points, edges (sides), or angles in congruent or similar figures that are arranged in similar ways. For instance if $\triangle ABC$ is similar to $\triangle DEF$, then side AB corresponds to side DE and angle C corresponds to angle F. (229)

cross multiplication: A way to find a missing numerator or denominator in equivalent fractions by multiplying diagonally across the equal sign to get an equivalent equation without fractions.
Example: In $\frac{a}{b} = \frac{c}{d}$, after cross multiplication the equation would be $ad = bc$. (212)

cube: A rectangular prism with 6 congruent faces, all squares.

cubic unit: A cube each of whose edges measures 1 unit in length. Volume is measured in cubic units. (293)

cylinder: Commonly, a three dimensional object with two circular, congruent, and parallel bases. (319)

decimal point: The dot separating the ones and tenths places in a decimal number.

denominator: The lower part of a fraction which tells into how many equal parts the whole is divided. (108)

dependent events: Two events are dependent if the outcome of the first event affects the outcome of the second event.

diagonal: A segment that joins two vertices of a polygon and is not one of the sides.

diameter: A line segment that has its endpoints on the circle and passes through the center. The longest chord in a circle. (222)

difference: The answer to a subtraction problem. (58)

digit: One of the ten numerals: 0, 1, 2, 3, 4, 5, 6, 7, 8, 9.

distributive property: For any a, b, and c, a(b + c) = ab + ac. Example: 10(7 + 2) = 10 · 7 + 10 · 2 (159)

dividend: A quantity to be divided. See divisor.

divisible: A number is divisible by another if their remainder is zero.

division: The inverse operation to multiplication. The operation which creates equal groups. (75)

divisor: The quantity by which another quantity is to be divided. dividend ÷ divisor = quotient (262)

dodecagon: A polygon with 12 sides. (411)

edge: The line segment where two faces of a solid figure meet. (369)

endpoint: Either of the two points which mark the ends of a line segment. (409)

enlargement ratio: The ratio of similarity comparing a figure to a similar larger one is often called the enlargement ratio. This number tells you by what factor the first figure is enlarged to get the second.

equal: Having the same value.

equal ratios: Two equivalent fractions; a proportion. (208)

equation: A mathematical sentence relating two mathematical expressions with an equal sign (=). (173)

equilateral triangle: A triangle with all three sides the same length. (408)

equivalent: Naming the same amount with a different name. (91)

evaluate (an expression): To evaluate an expression, substitute the value(s) given for the variable(s) and perform the operations according to the order of operations. (129)

even number: A whole number which is divisible by two with no remainder.

event: One or more results of an experiment.

exponent: In the expression 2^5, 5 is called the exponent. The exponent indicates how many times to use the base as a multiplier. (298)

expression: See algebraic expression.

face: A flat side of a three-dimensional figure. (309)

factor: When two or more numbers are multiplied, each of the numbers multiplied is a factor of the product. (158)

factored form: The result of writing an algebraic expression as a product. Example: $4x^3 + 12x^2 + 8x = 4x(x + 1)(x + 2)$ (137)

formula: An equation that shows a mathematical relationship. (279)

fraction: A number expressed in the form $\frac{a}{b}$ where a and b are integers and b is not equal to 0. (4)

frequency: The number of times something occurs in an interval or in a data set.

graph: A visual display of information in an organized manner. (6)

greatest common factor (GCF): The largest number which will divide evenly into two or more numbers. Example: 6 is the greatest common factor of 12 and 18.

guess and check table: A problem solving strategy in which you begin by making a guess and then check whether or not your answer is correct. In the process of checking, you gain information about how close your guess might be and make adjustments to your guess. Being organized is crucial to the success of this method, as well as writing a usable table. Guess and check leads to writing equations to represent word problems. (15)

height (altitude): The perpendicular distance between two bases, or between a vertex and a base. See altitude. (215)

hexagon: A polygon with six sides. (411)

horizontal: Parallel to the horizon. The x-axis in a coordinate grid is the horizontal axis. (45)

hypotenuse: In a right triangle, the longest side of the triangle, opposite the right angle, is called the hypotenuse. (291)

identity property of addition: Zero is the identity for addition. It does not change the value of a number when added to the number. (401)

identity property of multiplication: One is the identity element for multiplication. Multiplying by one does not change the value of a number. (93)

impossibility: An event with a probability of zero.

independent events: Two events are independent if the outcome of the second event does not depend on the outcome of the first event.

inequality: A mathematical sentence which compares two quantities, showing they are not the same. The symbols used may be: < (less than), > (greater than), to), or ≠ (not equal to). (69)

integers: The set of numbers { . . .,-3, -2, -1, 0, 1, 2, 3,... } (49)

intersect: To meet or cross. The intersection of two sets consists of all the points or elements that belong to both sets.

interval: A set of numbers between two given numbers.

inverse operations: An operation that undoes another operation. Example: Multiplication is the inverse operation for division. (295)

irrational numbers: Numbers that cannot be written as the ratio of two integers. (225)

isosceles triangle: A triangle with at least two sides equal in length.

least common multiple (LCM): The smallest common multiple of set of two or more numbers. Example: The least common multiple of 4 and 6 is 12. (86)

leg of a right triangle: Either of the two shorter sides of a right triangle. (291)

like terms: Terms that have the same variable part and corresponding exponent. 5 and 19 are like terms, 3xy and 5xy are like terms, $6x^2$ and $-3x^2$ are like terms. (141)

line: An infinite set of points forming a straight path extending in two directions. (12)

line segment: A part of a line between two endpoints. (407)

linear equation: An equation whose graph is a line, generated by an equation with a linear expression in it. (344)

linear expression: An expression in the form of ax + b, where a and b are numbers.

literal equation: An equation with two or more variables. (250)

lower quartile: The median of the lower half of an ordered set of data is the lower quartile. (27)

lowest common denominator (LCD): The smallest common multiple of the denominators of two or more fractions. Example: The LCD of $\frac{5}{12}$ and $\frac{3}{8}$ is 24.

mean: A measure of central tendency often referred to as the average. See average. (26)

measure of central tendency: Mean, median, and mode are all measures of central tendency, reflecting specific statistical information about a set of data. (26)

median: The middle number of a set of ordered data. If there is no distinct middle, the average of the two middle numbers is the median. (26)

midpoint: The point on a line segment that divides the line segment into two congruent line segments. (409)

mixed number (fraction): A number with an integer component and a fraction component. Example: $2\frac{3}{4}$ (199)

mode: The number or numbers that occur the most often in a set of data. There can be more than one mode. (26)

multiple: The product of a whole number and any other (nonzero) whole number. Example: 15 is a multiple of 5.

multiplication: An operation which reflects repeated addition. Example: $3 \cdot 4 = 4 + 4 + 4$. (71)

natural numbers: The counting numbers beginning with one. Example: 1, 2, 3... (49)

negative correlation: A relationship between two sets of variables in which one generally increases as the other decreases. (33)

negative numbers: Numbers which are less than zero, designated with a $-$ sign. (49)

negative slope: Lines that slant downward from left to right showing a negative ratio when comparing the vertical change to the horizontal change. (339)

net: A two dimensional one-piece plan which can be folded into a three dimensional shape. (321)

non-linear: A set of points which do not lie on a straight line when connected.

number line: A diagram representing all real numbers as points on a line. (12)

numeral: An expression (which is not a variable) that names a particular number.

numerator: The number above the bar in a fraction which tells the number of parts in relationship to the number of parts in the whole. (91)

obtuse angle: An angle whose measure is greater than 90° and less than 180˚.

octagon: A polygon with eight sides. (411)

odd number: An integer which cannot be evenly divided by two. (34)

operation: In mathematics, addition, subtraction, multiplication, division, raising to a power and taking a root are operations.

order of operations: Rules which define in what sequence operations will be completed when an expression is presented for evaluation. Expressions inside parentheses are evaluated first, then multiplication or division (left to right) followed by addition and subtraction (left to right). Exponents are a form of multiplication. (131)

origin: The point assigned to zero on the number line or the point where the x- and y-axes intersect in a coordinate system. (28)

ordered pair: A pair of numbers (a, b) used to indicate a position on a coordinate plane. The first number indicates the horizontal coordinate; the second number indicates the vertical coordinate. Syn: coordinate. (28)

outcome: Possible result in an experiment or consequence of an action. (85)

outlier: A number in a set of data that is much larger or much smaller than the other numbers in the set. (14)

parabola: A graph of the equation $y = ax^2 + bx + c$ with $a \neq$ zero. (79)

parallel: (‖) Two straight lines on a two-dimensional surface which never intersect and are the same distance apart are said to be parallel. (215)

parallelogram: A quadrilateral with opposite sides parallel. (215)

pentagon: A polygon with five sides.

percent: (%) A ratio that compares a number to 100. (119)

perfect square: The product of an integer times itself gives a perfect square. Examples: 1, 4, and 9 are perfect squares because $1 = 1 \cdot 1$; $4 = 2 \cdot 2$; $9 = 3 \cdot 3$; $16 = 4 \cdot 4$... (298).

perimeter: The distance around a figure on a flat surface. (11)

perpendicular: (⊥) Lines, segments, or rays that intersect to form right angles.

perpendicular bisector: A line, ray, or segment that divides a segment into two congruent segments and is perpendicular to the segment. (409)

pi (π): The ratio of a circle's circumference to its diameter. An irrational number, it is common to use the approximation of 3.14 or $\frac{22}{7}$ if you are not using a scientific calculator with a π key. (223)

place value: The value of a position of a digit in a number.

plane: A flat surface that extends infinitely in all directions. It has no thickness.

point: An exact location in space. In two dimensions, an ordered pair specifies a point in a coordinate plane. (28)

polygon: A two-dimensional closed figure made of straight line segments (sides or edges) connected end to end (at vertices). The segments may not cross. Examples: triangle or quadrilateral. (309)

polyhedron: A three-dimensional figure with no holes in which all faces are polygons.

population: A collection of objects or group of people about whom information is gathered.

positive correlation: A relationship between two sets of variables in which one generally increases as the other increases. (33)

positive slope: Lines that slant upwards from left to right showing a positive ratio when comparing the vertical change to the horizontal change of the line. (339)

positive numbers: Numbers that are greater than zero.

power (exponent): See exponent.

prime: A number with exactly two factors. Examples: 2, 3, 5, 7...

prime factorization: The expression of a number as the product of prime factors.

prism: A three-dimensional figure composed of polygonal faces and two parallel, congruent faces called bases. No holes are permitted in the solid. The remaining faces are parallelograms (or rectangles). A prism is named for the shape of its base. (309)

probability: The chance of an event happening. When the outcomes are equally likely, it equals the number of event outcomes divided by the total number of outcomes. Example: when rolling a number cube, the probability that you will roll a 3 is: $\frac{1 \text{ way}}{6 \text{ possible outcomes}} = \frac{1}{6}$. (85)

product (·): Result of multiplying. Example: 72 is the product of 8 · 9. (71)

proportion: An equation of two equivalent ratios. Example: $\frac{1}{3} = \frac{3}{9}$ (208)

pyramid: A polyhedron with a polygonal base and whose other faces are triangles with a common vertex. A pyramid is named for the shape of its base.

Pythagorean Theorem: The sum of the squares of the lengths of the legs of a right triangle is equal to the square of the length of the hypotenuse. (294)

quadrants: The four sections of a coordinate grid. (46)

quadrilateral: A polygon with four sides.

quartile: Along with the median, the quartiles divide a set of data into four groups of the same size. (27)

quotient: The result of a division problem. (74)

radius: (plural: **radii**) The distance from the center to a point on the circle. (225)

random sample: A sample in which each item in the population or sample space has an equal chance of being selected.

range: In statistics, the difference between the least and greatest values in the data set. (14)

rate: A ratio comparing two quantities, often a comparison of time. Example: miles per hour. (337)

rate of change: see slope (337)

ratio: A comparison of two numbers which can indicate division. It can be written three ways: 2 boys to 5 girls, 2 boys : 5 girls, or $\frac{2 \text{ boys}}{5 \text{ girls}}$. (207)

ratio of similarity: The ratio of similarity between any two similar figures is the ratio of any pair of corresponding sides. In this course ratios will always be listed in the order that compares the "new" to the "original" figure. This ratio is also known as the enlargement or reduction factor in this course. (233)

rational number: A number that can be written in the form $\frac{a}{b}$ with a and b integers and b ≠ zero.

ray: A portion of a line that has one endpoint and extends forever in one direction.

real numbers: The set of rational and irrational numbers. (All the numbers on the number line.)

reciprocals: Two numbers which have a product of 1. Example: 2 and $\frac{1}{2}$ are reciprocals of each other. (256)

rectangle: A quadrilateral with four right angles. Its two pairs of opposite sides are parallel and congruent. (11)

reduce: To put a fraction into simplest form. (99)

regular polygon: A polygon in which all sides are congruent and all angles have the same measure.

representative sample: A subset (group) of a given population with the same characteristics as the population.

rhombus: A quadrilateral with four congruent sides.

right angle: An angle whose measure is 90°. (291)

right triangle: A triangle with one right angle in it. (291)

root: A number that can be used as a factor a given number of times. Example: The square root of 16 is 4 because $4 \cdot 4 = 16$. $\sqrt{16} = 4$ (298)

scale factor: A ratio between two sets of measurements. (229)

scale (scaling): An arrangement of numbers in uniform intervals. (12)

scalene triangle: A triangle with no two sides of equal length.

scatter plot: Two related sets of data graphed as points, often in a coordinate plane. See positive and negative correlation. (30)

scientific notation: A method of writing very large or very small numbers as a product of a power of ten and a number greater than or equal to one and less than 10. Example: $124,500 = 1.245 \cdot 10^5$ (386)

sector: A part of the interior of a circle bounded by two radii and the arc between their endpoints.

semi-circle: Half of a circle.

set: A collection of items. (313)

similar figures: Figures which are similar have the same shape but not necessarily the same size. The lengths of the corresponding sides are proportional to one another; the corresponding angles are congruent. (229)

simple interest: Interest paid only on the principal (the amount invested). It is found by multiplying the principal, the rate, and the time in years. (265)

simplest form of a fraction: A fraction whose numerator and denominator have no common factor greater than one. (99)

simplify: To combine like terms; to express the quantity using as few symbols as possible; to put a fraction in lowest terms. (99, 106)

slope: A way to specify the steepness of a line defined as the ratio of the vertical distance divided by the horizontal distance between any two points on the line. (339)

solution: Any value for a variable that makes an equation true. (176)

square: A quadrilateral with four congruent sides and four right angles. (410)

square number: Any number which is the product of two identical integers. Examples: $1 \cdot 1 = 1$, $2 \cdot 2 = 4$, $3 \cdot 3 = 9$ ... (298)

square root: See root.

square measure: The units used to describe the measure of an area in the form of 1 x 1 unit squares. (293)

stem and leaf plot: A frequency distribution made by arranging the data. (19)

straight angle: An angle whose measure is 180°.

subproblems: A problem solving strategy which breaks a problem into smaller parts which must be solved in order to solve the original, complex problem. (304)

substitution: Replacing one symbol by another (a number, a variable, or other algebraic expression) without changing the value of the expression.

subtraction (-): An operation that gives the difference between two numbers. (57)

sum: An answer to a addition problem. (49)

supplementary angles: Two angles whose measurements give a sum of 180°.

surface area: The total area of all faces and bases of a polyhedron, cylinder, cone, or pyramid. (315)

term: Each part of the expression separated by addition or subtraction signs is a term. (131)

tetrahedron: A polyhedron with four faces.

tick mark: An indicator that a number line has been divided into intervals of equal length. (46)

trimodal: A set of data that has three modes. (18)

truncate: To cut off or shorten.

trapezoid: A quadrilateral with exactly one pair of parallel sides. (221)

triangle: A polygon with three sides. (221)

unit price: The cost of one item or one measure of an item. Example: cost for one pound or one gallon.

unit rate: A rate with a denominator of one.

units digit: The numeral in the ones place.

upper quartile: The median of the upper half of an ordered set of data. (140)

variable: A symbol or letter that represents a number. (140)

vertex: The point at which two rays, line segments, or lines meet.

vertical: At right angles to the horizon. In a coordinate grid, the y-axis runs vertically. (45)

vertical angles: The angles opposite each other when two lines intersect.

volume: The number of cubic units inside a three dimensional object. (311)

x-axis: The horizontal number line on a coordinate grid. (28)

x-intercepts: The point(s) where a graph intersects the x-axis. An x-intercept always has coordinates (x, 0). (54)

y-axis: The vertical number line on a coordinate grid. (28)

y-intercepts: The point(s) where a graph intersects the y-axis. The y-intercept always has coordinates (0, y). (54)

INDEX

Chapter Prefixes

Many of the page numbers listed here contain the definitions or examples of the topic listed. It may be necessary, however, to read text on preceding pages or the pages following to understand the topic fully. Also, on some page numbers listed here you will find "good examples" of the topic, but they may not offer any explanation. It is very important, therefore, for you to be sure you correct and complete your homework and keep it organized. Your record of the problems related to these topics may be your best index to understanding the mathematics of this course.